Smart Sustainable Cities

Transformation towards Future Cities

MAYSOUN IBRAHIM

Smart Sustainable Cities:
Transformation towards Future Cities

ISBN   978-1-912043-00-2 Paperback
            978-1-912043-72-9 Electronic version

First published June 2020
Mobi Publishing Ltd
Chichester, UK

Froward

Over half the world's population currently live in urban centres. Over the next few decades, according to the United Nations (UN), that proportion is set to rise to two thirds of the world's population. Urban centres are growing in size and complexity on every continent. We are seeing the emergence of mega cities, such as Tokyo, Shanghai, New Delhi, Mexico City, São Paulo, Cairo, Dhaka, London, Moscow, Istanbul and Lagos. 'Cities' in all their forms are clearly a very fertile area to research and understand. Indeed, sustainable futures for humanity will depend, to a large extent, on achieving sustainable living within these large urban centres – the cities that often form the backbone of economic, social and cultural activities for countries around the world. As such, the work that Dr Maysoun Ibrahim presents here provides an important contribution towards this sustainable future.

Cities are very complex entities. They require a vast network of infrastructure, resources and services. They also rely upon a lot of technology, management and planning to maintain the city's economy, and movement of goods, people and waste to keep the city functioning. Big challenges for cities are how to efficiently keep all these infrastructures running efficiently and increasingly in the context of global warming, reduced natural resources and other pressures on the globe, and how to do all this sustainably. This is the realm of smart and sustainable cities. Maysoun captures many of these complexities collating them together within the smart city's dimensions. This provides a base for planners, researchers and analysts to consider cities in a coherent and holistic model.

Maysoun's work is based on a significant body of research. The insights generated have both practical and theoretical use. Maysoun takes a Theory of Change approach to researching smart sustainable cities, from which she develops a practical road map of *things that need to be in place* to help a city move towards improving smartness and sustainability. It is informed with research using insights from decision makers and planners engaged in city transformation projects. The research formed the main body of Maysoun's PhD thesis, providing a robust and well-founded piece of research.

I wish the book the broad dissemination it deserves and Dr Maysoun Ibrahim all the best for her career.

Dr Carl Adams

Chichester, UK

Acknowledgement

First and foremost, praises and thanks to Allah, for His showers of blessings throughout my research work to complete the research and publish this book successfully.

I am extremely grateful to my parents, Mohammad and Zahira, for their love, prayers, caring and sacrifices for educating and preparing me for my future and to be the person who I am today.

I also express my special thanks and love to my brothers, Ashraf and Ramzi, for their continuous and endless support.

Finally, my love to my nephews, Mohammad, Omar, Naya, and Nataly, and to my sister in law, Yafa.

Executive Summary

The challenges related to the growing urbanization has been directing city planners towards seeking innovative ways to transform traditional cities into Smart and Sustainable Cities (SSC). This transformation requires an adequate roadmap and framework. The research community and practitioners exerted considerable efforts to come up with the desired roadmap and framework that would assist throughout this transformation process. However, these approaches lack comprehensiveness. A thorough analysis of the literature shows that selected approaches fall short in terms of analyzing the current economic, social, environmental, and political state and challenges of a city; others neglect one or more of the six dimensions of the SSC. A common limitation among existing approaches is ignoring the city's readiness for change before planning a smart urban transformation process. This highlights a conceptual gap in knowledge that this research addresses via the introduction of a holistic approach to guide the transformation process of cities into SSCs.

This book adopts a hybrid approach based on the Theory of Change (ToC) and the sustainable urban development approach. It introduces a novel theoretical logic model for the transformation towards SSCs through linking the ToC to SSCs. This logic model constitutes the foundation for introducing a comprehensive and systematic transformation roadmap, which captures the aspects of SSCs holistically including the cross-cutting readiness of a city along its different infrastructures. To realize this roadmap, a novel framework specifying the tools needed is introduced. This research book validates its contributions by capturing the insights of experts in the area responsible for top SSC projects from different countries around the world.

TABLE OF CONTENTS

LIST OF TABLES

CHAPTER ONE: INTRODUCTION

The world is experiencing the largest wave of urban growth in history. Over half of the world's population is now living in cities and according to the United Nations estimates, 65-75% of the total world's population is expected to be urban by 2050 (UN, 2014a). This creates enormous social stresses and poses major challenges for cities' sustainability at the economic, environmental, and social levels. The challenges include but are not limited to the poverty expansion, social stresses, aging infrastructure, environmental degradation, shortages in natural resources, spatial dynamics, and urban pollution along with its effects on the climate change (Choucri et al., 2007, ITU-T FG-SSC, 2014a).

The unprecedented urbanization growth along with the increasing awareness on sustainability issues is setting off the wave for the revitalization and expansion of existing cities and developing and creation of new ones. To meet this, cities need a new operating paradigm that is able to provide the solutions required by urban residents. These solutions should be economically viable, environmentally sustainable, and socially inclusive. Economically viable refers to solutions that are financially self-sustaining while environmental sustainability aims at ensuring the protection of current resources for future generations. By social inclusion, the access to benefits is equitable across population segments without any discrimination (PwC, 2010). Many governments and city planners are starting to recognize the role of Information and Communication Technologies (ICTs) in meeting these objectives. In this context, the ICT components can be used as an enabler in designing cities to be smarter and more sustainable, offering better quality of life for citizens through environmentally friendly and viable solutions (Ibrahim et al., 2015a).

Recently, the concept of Smart Sustainable Cities (SSCs) is getting global attention rapidly as a desired goal for present and future urban development (PwC, 2015b; ITU-T FG-SSC, 2016). It is emerging as a solution for various current urban problems. Many city planners, decision makers, and key stakeholders are currently seeking to transform their cities into SSCs aiming at improving the quality of life of their citizens and enhancing the sustainability issues of their cities. SSCs are also attracting the attention of many researchers and practitioners around the globe (Nam & Pardo, 2011). Their challenge is to ensure that cities are offering, for current and future generations, improved living conditions. To do so, they are working on proposing relevant transformation models to facilitate the development of the next generation of cities, using ICTs and other means such as new national policies, laws, and regulations.

1.1   Smart Sustainable City Concept, Characteristics, and Benefits

A SSC is an aggregate concept, in which the three constituents "city", "sustainable", and "smart" are important (Höjer and Wangel, 2014; ISO/IEC, 2015). In this context:

1. **City** is a complex system of systems area where people live and work. Each city has a unique history and consists of a specific social and environmental context, deferring it from others. All city actors are responsible for its flourish. They must work together to find the best ways of using its resources, overcome existing challenges, and grasp the opportunities it may face. In the context of SSCs, the word city is used to identify the type of human structures over which the smart and sustainable solutions are to be planned and delivered.

2. **Sustainable** or sustainability is related to the sustainable development concept, which is focusing on meeting the needs of current generations without compromising the needs of future generations. In SSCs, considering the sustainability of cities is a must and this is the main reasons for which the United Nations International Telecommunication Union Focus Group on SSCs (ITU-T FG-SSC, 2014a) added the word "Sustainable" to the concept of "Smart Cities"; aiming at ensuring that the sustainability aspect is not overlooked in smart cities.

3. **Smart** term in SSCs used as an instrumental concept, not a normative one. It describes the ability of a city to bring together all of its resources to achieve its urban development goals and objectives effectively. The smartness of a city describes how all different city systems and the organizations, facilities, people, finances, and infrastructures are working individually efficiently as well as acting together in a coherent and integrated way; enabling the city to function holistically and to facilitate growth and innovation.

A SSC is defined as *"an innovative city that uses ICTs and other means to improve quality of life, efficiency of urban operation and services, and competitiveness, while ensuring that it meets the needs of present and future generations with respect to economic, social and environmental as well as cultural aspects"* (ITU-T FG-SSC, 2016). It is also defined across six dimensions, namely, smart economy, smart environment, smart governance, smart living, smart mobility, and smart people. It is worth noting that the ICTs have a major role in realizing each of these dimensions though appropriate solutions. Figure 1.1 illustrates the SSC six dimensions along with the ICTs as an enabler.

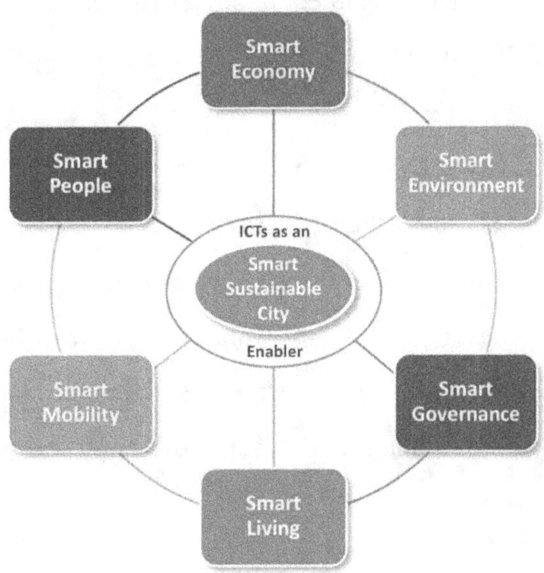

Figure 1.1: Six dimensions of a Smart Sustainable City along with the role of ICTs

The focus of SSCs is to enable the integration of city systems, aiming at providing benefits to a city as a whole and to individual citizens in specific. To implement this, a set of key characteristics must be realized while developing a SSC these are (ISO/IEC, 2015):

- Restructure the city as an instrument of collecting data about all its daily life activities.

- Aggregate city data from different sources and systems to be available for future analysis, providing the insights needed about what is going on in the city.

- Analyze data in a way that allows it to be presented in different types of formats depending on the context over which it will be used and on the person or technical system needing it. This ensures the simplicity of visualizing and accessing the analyzed data and thus, making it more useful when needed.

- Ensure that detailed and measurable real-time knowledge from the collected data are available at every level of a city, enabling various persons and technical systems to use it to meet their daily needs. This real-time knowledge should be available for analytics and decision-making systems, supporting real-time decision making by city planners, managers, and relevant citizens; enabling faster and accurate actions to be taken.

- Automate the city as much as possible, enabling different city operations and services to be delivered effectively and reliably, reducing the need of the direct human intervention.

- A city should have a network of collaborative spaces, enabling local innovations and growth and enhancing citizen's quality of life.

- A city should be able to provide the needed interaction between its physical and digital infrastructures, enabling the SSC solutions to be delivered easily to all city levels, allowing decision-makers, businesses, and citizens to work together effectively with the aim of managing the life of their city for the benefit of all.

A city that can be transformed into a SSC can provide various types of benefits to its citizens, businesses, institutions, and administration bodies. This includes:

- Better city governance.
- Better quality of life for citizens.
- More convenient and better urban services and operations.
- Better and sustainable environmental conditions.
- More intelligent and smarter infrastructures.
- Modern and innovative industry.
- Better, innovative, and dynamic economy.

To realize these benefits, cities needs to be transformed from their current traditional form into smart and sustainable ones, following a coherent, systematic transformation process.

1.2 Highlights on the Transformation Process

Transforming cities into SSCs requires an efficient and effective transformation process. The latter should take into consideration the city context, needs, and local aspirations, quality of life of citizens, readiness of a city for the change, and essential smart and sustainable change activities (i.e. solutions) to be applied at all city levels (Ibrahim et al., 2016). This book defines the transformation towards SSCs as *"a complex multidimensional process through which changes are applied at all city levels; aiming to enhance the sustainability of a city and provide a high quality of life for its citizens through the use of ICTs and other means"* (Ibrahim et al., 2016).

The transformation process is often represented by two types of diagrammatic forms known as (1) the roadmap and (2) the framework. The roadmap provides a diagrammatic illustration of the general directions (i.e. phases) and priorities of a transformation process (Withers et al., 2012). It guides the SSC team and key stakeholders to critical decision points throughout a transformation journey. In this book *"a smart sustainable city roadmap provides a high-level view of the objectives and goals of the transformation process and identifies the transformation phases and milestones in order to realize the city's vision for being smart and sustainable"*. Therefore, a generic SSC roadmap should be clear, understandable, achievable, and as comprehensive as possible. It should also take into consideration the specificity of each city, its context, attributes, and characteristics.

The framework, in turn, provides a diagrammatic form highlighting the needed tools to be used for turning the transformation phases into actions (Di Biase, 2014; Borowik et al., 2015). It simply aims at providing answers to how to realize a SSC transformation roadmap. This book defines a SSC framework as *"a layered structure that leads city planners and relevant stakeholders throughout a transformation process by providing guidance on city readiness for change and the innovative solutions needed to grant urban sustainability and high quality of life for citizens"*.

According to the literature, different roadmaps and frameworks currently exist but each focuses on a selected lens (Ibrahim et al., 2015b). The latter includes CISCO framework (2012), European Platform for Intelligent Cities roadmap and framework (EPIC, 2013), British Standards Institute roadmap and framework (BSI, 2014), Huawei roadmap (2014), Masdar city development process (2014), ITU-T FG-SSC roadmap (2015b), Smart Cities Council roadmap (SCC, 2015), Deloitte framework (2015b), and PricewaterhouseCoopers framework (PwC, 2015a). Each of these proposed models tackles a transformation process from its point of view. The analysis shows that they are not providing a strong base for their suggested phases, stages, guidelines, and tools. In addition, all of them are neglecting some essential components that should be considered during a transformation process, which sheds light on a gap in knowledge.

It is worth also nothing that the transformation of cities from traditional ones to SSCs has not happened yet (Deloitte, 2015a). This is related to the long-term nature of the transformation process as a journey of continuous improvements. Accordingly, none of the proposed models (i.e. roadmaps and frameworks) in the literature was validated on real cases. Some are being applied on existing cities, without reaching the final stage of a transformation process. These models, such as the case of the ITU-T FG-SSC roadmap adopted by Dubai city, are still being modified and updated to meet the context and needs of cities over which they are being applied and tested.

Using a transformation model that does not take into consideration all aspects of a SSC leads to an incomplete transformation process. Without a comprehensive transformation roadmap and framework, the city planners, policy makers, and key stakeholders will not have a concrete base to follow during their transformation journey. Consequently, the possibility of neglecting essential aspects while transforming a city into a SSC becomes high, or at worst, it may cause the whole transformation process to fail (Edwards et al., 2000). Therefore, a generic comprehensive transformation roadmap and framework that could be customized based on the city context, attributes, and needs are needed. The models should also consider all objectives and aspects of SSCs.

1.3 Research Questions

Primarily, the research question of this book is focusing on seeking a deep understanding of the phenomenon of transforming cities into SSCs, identifying a gap in knowledge in existing transformation models, and closing this gap using a theoretical, systematic approach. They are aiming at facilitating the realization of the identified problem statement

The overall research question of this book is as follows: *"What are the aspects that should be considered to ensure a comprehensive, systematic transformation process of traditional cities into Smart Sustainable Cities?"*. To answer this question, we can break down the task to the following sub questions:

1. What is the Smart Sustainable City concept and why is it needed?
2. Is there an agreed definition and dimensions of the SSC concept to be adopted? If yes, what are the justifications behind this selection?
3. How can the ICTs contribute in transforming cities into smart and sustainable ones?
4. Are there any existing SSC initiatives around the globe in general and in the Arab world specifically? What are their related transformation challenges?
5. How existing roadmaps and frameworks are representing a SSC transformation process?
6. Is there a gap in knowledge in existing SSC transformation models? if yes, what are the main constituents of this gap?
7. Are there any existing SSC initiatives around the world in general and in the Arab region in specific?
8. What are the challenges faced by cities during their transformation journey?
9. Is there a specific theory for the transformation towards SSCs? If not, which of the existing theories could be linked to a SSC concept and how could it be applied on this area of research?
10. How to close the identified gap in knowledge in existing transformation roadmaps and frameworks?
11. What are the contributing phases, components, and tools proposed to enhance a SSC transformation process?
12. What is the most appropriate method to be used to validate the proposed innovative transformation roadmap and framework?
13. What are the limitations associated with the validation process of these innovative models?
14. What are the overall limitations faced by this research?
15. How others can benefit from the proposed innovative SSC transformation roadmap and framework?

By answering these questions, this book provides an overall answer to the previously stated research question, giving the readers a high-level overview of the transformation process requirements, needs, and phases.

1.4   Book Objectives

The aim of this research is closing the gap in knowledge in relation to the transformation towards SSCs. Stemming from the research question and its related sub-questions, the primary objectives of this book research are summarized as below:

1. To assess the knowledge level among existing roadmaps and frameworks dedicated to the transformation towards SSCs.
2. To analyze phases, components, and tools of existing models and identify any existing gap in knowledge.
3. To close identified gap(s) by proposing an innovative transformation roadmap and framework that consider the city context, current city challenges, and readiness level of a city for the transformation journey.
4. To propose new tools or highlight existing ones that can be used to realize the proposed transformation phases.

In summary, this book aims at closing the identified gap in knowledge by introducing a novel transformation roadmap and framework that consider all mentioned aspects of a SSC. The resulted innovative models provide guidance to city planners, policy and decision makers, and key stakeholders to understand the essential stages and components to consider while transforming their cities into smart and sustainable ones.

1.5   General Research Methodology

The methodology followed by this book is hybrid. It is a mix of the inductive and deductive approaches. The inductive approach (i.e. qualitative or bottom-up approach) was used to explore and understand the phenomenon of SSCs, study and analyze existing transformation roadmaps and frameworks in the literature, and select the appropriate theory to be used as a base to propose the desired SSC transformation roadmap and framework. After selecting the appropriate theory, the deductive approach (i.e. quantitative or top-down approach) was followed. The latter aimed at introducing new definitions for the concepts of transformation, roadmap, and framework in the context of SSCs, proposing the novel transformation roadmap and framework based on the selected and expanded theory and theoretical model, and validating these models using a data driven validation approach, as illustrated in Figure 1.2.

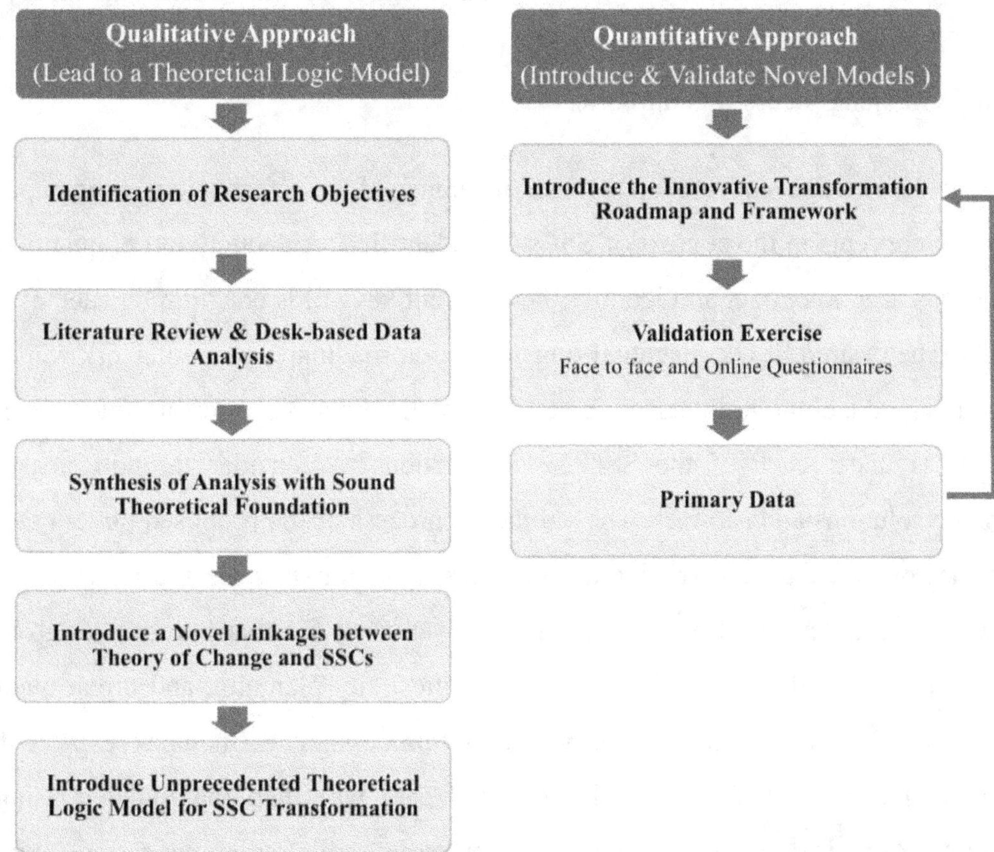

Figure 1.2: Overall Research Methodology – Hybrid Approach

The book starts by exploring the concept of SSCs, its definition, dimensions, factors, characteristics, and expected benefits. This inductive (i.e. qualitative) desk research technique, which is also known as a literature-based method, was used to provide the needed insights into the phenomenon of SSCs. The same approach was then used to conduct an extensive review on existing SSC transformation roadmaps and frameworks. The main components constituting the studied and analyzed transformation models were extracted and highlighted. The dimensions and factors over which each transformation model is being built were tabulated and mapped to the SSC six dimensions and their related factors, helping in identifying a gap in knowledge in existing models. Given the lack of a theory for the transformation towards SSCs, an extensive literature review on existing theories from neighboring disciplines were conducted. The examined theories were analyzed to find an appropriate one to be linked to a SSC transformation process. According to the nature of a SSC transformation process as a means of change, the Theory of Change was selected as a theoretical foundation for this work. This theory was linked to the concept of transforming cities into SSCs and a theoretical logic model for the transformation process was introduced as well.

A gap in knowledge in relation to the meaning of transformation, roadmap, and framework concepts in the context of SSCs was identified. A deductive (i.e. quantitative) analysis was used to extract and identify the different keywords constituting each of these concepts. The desired SSC conceptual transformation roadmap and framework were then proposed. The quantitative intersection research method was used to introduce a generic list of areas under each of the SSC six dimensions to consider through smart and sustainable solutions and services. The validation process of the proposed novel roadmap and framework was then carried out following a quantitative data driven validation approach. The survey questionnaire instrument was used for this purpose. A group of experts in the areas of sustainable cities, smart cities, city planning, and urban planning were contacted to contribute to the validation process. This includes experts from different countries around the world. Collected data was then manipulated using an appropriate statistical method. Finally, discussions and recommendations on the validation findings were provided.

1.6   Significance of the Book

This book aims at closing the mentioned gap in knowledge in relation to the transformation towards SSCs. Analysis of the literature show that most cities undergo this transformation process in an intuitive way rather than in a systematic, clearly structured manner. Using a structured method will not only improve efficiencies of the city infrastructures, but will also enable transparencies into how cities work. With this aim of having a clear structured method, this book records different contributions.

Through analytical review of the literature, this book provides a comprehensive definition of the concepts of transformation, roadmap, and framework in the context of SSCs. It also proposes a novel linkage between the Theory of Change (ToC) and SSCs and use this link to introduce an unprecedented theoretical logical model for the transformation towards SSCs. This book argues that checking the city's readiness for change prior to planning a transformation process is a must to ensure a sustainable transformation process, noting that none of the proposed models in the literature is taking this aspect into consideration. In addition, this book shows that any transformation roadmap and framework should consider the six dimensions of a SSC, namely, smart economy, smart environment, smart governance, smart living, smart mobility, and smart people. It also argues that any transformation activity should be sustainable thereby ensuring a proper quality of life, enhancing the urban operations and services, and improving the competitiveness.

The proposed roadmap and framework aim at providing a thorough guidance for city planners, policy makers, and key stakeholders in understanding the required components to be addressed throughout a SSC transformation process. The latter also includes providing the needed tools to be fully or partially adopted throughout a transformation journey. For example, this book introduces a generic list of areas under each of the SSC six dimensions to consider when transforming a city into a SSC. This list, subdivided into sub-lists, can be customized by any SSC project team based on the city's context, needs and local aspirations and used as a reference in a transformation process.

1.7   Research Complexity

This section presents a series of challenges related to this area of research, highlighting its complexity. One of these challenges is related to the conceptual ambiguity and fuzziness of the "Smart Sustainable City". There is a general agreement on the fuzziness of the concept in the literature with no agreement on its definition and dimensions yet (O'Grady and O'Hare, 2012). To overcome this challenge, a numerous research on the meaning of the concept was conducted, giving the ability to select the appropriate definition and set of dimensions of the concept (Sections 2.2.2 and 2.2.3) along with the needed justification (Section 2.2.4). Moreover, the absence of a theory dedicated to the SSC concept forms another challenge. To overcome this challenge, the author originates an unprecedented linkage between the Theory of Change (ToC) and SSCs. This link is used to create a novel theoretical logic model for the transformation towards SSCs (Chapter 4).

Another challenge is related to the selection of a trustful technique to capture the significance of the proposed innovative models. There are different techniques that researchers may adopt for this purpose. These includes applying the proposed models on real cases; conducting surveys; undertaking interviews with experts; among others. Given the conceptual nature of this book, it becomes important to validate its findings by capturing the insights of experts in the field on different components of the innovative models before applying them on real cases. Therefore, the survey questionnaire method was used to confirm the components of the proposed roadmap and framework. The challenge that emerged from this step was the ability of getting access to key people with experience and knowledge in the area of SSCs. There are many SSC projects taking place globally; however; there was difficulties in contacting such experts, especially in the Arab region. To overcome this challenge, the validation process took place in the United Kingdom, during which a group of experts from different countries around the world were contacted to validate the innovative roadmap and framework (Section 8.5). This includes Canada, Colombia, Estonia, Italy, Japan, Russia, South Korea, United Kingdom, and United States. The validation process resulted in enriching and strengthening the outcomes of this book.

1.8 Book Organization

The organization of this book is summarized as follows. Chapter Two discusses the underlying definitions and dimensions of the SSC concept as represented in the literature. The chapter investigates existing SSC transformation roadmaps and frameworks and provides a mapping of each to the SSC dimensions and factors. It shows how the ICTs are used as an enabler to facilitate the transformation towards SSCs. It explores existing SSC initiatives around the world with a focus on the Arab countries; summarizing the challenges facing the transformation processes in general and in the Arab world in specific. The chapter findings, specifically these related to the SSC definition, dimensions, and Arab region SSC initiatives and challenges were published in the 15th European Conference on eGovernment (Ibrahim et al., 2015a). The article that tackles the analysis of existing transformation models in the literature was published in the Journal of Information Systems and Technology Management (Ibrahim et al., 2015b).

The research methodology used is highlighted in Chapter Three while Chapter Four is dedicated to the theoretical foundation. In this chapter, an unprecedented linkage between the ToC and SSCs is proposed. This link is used to introduce a novel theoretical logic model for the transformation towards SSCs. The findings of this chapter were published in the IEEE Xplore Digital Library (Ibrahim et al., 2017b).

Chapter Five provides new definitions for the concepts of the transformation, roadmap, and framework in the context of SSCs. The proposed definitions were published in the 5th International Conference on Smart Cities, Systems, Devices, and Technologies (Ibrahim et al., 2016).

Chapters Six and Seven are dedicated to the proposed SSC transformation roadmap and framework, describing in details the phases and components of each. Chapter Six focuses on the proposed novel roadmap. Chapter Seven, in turn, is devoted to the proposed innovative framework. It also introduces new models that can be used as tools to realize the novel transformation roadmap. It is worth noting that one of the proposed models, the SSC Stakeholders' Engagement Model, was published in the IEEE Xplore Digital Library (Ibrahim et al., 2017a). The novel roadmap was published in the Sustainable Cities and Society Journal (Ibrahim et al, 2017c) while the innovative framework was published in the International Conference on Information Society and Smart Cities (Ibrahim et al., 2018) and the International Conference on Smart Applications, Communications and Networking (Ibrahim et al., 2019).

Chapter Eight is dedicated to the validation process and its findings. In this chapter, a relevant statistical method to analyze the collected data from the survey questionnaire is identified and used. The data is then tabulated and illustrated using appropriate and meaningful formats. The chapter concludes with a discussion on the findings. Chapter Nine is devoted to the discussion and limitations. The book concludes with the key points emerging from its findings in the Conclusion and Future Directions. Briefly, the proposed innovative roadmap and framework are presented and results of the validation process are pointed out. A set of recommendations along with future directions are highlighted as well.

1.9 Conclusion

SSC is an emerging concept to enhance the urban development of cities, overcoming existing urban problems and challenges. Because of its various benefits, many cities around the globe are seeking to be transformed into smart and sustainable ones. A complete transformation from the traditional city to a SSC has not happened yet. All existing attempts are in the planning or development stage. This book focuses on coming up with a conceptual roadmap and framework for the transformation towards SSCs, which are gaining global attention rapidly as hundreds of SSC initiatives are taking place around the globe.

The next chapter presents a literature review on a SSC definition and dimensions, existing transformation roadmaps and frameworks, and existing SSC initiatives around the world and in the Arab region.

CHAPTER TWO: LITERATURE REVIEW

2.1 Introduction

This chapter presents a literature review on the SSC concept and its transformation models, focusing on both the transformation roadmap and framework. The dimensions and factors over which each transformation model was build are identified, tabulated, and mapped to the SSC six dimensions along with their related factors. The latter aims at identifying a gap in knowledge in existing models in relation to the consideration of the SSC dimensions and factors. The role of ICTs as an enabler to foster the transformation of cities into SSCs is also highlighted. The chapter also provides a review on existing SSC initiatives around the world including the Arab region, shedding light on the challenges facing a SSC transformation process in general and in the Arab region specifically.

The literature review disclosed that the SSC term is being used in many sectors with no agreement upon its definition and dimensions. This has led to confusion among city planners, policy and decision makers, and key stakeholders, who are hoping to transform their cities to be smarter and sustainable. The concept of a SSC is far from being limited to the application of different types of technologies to cities. It includes many other issues that should be considered and reflected in its definition and dimensions.

A thorough review of the literature reveals that there is no harmony in the proposed components of existing SSC transformation models. Different roadmaps and frameworks currently exist but each focuses on a selected lens. This includes CISCO Systems framework (2012), European Platform for Intelligent Cities roadmap and framework (EPIC, 2013), British Standards Institution roadmap and framework (BSI, 2014), Huawei roadmap (2014), Masdar city development process (2014), ITU-T FG-SSC roadmap (2015b), Smart Cities Council roadmap (SCC, 2015), Deloitte framework (2015b), and PricewaterhouseCoopers framework (PwC, 2015a).

The rest of this chapter is as follows. A review on a SSC definitions and dimensions is provided in Section 2.2. In Section 2.3, existing transformation models are highlighted along with their mapping to the SSC dimensions and their related factors. The Role of ICTs in SSC is discussed in Section 2.4. Section 2.5 is devoted to the existing SSCs initiatives in the world with a specific focus on the Arab world along with the challenges related to a SSC transformation process. The chapter concludes in Section 2.6

It is worth noting that the status of SSCs in the Arab region along with the challenges related to the transformation process in the region were published in the 15th European Conference on e-Government under the title "Challenges facing E-Government and Smart Sustainable City: An Arab Region Perspective". Moreover, the findings of analyzing existing transformation models were published in the Journal of Information Systems and Technology Management.

2.2 Smart Sustainable City Definition and Dimensions

The SSC is an emerging and fuzzy concept with no standardized terminologies to comprehensively describing it. There is neither a single template of framing the concept, nor a one-size-fits-all definition of it (O'Grady and O'Hare, 2012). Depending on the lens or the viewpoint taken, there exist different definitions and dimensions of the concept used in ways that are not always consistent. However, all agree that a SSC is evolving as an urban space that tends to solve urban problems, making urban development more sustainable and improving the daily life of its citizens (Negre et al., 2015).

2.2.1 Lack of a Comprehensive Definition

Many definitions for a SSC exist in the literature with different naming, meaning and context (Chourabi et al., 2012). One of the reasons of this is that the concept is being applied to two different types of "domains". On one hand, it is being applied to "hard" domains, such as buildings, water and waste management, energy grids, natural resources, mobility, and logistics, where the ICTs have a crucial role in the functioning of these systems. On another hand, it is being applied to "soft" domains, such as culture, social inclusion, education, policy innovations, and governments, where the enforcement of ICTs is not usually crucial (Neirotti et al., 2014).

Another reason behind the lack of a common definition of SSCs is related to the availability of a number of terms that could be seen as similar to the term "Smart City" (SC), which is alternatively used in various studies to refer to the term "Smart Sustainable City" (Nam and Pardo, 2011; Anastasia, 2012; Albino et al., 2015). This includes the "digital city", "intelligent city", "virtual city", "ubiquitous city", "information city", and "knowledge city". To identify the difference between a SSC term and other terms, there is a need to understand what each term is referring to, as summarized below:

- *Digital city*: refers to *"a connected community that combines broadband communications infrastructure to meet the needs of governments, citizens, and businesses"* (Ishida, 2002). The final goal of a digital city is creating an environment for information sharing, collaboration, interoperability and seamless experiences that could be found and used anywhere in the city.

- *Intelligent City*: the notion emerges at the crossing of the knowledge society with the digital city (Yovanof and Hazapis, 2009). Intelligent cities use information technology in a wisely manner to transform life and work (Komninos et al., 2013). The term intelligent implies the ability to support technological development, innovation, and learning within cities. In this sense, every digital city is not necessarily intelligent, but every intelligent city has digital components. It is worth noting that an intelligent city does not include the "people" components.

- *Virtual city:* in this type of cities, functions of a city are implemented in a cyberspace, in which a city becomes a hybrid city that consists of a reality with its physical entities and real inhabitants and a parallel virtual city of counterparts of real entities and people (Albino et al., 2015). The latter is also one of the cases of SSCs (Nam and Pardo, 2011).

- *Ubiquitous city (U-city)*: a further extension of a digital city concept in terms of wide ubiquitous accessibility and infrastructure. The goal of a U-city is to make the ubiquitous computing available to urban elements everywhere; therefore; a citizen can get any service at anytime and anywhere by any device (Greenfield, 2006; Townsend, 2013). The U-city is different than the virtual city. The latter reproduces urban elements by vitalizing them within the virtual space. The U-city, in turn, is created by the inclusion of computer sensors and chips in urban elements (Lee et al., 2013).

- *Information city*: it is a digital environment in which information are collected from local communities and delivered to the public via web portals. The city is an urban center for social and civic services, commerce, and social interactions among businesses, people, and government institutions (Sairamesh et al., 2004; Sproull and Patterson, 2004).

- *Knowledge city*: refers to a city that is being designed to encourage the nurturing of knowledge, processes and economy. It is a geographical area with an expanding knowledge community, and with knowledge as a strong pillar of its economy (Edvinsson, 2006; Yigitcanlar et al., 2008; Baqir and Kathawala, 2008).

- *Smart Sustainable City*: is an innovative city that uses the ICTs and other means for the purpose of improving the quality of life of its citizens as well as the efficiency of its operations and services. It aims at meeting the needs of present and future generations while taking into consideration the economic, environmental, and social aspects of a city (ITU-T FG-SSC, 2014b).

According to (Caragliu et al., 2011; Deakin and Al Waer, 2011; Townsend, 2013; ITU-T FG-SSC, 2015a), the digital, intelligent, virtual, ubiquitous, and information cities refer to more specific and less comprehensive levels of a city, with the miss of people component that is shaped in a SSC concept through continuous interactions with citizens. Therefore, these terms are often included in the SSC concept (Albino et al., 2015). In relation to the knowledge city, the term is heavily related to knowledge economy, which is only one component of the overall vision on a SSC.

2.2.2   Towards a Comprehensive Definition

The origins of the term "Smart Sustainable Cities" returns back to the origins of the term "Smart Cities". The former was conceptualized by the International Telecommunication Union Focus Group on SSCs (ITU-T FG-SSC, 2014b) to ensure that the sustainability aspect in not overlooked in a Smart City (SC) concept. From a sustainability perspective, the use of ICTs is not needed as long as the city is sustainable, thus the concept of a sustainable city becomes sufficient. From an ICT perspective, as long as the smart solutions are considered, the concept of sustainability is not on the priority list, thus the concept of a smart city becomes sufficient. However, from a comprehensive perspective, as illustrated in Figure 2.1, the concept of a "Smart" and "Sustainable" city is must.

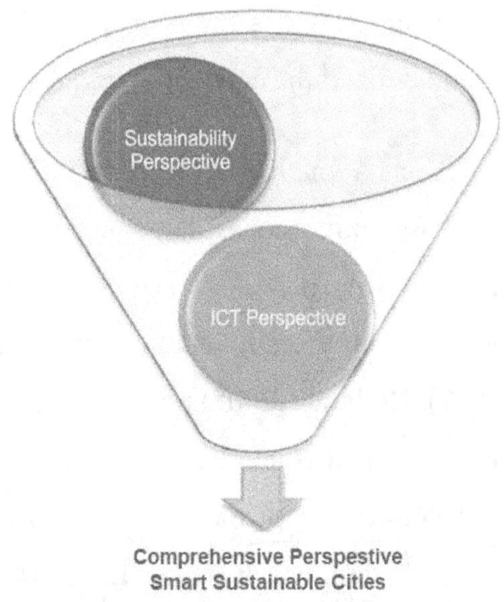

Figure 2.1: A SSC as a comprehensive solution

Many international organizations start using the term SSCs to point out the necessity of considering the sustainable development of a city during its transformation process to become smarter. This includes but limited to the United Nations, European Commission, American National Standards Institute (ANSI), Swedish Institute of Computer Science, among others. It is worth underlining that all selected SCs definitions in this book are considering the sustainability aspect in their context; therefore; all used definitions could be considered as definitions for the SSC concept.

The term "Smart Cities" (SCs) was first used in the 1990s during which the focus was on the significance of new ICTs with regards to modern infrastructure within cities (Albino et al., 2015). The first attempt to define the concept returned back to Hall (2000), who provided a deep analysis on the vision of future cities to be named as SCs. In his study, a SC was described as an urban center of the future that should monitor and integrate conditions of its entire critical infrastructure, plan its preventive maintenance activities and monitor security aspects while maximizing services to its citizens. It was defined as: "*A city that monitors and integrates conditions of all of its critical infrastructures, including roads, bridges, tunnels, rails, subways, airports, seaports, communications, water, power, even major buildings, can better optimize its resources, plan its preventive maintenance activities, and monitor security aspects while maximizing services to its citizens"*. Few years later, researchers start asking for a real SSC to stand up and many studies have conceptualized and defined the concept in various context and meaning.

In 2007, the University of Vienna published a study of ranking 70 medium-sized European smart cities using six dimensions. They define a SSC as a city that is performing in a forward-looking way. The latter takes into consideration issues related to awareness, flexibility, transformability, individuality, self-decisiveness, and strategic behavior (Giffinger et al., 2007). Hollands (2008) points out that a SSC is more than using of ICTs in the city operations, rather, it is the use of networked infrastructure as a means to enable the sustainable development with the use of ICTs to achieve this view. The International Data Corporation Government Insights (IDC, 2009) shows up the need for cities to start adopting SSC solutions in order to develop sustainably, resulting in attracting various investments to meet the expectations of their citizens. This is achievable using the ICTs with the aim of not only delivering high-quality services to citizen but also affecting government workers and city businesses as well.

The European Parliament (2014) denotes that a SSC must provide ICT-based solutions to address public issues and to improve competitiveness to ensure a more sustainable future of the city. According to the British Standards Institutions (BSI, 2014), a SSC must deliver a sustainable, prosperous and inclusive future for its citizens through an effective integration of its digital, physical and human systems. The ITU-T FG-SSC (2014b) highlights the necessity of adding the word "Sustainable" to the term "Smart City" and start using the term "Smart Sustainable City" instead, to ensure that the sustainability aspect in SCs is not overlooked. After analyzing more than a hundred definitions of SCs, SSCs, and sustainable cities, they define a SSC as *"an innovative city that uses ICTs and other means to improve quality of life, efficiency of urban operation and services, and competitiveness, while ensuring that it meets the needs of present and future generations with respect to economic, social and environmental aspects"*. In 2016, the ITU-T FG-SSC expanded the definition to capture the cultural aspect of the city to be read as *"A SSC … with respect to economic, social and environmental aspects as well as cultural aspects"*.

Höjer and Wangel (2014) investigate the concept of SSCs and define it as a city that meets the needs of its present inhabitants through the use of ICTs without compromising the ability for other people or future generations. From their point of view, a SSC is an aggregate notion in which each of the constituent concepts, namely, smart, sustainable, and city is important. An entity is qualified as a SSC if all three parts are presented. If not, the entity is then a sustainable city, a case of smart city, a case of sustainable city or something else. The International Organization for Standards Technical Management Board (ISO TMB) Smart Cities Strategic Advisory Group defines a SSC as a city that needs to improve its social, economic, and environmental outcomes in a sustainable manner in order to response to city challenges and provide better services and quality of life to its citizens (ISO/IEC, 2015). Last but not least, for Hirani and Yavatmal (2015), a SSC is a transformation of existing urban development and its infrastructure into a more attractive city to improve the economic and political efficiency of a city using the ICTs.

In conclusion, the concept of SSCs has been gradually changing its meaning over the years. Mosannenzadeh and Vettorato (2014) and De Santis et al. (2014) analyzed existing literature on the concept, showing that it is being developed and defined in three main areas: Academia, Industries and Governments. Each area has its own view regarding the concept, which derives from the different interests of each domain and how the word "Smart" is being interpreted. From their point of view:

- Academia is mostly oriented in defining the concept in an organic theoretical framework; therefore; the term "Smart" covers a set of technological characteristics such as self-healing, self-configuring, self-optimizing, and self-protection.

- For industries, a SSC concept is related to the quality of life and this should be reflected in its definition. In this case, the term "Smart" refers to artificial intelligence, thinking machines, and intelligent-acting products and services that can be used to support the sustainable urban development.

- Governments and enterprise institutions are mainly oriented to network infrastructures and ICT services/products to citizens. The term "Smart" is related to the "Smart Growth" concept with the aim of making the development decisions predictable, fair, and cost effective.

2.2.3 Smart Sustainable City Dimensions

Transforming a city into a SSC requires a full understanding of the city dimensions over which the smart and sustainable solutions will be planned and delivered. The identification these dimensions is a critical step after its definition as they form the base of building a comprehensive transformation process towards SSCs.

Different point of views exists in the literature regarding the identification of a SSC dimensions. Dirks and Keeling (2009) insists the importance of the organic integration of the city's various systems in a process of creating SSCs. In this case, a city is viewed as a system of systems environment. Researchers who agree with this integrated view underline that in this type of dense environment no system can operate in isolation. In turn, Kanter and Litow (2009) affirm that instill intelligence into each subsystem of a city (i.e. one by one) is insufficient to create a SSC. From their point of view, this should be treated as a one block. Therefore, to clarify what constitute a SSC, many researchers start identifying a SSC by a series of dimensions.

Giffinger et al. (2007) define a SSC across six dimensions, namely, Smart Economy (competitiveness), Smart Environment (natural resources), Smart Governance (participation), Smart Living (quality of life), Smart Mobility (transport and ICT), and Smart People (social and human capital). The dimensions, as illustrated in Table 2.1, are divided into 33 factors to reflect the most important aspects of every dimension. Every factor is defined through a group of corresponding indicators with a total number of 74 indicators to be used to evaluate the smartness degree of a city. Each factor is realized through a well-planned and delivered services and solutions.

Leydesdorff and Deakin (2011) introduce a triple helix model of SSCs in which cities are considered as densities of networks among three relevant dimensions (i.e. dynamic spaces), namely, intellectual capital of universities, wealth creation of industries, and democratic government of civil society. These dimensions can be understood as spaces of ubiquitous ICTs, where knowledge is the key for developing the needed innovation systems for SSCs. Nam and Pardo (2011) in turn suggest three conceptual factors of a SSC that are: Technology, People, and Institutional factors. The technology is a key factor to transform the life and work within a SSC in a significant and fundamental way. However, a SSC cannot be built only through ICTs, meaning that the role of human capital, human infrastructure, and education in urban development and the support of government and policy for SSC governance should also be considered as factors. Each factor, as illustrated in Table 2.2 (Nam and Pardo, 2011; Khansari et al., 2013; EP, 2014), consists of a set of components, forming a holistic vision of a SSC.

Table 2.1: Dimensions and factors of SSCs proposed by Giffinger et al.

Dimension of a SSC		Related Factors
Smart Economy	**Competitiveness**	Innovative spirit Entrepreneurship Economic image and trademarks Productivity Flexibility of labour market International embeddings Ability to transform
Smart Environment	**Natural resources**	Attractive natural conditions Pollution Environmental protection Sustainable resource management
Smart Governance	**Participation**	Participation in decision-making Public and social services Transport governance Political strategies and perspective
Smart Living	**Quality of life**	Cultural facilities Health conditions Individual safety Housing quality Education facilities Touristic attractivity Social cohesion
Smart Mobility	**Transport and ICTs**	Local accessibility (Inter)-national accessibility Availability of ICT infrastructure Sustainable, innovative, safe transport systems
Smart People	**Social and Human Capital**	Level of qualification Affinity for life-long learning Social and ethic plurality Creativity Flexibility Cosmopolitanism/open-mindedness Participation in public life

Table 2.2: Three Conceptual Factors of SSC Components

Technology Factors	Human Factors	Institutional Factors
Digital networks	Human infrastructure	Governance
Mobile technologies	Social capital	Policy
Physical infrastructure		Regulations and directives
Smart technologies		
Virtual technologies		

Anastasia (2012) indicates that a SSC offer local business and citizens a range of tools and ICT applications that can motivate innovations within the city. The latter are developed based on six dimensions, namely, e-Information, e-Business, e-Marketing, e-Government, e-Innovations, and e-Participation. The study also provides a link between the six digital dimensions to the six dimensions identified by Giffinger et al. (2007).

Lombardi et. al. (2012) in turn associate the six dimensions of Giffinger et al. (2007) with different aspects of urban life, as illustrated in Table 2.3. In this study, the economic dimension is associated with the presence of smart industries in the field of ICT and with industries that employing ICT in their production process. Smart environment is linked to the green, sustainable, and efficient energy while smart governance refers to e-governance or e-democracy. Smart living refers to security/safety and quality of life of citizens; smart mobility refers to the use of ICT modern transport technologies, logistics, and new smart transport systems; and smart people is linked to the educational grade.

Table 2.3: Dimensions of SSC and Related Urban Life Aspects

SSC Dimensions (Giffinger et al., 2007)	Related aspects of Urban Life (Lombardi et. al., 2012)
Smart Economy	Industry
Smart Environment	Green, sustainability and efficiency
Smart Governance	e-Government or e-Democracy
Smart Living	Security/safety and quality of life
Smart Mobility	Logistics and smart transport systems
Smart People	Education

According to Dameri (2013), the implementation of SSC initiatives should be based on four dimensions, including the land over which the project will be established;

technologies; citizens; and government. The European Parliament (EP, 2014) maps the conceptual factors of Nam and Pardo (2011) to the six dimensions of Giffinger et al. (2007). The conceptual factors are used to represent the components of a SSC while dimensions refer to its characteristics. From their point of view, as illustrated in Figure **2.2**, the technological, human, and institutional conceptual factors underpin all dimensions of a SSC without a need of mapping each component onto a specific dimension. In some cases, a dimension can fully describe the initiative by displaying what the initiative is about, the priorities of its participants and direct beneficiaries. In other cases, dimensions are the vehicle for the components while the initiative is primarily a way to bring people together and create new ways of collaborating.

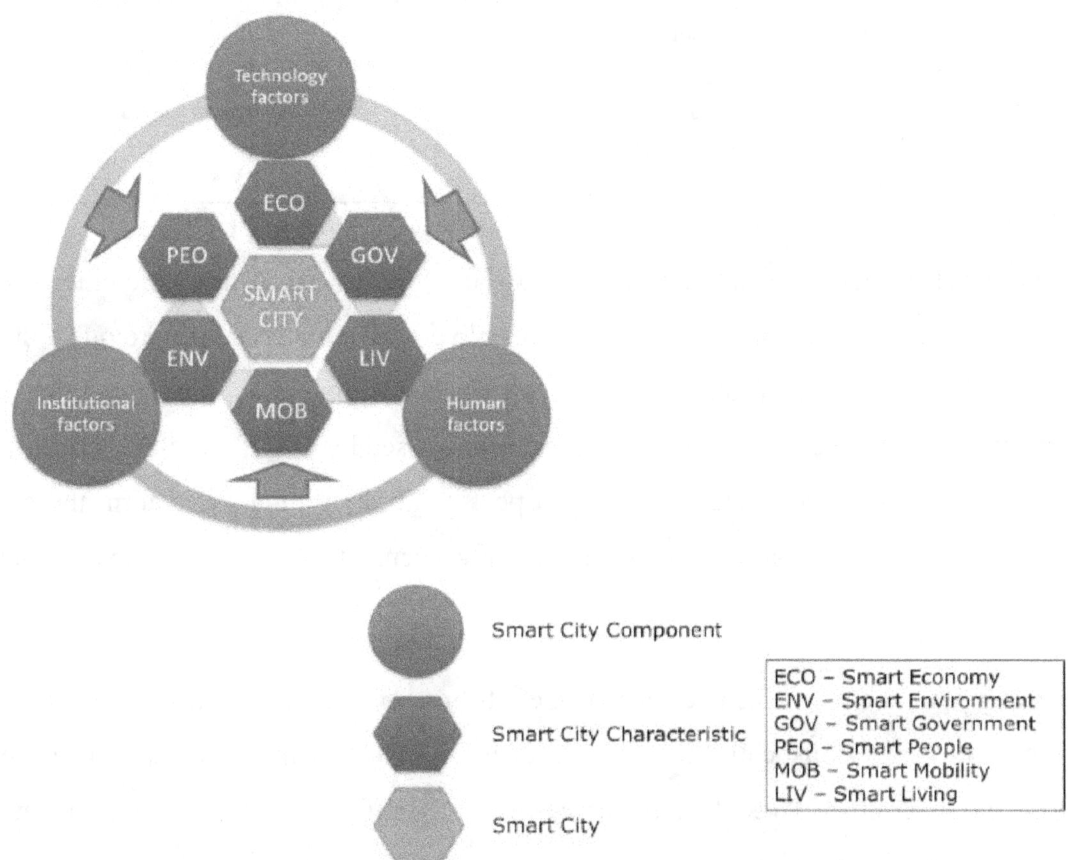

Figure 2.2: Mapping Nam & Pardo Factors to Giffinger et al. Dimensions

The ITU-T FG-SSC (2014b) reclassify the three city dimensions, namely, environment and sustainability, city level services, and quality of life, into four themes to be used as core pillars (i.e. dimensions) in SSCs. These are economy, environment, governance, and society pillars, as illustrated in Table 2.4. They also relate the sustainability aspect of a city to environment pillar.

Table 2.4: ITU-T FG-SSC's Core Pillars and Attributes

Core Pillars			
Economy	**Environment**	**Governance**	**Society**
• Employment	• Regulatory	• Sustainable	• People
• GDP	• Compliance	• Renewable	• Culture
• Market – Global/Local	• Processes	• Land use	• Social networks
• Viability	• Structure	• Biodiversity	• Tech Savvy
• Investment	• Authority	• Water/Air	• Demographics
• PPP	• Transparency	• Waste	• Quality of life
• Value chain	• Communication	• Workplace	• User experiences
• Risk	• Dialogue		• Equal access
• Productivity	• Policies		• End consumers
• Innovation	• Standards		• Community needs
• Compensation	• Citizen services		• The city as a database

** GDP = Gross Domestic Product, PPP = Public Private Partnership*

Last but not least, the PricewaterhouseCoopers (2015) indicate that the future cities need to be both smart and sustainable to ensure easy delivery of services and to provide a high quality of life for citizens. From their point of view, the sustainability aspect of a SSC is not related only to the environment dimension, as proposed by ITU-T FG-SSC (2014b), it also has economic, governance, and social aspects. The three pillars that form the core foundation of a SSC are sustainable economic advancement, political participation, and social emancipation.

Stemming from the above, it is clear that the attribute of "smart and sustainable" is not attributed to a city holistically, rather, it is distributed across many features of a city, mainly, its dimensions. These features range from economic and social to environmental and governmental dimensions.

2.2.4 Justification of the Adopted SSC Definition and Dimensions

To transform a city into a SSC, a standard definition of a concept is needed. After studying the literature, this book adopts the definition proposed by the ITU-T FG-SSC for the following reasons:

- The definition is a result of studying and analyzing around one hundred existing definitions of SCs, sustainable cities, and SSCs in the literature.

- The definition considers the sustainability aspects of a city, namely, the economic (i.e. the city must be able to grow economically and financially), environmental (i.e. the city functionality should be sustainable for present and future generations), and social (i.e. the city is for its citizens) aspects. In addition to the governance aspect (i.e. the city must be robust in developing and administrating its policies).

- A systematic approach was used to come up with this definition. The used methodology started by collecting a database of existing definitions in the literature. For each definition, a set of top keywords and characteristics that make a SSC were extracted and tabulated. Following a quantitative analysis technique, 50 keywords that have multiple references across all the studied definitions were identified and a graphical representation to illustrate the relative importance of each keyword was developed. For the identified keywords, all related keywords were grouped logically into one category. For example, the keywords: ICT, communications, intelligence, and information were grouped into one category. Based on this analysis, a standardized definition of SSC based on 30 key terms and 8 categories was proposed.

- At its 5th meeting in June 2014, the ITU-T FG-SSC in parallel with many international organizations agreed on the proposed definition. The meeting was held in Genoa, Italy with attendances from academia, top policy-makers, government officials, regulators, engineers, designers, planners, standards experts, among others.

- Different researchers and institutions, such as EUREKA (2014) and Budden (2015), start using this definition. Additionally, one of the external partners of the IEEE (2015) regarding SSCs is the ITU-T.

In relation to the dimensions, the six dimensions proposed by Giffinger et al. (2007) are adopted. The meaning of each dimension is summarized as below (Giffinger et al., 2007; Staffans and Horelli, 2014):

- *Smart Economy*: refers to the transformative, responsible, and holistic economic transactions that lead to flexible and effective production of services and goods with an innovative spirit for new business models, enhanced by connectivity through ICTs.

- *Smart Environment*: refers to the care of natural resources and the planetary culture. It comprises environmental protection, sustainable resource management, and reduction of pollution. This includes green energy production, green urban planning, and green buildings construction.

- *Smart Governance*: refers to political policies and strategies that enable the co-production of public services. It is about the use of technology to support and facilitate better planning and decision making. The aim of smart governance is to improve democratic processes and deliver public services electronically. Ideally, smart governance is a transparent deliberative system.

- *Smart Living*: refers to the quality of life of citizens in livable and safe settings. It comprises a supportive infrastructure of everyday life. This includes decent housing options, opportunities for work or meaningful activities, good health conditions, access to nature, and cultural and educational facilities embedded in social cohesion.

- *Smart Mobility*: refers to sustainable and innovative ICT-aided transport, communication systems, and logistics with local and (inter)-national accessibility. Smart mobility allows efficient, flexible, and seamless travel across different modes. The real-time information to be collected and sent to citizens via online applications will enhance both public and personal mobility management; which in turn will increase the use of appropriate mobility choices and chains such as trams, trains, metros, buses, cars, bicycles, etc.

- *Smart People*: refers to human and social capital and the qualification level of women and men with different backgrounds, who are motivated to learn and participate in the co-creation of public life. Some of the values are creativity, tolerance, equity, and cosmopolitanism.

The six dimensions are adopted for the following reasons:

- Many researchers in the literature such as (Soom, 2009; Girard et al., 2009; Cohen, 2012; Anastasia, 2012; Lombardi et al., 2012; Khansari et al., 2013; EP, 2014; EPIC 2014; Deloitte, 2015b; IEEE, 2015) have already agreed on the six dimensions proposed by (Giffinger et al., 2007) and based their research and/or proposed SSC transformation roadmaps and frameworks on them.

- Although the ITU-T FG-SSC (2014b) suggests changing the name of "Smart Environment" dimension into "Smart Environment and Sustainability", the sustainability issue is being taken into consideration within the "Smart Environment" dimension through the "sustainable resource management" factor (Table 2.1).

- ISO/IEC (2015) is planning to develop a set of Key Performance Indicators (KPIs) for SSCs based on the dimensions and factors of (Giffinger et al., 2007).

- Most of the proposed dimensions by different researchers are centers around the six dimensions of (Giffinger et al. (2007). For example, Barrionuevo et al. (2012) define a SSC around ten dimensions, namely, Economics, Environment, Governance and Civic Participation, Human Resources, International Presence, Mobility and Transportation, Public Management, Social Cohesion, Technology, and Urban Planning. Results of studying and analyzing these dimensions show that they are already covered in the six dimensions defined by Giffinger et al., (2007), as illustrated in Table 2.5.

Table 2.5: Linking Barrionuevo et al. (2012) Dimensions to Giffinger et al. (2007) Ones

Dimension	Description	Related dimension in (Giffinger et al., 2007)
Economics	Factors that contribute to the city's economic development, including local development frameworks, transition plans, business strategies, formation of industrial clusters and the presence of innovation and entrepreneurship.	Smart Economy
Environment	This includes tackling pollution, managing water efficiently and supporting green buildings and alternative energy for cities to become cleaner, more pleasant places to live, while at the same time drastically reducing their energy bills.	Smart Environment
Governance & Civic participation	The consideration of citizens' participation, the ability of authorities to engage business leaders and local residents and the implementation of electronic government/e-government plans.	Smart Governance

Dimension	Description	Related dimension in (Giffinger et al., 2007)
Human resources	This includes the raise of local education standards and promotes creativity and research.	Smart People
International Presence	Building international presence to attract tourism and foreign investment, which requires bold initiatives to boost the city's overseas representation and global positioning	Smart Economy
Mobility & transportation	Making it easier for people to get around town and access public services.	Smart Mobility
Public management	The improvement of the efficiency of local government institutions; focusing on the design of new organizational and management models. This area presents major opportunities for the private sector, whose experience of optimizing efficiencies is invaluable.	Smart Governance
Social cohesion	This includes improving a city's social environment, which requires extensive research and action in areas such as immigration, community development, elder care, health care and public safety.	Smart Living
Technology	The use of ICT as an essential driver of a community's economic and social development.	Enabler for all dimensions
Urban planning	The need of launching a local master plans focusing on the design of green areas and public spaces.	Smart Environment

2.3 Existing SSC Transformation Roadmaps and Frameworks

This section reviews existing SSC transformation roadmaps and frameworks in the literature. A mapping of studied solutions to the SSC six dimensions and their related factors is carried out followed by a discussion on identified gap(s) in knowledge in the studied and analyzed models.

2.3.1 CISCO Framework

CISCO framework aims at providing a simple decision methodology, resulting in a feedback loop, as illustrated in Figure 2.3, to enable city leaders and private sector to understand best practices of other SSC initiatives and to plan and implement SSC projects effectively. The framework consists of 4 layers, summarized as bellow (CISCO, 2012):

- *Layer 1 - City Objectives*: in its first layer, the city objectives are identified with the aim of improving the social, economic, and environmental aspects of a SSC.

- *Layer 2 - City Indicators*: this layer matches the city objectives to existing city indicators that are used to measure cities using specific and defined methodologies. As cities are complex and their objectives and priorities differ, each city should use a set of indicators that closely match its objectives.

- *Layer 3 - City Components*: this layer details city physical components, namely, transportation, real estate, utilities, and city services; and link them to city objectives, indicators, and contents. Each component forms a hierarchy where the component itself resides at the top level followed by a set of subcomponents at different levels of the hierarchy. For example, transportation component includes four sublevels/ subcategories named as road, rail, air, and logistics.

- *Layer 4 - City Content*: this layer encompasses the question of "how" SSC solutions could be implemented. It maps city objectives to best SSC practices and policies.

Figure 2.3: CISCO SSC Framework Layers (from bottom to top)

2.3.2   European Platform for Intelligent Cities' Roadmap and Framework

EPIC roadmap and framework are designed to guide the transformation process throughout the EPIC platform. The latter offers a series of web-based services over a cloud. The roadmap describes for a city a series of planned steps, actions, and tasks to be taken to become a SSC. The framework is used by a city to help in developing its SSC strategy. It is worth noting that all EPIC services are delivered as PaaS (Platform as a Service) and SaaS (Software as a Service) models and controlled by the EPIC team. EPIC roadmap is divided into six phases, as illustrated in Figure 2.4 (EPIC, 2013), that are:

- *Vision Phase*: in this phase, a SSC strategy is developed by the city administration and key stakeholders. This strategy is then used as a base to define a series of objectives and goals to be achieved within a specific period.

- *Plan Phase*: this phase aims at developing the project and program plans for business cases and strategic objectives. During this phase, the project definition, master plan, and budget are developed. This helps in defining and describing the project goals, expected benefits, scope, approach, risk issues, and key milestones.

- *Design Phase*: to document business requirements and create a detailed design for public smart services. The design will consider the business processes, change impacts, software configurations, applications security, and technical infrastructure. A proof of concept prototype, to demonstrate the feasibility of the used design, will be developed in order to show how city administrations, businesses, and citizens can use and operate the SSC services on the EPIC platform.

- *Build Phase*: during this phase, the SSC services are implemented using EPIC platform and tested using the test management plan. This also includes developing of the end-user training materials and guidelines.

- *Deliver Phase*: during this phase, SSC solutions are prepared and executed to be transformed to the operational environment. This includes performing end-user training, conducting user-acceptance testing and evaluation, and establishing of the support organization that provides the needed support to end-users.

- *Operate Phase*: the actual operation and support of the SSC solutions is in place.

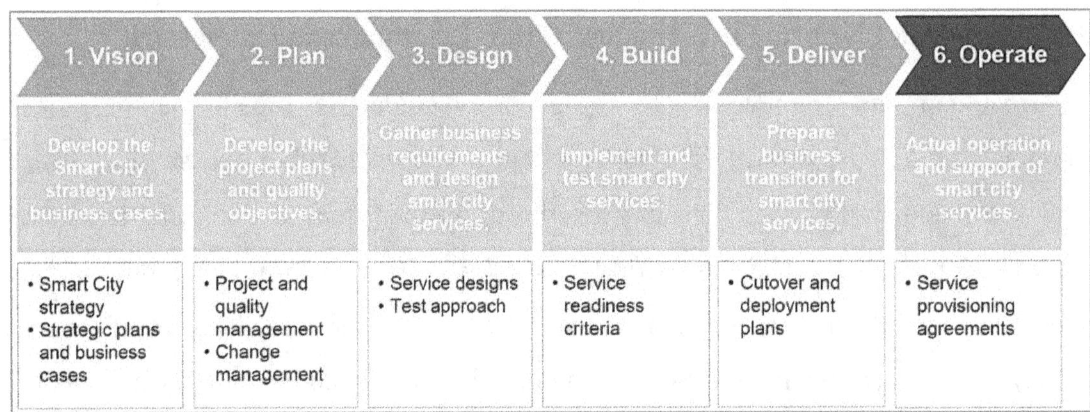

Figure 2.4: Overview of EPIC Roadmap

The EPIC framework, as illustrated in Figure 2.5 (EPIC, 2013), consists of six strategic domains; namely, smart governance, smart economy, smart mobility, smart living, smart people, and smart environment; and six strategic characteristics namely, strategic mindset, awareness, commitment, flexibility, synergy, and self-decisiveness. The latter aims at describing to cities the required goals and initiatives needed to become SSCs.

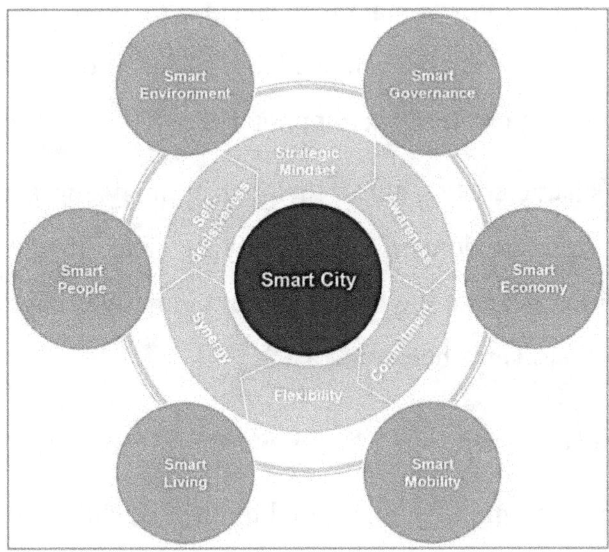

Figure 2.5: Overview of EPIC SSC Framework

Each strategic domain describes an area of focus for which initiatives and goals are identified to support the transformation towards SSCs as below (EPIC, 2013):

- *Smart Economy*: the aim of this domain is to benefit from resources available at the community level to build a community trademark. This process is facilitated and supported by the use of technology.

- *Smart Environment*: the domain aims at providing the SSC services in a sustainable environment with the support of technology. This includes saving of water resources, ensuring the balance between built and green areas, energy saving, and others.

- *Smart Governance*: the aim of this domain is to ensure the involvement of all relevant key stakeholders in the implementation and policy making process. The technology is used to facilitate and support achieving domain goals and initiatives.

- *Smart Living*: the aim of this domain is to simplify the access and maximize the benefits of housing, education, and healthcare facilities. The role of technology is to provide smart solutions to citizens that meet the goals and objectives of this domain.

- *Smart Mobility*: the aim of this domain is to embed mobility services in the life of city community in a natural way. This includes minimizing related costs and required investment in resource planning and operation as well as in service customization.

- *Smart People*: the aim of this domain is to enhance the participation of citizens in the community life. This could be achieved by social and ethnic plurality, lifelong learning, and support of creativity at community.

Finally, the strategic characteristics aim at helping in analyzing and improving the city maturity within each strategic domain and identifying areas of improvements. They are used to give an indication whether the SSC goals and initiatives have a positive impact on the strategic growth path towards becoming a SSC.

2.3.3 British Standards Institution's Framework and Roadmap

The BSI proposed a SSC framework to be used by the UK cities' leaders to develop and deliver their SSC strategies with the aim of meeting the future challenges and aspirations. In its high-level view, the proposed framework consists of four components, as illustrated in Figure 2.6, as summarized below (BSI, 2014):

- [A] *Guiding Principles*: a statement of values that can be used by city leaders to steer business decision-making while they are implementing a SSC strategy.

- [B] *Key Cross-City Governance and Delivery Processes*: a set of practical guidance notes used to show how to address city-wide challenges caused by joining-up different city systems.

- [C] *Benefit Realization Strategy*: a guide on how to ensure that the intended benefits of a SSC strategy are clearly articulated, managed, delivered, measured, and evaluated in practice.

- [D] *Critical Success Factors*: a checklist that should be regularly monitored by a city to ensure that it is on track in delivering its SSC program and effectively managing the major strategic risks.

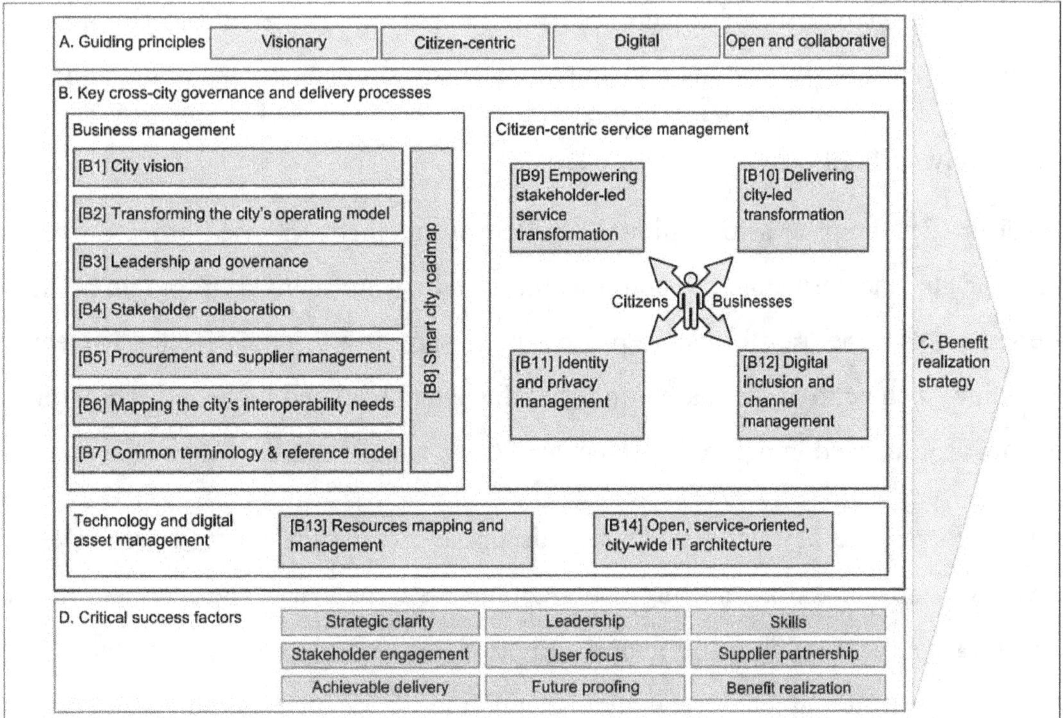

Figure 2.6: The BSI High-Level Structure of a SSC

One of the activities of the [B] component of the proposed framework is to establish a deliverable phased roadmap that consists of five main phases as summarized below:

- *Plan phase*: to ensure that the business case is fully articulated and all key stakeholders are on board. The key output of this phase includes the guiding principles, city vision, benefit realization framework, and SSC roadmap.

- *Initiate phase*: in this first phase of delivery, the focus is to maximize the benefits and minimize the delivery risks. This means focusing on (1) the quick wins to demonstrate progress and early benefits aiming at accelerating the believes of stakeholders and (2) embedding the roadmap in governance processes and structures.

- *Deliver phase*: during this phase, some of the more significant investments start coming on stream. For instance, the first wave of smart services and applications.

- *Consolidate phase*: longer-term strategic solutions are developed to focus shifts towards driving take-up of the initial SSC services and applications, learning from smart data and user feedback, and using that feedback to specify changes to the business and technology architectures.

- *Transform phase*: includes building out the broader range of SSC projects and complete the transition to the full strategic IT platform to guarantee future agility.

2.3.4 Huawei Roadmap

Huawei defines the process of building SSCs as an interactive phased process that must have clear guidance principles, vision, roadmap, and a set of delivery programs. The city leaders must start the transformation process by designing a SSC vision that is clear (i.e. measurable), competitive (i.e. based on local characteristics) and inclusive. The proposed roadmap, as illustrated in Figure 2.7 (Huawei, 2014), consist of five phases as below:

- *Plan Phase*: the key deliverables of this phase include the guiding principles, city vision, framework for realizing benefits, and SSC roadmap. The roadmap includes setting up a leadership team, identification of ICT and digital assets, transformation of procurement and supply models, formulation of risk management strategies, and priority action plan that reflects the city's interoperability needs.

- *Initiate Phase*: focuses on two main issues. The first is to obtain quick result with the lowest technical costs to enhance stakeholders' confidence. The second is to rapidly integrate the roadmap with city governance structures to support future investments.

- *Deliver Phase*: the early investments will start taking effects. This may include introducing of a one-stop portal that provides online public services to citizens and opening of an information-sharing platform to support the city data transparency.

- *Consolidate Phase*: the aim of this phase is to deliver additional SSC applications and services; learn from user feedback and shared data; and develop long-term technology architecture strategies and business solutions.

- *Transform Phase*: after delivering most of the SSC services, there is a need to expand the scope of a SSC project. This includes improving a city platform to ensure that it is fully complies with a city vision. A platform should be flexible and responsive to any future requirements emerged from changing business and customer needs.

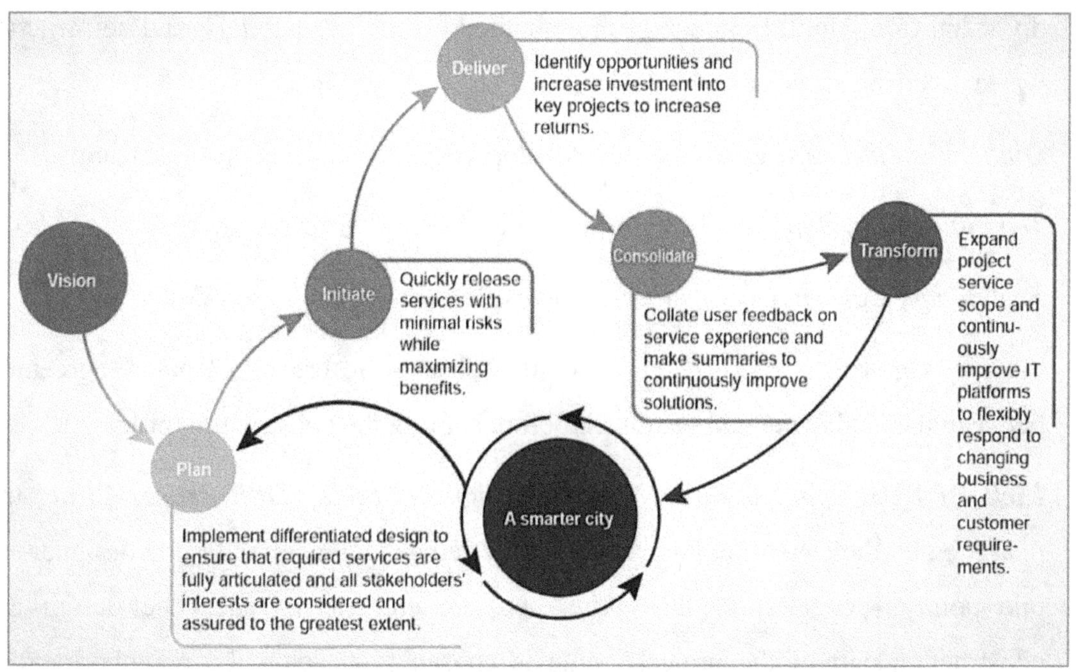

Figure 2.7: Overview of Huawei SSC Roadmap

2.3.5 Masdar City Development Process

Masdar city, a new planned city project near Abu Dhabi city in the United Arab Emirates (UAE), is a clean-technology cluster being built with the aim of becoming one of the smartest and sustainable cities in the Arab region and the world. As illustrated in Figure 2.8 (Masdar, 2014), the development process of Masdar consists of 12 integrated phases as below:

- *Vision Phase*: the vision of Masdar city is *"to develop a smart and sustainable city that incorporates the highest quality of life with the lowest environment footprint"*.

- *Pre-design Studies and Assessments Phase*: variety of sites and regional studies are undertaken to inform the design response and integration of the city within its context: environmentally, socially, and economically.

- *Master Plan Phase*: aims at designing a master plan of the project based on four pillars/ dimensions: sustainable environment, economic, social, and cultural pillars.

- *Resource Budget and KPIs Phase*: a set of Key Performance Indicators (KPIs) are developed to assess the development process. The indicators are used to measure the provision of renewable energy, interior water demand reduction, operational waste diversion from landfill, reduction in embodied carbon in materials, and construction waste diversion recycled.

- *Guidelines Phase*: the guidelines are developed and issued to the project team.

- *Tenant/ Sub Developer Interest Phase*: (no explanation from the source)

- *Preliminary Concept Options Phase*: (no explanation from the source)

- *Tenancy Agreement Phase*: the aim of this phase is to create a tenancy agreement between the landowner and the tenant before starting the construction process.

- *Kick off Design and Build (D&B) or Design-Bid-Build (DBB)Phase*: during this phase, either the D&B (i.e. joint venture between general contractor and designer and one point of contact) or DBB (i.e. separate entities for each the design and construction part of the project) route is chosen to develop the neighborhood or building projects to improve delivery efficiency and control of design integrity to suit individual projects.

- *Project Design with Gateway Review Phase*: aims at ensuring the capturing and incorporating commentary from all stakeholders and promoting further collaboration that may lead to synergies among the owner, architects, engineers, and end-users.

- *Construction Phase*: this phase includes third part commissioning verification, integrated systems testing, constructing supervision, infiltration testing, mockups, sample testing, construction/waste/supply chain management to ensure their compliance with the guidelines and verification of implementation and performance.

- *Operation Phase*: the city will be ready for operation and use. The pre-identified guidelines will be tested to ensure the stability and continuity of all systems.

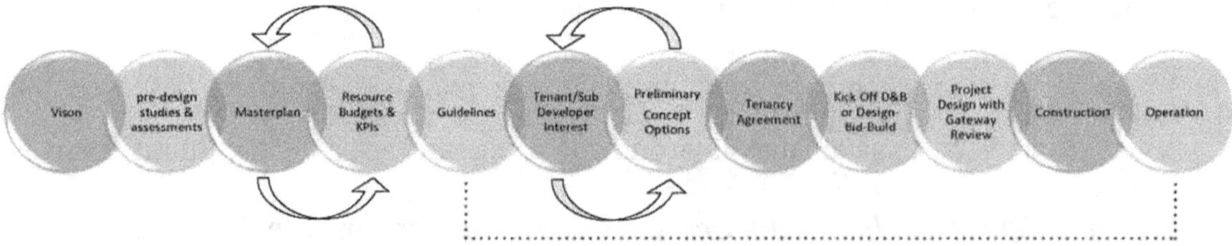

Figure 2.8: Overview of Masdar City SSC Development Process

2.3.6   ITU-T Focus Group on Smart Sustainable Cities Roadmap

The ITU-T FG-SSC proposed a six steps roadmap for a SSC transformation process, as illustrated in Figure 2.9 (ITU-T FG-SSC, 2015b). The roadmap can be used to assist city decision makers to re-define the ways of building city's infrastructure, offering services, engaging citizens, and linking systems. The six proposed steps are summarized as below:

- *Set the Vision*: this step includes the identifying of a SSC vision that meets the city's identity, long-term strategy, and political priorities. This also includes checking the ICT infrastructure capacities; identifying mechanisms for citizens' engagement, multi-stakeholders' involvement, communication and information sharing; and identifying existing governance mechanisms that could be used to manage the SSC solutions.

- *Identify SSC targets*: identify the SSC services to be developed. This includes developing of the SSC infrastructure and integrated platform, defining the KPIs, and educating stakeholders on SSC advantages.

- *Achieve Political Commitment*: during this step, local government obtains the required political approval and support to ensure the continuity of a SSC programme.

- *Build the SSC*: the actual establishment of a SSC takes place during this step. This may require significant improvements of existing infrastructure by integrating the required ICT applications or by building new infrastructure from scratch.

- *Measure City Progress*: this includes monitoring and evaluation of the working process required to achieve the SSC targets by using the relevant set of KPIs.

- *Ensure Accountability and Responsibility*: the focus of this step is on reporting, evaluating, and learning from a SSC process and its related experiences. This includes an assessment of the implementation process and its strengths and shortcomings.

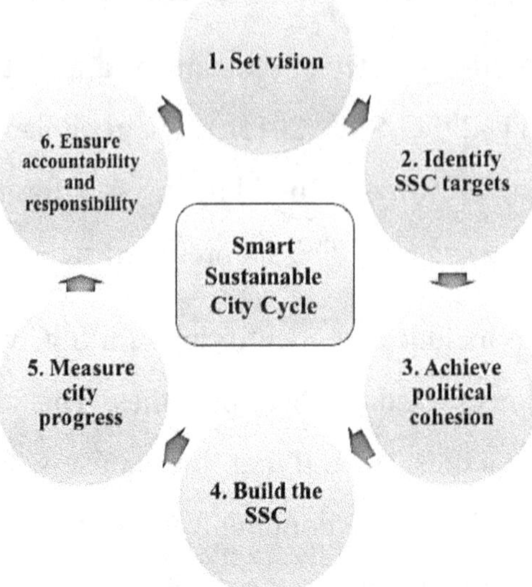

Figure 2.9: Overview of ITU-T FG-SSC SSC Roadmap

2.3.7   Smart Cities Council Roadmap

The SCC suggested an abstract roadmap that can be used by city leaders in transforming their cities into SSCs. From their point of view and as illustrated in Figure 2.10 (SCC, 2015), any roadmap should include at least the following five phases:

- *An Assessment*: which provides a clear picture of the current state and challenges of the city regarding its economic, social, environmental, and political aspects.

- *Vision*: the vision should provide a clear picture of the required outcomes of a SSC project based on citizen benefits and expectations. In addition to the technical achievements, the vision should be expressed in term of improving the city lifestyle and work style. It should also be built with citizen involvement.

- *Project Plan*: it is the blueprints for the most important components of a SSC, such as master plans for the ICT infrastructure, land use and built environment, transportation, city data and information, business and commerce, and city services.

- *Milestones*: these are the waypoints at which the transformation process is measured, lessons learned are shared, and corrections and strengthen commitments are discussed.

- *Metrics*: this phase should use the KPIs to measure the success of a SSC transformation process. The KPIs could be used for example to measure the energy efficiency achievements, carbon footprint, percentage of online services, water efficiency achievements, education level, among others.

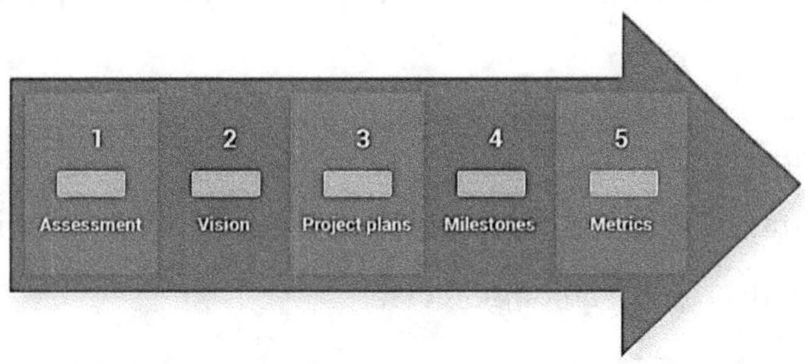

Figure 2.10: The Smart Cities Council SSC Roadmap

2.3.8   Deloitte Framework

For the purpose of building 100 SSCs in India, Deloitte proposed an integrated SSC framework to facilitate the implementation of these cities. The framework, as illustrated in Figure 2.11 (Deloitte, 2015b), consists of six enablers, namely, smart economy, smart governance, smart mobility, smart living, smart people, and smart environment.

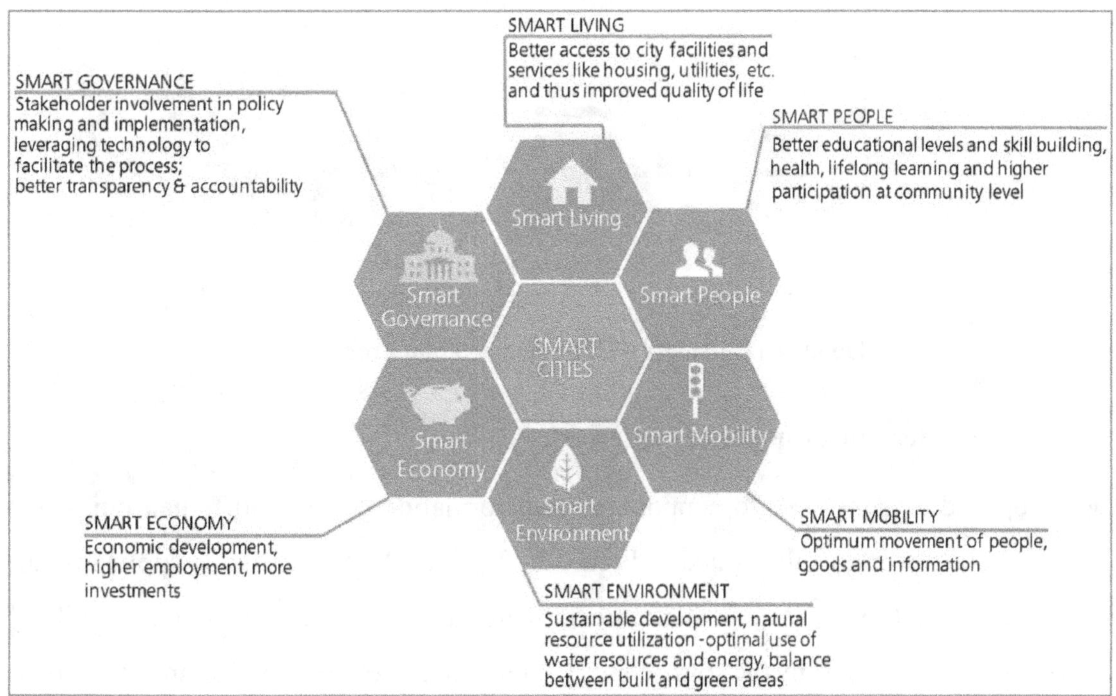

Figure 2.11: Deloitte SSC Integrated Framework

The framework is used to develop the implementation framework of a SSC, which provides guidance on how to build the smart infrastructure and solutions. It enables public and private sectors to provide services to citizens through a cloud-based infrastructure. As illustrated in Figure 2.12 (Deloitte, 2015b), the implementation framework comprises the following:

- *City Level Infrastructure and Associated Services*: including all city infrastructure such as transportation systems, water and sewerage network, mobile network, Global Positioning Systems (GPS), among others.

- *Cloud based back end ICT Platform*: this platform is able to collect data from all city levels, processing it and then generate responses in an intelligent matter.

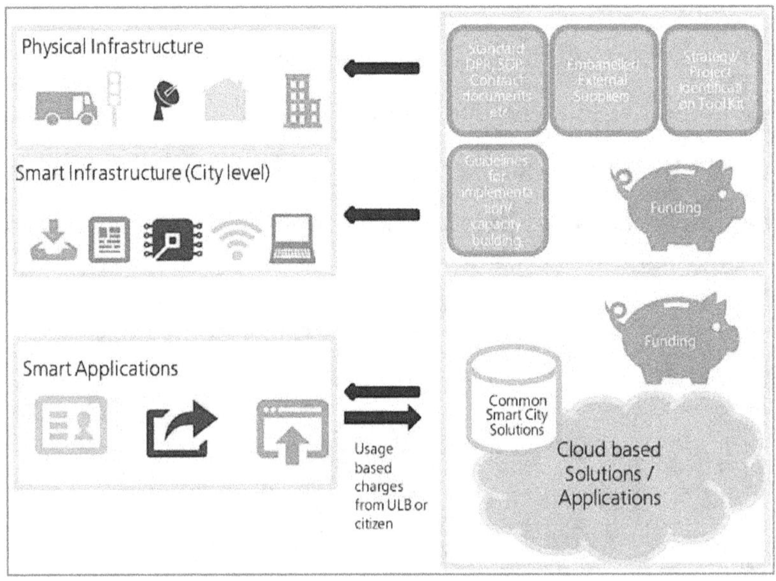

Figure 2.12: Deloitte SSC Implementation Framework

2.3.9 PricewaterhouseCoopers Framework

PwC proposed a framework to support the transformation of the 100 Indian cities into SSCs. The framework, as illustrated in Figure 2.13 (PwC, 2015a), could be applied on the Brownfield cities (i.e. existing Indian cities), Whitefield cities (i.e. Indian cities built by European and Eurasians in the 19th century), Greenfield cities (i.e. Indian cities to be built from scratch). The framework consists of 3 main layers as summarized below:

- *City Planning Layer*: in which the transformation plan is developed based on the type of the city over which it will be applied.

- *Urban Development Layer*: in which the physical and social infrastructures, utilities provisioning, business models and governance models of a SSC are identified and developed (PwC, 2014b).

- *ICT Plan Layer:* focuses on the areas where the ICTs can be used to transform a city into a SSC. This includes designing and finalizing the ICT plan, implementing the ICT platform, and drafting legislations for implementing and governing of the SSC initiatives (PwC Connect, 2015).

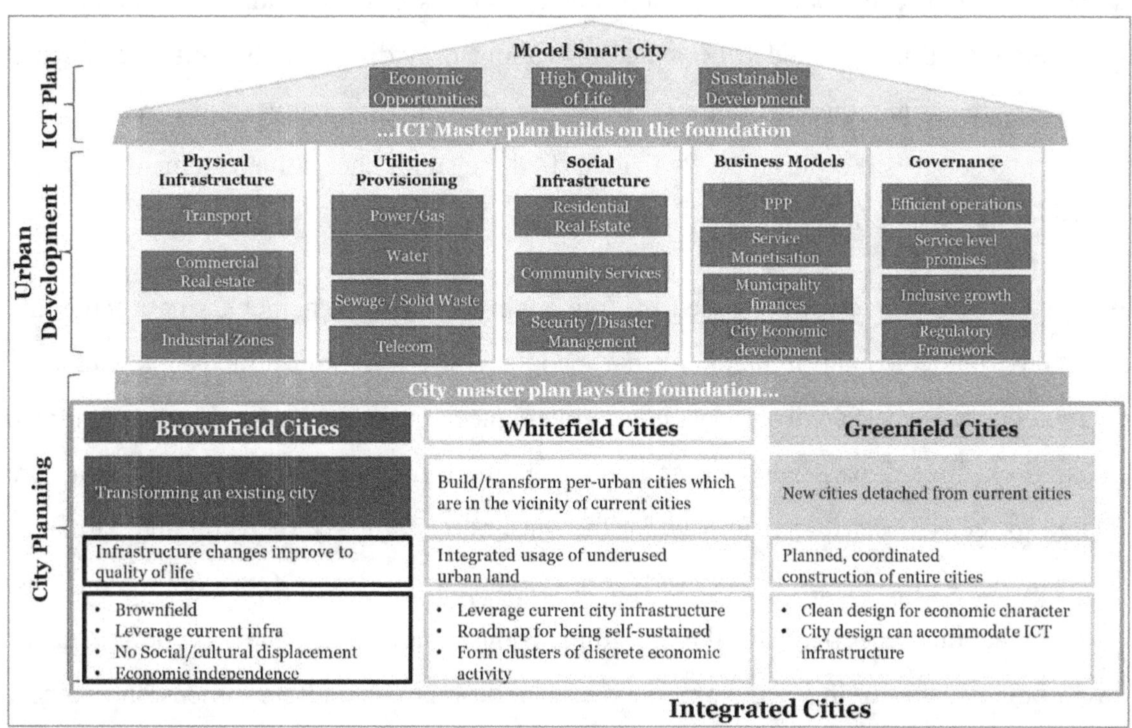

Figure 2.13: Overview of the PricewaterhouseCoopers SSC Framework

2.3.10 Mapping SSC Dimensions and Factors to Existing Models

Different roadmaps and frameworks exist in the literature; each tackles a transformation process from a specific lens. Most of them neglect one or more of the SSC six dimensions, which denote a gap in knowledge. This Section aims at providing a holistic mapping of studied and analyzed transformation models to the SSC six dimensions along with their related factors. This part is carried out following the literature-based method approach to identify a gap in knowledge in existing models.

For each studied transformation model, an in-depth analysis on the dimensions and factors over which the proposed model is based is performed. Collected data are then tabulated and mapped to the SSC six dimensions and their related factors. Finally, two comparison matrices, one for the dimensions and the other for the factors, are created as illustrated in Table 2.6 and Table 2.7 respectively. Analysis shows that none of the studied models is fully considering the six dimensions of a SSC and their related factors. Only EPIC (2014) and Deloitte (2015b) highlighted their consideration of these dimensions. However; both do not consider all factors defined under each dimension. Additionally, all models added new factors without providing any theoretical or logical evidences regarding these additions. Some are also mixing between the meaning of factors and services. For instance, PwC identified the smart energy management, which is a service, as a factor under the smart environment dimension.

In sum, CISCO framework is based on four main dimensions, namely, smart economy, smart environment, smart living, and smart people. BSI covers four dimensions, including smart economy, smart environment, smart governance, and smart living. Huawei roadmap is based on three dimensions; two of them; the smart governance, and smart living; are related to the SSC six dimensions while the third one is a new dimension and named as smart industry. Masdar City has based its development process on four core dimensions; three of them are related to the six dimensions; they: are smart economy, smart environment, smart living, and smart people; in addition to the culture dimension as a new one. The ITU-T FG-SSC roadmap considers five core pillars, the smart economy, smart environment, smart governance, smart living, and smart people. The PwC based their framework on four core dimensions, named as: sustainable economic advancement (i.e. smart economy), political participation (i.e. smart governance), social emancipation (i.e. smart people), and smart environment. Finally, the SCC roadmap takes into consideration eight newly identified dimensions, namely, smart transportation, energy efficiency, smart grids, smart water networks, smart street lights, public safety, digital government services, and smart payments. All of which are services, not dimensions.

Table 2.6: Covered SSC Dimensions in Selected set of existing Transformation Solutions

Study Name	Core Dimensions Smart						Other Dimensions
	Economy (Competitiveness)	Environment (Natural resources)	Governance (Participation)	Living (Quality of life)	Mobility (Transport & ICT)	People (Social & Human Capital)	
CISCO	YES	YES	-	YES (i.e. named as Smart Society)	-	YES (i.e. named as Smart Society)	-
EPIC	YES	YES	YES	YES	YES	YES	-
BSI	YES	YES	YES	YES	-	-	-
Huawei	YES	YES	YES	YES	-	-	- Smart Industry (includes: Smart Tourism and Smart Park)
Masdar	YES	YES	-	YES (i.e. named as Smart Society)	-	YES (i.e. named as Smart Society)	- Culture dimension
ITU-T FG-SSC	YES	YES	YES	YES (i.e. named as Smart Society)	-	YES (i.e. named as Smart Society)	-
Smart Cities Council	-	-	-	-	-	-	- Smart Transportation, - Energy Efficiency, - Smart Grids, - Smart Water Networks, - Smart Street Lights, - Public Safety, - Digital Government Services, - Smart Payments.
Deloitte	YES	YES	YES	YES	YES	YES	-
PwC	YES (i.e. named as Sustainable Economic Advancement)	YES	YES (i.e. named as Political Participation)	-	-	YES (i.e. named as Social Emancipation)	-

Table 2.7: Covered SSC Factors in Selected set of existing Transformation Solutions

SSC Solutions		Core Dimensions					
		Smart Economy	Smart Environment	Smart Governance	Smart Living	Smart Mobility	Smart People
CISCO, BSI, Masdar, SCC		**No Supporting Data from the Source**					
EPIC	**Common Factors**	- Innovation spirit - Entrepreneurship - Productivity - Flexibility of labour market - International embeddedness	- Attractivity of natural conditions - Pollution - Environmental protection - Sustainable resource management	- Participation in decision-making - Public and social services - Transparent governance - Political strategies & perspectives	- Cultural facilities - Health conditions - Individual safety - Housing quality - Education facilities - Touristic attractivity - Social cohesion	- Local accessibility - (Inter-)national accessibility - Availability of ICT-infrastructure - Sustainable, innovative and safe transport systems	- Level of qualification - Affinity to lifelong learning - Creativity - Cosmopolitanism/ Open-mindedness - Participation in public life
	Missed Factors	- Economic image and trademark - Ability to transform	-	-	- Education facilities	-	- Social and ethic plurality - Flexibility
	Added Factors	- Branding	-	- Financial management	-	-	- Education facilities
Huawei	**Common Factors**	-	-	- Smart government including: - Participation in decision-making - Public and social services - Transparent governance - Political strategies & perspectives	- Education facilities: named as Smart education - Health conditions: named as Smart hospital - Touristic attractivity: named as Smart tourism in Smart Industry dimension	-	-

SSC Solutions		Core Dimensions					
		Smart Economy	Smart Environment	Smart Governance	Smart Living	Smart Mobility	Smart People
	Missed Factors	- Innovation spirit - Entrepreneurship - Economic image and trademark - Productivity - Flexibility of labour market - International embeddedness - Ability to transform	- Attractivity of natural conditions - Pollution - Environmental protection - Sustainable resource management	-	- Cultural facilities - Individual safety - Housing quality - Social cohesion	- Local accessibility - (Inter-)national accessibility - Availability of ICT-infrastructure - Sustainable, innovative and safe transport systems	- Level of qualification - Affinity to lifelong learning - Social and ethic plurality - Flexibility - Creativity - Cosmopolitanism/ Open-mindedness - Participation in public life
	Added Factors	-	-	- Safe city - Emergency - Command - Environmental protection - Energy management	- Smart transport	- Smart Park from Smart Industry dimension	-
ITU-T FG-SSC	**Common Factors**	- Innovation spirit - Productivity - Flexibility of labour market (i.e. named as Market – Global/Local) - International embeddedness (i.e. named as Market – Global/Local)	- Sustainable resource management (i.e. named as Sustainable Environment)	- Public and social services (i.e. named as Citizen Services) - Transparent governance (i.e. named as Transparency)	- Cultural facilities (i.e. named as Culture)	-	- Level of qualification (i.e. named as user experiences) - Social and ethic plurality (named as Demographics) - Participation in public life (i.e. named as Social networks)
	Missed Factors	- Entrepreneurship - Economic image & trademarks - Ability to transform	- Attractivity of natural conditions - Pollution - Environmental protection	- Participation in decision-making - Political strategies & perspectives	- Health conditions - Individual safety - Housing quality - Education facilities - Touristic attractivity - Social cohesion	- Local accessibility - (Inter-)national accessibility - Availability of ICT-infrastructure - Sustainable, innovative & safe transport systems	- Affinity to lifelong learning - Flexibility - Creativity - Cosmopolitanism/ Open-mindedness

SSC Solutions		Core Dimensions					
		Smart Economy	Smart Environment	Smart Governance	Smart Living	Smart Mobility	Smart People
	Added Factors	- Employment - GDP - Viability - Investment - PPP - Value chain - Risk - Compensation	- Renewable - Land use - Biodiversity - Water/Air - Waste - Workplace	- Regulatory - Compliance - Processes - Structure - Authority - Communication - Dialogue - Policies - Standards	- Tech Savvy - Quality of life - Community needs - The city as a database	-	- People - Equal access - End consumer
Deloitte	Common Factors	- Flexibility of labour market: named as Labour market	- Pollution - Sustainable resource management	-	- Housing quality: named as Housing - Individual safety: named as Citizen Safety	Transport: - Local accessibility: named - (Inter-)national accessibility - Sustainable, innovative and safe transport systems ICT: - Availability of ICT-infrastructure	- Affinity for life-long learning: named as Education - Social and ethic plurality: named as Participation of communities/ Advocacy - Participation in public life
	Missed Factors	- Innovation spirit - Entrepreneurship - Economic image and trademark - Productivity - International embeddedness - Ability to transform	- Attractivity of natural conditions - Environmental protection	- Participation in decision-making - Public and social services - Transparent governance - Political strategies & perspectives	- Cultural facilities - Health conditions - Education facilities - Touristic attractivity - Social cohesion	-	- Level of qualification - Flexibility - Creativity - Cosmopolitanism/ Open-mindedness
	Added Factors	- Income level - Poverty level	-	- Revenue management - Administration - Grievance management - Policy	- Sewerage and sanitation - Water supply - Electricity - Storm water drainage	-	- Health - Inclusive development
PwC	Common Factors	- Competitive economy including: - Employment	- Attractivity of natural conditions - Pollution	- E-governance and citizen services including:	-	-	- Affinity of lifelong learning: named as Smart education

SSC Solutions		Core Dimensions					
		Smart Economy	Smart Environment	Smart Governance	Smart Living	Smart Mobility	Smart People
		- growth and opportunity (i.e. economic growth) - Productivity	- Environmental protection - Sustainable resource management	- Participation in decision-making - Public and social services - Transparent governance - Political strategies & perspectives			- Social and ethnic plurality: named as Human rights - Participation in public life: named as Social inclusion, stakeholder engagement and participation
	Missed Factors	- Innovation spirit - Entrepreneurship - Economic image and trademark - Flexibility of labour market - International embeddedness - Ability to transform	-	-	- Cultural facilities - Health conditions - Individual safety - Housing quality - Education facilities - Touristic attractivity - Social cohesion	- Local accessibility - (Inter-)national accessibility - Availability of ICT-infrastructure - Sustainable, innovative and safe transport systems	- Level of qualification - Flexibility - Creativity - Cosmopolitanism/ Open-mindedness
	Added Factors	- Incubators, skill development centers, specialized business parks, hubs, etc. - Affordable housing - Governance	- Smart energy, water, waste & natural resources Management; - Urban mobility; - Smart communications; - Smart spaces & surveillance; - Climate change mitigation & adaptation; - Green buildings; - Sustainable transport.	-	-	-	- Smart healthcare - Recreation: arts, sports, entertainment - Sanitation, public health and safety

2.3.11 Discussion on the Findings of the Studied Transformation Models

2.3.11.1 Existing Transformation Roadmaps

In relation to existing roadmaps; EPIC, BSI, Huawei, ITU, and SCC; the analysis shows that they are not solid and are not developed based on a systematic and theoretical logic. For example, the BSI roadmap defines the city vision during their proposed planning phase. Based on (KU, 2015), the first phase of any transformation process should be a vision phase during which a city vision is identified. The vision is then supported by a vision statement, mission statement, objectives, goals, and strategies. Following the vision phase, the transformation solutions are identified and prioritized during the planning phase.

Moreover, none of the proposed roadmaps takes into consideration checking the city's readiness for change before planning the transformation activities (i.e. solutions). The city's readiness in this context refers to the current city capacities regarding its hard, soft, and digital infrastructures as well as the level of existing digital literacy. Only the ITU-T FG-SSC and SCC provide some kind of city assessment in their developed roadmaps. Although one aspects of the earliest stage of the ITU-T FG-SSC (2015b) roadmap is collecting the relevant data in relation to the city's ICT infrastructure status and its usage at a city-level, the ICT-based infrastructure is not the only resources that are required in the transformation process (Ruhel, 2014; Vogel, 2012; Kohel, 2016). Existing non-ICT based infrastructure, such as policies, laws and regulations and healthcare, education, and government systems are essential and should be assessed as well. In relation to the SCC (2015), the proposed roadmap includes an assessment phase focusing only on assessing the current state of a city in relation to available SSC initiatives and goals, which is also not adequate.

On another note, none of the studied and analyzed solutions is based on a theoretical foundation or systematic logic to be followed while developing the proposed roadmaps; neither identifying their point of view behind the techniques used for selecting the proposed phases, ordering of phases, and identification of each phase's components.

Finally, none of the studied roadmaps is taking into consideration the six dimensions of a SSC. Only EPIC (2012) indicates their consideration of the six dimensions; however; EPIC provides all SSC solutions and services over EPIC platform based on cloud computing techniques using PaaS and SaaS delivery models. All suggested services are web-based services and controlled by EPIC team. According to its various downsides (Apostu et al., 2013), developing a city into a SSC based only on cloud computing techniques is insufficient. Moreover, ICTs are only an enabler or purveyor which allow providing solutions that enhance the smartness level of a city (BSI, 2014, ISO/IEC, 2015, ITU-T FG-SSC, 2016). There are many issues to be considered at all city levels that have nothing to do with ICT, e.g. government policies, laws and regulations.

2.3.11.2 Existing Transformation Frameworks

The results of analyzing existing frameworks, the CISCO, EPIC, BSI, and PwC, show many shortages in them. This includes not following a solid logical structure while defining their proposed layers and components, neither considering all aspects needed for an effective and efficient transformation process, which constitute a gap in knowledge. To start with, some frameworks neglect the necessity of identifying a SSC vision and transformation strategies at an early stage of a transformation process such as the case of CISCO (2012). Many studies including (KU, 2015; ITU-T FG-SSC, 2016) emphasize the necessity of identifying the city vision of any transformation process at its first stage, as it provides an overall picture for locals about how their city will look like in the future after applying a series of significant changes at all city levels. It also motivates all types of stakeholders (e.g. citizens, public and private sector organizations, civic organizations, and others) to participate in the transformation process and increase their buy-in. This vision is then supported by a set of transformation objectives, goals, and strategies to be used as a base while planning the transformation solutions and services.

Moreover, none of the proposed frameworks provides any guidance or tools regarding checking the city readiness for change before planning and implementing the SSC services and solutions. In this context, checking the city readiness for change refers to the examination of existing city assets regarding its current hard, soft and digital infrastructures and level of the digital literacy of a city. Only CISCO provides some kind of city assessment in their developed framework. Although the third layer of CISCO framework aims at detailing the current city physical components regarding its transportation, real estate, utilities and city services, these physical components are not the only components to be examined. There are also a need to check the current state of the city regarding:

(1) ICT-based infrastructure including the hardware and software components of a city, such as the network infrastructure, access devices, and social applications (Nam and Pardo, 2011; ISO/IEC, 2015; ITU-T FG-SSC, 2016),

(2) Non-ICT based soft infrastructure, such as existing policies, financial systems, and healthcare and education systems (Rubel, 2014; Vedashree and Bose, 2015), and

(3) level of digital literacy, such as ICT skills and knowledge skills (Kirkman, et al., 2002; Lorenz et al., 2013; Baller et al., 2016).

On another note, none of the proposed frameworks takes into account the six dimensions of a SSC except EPIC (2013). The previous sub-section discussed the disadvantages of the EPIC solutions. It is worth noting that there are many issues to consider and solutions to deliver that have nothing to do with ICTs. The latter is mainly used as an enabler to enhance the smartness level of a city and to provide solutions that are environmentally friendly and viable (BSI, 2014; ISO/IEC, 2015; ITU-T FG-SSC, 2016).

In addition, none of the proposed frameworks is following a systematic logic or theoretical foundation while selecting the proposed layers and components. In addition, none of the analyzed studies highlights their point of view regarding the techniques used for ordering the proposed layers and identifying their components. None highlights the mechanisms of how to contextualize their proposed framework based on the current city resources, needs, and local interests while taking into consideration the objectives of a SSC and city sustainability. Finally, none highlights or explains the tools to use to realize their proposed frameworks components.

2.4   The Role of ICTs in SSCs

The ICTs play a crucial role in SSCs. As an enabler, they provide the required infrastructure to connect various city systems, creating a system-of-systems or network-of-networks that facilitate the interaction between different city levels. They act as a digital platform from which a network of information and knowledge is created. Through this network, information and data are aggregated for the purpose of data analysis and understanding of how a city is functioning in relation to its services, consumptions, and lifestyle. This leads to significant improvements in the quality of life of citizens in specific and society in general.

A SSC, as highlighted by the European Parliament (EP, 2014), should provide at least one smart solution for each of its six dimensions, utilizing the ICTs as the key medium to ensure a sustainable future of a city. While ICTs provide smart and sustainable solutions to a diverse set of city challenges, the ICT infrastructure acts as the "glue" that integrates all SSC elements, as illustrated in Figure 2.14. The ICT infrastructure looks like a nerve center that orchestrates the interactions between the physical infrastructure of a city; such as buildings, roads, electric lines, water and gas pipelines; and different city systems.

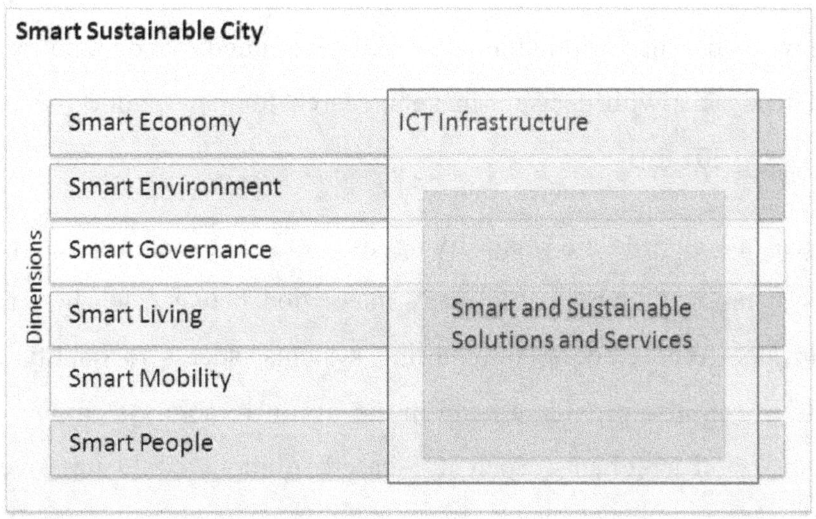

Figure 2.14: Smart Sustainable Cities and ICT Infrastructure and Services

The importance of the ICTs is that they stand on all dimensions of a SSC. To start with, they can play a central role in achieving the smart economy objectives (Factors of Table 2.1). For example, the ICT-based solutions and services have the potential to create jobs, empower small businesses and innovative entrepreneurs, increase productivity, and accelerate economic growth. According to the World Bank Group, firms that are using ICTs are more productive, profitable, and grow faster than those that do not use ICTs (WBG, 2012). The smart environment in turn can benefit from the ICT solutions to enhance the environmental conditions and tackle the climate change phenomenon. For instance, implementing the smart solutions to manage building energy, greenhouse gas emissions, utility supply, security, safety, and others can lead to environmentally sustainable properties and improve the energy efficiency and quality of life of citizens. In relation to climate change, the ICTs can track, predict, and analyze such changes and develop the convenient management and communication strategies (OECD, 2010).

The aim of the smart governance is to improve the democratic processes and deliver public services electronically. It is about enhancing accountability and transparency, improving the performance of administration, implementing political strategies and perspectives, and providing public and social services for citizens. In this case, the ICTs provide the tools needed to achieve all these goals. For example, the government can provide a portal to facilitate the engagement and participation of citizens in public policy making, allowing them to access government shared information. The citizens, therefore, will know how to use the information to hold government accountability, share their opinions and feedbacks with decision-makers, search for new public job opportunities, among others (UN, 2014b).

The ICTs have a key role in smart living as well. They contribute in developing educational systems that support a two-way interaction between teachers and students. This could include remote access, monitoring systems, access to quality content, and others. The ICTs can also provide a hand in the use of remote systems in hospitals for disease diagnosis and treatments. Such ICT-based solutions could improve emergency responses as well as enhance patient experience and penetration of direct care (PwC, 2010). As for smart mobility, the ICT-based solutions help in improving the transportation efficiency through reducing congestions, enhancing public transportation, and minimizing environmental impact. For example, the intelligent transport systems can be used to monitor traffic on roads and direct the flow based on real-time information (PwC, 2010).

Finally, the smart living refers to human and social capital and the qualification level of women and men with different backgrounds, who are motivated to learn and participate in the co-creation of public life. Some of the values are creativity, tolerance, equity and cosmopolitanism. The ICTs, for example, can enhance the long-life learning of citizens through online distance learning (i.e. e-learning), e-book loans, online tourist orientation and guidance, forums to get expert advices, among many others (Toppeta, 2010).

In sum, the ICTs play a central role in the transformation towards SSCs. The transformation process can use ICTs to transform the city core systems and services for greater development impact, optimize finite resources, and help in cleaning the environment. This results in enabling more sustainable citizen services, providing them with a high quality of life. Smart technologies will help city leaders, who are responsible about the transformation process, to develop smarter and more sustainable cities.

2.5 Smart Sustainable Cities in the Arab Region

The Arab region, as a miniature model of the world, consists of a widely diverse group of countries in terms of demographic, economic, natural resources, and technological infrastructure. The latter is also the case between cities within the same country. In Arab countries, there are several situations where land use and the access to services, infrastructure, education, and health are widely different from one city to the other. This depends mostly on what regions of the Arab world is being addressed. For example, the Gulf region has a higher petroleum outcome than others. As a result, the Gulf cities are well established in general and some of them are currently being considered as examples of SSCs (e.g. Masdar City in the United Arab Emirates). However, many other countries in other parts of the Arab region have serious problems in relation to their economic and infrastructure conditions.

In what follows, a research study on existing urban life challenges in the Arab region that forces the transformation towards SSCs is provided. An overview of the challenges of

Arab SSCs transformation is highlighted as well. Finally, a literature review on existing Arab SSCs initiatives is laid out.

2.5.1   Urban Life Challenges in the Arab Region - the need for SSC Initiatives

The move towards urbanization allows cities to gain better control over their economic and political development. Cities, as well, are empowered technologically, enabling new levels of intelligence and allowing city's systems to become more instrumented and interconnected. In parallel, cities start facing different challenges and threads to their sustainability that they need to address holistically. The latter include sustainability issues related to people and business systems and core infrastructures such as energy, water, transport and communication. Therefore, to seize opportunities and build sustainable growth, cities need to become "Smarter" (IBM, 2009) and "Sustainable".

Governments and communities in the Arab region, like others around the world, are facing intractable challenges in relation to urban life and sustainability of their cities that are (CISCO, 2012; Government Summit, 2015; UN-HABITAT, 2015):

- *Rapid Urbanization*: in the Arab countries, the urban population grew by more than four times from 1970 to 2010, and is expected to be doubled from 2010 to 2050. In 2010, the international statistical studies showed that 56% of residents in the Arab countries were living in cities; by 2050, the rate will be around 68%, causing an urbanization boom within cities. Because of this rapid urbanization, the sustainable development in the region will be affected dramatically and will be gained or lost in cities.

- *Environmental awareness*: environmental awareness has not been widely diffused across the Arab region, resulting in poor response to international environment standards as well as the lack of legislation and/or implementation of environment protection regulations. Moreover, desertification, caused by the climate change and the associated threats of future water and food insecurity, are key problems of the region.

- *Increased Greenhouse-Gas emissions* (GHGs): rather than using renewable energy, most countries in the region depend heavily on oil and gas derivatives to meet local energy demands, resulting in increasing the greenhouse emissions. The latter have increased in most Arab countries due to the use of fossil fuels in industries and the use of inefficient public transportation and ageing vehicles.

- *Urban Economic*: economic performance in the region varies from one country to another, ranging from exceptional to modest or poor economic performance. Despite the fact that the rate of recent economic growth of Arab countries tends to exceed the global average, countries are still suffering from highly non-diversified national economies. Moreover, the economics of some parts of the region are highly dependent on natural resources such as hydrocarbons; therefore; changing in international prices may cause economic shocks, which in turn affect employment and economic stability of these countries.

- *Employment opportunities*: many Arab countries have not been able to provide employment opportunities for large sections of the population. Unemployment rates remain high in the region, especially among youth and women. Governments do not have policies to help creating enough suitable and decent jobs for graduated youth as well as for women. In addition, a mismatch between existing opportunities in the labor market and educational qualifications of youth also is a key problem.

- *Urban services and infrastructure*: in most Arab countries, governments are facing the challenge of providing the sufficient services and infrastructure for their citizens in all areas of the country. In general, access to services and infrastructure such as public, education and health facilities; energy and water services; transport and ICT networks and infrastructures are better in cities than in rural areas.

In sum, the challenges that affect the sustainability of a city can be mitigated through adoption of scalable solutions, taking advantages of ICTs to increase efficiency, reduce costs and enhance citizens' quality of life. The latter can be highly and effectively achieved through SSC initiatives.

2.5.2 Challenges of Arab SSCs Transformation

Different challenges are facing the transformation of cities into SSC. This varies from one region to another and between countries within the same region. The challenges range from economic and social to technological and regulatory ones and could be summarized, world widely, as below (EC-Europa, 2014; EP, 2014; Ibrahim et al., 2015a):

- *Complexity challenges*: SSCs require creation of a sustainable system of systems capable of generating opportunities for cities and their citizens. This can be achieved through horizontal and vertical integrations of city's independent infrastructure, data and services. This integration increases the complexity of how to plan, operate, regulate and finance SSC projects. It also includes issues related to administration; integration and convergence; standardization and interoperability; management of open data; data privacy and security; integrity of data and others.

- *Economic challenges*: a sustainable financial investment to create and/or renovate the technological and physical infrastructure and to invent the digital solutions is one of the big challenges of any SSC project. The latter is highly dependent on the economic status of a country, thereby a city. Therefore, a plan of a SSC project needs to identify how SSC services will be delivered (i.e. operation model) and how these services will be funded (i.e. business model).

- *Social challenges*: one of the emerging social challenges results from the necessity to adopt SSC services to the specific needs of each user (i.e. citizen). Therefore, it is necessary to know the user expectations and preferences of each service. This requires integration of security and privacy-preserving mechanisms. Social challenges also refer to the lack of skilled people in the field of SSCs, lack of collaboration between research and development firms, misunderstanding of the impact of smart technologies on the city's daily administrative level, the need for greater citizens' engagement, insufficient attention to citizens, among others.

- *Governance challenges*: switching to SSCs means, at citizen's level, a change of behavior for public administration rules and processes as well as concerning the industry mind-setting. The inherent nature of a SSC as a complex system of systems highlights the need for administrative silos including long-term and holistic policies to enable institutional and governance mechanisms for SSCs initiatives. This requires coordination and integration between public, private, and civil bodies in addition to the collaboration with different stakeholders for making a city function as one organism in an efficient and effective manner.

- *Technological challenges*: SSC solutions require huge amount of data (i.e. big data), which are a valuable tool for developing applications. As a result, there is a need to make sure that used data are accessible and trustworthy. In SSCs, systems from different sectors; such as energy, transport, and government need to interconnect and communicate with each other. Therefore, inter- and intra- system interoperability must be considered in SSCs. Moreover, technological obsolescence is one of the challenges facing the adoption of SSCs. Solutions to be deployed today may be replaced later to make them interoperable with future systems and requirements. The technological challenges include but not limited to the operating cost, security and privacy and out lack or datedness of ICT infrastructure.

In addition to the above challenges, there are additional long-term challenges to SSCs development in the Arab region. Some of these challenges are strongly critical. The major challenges facing the Arab countries, thereby cities within these countries are highlighted below (Government Summit, 2015):

- *Unemployment challenges*: the rate of youth unemployment in the Arab region is very high comparing to other regions in the world (Eide and Rösler, 2014). This can be considered as a problem caused by the labour market rigidities and growing mismatch between the skills of young graduates and the needs of industries and businesses in the region (Mesiano, 2014). This will not only affect the economy of the country but also the financial well-being of citizens. The latter will place huge budgetary constraints on cities, therefore, affecting the adoption of SSCs solutions.

- *Environmental Challenges*: this includes the growing inflation pressures; water scarcity; climate change that induced temperature increases and precipitation declines; food insecurity; and lack of greenery.

- *Other challenges*: there are additional challenges that could affect the transformation process towards SSCs in the Arab region. The latter includes but not limited to the political instability; lack of developed and well managed transportation networks; shortage in access to ICT; and high dependence on petroleum outcomes to support national economy, which is the case in selected Arab countries such as the Gulf region (Doherty, 2014).

Despite these challenges, some Arab countries start their journey towards SSCs, either by building SSCs from scratch or by adopting and applying SSCs solutions on the top of existing ones. The next section highlights SSCs initiatives in the Arab region.

2.5.3   SSC Initiatives in the Arab Region

SSC initiatives usually differ from one country to another and between cities within the same country depending on the investment requirements, availability of technological infrastructure, driving forces, and stakeholders involved (Amitrani et al., 2014).

The transformation process is often based on two different development models named: Brownfield model, which is applied on existing cities, and Greenfield model, by which cities are created from scratch (Amitrano, 2014). The International Electrotechnical Commission (IEC, 2014) defines Brownfield initiatives as existing industrial areas that are being rebuilt and developed for a new purpose. The Brownfield approach is used to define the processes and related actions to turn existing urban infrastructures into SSCs of the future. In this case, the transformation or replacement of existing infrastructures should consider the needs of citizens and features of cities. In contrast, Greenfield initiatives refer to new sites that have not been previously used for an industrial purpose. The Greenfield approach is simply used to build SSCs from scratch. It is important noting that Greenfield cities require large investments in ICT technologies for the development of new builds while Brownfield ones require an evolution or transformation of existing ICT capacities. Figure 2.15 illustrates the difference between Greenfield and Brownfield approaches.

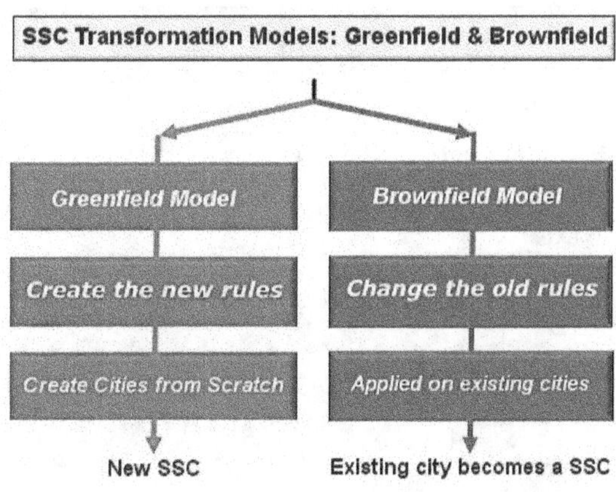

Figure 2.15: Greenfield versus Brownfield SSCs

According to IEC (2014), a Brownfield approach is applicable on industrialized or developed countries. This requires integration of existing infrastructure and, therefore, the transformation process may stretch beyond a decade. A Greenfield approach, in turn, is often adopted in emerging or developing countries. It is applicable on industrialized and developed countries, where new SSCs are planned in an integrated fashion. Regarding the final results, there are no major differences between both approaches; the only thing to be considered is the path and time needed to achieve the objectives of a SSC. A selected list of existing Brownfield and Greenfield SSC initiatives from different regions in the World, except the Arab region, is illustrated in Table 2.8 (Alcatel-Lucent, 2012).

Table 2.8: Examples of Brownfield and Greenfield SSC initiatives - Worldwide

Country	SSC Project	Used Approach
Australia	Ballarat, Gold Coast City, and Ipswich	Brownfield
Austria	Vienna Salzburg	Brownfield
Brazil	Curitiba, Porto Alegre, and Recife	Brownfield
	Pedra Branca	Greenfield
Canada	Moncton, Ottawa, Quebec City, Toronto, Windsor-Essex, and Winnipeg	Brownfield

Country	SSC Project	Used Approach
China	Shanghai, Shenyang, Urumqi, and Wuxi	Brownfield
	Dongtan, and Tianjin Binhai,	Greenfield
Denmark	Copenhagen, and Kalundborg	Brownfield
Estonia	Tallinn	Brownfield
France	Besançon, Issy-les-Moulineaux, and Lyon	Brownfield
Germany	Frankfurt, and	Brownfield
	Bottrop Innovation City Ruhr	Greenfield
Greece	Trikala	Brownfield
Hungary	Sopron	Brownfield
India	Gujarat International Financial Tech-city (GIFT), and Lavasa	Greenfield
Ireland	Dublin	Brownfield
The Netherlands	Amsterdam, Eindhoven, and Rotterdam	Brownfield
Norway	Trondheim	Brownfield
Poland	Gdansk	Brownfield
Portugal	PlanIT Valley (Paredes)	Greenfield
Spain	Malaga Barcelona	Brownfield
South Africa	Cape Town	Brownfield
South Korea	Suwon	Brownfield
	Songdo	Greenfield
Sweden	Malmö	Brownfield
Taiwan	Taoyuan	Brownfield
United Kingdom	Birmingham, and Manchester	Brownfield
United States of America	Bristol, Chattanooga, Cleveland, Dakota County, Dublin, and Riverside	Brownfield

To face globalization challenges and the need for a sustainable urban development, selected cities in the Arab region start adopting Brownfield and/or Greenfield SSCs solutions. These cities include but are not limited to Masdar City and Dubai Silicon Oasis in the United Arab Emirates, Smart Village in Egypt, King Abdullah Economic City in Saudi Arabia, Tunisia Economic City in Tunisia, Rabat City in Morocco, and Lusail City in Qatar. In contrast, many other cities in the region are still suffering from a knowledge gap in relation to the transformation towards SSCs (Ibrahim et al, 2015a).

To start with, Masdar City is a Greenfield modern Arabian eco-city that is being built in the United Arab Emirates (UAE). It is located in the desert near Abu Dhabi, only 15-kilometers from Dubai. The city is a model of a smart and sustainable urban development and planned, by year 2020, to deliver a high quality of life and working environment for its citizens with the least negative impact on the environment. Masdar city is designed to use low carbon technologies and to be a hub for many international telecommunication companies (Manghnani and Bajaj, 2014).

Dubai Silicon Oasis (DSO) is a Greenfield state-of-the-art technology city in the UAE. It is one pilot project of Dubai SSC initiative and wholly owned by the Government of Dubai. The city is designed to provide smart and sustainable living and working environments for its citizens with a mission of promoting and facilitating technology-based research, development and industries within a community that is fully integrated. It is being built to become equivalent to California's Silicon Valley with a vision of incubating leading technological centers. The five main pillars under which the city has been build are education, public facilities, industry, commercial and living and residence (Doherty, 2014).

The Kingdom of Saudi Arabia starts large and medium scale "Economic City" projects, referred to as SSC initiatives. Six new Greenfield SSCs (i.e. economic cities) are emerging from the kingdom's stands. Two of them are still in the planning phase; one to be built in Tabouk city and the other in the eastern province. The remaining four cities; King Abdullah Economic City in Rabigh, Knowledge Economic City in Madinah, Prince Abdul Aziz Bin Mousaed Economic City in Hail, and Jazan Economic City in Jazan; are under development (Osec, 2015). The largest one from the latter denoted cities is King

Abdullah Economic City (KAEC), to be completed in 2020. The city envisioned as a world-class, integrated lifestyle SSC. It is being designed to be economically sustainable and capable of generating many new job opportunities. Using state-of-the-art solutions and technologies, the city is planned to improve public health and safety, lower the carbon emissions, provide a high quality of life and support innovations (Delivered, 2014). It will contain an industrial zone, a resort district, a central business district, residential communities, an educational zone and a seaport that is expected to be the largest in the world on completion.

Lusail City is located about 15 kilometers north of Doha on the Qatari coast. It is a Greenfield SSC project, which will create a modern and aspirant society to face the rapid urbanization of Qatar. To reflect its vision; which is based on four pillars named: future, business, people and integration; the city will provide various smart services in order to satisfy the needs of its residents and visitors (Tok et al., 2014). The latter includes the integrated ICT infrastructure to enable the SSC to function; smart operations to enable integration, management and monitoring of integrated smart service systems; smart energy to improve the efficiency of the electricity network and water usage; and others (Ooredoo, 2014). The city, through green technologies, will also reduce air and water pollutions, carbon emissions and facilitate conservation of soil.

Finally, Tunisia officially announced its first SSC project at the end of 2014. The Tunisian Economic City will be built in the Enfidha district of Tunis city as an integrated SSC with strong base in commerce, education, culture and tourism. The project is still in its planning phase with a vision of contributing in the formulation of the overall economic and future sustainable development map of Tunisian Republic. The objectives of the project include facilitating commercial trade, attacking Arab and international investment, improving tourism sector, attracting students from Arab and African countries, creating job opportunities, providing high quality of life for citizens and others (TunisiaEC, 2014).

Despite the fact that the mentioned examples above refer to SSC initiatives being built from scratch; some large and medium scale Brownfield initiatives have been announced by different governments in the region. The latter includes cities in UAE, Qatar, Kingdom of Saudi Arabia (Doherty, 2014), Kuwait, Oman, Bahrain (MEED, 2015), and Rabat in

Morocco (Wheatley, 2012). These cities start adopting SSC solutions in order to provide a sustainable and a high quality of life for their residents and visitors as well as to empower their economics and business environments. Table 2.9 summarizes the status of SSC initiatives in the Arab region (Ibrahim et al., 2015a). The dash character indicates the lack of any SSC initiative in the selected country.

Table 2.9: Brownfield and Greenfield SSC Initiatives in Arab Region

Country	Are there any SSC initiatives	Used Approach	Example of a SSC Initiative
Algeria	YES	Brownfield Greenfield	Algiers Cyberpark City of Sidi Abdellah
Bahrain	YES	Brownfield	Manama
Comoros	NO	-	-
Djibouti	NO	-	-
Egypt	YES	Brownfield Greenfield	Cairo Smart Village
Iraq	NO	-	-
Jordan	YES	Brownfield	Amman
Kuwait	YES	Brownfield	Kuwait City
Lebanon	YES	Brownfield	Beirut
Libya	NO	-	-
Mauritania	NO	-	-
Morocco	YES	Brownfield	Rabat
Oman	YES	Brownfield	Masqat
Palestine	YES	Brownfield Greenfield	Ramallah Techno Park
Qatar	YES	Brownfield Greenfield	Doha City Lusail City
Saudi Arabia	YES	Brownfield / Greenfield	King Abdullah Economic City Knowledge Economic City Prince Abdul Aziz Bin Mousaed Economic City Jazan Economic City
Somalia	NO	-	-
Sudan	YES	Brownfield	Khartoum
Syria	NO	-	-
Tunisia	YES	Brownfield Greenfield	Tunisia Tunisia Economic City (in planning stage)

Country	Are there any SSC initiatives	Used Approach	Example of a SSC Initiative
United Arab Emirates	YES	Brownfield Greenfield	Dubai City Abu Dhabi City Masdar City Dubai Silicon Oasis
Yemen	NO	-	-

2.5.4 Discussion on the Findings of SSC Initiatives in the Arab Region

Many Arab countries, thereby cities, are still suffering from a gap in knowledge in relation to the transformation towards SSCs. This gap occurs due to a set of constraints exists at a country and/or a city level. The latter includes but not limited to the socio-economic inequality, inappropriate ICT infrastructure, unstable political situations, lack of developed and well-managed transportation networks, and youth unemployment. As a result, a need for a comprehensive SSC's transformation framework that can be customized to meet the characteristics of each city is emerged.

2.6 Conclusion

SSC is a fuzzy concept with no standardized terminologies that can be used to comprehensively describing it. Despite the absence of an agreed upon definition, a SSC is evolving as an urban space that tends to solve urban problems, making the urban development more sustainable while improving the daily life of citizens. As a result, many cities around the globe, including selected cities in the Arab region, start their move towards SSCs. The latter requires a holistic, systematic transformation process that leads to different changes at all city levels. The literature shows that existing transformation models are neglecting essential objectives of a SSC. For instance, the inconsideration of checking the city readiness for change before planning the SSC solutions and the negligence of one or more dimensions of a SSC. This constitutes a gap in knowledge, that can be closed by introducing a robust transformation roadmap and framework.

The ICTs play a crucial role in SSCs. They provide the required infrastructure to connect various city systems, creating a system-of-systems to facilitate the interaction between different city levels and services. The SSC digital platform helps in analyzing the city data collected from different sources for understanding how a city is functioning in relation to its services, consumptions, and lifestyle. This also allow sharing knowledge between different levels of a city, leading to significant improvements in the urban quality of life. A SSC should provide at least one smart solution for each of its six dimensions, utilizing the ICTs as the key medium to ensure a sustainable future of a city.

On a final note, many cities are still suffering from a knowledge gap in relation to the transformation towards SSCs; due to a set of constraints that exists at a country and/or a city level. This chapter overviewed these challenges and explored practices from around the globe in general and the Arab region in specific in relation to the realization of the transformation towards SSCs.

The next chapter provides a detailed discussion on the followed methodology.

CHAPTER THREE: RESEARCH METHODOLOGY

3.1   Introduction

In this chapter, the methodology followed by this book is described. To elaborate, this chapter provides an overall understanding of the research philosophy, approach, design, strategy and data collection. The used data analysis methods are explained as well.

3.2   Research Philosophy

Research philosophy is related to the development of knowledge about a particular field. It contains assumptions that will underpin the research strategy and the methods used under this strategy (Saunders et al., 2009). There are different research philosophies, but the most popular approaches are the positivism and interpretivism.

Positivism is a scientific method that includes the systematic description and observation of a phenomenon contextualized within a theory or a model. It also focuses on testing the proposed research using inferential statistical methods, such as surveys, and interprets the statistical results in the light of the used theory or model. The interpretive philosophy, in turn, concerns with the understanding of what is interesting, specific, and unique in a phenomenon and how this understanding is changed based on time, context, and culture (Ponterotto, 2005). It provides the understanding needed regarding a phenomenon based on the meanings given to it by other people. Doing so requires entering the social world of the research area and understand how others are interpreting this area from their point of view (Saunders et al., 2009). Saunders et al, (2009) indicate that none of these philosophies can be considered as a 'better' one to be adopted for a specific research area. The philosophy selection is highly dependent on the nature of the research question(s). Moreover, in practical reality both philosophies are used together, in a mixed fashion, to serve in answering the research question(s).

Stemming from the above, this research selects a mixed philosophy. The nature of this research, which focuses on understanding the world point of view regarding the concept of SSCs and its related transformation process along with the aim of proposing a new thorough transformation models, is consistent with an interpretivist position and a positivism orientation.

3.3   Research Approach

There are two types of approaches used to conduct a research, the deductive and inductive approaches. In a deductive or quantitative (i.e. top-down) approach, a clear research theoretical position (i.e. conceptual model) is developed prior to the data collection. In an inductive or qualitative (i.e. bottom-up) approach, a theory is developed after collecting and analyzing the data (Saunders et al., 2009).

Saunders et al. (2009) indicate the necessity of not to start a research using a predetermined theories or conceptual models (i.e. deductive approach) even if a research purpose with its research question(s) are clearly defined. Instead, there is a need first to review the literature to collect a competent knowledge on the area under research. Although it is impossible to review every single piece in the literature before collecting the research data, it is recommended to review the most significant and relevant researches in the subject area. This helps in identifying any issues that have been overlooked in other researches (i.e. gaps) as well as lead to the identification of theory(ies) that no one else has thought about before.

Hinkin (1998), in turn, suggests that if the followed theoretical foundation of a research provides adequate data and information to generate a set of overlooked items in other researches, the deductive approach should then be followed. He also emphasizes the necessity of understanding the phenomenon to be investigated through reviewing the literature. This review helps in developing the theoretical model of the items to be proposed throughout the research study.

Arising from the above, this research follows a hybrid approach using both, deductive/quantitative and inductive/qualitative approaches. The first part of this research is exploratory in nature, which fits with the inductive/qualitative approach. This approach concerns with understanding and interpreting a phenomenon in question through its meanings in the literature. It helps in reviewing, investigating the literature regarding the phenomenon of SSCs and studying, analyzing existing SSC transformation roadmaps and frameworks. It also helps in selecting an appropriate theory to be used as a theoretical foundation for this research. Note that this approach relates to the interpretivist philosophy.

The deductive/quantitative approach is then followed to generate observations on existing transformation models and to introduce a theoretical logic model for the transformation towards SSCs. This also includes introducing new definitions for the concepts of transformation, roadmap, and framework in the context of SSCs. The theoretical model is then used to propose the desired SSC transformation roadmap and framework. Both models are then validated using a data driven validation method. Note that this approach relates to the positivism approach (Saunders et al., 2009).

3.4   Research Design

Research design, as defined by Saunders et al. (2009), is dedicated to the overall plan of a research. This plan should be clear and consistent with the research objectives and its desired results. It often consists of a number of closely related activities that may overlapped with each other on some stages of the research. Figure 3.1 summarizes the overall plan of this research.

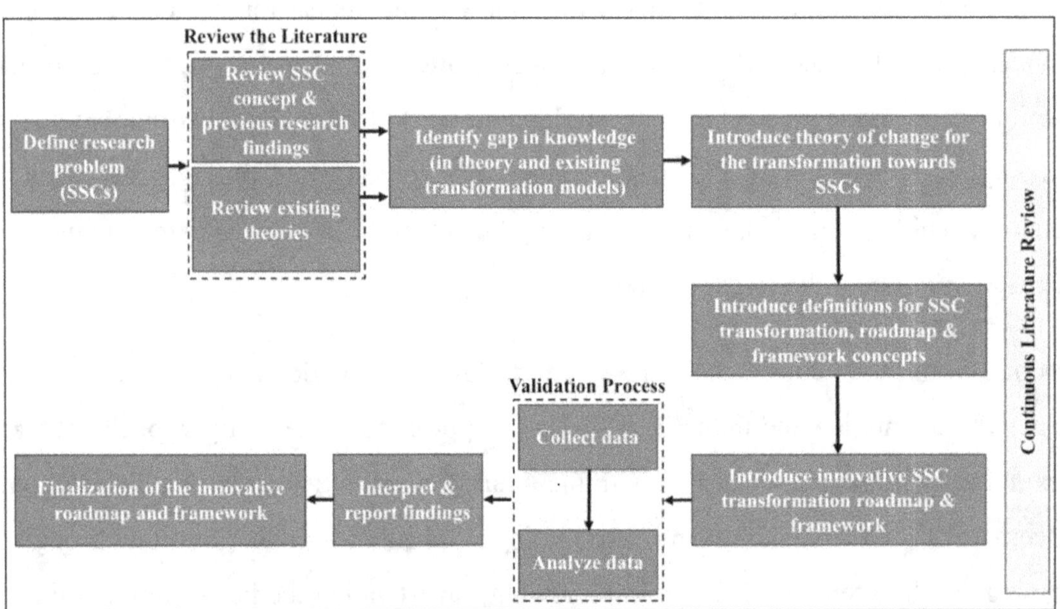

Figure 3.1: Research Design/Plan

The research plan starts by defining the research problem and its related research question, specifically, *"What are the aspects that should be considered to ensure a comprehensive, systematic transformation process of traditional cities into Smart Sustainable Cities?"* The research process then continues moving from reviewing the literature regarding existing transformation models and theories up to the validation of the proposed innovative transformation roadmap and framework using an appropriate data driven method. This research enriches its understanding to different aspects related to the SSC concept and its related transformation roadmap and framework through continuous review of the literature. This helps in selecting an appropriate theoretical foundation, identifying gaps in existing transformation models, linking SSC concept to urban development, selecting an adequate validation method, among others.

3.5   Research Strategy and Data Collection

Research strategy is concerned with the tactics used to collect and analyze the research data (Saunders et al., 2009). In the context of this book, there are two types of collected and analyzed data. The first type focuses on capturing a gap in knowledge in existing transformation roadmaps and frameworks in the literature. The second is related to the validation process of the proposed innovative roadmap and framework. For the former, the data are collected using a desktop research method strategy. This helps in collecting data from existing resources for the benefit of the following:

1. Review a SSC concept in relation to its definition and dimensions along with their related factors. Collected data is used to compare existing SSC definitions and dimensions to select the most appropriate ones based on relevant justifications. It is worth noting that this type of data is known as secondary data as it is collected from secondary sources (i.e. from the literature) and does not report any new contributions.

2. Review previous research findings, specifically, in relation to existing SSC transformation roadmaps and frameworks and collect data regarding their identified phases and components. Collected data, which is also secondary data as in point 1, provides the knowledge needed to understand the transformation directions in the context of SSCs, identifying main elements and components to consider during a transformation process. It also helps in identifying the overlooked SSC dimensions and factors in these models.

3. Review existing SSC initiatives globally with a focus on the Arab region, highlighting their related transformation challenges in general and in the region in specific.

4. Review the literature to select a relevant and significant theory that can provide the needed theoretical foundation of this book. Collected data from the selected theory, which is secondary data, helps in identifying the neglected essential elements and components in existing studied transformation models in the literature. It also helps in introducing a theoretical logic model for the transformation towards SSCs. This model provides the basis for proposing a comprehensive, systematic SSC transformation roadmap and framework with the aim of closing the identified gap in knowledge in existing models.

5. Review definitions of the concepts of transformation, roadmap, and framework in the context of SSCs to identify their existing knowledge gap. This stage is based on the secondary data collection method and keywords extraction method. The former is used to review existing definitions of the three concepts in the literature. The keyword extraction method is then used to extract the keywords that are being used in describing each definition (Mihalcea and Tarau, 2004) and identifying existing gap in knowledge, which closed by proposing a new definition for each concept.

The second type of data is related to the validation of the innovative SSC transformation roadmap and framework. For this purpose, the survey strategy is applied. Validation data is collected using a survey questionnaire instrument and analyzed using an adequate data analysis software. The survey strategy is most frequently used to answer what, where, who, how much, and how many questions. It provides the needed evidences on particular relationships between variables of the model(s) being validated (Saunders et al., 2009).

It is worth noting that the validation process followed by this book is based on the quantitative (i.e. deductive) approach, to which the survey strategy is often associated (Saunders et al., 2009). The survey strategy is one of the types being used by many researchers to validate the models proposed in different research areas related to social and urban development studies (Sharp et al., 2002), such as the case of this book. This type of model needs a long period to be applied on real cases. Therefore; the survey strategy helps in check the robustness of these models (Robinson, 1997). This helps in collecting data that can be analyzed quantitatively using inferential and descriptive statistics.

3.6   Analysis Methods

This book uses different types of data analysis methods based on the type of the collected data. The latter are analyzed for the aim of (1) mapping existing transformation models to the SSC six dimensions and their related factors, (2) proposing new definitions for the concepts of transformation, roadmap, and framework in the context of SSCs, (3) proposing new SSC transformation roadmap and framework, and (4) validating the two proposed models.

3.6.1   Mapping existing Models to the SSC dimensions and Factors

For each studied transformation roadmap and framework in the literature, a list of dimensions and factors over which it is being proposed has been identified. Each list was compared to the SSC six dimensions, namely, smart economy, smart environment, smart governance, smart living, smart mobility, and smart people along with their related factors. Results were tabulated in two different tables showing overlooked dimensions and factors in each model. The first table was dedicated to the dimensions and the second to the factors.

3.6.2   New Definitions

After conducting the literature review on existing definitions of transformation, roadmap, and framework concepts in the context of SSCs, a set of keywords that constitute each definition of each concept was created. Meaning that, for the transformation concept, a list of key terms used to identify the concept of transformation in the context of SSCs was created. The same technique was applied on the roadmap and framework concepts. Extracted keywords for each concept were compared to others, creating a list of most frequently used terms for that concept. The list was compared to the objectives of a SSC, identifying a gap in knowledge in existing definitions for each concept. This gap is then closed by proposing new thorough definitions.

3.6.3   Innovative Transformation Roadmap and Framework

In order to propose a thorough transformation roadmap and framework, there was first a need to identify a gap in knowledge in existing models in the literature. Accordingly, an extensive literature review on existing SSC transformation roadmaps and frameworks was conducted. Due to the lack of a theory for the transformation towards SSCs, an extensive literature review on existing theories from neighboring disciplines in addition to theories of change was conducted. This includes theories related to sustainable urban development, human systems integration, Theory of Change (ToC), theory of cities, and theory of quality of life. After selecting the appropriate theory, which is the ToC, the analysis of collected data from the literature proceeded as below:

1. For the transformation roadmap:
    a. The main phases and components constituting each studied roadmap were extracted and tabulated.
    b. Common phases and components between all roadmaps were tabulate, creating a list of essential stages and elements to consider in the proposed roadmap.
    c. Based on the selected theory and other related studies from neighboring disciplines, the overlooked phases and components in studied roadmaps and existing gap in knowledge were identified and listed.
    d. For each phase in the innovative roadmap, the list of common components was considered and overlooked ones were added with relevant justification.
    e. A comparison between the proposed roadmap and existing roadmaps was tabulated, highlighting the significance of the proposed one comparing to others.

2. For the transformation framework:
    a. The main layers and tools constituting each studied framework were extracted and tabulated.
    b. Common layers and tools were tabulated, creating a list of essential layers and tools to consider and use in the innovative framework.
    c. Overlooked components and tools in existing frameworks were either adopted from existing studies or proposed.

d. As the aim of the framework is to realize the transformation roadmap and put its stages into action, this book identified the layers and tools needed to realize the added phases and components of the proposed novel roadmap.

e. A comparison between the proposed framework and existing frameworks was tabulated, highlighting the significance of the proposed one compared to others.

3.6.4   Validation of the Innovative Models

A survey questionnaire was selected as a data collection instrument for the validation process. Data was collected to validate the proposed SSC transformation roadmap and framework based on experts' knowledge and views. The questionnaire was in English language and questions were formulated using simple language for ease of understanding. Information assessing knowledge regarding the research objectives and some used terms were included. The validity of the questionnaire was based on the advisors' knowledge and views. The questionnaire was distributed personally either by hand or via emails and the data was collected over a period of three months.

The questionnaire consisted of two types of questions, close-ended and open-ended questions. The majority of questions were close-ended; each has an open-ended section to allow experts to provide their comments if they have any. Close-ended questions were analyzed using the Microsoft Office Excel 2015 for Mac machines. The application supports all needed mathematical and statistical equations to analyze collected data. It also provides different types of charts to represent analyzed data graphically, allowing graphical comparison of results. For standalone questions (i.e. questions with no sub-questions), pie charts were used as they are appropriate to show relative values. Meaning that, answers of such a question are dedicated to only one question statement, where a single answer is needed out of less than six options (Fryrear, 2015). Column charts were used for questions where respondent can select more than one option to the same question (i.e. multiple-choice questions with multiple answers). In this case, vertical column charts provide visualization of grouped data along with their ranking values (i.e. percentages) (Fryrear, 2015). For questions that were divided into a series of sub-questions (i.e. categories), horizontal stacked bar charts were used. This type of charts is useful when a question has many categories that cannot be illustrated well using vertical column charts.

It helps in showing the differences of answers regarding each category. Data can also be represented as positive and negative data, separating agreeing answers from disagreeing ones (Fryrear, 2015).

Open-ended questions were analyzed by the researcher by extracting the main idea behind each answer to be used for recommendations and future directions.

3.7   Ethical Consideration

This book was subject to certain ethical issues. To render the research ethics, the rights to informed consent, anonymity, confidentiality, voluntary participation and privacy, and preventing harm were observed (Saunders et al., 2009). All participants were asked to report their acceptance to contribute to the validation process by signing a consent form letter. This letter aimed at reassuring participant that their participation in the research is voluntary and only for research purposes with their right to withdraw from it at any time. The ethical issues of this book were addressed as follows:

1. *Informed Consent*: the researcher informed explicitly each participant about the nature of the research, its objectives, purposes, and outputs and the reasons behind the questionnaire as a validation instrument. After this, each participant was asked to sign a consent form.
2. *Anonymity*: this book ensures that the participants' names and their personal information were not disclosed in the research reports; it also detached the signed consent from the questionnaire. No identify information was entered into the data analysis software, and experts were only represented using abbreviations (e.g. P1, P2, P3, …) in the used application.
3. *Confidentiality*: this book made it clear, as stated in the consent form, that the participants' answers would only be used for research purposes and for the benefit of this book only. Participants' identity was not revealed when documenting or publishing the book as well.
4. *Voluntary Participation and Privacy*: it was stated clearly in the consent form that participation in the validation process is voluntary and that the participant has the right to withdraw from the research at any time. They were also able to refuse revealing certain personal information about themselves.

5. *Preventing Harm*: this research made it sure that participants were not put in a situation to be harmed or abused either physically or psychologically during the conduction of the validation process.

3.8   Conclusion

This chapter explained the research philosophy, approach, design, and strategy and data collection and analysis methods. It sets out different steps to be followed in proposing a new thorough SSC transformation roadmap and framework. For this purpose, the research of this book follows a hybrid approach, using deductive/quantitative and inductive/qualitative approaches. The survey questionnaire instrument was used to validate the innovative models while considering certain ethical issues.

The following chapter presents the theoretical foundation of this book research.

CHAPTER FOUR: THEORETICAL FOUNDATION

4.1   Introduction

A theoretical foundation of a research serves as a crucial basic for explaining, describing, and predicting the phenomena it relates to. It provides answers to what is behind the scenes to understand the phenomenon in question (Whetten, 1989). Such understanding allows researchers and practitioners to realize the underlying conceptual structure of the phenomenon and enable them to take meaningful and purposed actions. A theory could be considered as an input and as an output of a research. As an input, it helps in conceptualizing a given phenomenon of interest and capturing it in the proposed observations. As an output, a theory assists in documenting what is known about the phenomenon based on the research consequences to inform others about the findings (Muller and Urbach, 2013).

Transforming a city into a SSC is a complex, multidimensional process that cannot be achieved overnight. This process leads to different changes at all city levels, including economic, social, environmental, and governance levels. Many factors should be considered before and during a transformation process to ensure its success. The latter includes understanding the concept of change in the context of SSCs, why it becomes a need, and how it will be applied all city levels. Therefore, a theoretical foundation of a change concept in the context of SSCs is needed. However, with a lack of a standardized theory for SSCs, theories from neighboring disciplines, such as the Theory of Change (ToC), can be used for this purpose.

This chapter aims at providing a strong theoretical foundation for the innovative models to be proposed by this book. It starts by providing a novel link between the ToC and SSCs and use this link to propose an unprecedented theoretical logic model for the transformation towards SSCs. The proposed link along with the novel theoretical logic model were published in the paper titled: "Theory of Change for the Transformation towards Smart Sustainable Cities" in the International Conference on Sensors, Networks, Smart and Emerging Technologies (Ibrahim et al., 2017b).

The structure of this chapter is as follows. In Section 4.2, the reason behind selecting the ToC along with its definition, elements and stages are carried out in addition to the importance of the change readiness in the ToC. Section 4.3 sheds light on the introduced linkage between the ToC and SSCs. The need of the technological change in the field of SSCs is presented in Section 4.4. Section 4.5 is devoted to the proposed theoretical logic model for the transformation towards SSCs. The chapter concludes in Section 0.

4.2   Why Theory of Change?

ToC emerged in the mid 1990s from the fields of evaluation theory and social change theory (i.e. practices of community initiatives) with the aim of providing new ways of analyzing and evaluating programmes and initiatives related to social and political changes (James, 2011; Stein and Valters, 2012; Vogel, 2012a). There is also a strong link between the ToC and the planning theory (i.e. planning process), as the former is widely used as a tool for strategic planning (Anderson, 2004; NPC, 2012; Vogel, 2012a; Inness & Booher, 2014). ToC provides the methodological and logical thinking and models required to identify the current context and situation, address the needs, and achieve these needs through a series of change events/activities (NPC, 2012; Rogers, 2014).

From the development perspective, ToC is used as a way to focus on the theoretical underpinning of a project, identify linkages between project inputs and outputs, and explain how a project is expected to work. It helps in developing the required logical planning model of an initiative and programme (Vogel, 2012). From the evaluation perspective, the ToC has emerged to model and evaluate social programmes and community initiatives including complex ones (Stein and Valters, 2012; Vogel, 2012). As a result, the ToC could be considered as a central building block that lays the foundation for the strategic planning, measurement, learning, and evaluation planning and design of an initiative and programme (ORSIMPACT, 2015).

ToC has strong roots in a number of disciplines. The latter includes sociology, political science, communications, environmental and organizational psychology (Stachowiak, 2013), education, public health (Laing and Todd, 2015), and community, urban and international development (Stein and Valters, 2012, Vogel, 2012a, Vogel, 2012b; Laing and Todd, 2015). These strong roots come from the power of the ToC to focus not only on generating the required knowledge about the effectiveness of programmes and initiatives, but also on explaining the methods that are needed to be used to make a programme and initiative effective (Chris et al., 2011).

Given the fact that implementing a SSC initiative introduces changes at the different dimensions of a city, this book justifies its novel contributions to knowledge based on the "Theory of Change". More details regarding this issue are provided in Section 4.3.

4.2.1   Theory of Change Definition

There are various definitions of the ToC depending on the area of research over which it will be applied; however; it is commonly realized as a term of why and how a given intervention will lead to a specific change taking into consideration the context over which a change will take place. In an early attempt to define the concept, Weiss (1995) describes the ToC as a theory of why and how an initiative works. It is a way of describing a set of assumptions that are used to explain both a set of mini-activities that leads to the long-term goals and the connections between these activities and the desired outcomes of a programme or initiative (Weiss, 1995).

Anderson (2005) defines the ToC as a tool that can be used to develop solutions for complex social problems. It articulates explicitly the assumptions about the process through which changes will take place. It specifies the ways in which the required outcomes that are needed to achieve the desired long-term change will be announced and documented when they occur. The Organizational Research Services (ORS, 2007) defines the ToC as a conceptual model that is used to achieve a common vision. It is usually expressed in a visual diagram to address the linkages between strategies, goals, and outcomes, along with the logical interconnection between them. It provides an overall map of how to get from one state to another. It can be named as a blueprint, a roadmap, a theory of action, an engine of change and others. James (2011) defines the ToC as an ongoing process of reflections to explore a change and how it happens in a particular context. It allows a programme to analyze how change comes about, articulate the understanding of change, draw external learning about development, and acknowledge the change complexity. It is often represented in a diagrammatic form with an appropriate narrative summary.

The Ecosystem Services for Poverty Alleviation (ESPA) defines the ToC as a dialogue-based process that is used to generate a description of a sequence of events expected to lead to a desired outcome in a particular context. The description is often presented in a diagrammatic form and narrative summary to provide a guiding framework of the change model showing the project team and stakeholders how and why the desired goals can be reached (Vogel, 2012a). A research study proposed for the UK Department of International Development defines the ToC as an outcome-based approach that applies a critical thinking to the design, implementation, and evaluation of programmes and initiatives intended to provide changes in their context. The research study shows that the ToC is being used increasingly in international development by many governmental development agencies, non-governmental organizations, civil society organizations, and research programmes aiming to support the development process outcomes (Vogel, 2012b).

Based on the Center for Theory of Change, the ToC can be seen as a comprehensive description and illustration of why and how a required change is expected to happen in a particular context. It provides a mapping between change programme/initiative activities and the desired goals to be achieved by first identifying the desired long-term goals and then work backward to identify a set of activities that are needed to achieve these goals. The latter is presented and mapped out in outcomes framework (Center for ToC, 2013). Finally yet importantly, a research study on using theories of change for development, research, and evaluation defines ToC as a theory-based approach for designing, implementing, and evaluating changes at different levels including individual, organizational, and community levels. It can articulate how a programme or initiative could achieve its desired outcomes through a set of actions, considering its context (Laing and Todd, 2015).

Putting this all together, the ToC, as illustrated in Figure **4.1**, is a dialogue-based process used to generate a description of how and why a set of activities (i.e. actions) can lead to a desired change in a particular context. The description is usually presented in a diagrammatic form and narrative summary (Vogel, 2012a).

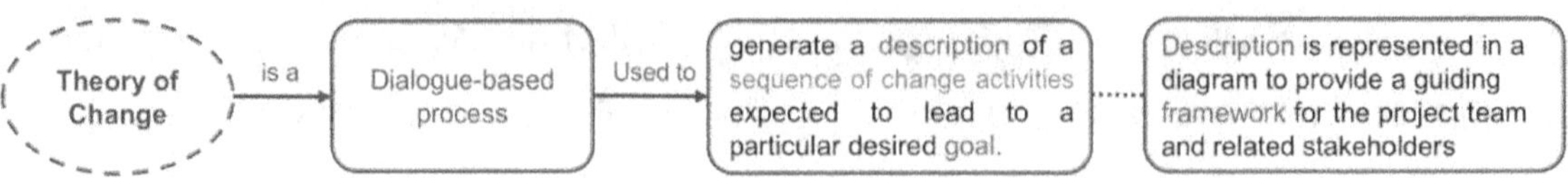

Figure 4.1: Theory of Change in its Simplest Form

To clarify the usage of the ToC, the following example is provided. As illustrate in Figure 4.2, if the long-term goal of city planners is to reduce the level of pollution of their city, then city planners and key stakeholders should at first have a dialogue together about the pollution phenomenon and its effect on the overall city environment and citizens. Following step is to agree on a set of change activities that should be taken to face this problem. For instance, this may include activities such as start using of solar systems to produce lights, using of wind energy to produce electricity, planting more trees to enhance air recycling process, and using of eco-cars and bicycles to reduce CO_2 emission. Finally, a transformation process should be represented in a diagrammatic form with narrative summary to facilitate the management, monitoring, and evaluation of a change process.

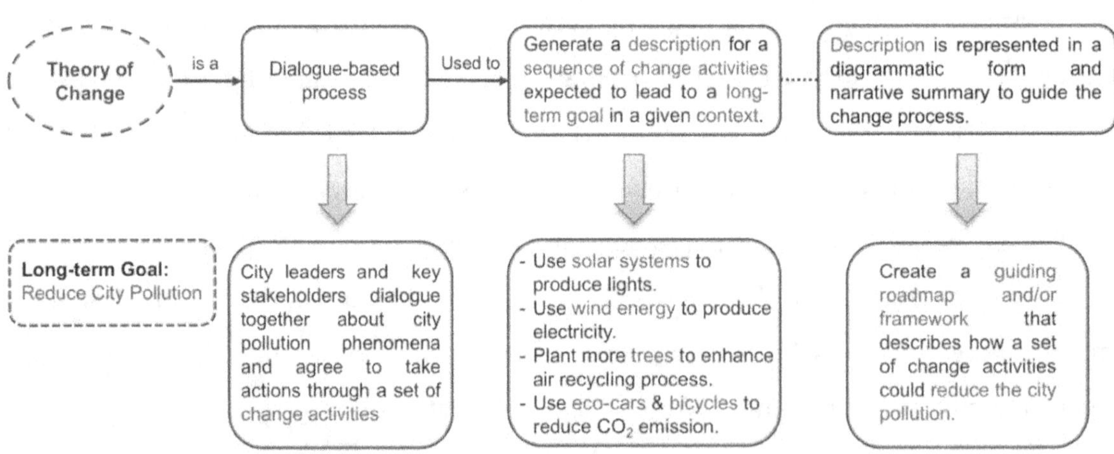

Figure 4.2: Reflecting a ToC Definition on a City Pollution Phenomena

4.2.2   Theory of Change Elements and Stages

ToC is an ongoing process of analysis and reflection. It is not a one-off exercise to design and/or evaluate a programme and initiative; rather it means an ongoing cycle of learning and adaptation (Weiss, 1995; Anderson, 2005; James, 2011; Vogel, 2012a). To reach a better understanding of a programme or initiative, the ToC process provides five essential elements that should be addressed in order, as stages (i.e. phases), namely: (1) context of the initiative, (2) long-term change, (3) sequence of events, (4) assumptions, and (5) change diagram and narrative summary (Vogel, 2012; Allen, 2016). The required activities under each element are described below:

- **Stage 1: Initiative Context**: this includes analysis of the current state of the economic, social, environmental, technological, and political conditions of the problem the initiative is seeking to influence in addition to other actors that may influence the change (e.g. stakeholders, institutions, target groups, among others). Identifying the availability of required resources for a change is necessary as well. The project team should answer a list of questions related to the initiative context to be planned, designed, and implemented. Examples of these questions are as below:

    - Which communities are to be affected by the initiative (e.g. individuals, groups, households, geographical areas, communities)?

    - What are the main economic, social, political and technological factors that affect the change in this context?

    - Which ecosystems are to be affected?

    - What are the key ecosystem pressures?

    - What are the existing policies, resources, practices, attitudes and beliefs that can be used to support the change and what is the gap?

    - Who can affect the key desired changes?

    - What relationships exist between stakeholders?

- **Stage 2: Long-term Change**: this includes identifying a clear statement of a long-term change the initiative is seeking to support and for whose ultimate benefit. Examples of questions to be considered by the project team are as below:

  - What is the most essential change that must be seen in the context, without which the project has no meaning?

  - What are the short-term and medium-term changes that are needed to be accomplished to facilitate the achievement of a long-term change?

  - Why is/are this (these) desired change(s) being the most essential?

  - What are the positive outcomes that might be seen as a result of this change?

  - What is approximately the lasting timeframe of the change after the project?

- **Stage 3: Sequence of Events**: this includes the identification of the sequence of activities/actions that may lead to the desired long-term outcome(s) in a given context. This stage is not a literal prediction of the future; rather it should be approached as a conceptual exercise about the required steps that may lead to the desired impact of a project in a given context. Examples of questions to consider during this stage are:

  - What are the essential change activities (i.e. actions) that are needed to achieve the desired short-term, medium-term and long-term changes?

  - What strategies and resources are needed to support achieving the desired change (i.e. short, medium and long-term changes)?

  - For short-term change, who are the key stakeholders to engage in a change process?

  - What are the responsibilities of stakeholders in the project?

  - What type of collaboration and partnerships does the project team need to build?

  - What will these collaborations and partnerships bring to the project?

  - What are the other requirements needed to support the changes?

- **Stage 4: Assumptions:** this includes identifying a set of assumptions about how the change events might happen and whether their resulted outputs are appropriate for influencing the desired change in a given context. Making assumptions explicit takes time and requires dialogue with others. They are usually informed by professional experiences, organizational values, and individual beliefs, and influenced by analytical perspectives and particular intellectual traditions. The goal of this stage is to check and test the identified assumptions through the ToC process in order to improve them as needed and create new ways of addressing issues needed to the desired change. Examples of questions to considered by a project team during this stage are as below:

- What is the worldview that may enhance the understanding of the change process?

- What is the most essential change that would make the project fail if not achieved and why this essential change is important?

- Why do the identified short-term changes seem to be the most essential ones?

- Are there any other short-term changes that are missing?

- What else would be needed to happen in order to support the short-term change?

- **Stage 5: Diagram and Narrative Summary**: aims at representing the ToC sequence and capturing the discussion about a change process using diagrams and narrative summary. Creating a diagrammatical model and narrative summary is highly dependent on the resulted discussions on the previously accomplished four stages.

To simplify its understanding and requirements, this book introduces a graphical representation of the ToC elements and stages as illustrated in Figure 4.3.

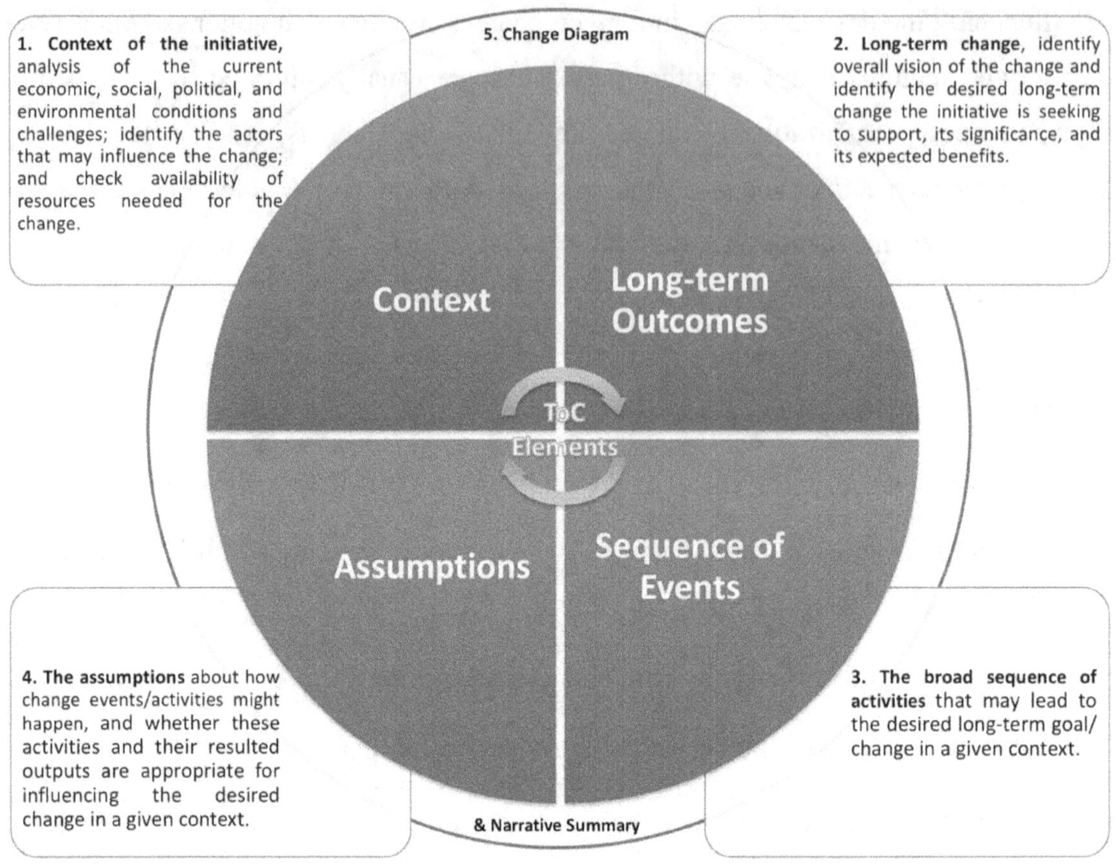

Figure 4.3: Theory of Change Elements and Stages

4.2.3   Theory of Change Management: Types of Change

Many types of change exist in the literature; however; they are most likely to be categorized into three key types, namely, developmental (incremental) change, transitional change, and transformational change. Each type of change is used based on the needs and selecting the required change could be determined through answering the following two questions:

- What is the complexity of the change (i.e. is it a simple or a complex change)?

- Is the change relatively predictable or not (i.e. are there clear solutions to the change)?

Answering these questions helps in selecting and applying the appropriate type of change depending on the complexity and predictability of the desired change. The difference between the developmental (incremental), transitional and transformational changes, as illustrated in Figure 4.4 (Anderson and Anderson, 2001), is summarized as below (Biech, 2008; Rikerjoe, 2009; Folke et al., 2010; Roggema et al., 2012):

- *Developmental Change (Incremental Change):* is a small-scale discrete change that is used when the desired outcomes are simple and predictable. It is a continuous adjustment and improvement of existing systems. With this type of change, the needed level of investment is fairly low. Little or no modifications are needed on existing systems, strategies, policies and procedures. Individual skills and abilities can be used to implement it. Developmental/incremental change, therefore, does not alter essential forms, fits or functions of existing system components.

- *Transitional Change:* is a restructuring and reorganizing change that is used when the desired outcomes are simple and unpredictable or complex and predictable. A transitional change focuses on designing and implementing a new state of a system aiming to solve its old state problem(s). Roggema et al. (2012) define it as *"a gradual, continuous process of societal change, changing the character of society (or a complex part) structurally"*. This type of change requires higher investment than that for developmental/incremental change and some modifications are needed on existing systems, strategies, policies and procedure. Individual skills and abilities can be used to implement it. Transitional change motivates and raises an examination and refinement of the system's mission, strategy and culture.

- *Transformational Change:* is a long-term change that is used when the desired outcomes are complex and unpredictable. Folke et al. (2010) define it as *"the capacity to transform the stability landscape itself in order to become a different kind of system, to create a fundamentally new system when ecological, economic, or social structures make the existing system untenable"*. This change requires the highest investment than others. Potential changes and radical modifications are needed on existing systems, strategies, policies, culture and procedures. To implement the change, new skills, abilities and ways of thinking are required. Transformational change requires a fundamental revision of one or more of the system's mission, strategy and culture.

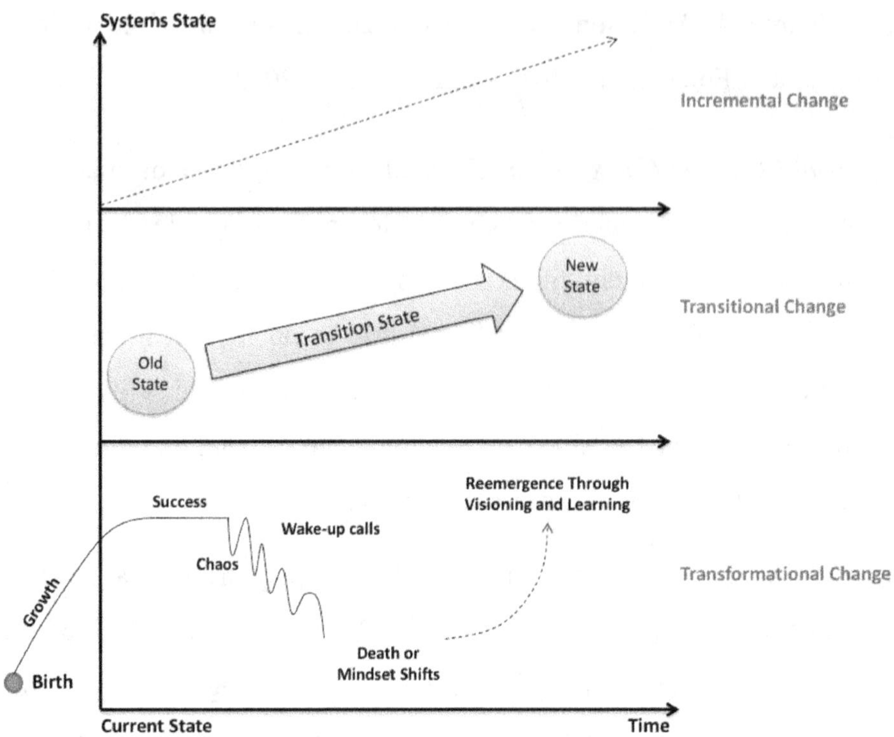

Figure 4.4: Developmental (Incremental), Transitional, and Transformational Changes

There are different issues to consider in selecting the appropriate type of change to use. A change is either occurs as a response to a certain event; such as the case of the developmental/ incremental change; or a change of strategies; such as the transitional and transformational changes (Roggema et al., 2012). Table 4.1 illustrates some examples of each type of these changes (Queensland Government, 2016).

Table 4.1: Examples of different types of changes

Types of Change		
Developmental/Incremental Change	**Transitional Change**	**Transformational Change**
• Improving existing billing and reporting methods. • Updating payroll procedures. • Refocusing marketing strategies.	• Introducing new services and/or products. • Implementing new technologies. • Minor system restructuring.	• Implementing major strategic and culture changes. • Adopting radically different technologies. • Major system restructuring.

On another note, the 'transitional' change has been used by many research studies in the notion of the 'transformational' change. Despite the existence of a certain similarity between both terms, there are three major differences between them as illustrated in Figure 4.5 and summarized below:

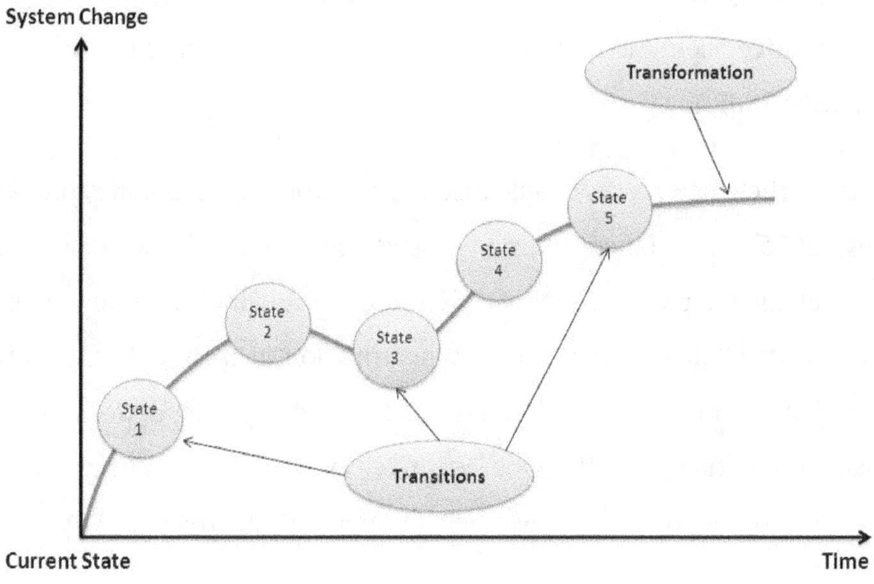

Figure 4.5: Transformational and Transitional Changes of a System

1. 'Transformation' is a continuous process that is about a new trajectory (i.e. new system), while 'transition' refers to a shift from one system state to another in term of dynamics in a system. It is about re-orientation of an existing trajectory (Yang, 2010).

2. From management perspective, 'transformation' is a well-planned process that is mainly driven by internal forces such as economic growth, poverty, governance strategies, technological growth, environmental degradation, and others. 'Transition', in turn, is a non-linear change process that is mainly driven by external forces such as fundamental change to political systems, global economic crisis, climate change, and others (Yang, 2010).

3. A transformational change usually involves both the developmental/incremental and transitional changes (Queensland Government, 2016) but not the opposite.

A transformation process, as illustrated in Figure 4.5, may include a set of transitional change processes to simplify achieving a transformational change long-term goal(s) in complex contexts (Policy Horizons Canada, 2012). A transitional approach, in turn, could help in achieving the transformational change short-term goal(s) by making an appropriate change plan for one or more short-term change(s) and working towards this plan (Daszko and Sheinberg, 2005). For example, in their transformational 2002 National Environmental Plan, Netherlands used a transitional change process to develop a set of activities to improve their transportation, agriculture and construction systems (Policy Horizons Canada, 2009).

A transformational change process could also benefit from the techniques provided by the ToC (Hivos, 2015). The latter helps at answering a set of questions related to a transformational change process, such as: what are the required programme analysis and why they are needed? How does a social transformation happen and what is the role of different stakeholders in it? Which analysis, values, and key assumptions are underlying decision makers' thinking? Why to choose to work on specific themes and why to make certain strategic choices? Among many others (Vogel ,2012a, Hivos, 2015).

The ToC usually takes place at the preparation or inception phase of a transformational change project (Hivos, 2015). It enables a broad analysis of a system to be transformed. It helps in identifying a project vision; long-term goal(s); current state, gap and change requirements; key actors; initial project design and strategic choices; critical assumptions; and change activities. It also forms the basis for monitoring, evaluating, and learning (MEL) from a transformational process (Hivos, 2015).

4.2.4   Theory of Change and Change Readiness

For a transformational change to success, examining the readiness of a city for a change before planning the transformation solutions and services is essential. Change programmes are likely to lead to only failure if they start before ensuring the readiness of a city for a change (Edwards et al., 2000). According to the Community Tool Box of the University of Kansas, the readiness for change differs from one city to another depending on its context. It also varies across city levels (KU, 2015). Some cities may be more than ready for the desired change while others being at a very earliest stage of readiness for that change.

The KPMG and Oxford Economics define a change readiness of a country, thereby a city, as *"the capability of a government, private and public enterprises, people and wider civil society to anticipate, prepare for, manage and respond to a wide range of change drivers, proactively cultivating the resulting opportunities, and mitigating potential negative impacts*". They also create an international index, named as the Change Readiness Index (CRI), to measure the capability of countries and cities to withstand and capitalize on change. Using this index; that was first raised in the 2010 World Economic Forum in Davos, Switzerland; governments, policy makers and other stakeholders can identify and address the capability gap of countries and cities to a change and accordingly being able to make more informed investment decisions (KPMG, 2015a).

The CRI is based on three main pillars, as illustrated in Figure 4.6 (KPMG, 2015a), namely, Enterprise Capability, Government Capability, and People and Civil Society Capability. Enterprise capability focuses on variables that affect the ability of businesses to function, such as economic policies, labor markets, innovation, and infrastructure. Government capability takes into account the ability of administration bodies to enforce laws and budgets among other capacities. Finally, people and civil society capability focuses on population's demographics, growth inclusivity and education. The CRI ranking allows countries and cities to know their local readiness for upcoming required changes and work toward overcoming existing obstacles and closing identified gaps.

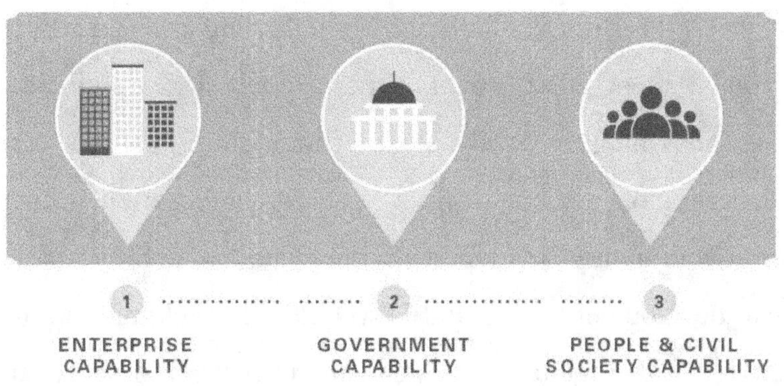

Figure 4.6: Three Pillars Underlie Change Readiness Index (CRI)

The purpose of assessing a city's readiness for change is to identify the level of preparedness of current conditions and resources of a city at all levels for the desired change. The greater the complexity of the desired change, the greater the importance of understanding whether and where there is a readiness for change at every city level. The latter could be critical to decide if the current conditions and resources are ready for the change. If yes, this would help in identifying the entry point and the types of actions to be taken to achieve the change. Once accomplished, a city will be ready for the desired transformation process.

Returning to the ToC, the first stage of the theory emphasizes the necessity of checking the readiness of a programme context before planning a series of change events. This requires answering a set of questions that help in understanding how a programme could achieve the desired long-term goal(s). One of the required questions focuses on analyzing existing policies, resources, practices, attitudes, and beliefs that are needed to support a change as well as identifying any existing gap. This gap analysis shows the weaknesses of existing policies and resources that are needed throughout a changing process. As the ToC takes place at the preparation or inception phase of a transformational change process (Hivos, 2005), the city readiness for change should take place at the preparation phase of a transformation process. Moreover, the city readiness gap should be identified before planning a transformation process (Vogel, 2012a). This gap could be then closed by a well-planned set of solutions.

4.3   SSCs and Theory of Change

The ToC is applicable to a range of disciplines including the community development discipline (Stein and Valters, 2012, Vogel, 2012a, Vogel, 2012b; Laing and Todd, 2015). A community can be a nuclear family, urban community, suburban community, rural community, national region, region within a state, or entire nation (Debertin and Goetz, 2008). As a type of community development, many national and international studies use the ToC for urban development (LTS and ITAD, 2012; Mackinlay et. al, 2013; Gottret, 2013; PD&R, 2013). In this matter, the ToC helps in developing an overall picture of a required urban change that could be achieved through a series of change activities to be applied at different city levels based on the city context and needs. It is worth noting that the change activities in the context of the ToC refer to any activity (i.e. solution) that may be identified for the benefit of achieving the desired long-term change and goals. In other word, they are a series of actions that may help in achieving the predefined and agreed on vision. For instance, one activity may focus on creating new policies to encourage citizens' engagement in the city governance, others may provide the needed solutions to reduce greenhouse gas emission, improve healthcare and education systems, and enhance transportation systems.

Urban development is the main constituent of cities' vision, particularly a SSCs' vision (PwC, 2015b; ITU-T FG-SSC, 2016). The main objectives of a SSC is to improve the quality of life of citizens, city services and operations, and competitiveness, taking into consideration the sustainability of a city with respect to its economic, social, and environmental aspects. These objectives are realized through a series of change events, applied at different levels of a city, specifically, over the SSC six dimensions. The SSC vision and objectives along with the mechanisms followed to realize them are highly related to the objectives of the urban development and its related change process (SSU, 2015). As a result, the ToC is applicable on SSCs discipline. In this regard, the ToC elements and tools are used to understand the flow of a SSC transformation process and its required elements/stages and components. Figure **4.7** illustrates how the ToC concept is applied on the urban development discipline and how it is linked to the transformation towards SSCs.

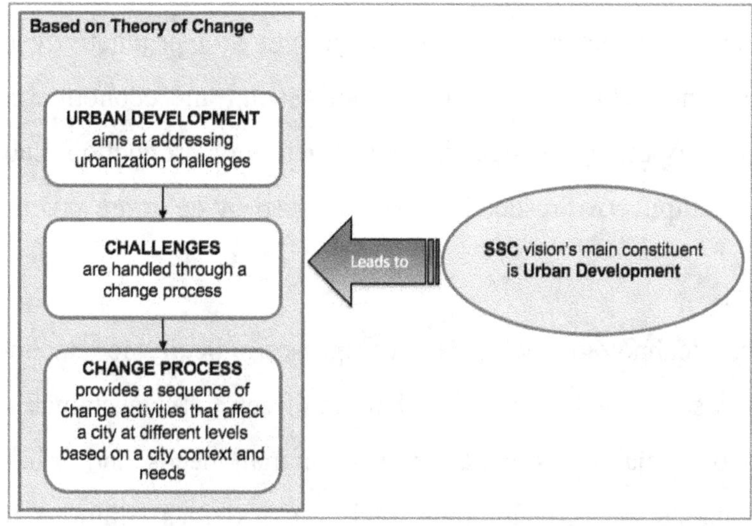

Figure 4.7: Applying Theory of Change on Smart Sustainable Cities

On a final note, a SSC is a complex system-of-systems (ISO/IEC, 2015). Moving in a direction of SSCs and urban development is a dynamic long-term process that needs changes at different city levels (GIZ, 2011; Dias, 2013). This requires a set of complex change activities while the outcomes are unpredictable (Webb, 2013). Therefore, developing a city into a SSC is being considered as a transformational change process (Daszko and Sheinberg, 2005; Wei, 2012; UN Rio+20, 2012). As discussed in Sections 4.2.4, for this transformation process to success, checking the city readiness for change is a prerequisite step before planning the transformation process.

4.4   SSCs and Technological Change

The technological change is one type of the transformational change (CEO, 2000; Palmer et al., 2008; Yang, 2010). It is a loose concept that has different meaning depending on the discipline over which it is being applied on. For sociologists, a technological change refers to new technologies; including tools, facilities and services; and their effects and changes on society. If used properly, a technological change increases the productivity of capital, labour and other production factors (Gerstenfeld, 1979). For economists, the meaning of the technological change is related to changes in production techniques and/or methods of production (i.e. industrial processes). It makes production more efficient by increasing the amount of output an economy can produce with the same amount of inputs. In other words, it is the ability to invent or improve a product or a process using the same resources to get a bigger reward. A technological change, in this sense, focuses on the industrial techniques as factors of economic growth and productivity (Godin, 2015). Finally, a technological change can refer to both social and economic changes. It is a change in productivity due to changes in input (factors of production: capital and labor) used to produce outputs with social impact (e.g. provide more work opportunities) (Godin, 2015).

In a city context, a technological change encompasses radically new technologies aiming at providing smart solutions for problems that are affecting the sustainability of a city. It is a redirection of social investments to meet human needs and urban development (McMichael et al., 2000). A technological change provides solutions to improve the quality of life of citizens; promote growth and competitiveness; manage the natural and social environments; create new employment opportunities; improve city governance, delivery of services, and energy and water use efficiency among others (UNSDN, 2013; UN, 2013). It mainly focuses on addressing economic, social, and environmental challenges faced by countries, thereby cities (UNTT, 2013; UN, 2013). A technological change should be applied at all city levels with appropriate actions that ensure present improvements and future sustainability (McMichael et al., 2000). It uses the ICTs as a crosscutting enabler for urban development.

In September 2015, the 2030 Agenda for the Sustainable Development was agreed at the United Nations Sustainable Development Summit. The 2030 Agenda is based on three main pillars of urban development, namely, economic, social, and environmental pillars. It consists of 17 Sustainable Development Goals (SDGs), as illustrated in Figure 4.8 (UN-DESA, 2015), to be achieved globally by 2030.

Figure 4.8: United Nations Sustainable Development Goals (SDGs)

In late 2015 and after the agreement on the SDGs, the Earth Institute at Columbia University and Ericsson published a report about how the technological change can be used to facilitate the transformation process towards the SDGs (Earth Institute and Ericsson, 2015). The report shows that the new innovative ICTs can be used as an accelerator for achieving the SDGs globally. Cities that adopt smart sustainable development practices (i.e. being transformed into SSCs) will be more likely to achieve the SDGs and meet their sustainability challenges (Ericsson, 2016). The PricewaterhouseCoopers (PwC, 2015b) demonstrate that the dimensions of a SSC are aligned, directly or indirectly, with the objectives of the SDGs. Therefore, it becomes a requirement for cities to be transformed into SSCs (ITU-T, 2016). A SSC could use the technological change as an enabler to the long-term vision of urban and sustainability development. The latter does not mean that all SSC projects should provide ICT-based solutions; rather, a transformation process can use the ICTs to provide solutions that are environmentally friendly and viable as needed.

As a type of a transformational change, the ToC is applicable on a technological change. The ToC helps a SSC project team to understand how to use a technological change to provide economic, social, and environmental ICT-based services and solutions. It provides the team with the required knowledge about the needed ICT infrastructure, availability of ICT resources and identifying existing gap, how and when to use ICTs, which ICT-based services and solutions to provide, among others.

For the purpose of this research, the meaning of a technological change that is related to the economic, environmental, and social changes will be adopted. In this sense, a technological change refers to the *"use of ICTs to provide innovative solutions at all city levels aiming at improving the living standards and ensuring the future sustainability of a city"*. Based on the ToC, the innovative solutions could be considered as input activities that can lead to the desired output of transforming a city into a SSC. Checking the technological readiness of a city is one of the essential steps to consider before planning a transformation process. A city should have a minimal set of ICTs before starting its transformation process, or providing ICT-based solutions maybe more likely to fail. The greater the technological readiness of a city is, the greater the success of providing smart solutions during a transformation process.

4.5 Proposed Theoretical Logical Model for the Transformation towards Smart Sustainable Cities

The development of a city into a SSC differs from one city to another and there is no 'one-size fits all' approach for a transformation process. Each city has its specific needs and context that refine its transformation journey (Government Summit, 2015, ITU-T FG-SSC, 2016). However, there are a set of general stages that should be taken into consideration while planning any transformation process. For example, each transformation process requires a set of change activities to be applied at different levels of a city aiming to improve its urban development process and sustainability (Backović et al., 2016) while taking into account its context. These general stages or bold lines could be used to create a theoretical model of a transformation process. Each city can use this theoretical model as a base for planning its transformation process based on its context, needs, priorities, and availability of resources.

With a lack of specific theory, this book introduces a Theory of Transformation towards SSCs (ToSSC) based on the ToC (Weiss, 1995; James, 2011, Vogel, 2012a, Center for ToC, 2013) and Transformational Change concepts (Hivos, 2015). In the context of SSCs, the long-term outcome or goal of a transformation process is transforming a city into a SSC. With this aim, the transformation process should cover five essential stages in sequence as below:

1. **Stage 1: City Context**: this includes analyzing the current state of a city regarding its economic, social, environmental, and political conditions. This also includes agreeing on a transformation vision, strategies, and list of key stakeholders to be involved in a transformation process as well as the list of the required resources needed and gap analysis. For instance, during this stage the analysis process generates information to decision-makers on the following issues:
   - Current city economic, social, environmental and political state and challenges.
   - Analysis of the city priorities in relation to local challenges that should be handled before the situation becomes worst.
   - The effect of the current state on citizens, businesses, ecosystems, governance, and other aspects of life within a city.
   - Agree on a city vision along with the transformation strategies to be followed during a transformation process.
   - The effect of a transformation process on the urban development process and sustainability of a city.
   - City existing policies, practices, strategies, physical or hard infrastructure, soft or social infrastructure, and technological capacities.
   - Gap analysis of missing resources, policies, legislations, awareness, services, among others.

- Identify the main actors (i.e. stakeholders) to be engaged in a transformation process. This includes citizens as a critical player, public/private sector organizations, Non-for-Profit Organizations (NGOs), international bodies, universities among others.

2. **Stage 2**: **Short, Medium and Long-term Changes**: this includes identifying clear statements of the short-term, medium-term and long-term outcomes of a transformation process. Transforming a city into a SSC is a long-term continuous process that is often divided into a set of initiatives to be applied at different levels of a city. Each initiative has a long-term outcome related to a problem the initiative is seeking to address. The set of the initiatives' long-term outcomes could be considered as short-term and medium-term outcomes of the overall transformation process. These short-term and medium-term outcomes should be identified and prioritizes in a way that helps in achieving the long-term outcome of transforming a city into a SSC. The city's decision-makers should be clear about the bold-lines of a transformation process and how each short-term and medium-term change could lead to the desired long-term outcome. The outputs of this stage include but are not limited to:

- Identify and prioritize the most essential short, medium and long-term changes that must be seen in the context, without which a transformation towards a SSC has no meaning.

- Clear explanation about the importance and impact of the desired changes on citizens' daily life, efficiency and effectiveness of city's systems, and city sustainability.

- A list of positive outcomes that might be seen as a result of these changes; including positive outcomes on quality of life of citizens, urban services and operation, and sustainability of a city.

- Identify the short-term and medium-term changes that are needed to be accomplished to facilitate the achievement of the long-term change (i.e. developing a city into a SSC).

3. **Stage 3**: **Sequence of Transformation Activities**: this includes a sequence of transformation activities; short, medium and long-term activities; that may lead to the desired long-term outcome of developing a city into a SSC. The aim of this stage is to

map out the connection between a transformation process and the desired long-term outcome. The mapping should represent a hierarchy of transformational changes starting from short-term changes to medium-term changes to long-term changes. The latter should be shown in a logical, reasonable progression from one set of changes to the next. Based on the ToC (Vogel, 2012a), this stage is not a literal prediction of the future; rather it could be seen as a conceptual exercise about the needed steps that may (or may not) lead to the desired impact of a transformation process. For instance, this stage generates information on:

- The essential change activities that are related to the short-term, medium-term and long-term changes in sequence.
- The connection between short, medium and long-term activities and how short-term and medium-term activities could help in transforming a city into a SSC.
- Identify a set of strategies and resources needed to support the short-term, medium-term and long-term changes' activities.
- Engage the key stakeholders in the change activities.
- Specify the responsibilities of each stakeholder in the change activities.

4. **Stage 4**: **Assumptions, Constraints, and Risks**: this includes the identification of a set of assumptions in relation to how the short, medium and long-term change activities might happen in a way that leads to the desired goal of transforming a city into a SSC. As assumptions are the most challenging to create, hard to make explicit and can be thought of as things that are believed to be true in the future (Vogel, 2012a), the city planners, decision-makers, professional experts and appropriate stakeholders should dialogue together in order to create a set of transformation assumptions that are both explicit and realistic. Assumptions are often supposed to be true, but in reality, they may turn out to be false and this could affect a transformation process significantly. Therefore, a transformation process team should make as many assumptions as possible (Usmani, 2013). This set of different assumptions can be used to suggest different pathways to a transformation process (Vogel, 2012a) and are useful to create a risk management plan (Usmani, 2013). Developing two or three pathways and being able to select between them can be a point of learning and reflection to open up new strategic choices and innovations throughout a

transformation process (Aragón and Macedo, 2010). Although the ToC does not mention the necessity of identifying them, there is also a need to identify a set of constraints and risks that may affect a transformation process and its change activities (Tayntor, 2002; Usmani, 2013, KU, 2015). The aim of defining the transformation constraints is to find a way to eliminate them or to work within the boundaries of these constraints (Usmani, 2013). The identification of possible risks helps in developing a risk management and mitigation plan to be used to mitigate risks through possible corrective actions and scenarios (Tayntor, 2002). The information to be generated during this stage include but not limited to:

- Study and understand the worldwide view of the transformation towards SSCs.

- Identify a set of values and norms that influence the understanding of a transformation process.

- Developing a set of different types of short-term, medium-term and long-term assumptions based on local actors' professional experience and national and international practices that are closed to the context of a city to be transformed.

- Identify a set of constraints (i.e. limitations such as budget, time, availability of resources and time) that may affect a transformation process and the possible ways of dealing with them (Usmani, 2013).

- Identify a list of possible risks that may face a SSC transformation process, such as natural calamities (Tayntor, 2002)

5. **Stage 5**: **Transformational Change Roadmap and Framework**: this stage uses the information generated during the previous four stages to create a SSC transformation roadmap and framework. This could be used by a SSC project team to facilitate understanding and following up the different stages of a transformation process.

Figure 4.9 illustrates the main elements to consider in the Theory of Transformation towards SSCs (ToSSC). The dashed lines used to surround the 'City Context" box is a visual design type used to represent something (i.e. a city in this case) in its transformational state (Malamed, 2011).

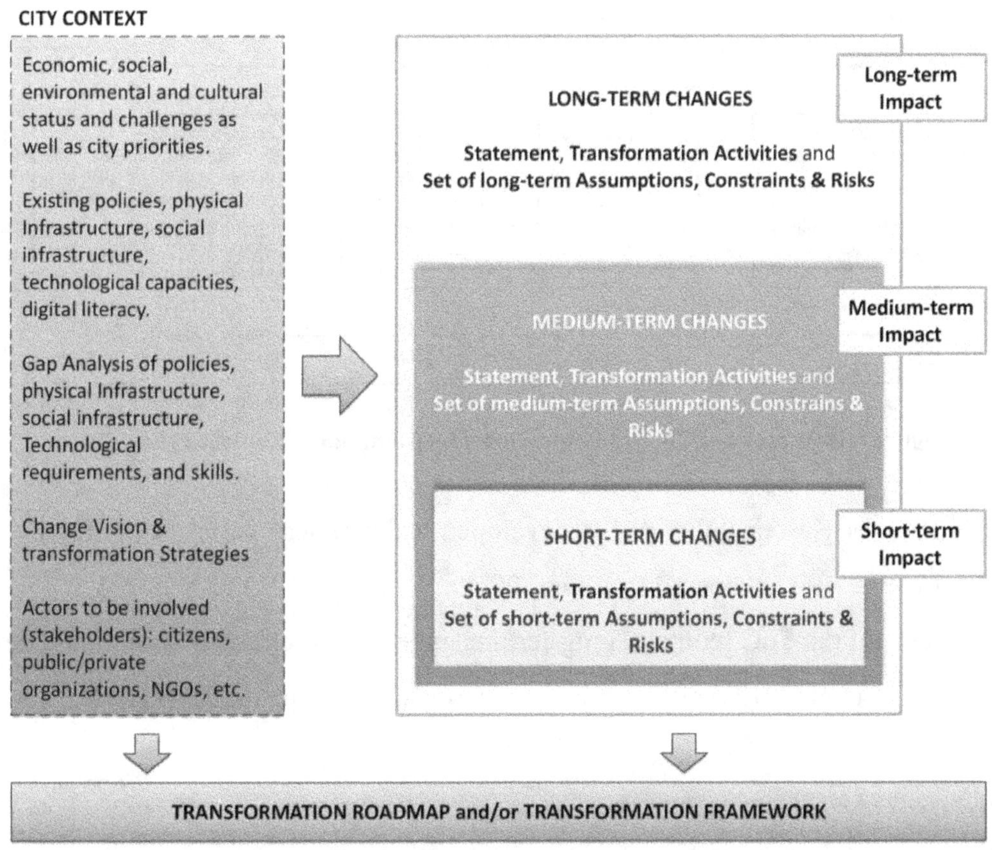

Figure 4.9: Theory of Transformation towards Smart Sustainable Cities

The next step after applying the ToC on any phenomenon is creating its theoretical logic model that must be broad and about the big picture of a change (WKKF, 2006; KU, 2015). The aim of this logic model is to link program outcomes; short, medium, and long-term; with program activities and assumptions (WKKF, 2006). The model provides directions and clarity by presenting a high-level view of a change along with the certain important details that must be considered during a change process (KU, 2015; Allen, 2016). The Community Tool Box introduces a theoretical logic model of the ToC based on the purpose, context, inputs, activities, outputs and effect elements of the ToC (KU, 2015), as illustrated in Figure 4.10. The model shows the continuity of a change process; using return arrows; and the sequence and flow from one element to another; using directed arrows.

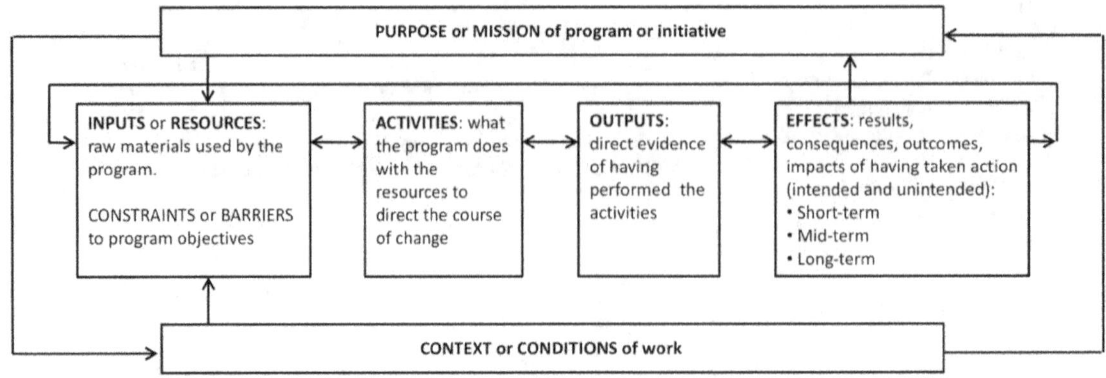

Figure 4.10: Theory of Change Logic Model by Community Tool Box (KU, 2015)

The Learning for Sustainability (LfS) developed a theoretical logic model for the ToC based on (Weiss, 1995; James, 11; Vogel, 2012a; Vogel, 2012b) taking into account the main elements of the ToC (context, long-term change, activities and assumptions) defined by the ESPA (Vogel, 2012a) as illustrated in Figure **4.11** (Allen, 2016).

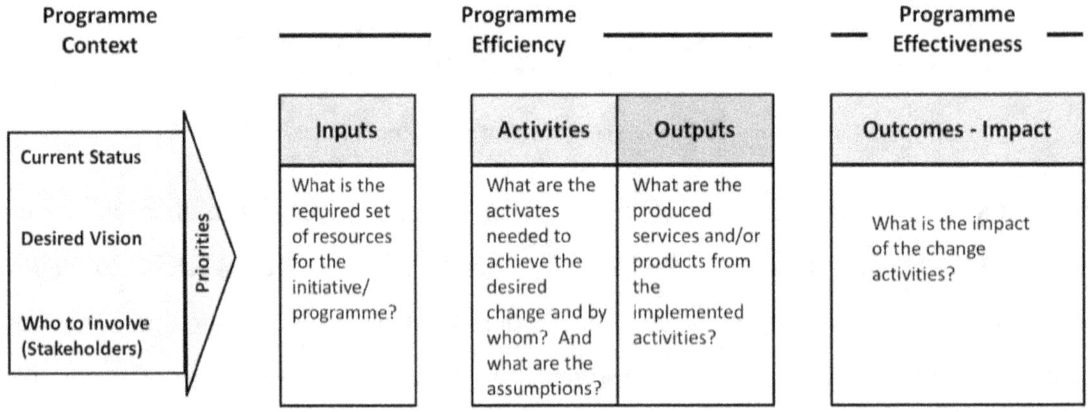

Figure 4.11: Theory of Change Logic Model by Learning for Sustainability (Allen, 2016)

The theoretical logic models of the ToC proposed by the Community Tool Box (KU, 2015) and Learning for Sustainability (Allen, 2016) are used as a reference to introduce a theoretical logic model for the proposed ToSSC considering the specificity of SSCs. The latter provides a high-level logical view of a transformational change process, capturing the main elements of the ToSSC along with their sequence as illustrated in Figure 4.12.

In the introduced model, the 'INPUTS' has a caption named 'Planning Resources' that is adopted form (KU, 2015; Allen, 2016) while the 'ACTIVITIES', 'OUTPUTS' and 'OUTCOMES-IMPACT' have captions named 'Planning Activities', 'Implement &

Monitoring' and 'Evaluation' respectively that are adopted from (WKKF, 2006; Vogel, 2012a). Return arrows from 'OUTCOME-IMPACT' stage to "CITY CONTEXT' and 'INPUTS' indicate the continuity of a change process. The double-headed arrows between 'INPUTS' and 'ACTIVITES, 'ACTIVITES' and 'OUTPUTS', and 'OUTPUTS' and 'OUTCOMES-IMPACT' indicate a bidirectional relationships and correlations between their elements that are neither predictive nor casual (Hair Jr et al., 2011), which is the case of a transformational change where the long-term outcomes of a change are complex and unpredictable.

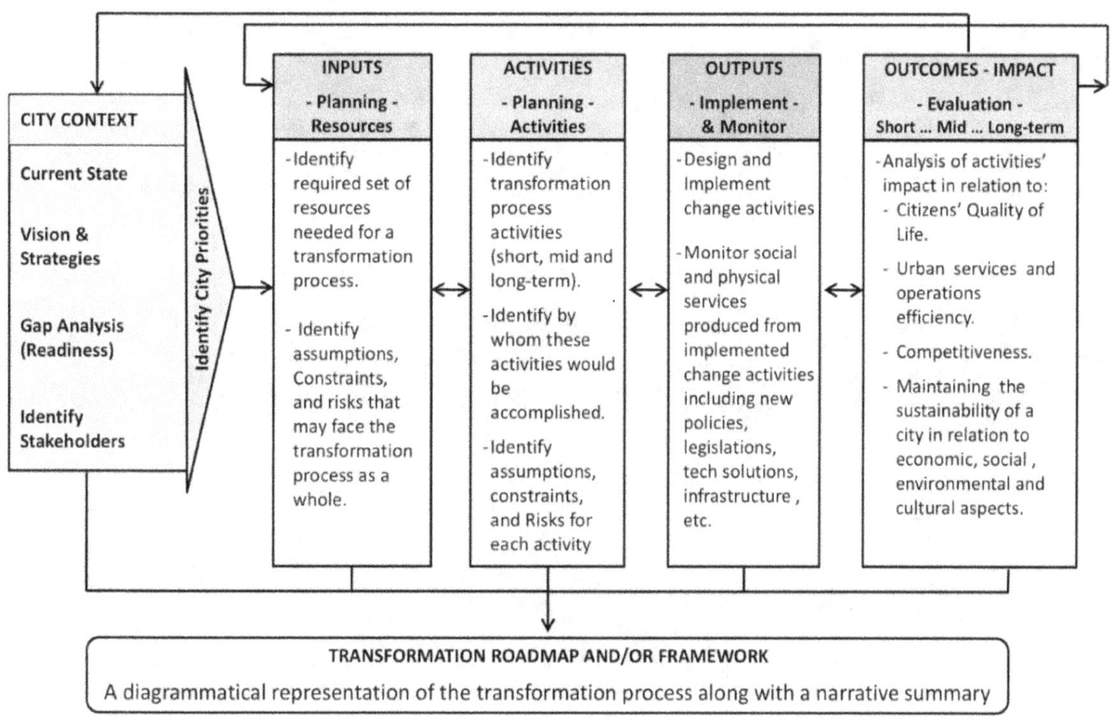

Figure 4.12: Theory of Transformation towards SSCs Logic Model

4.6 Conclusion

Planning a SSC project should consider all aspects needed to ensure an effective and efficient transformation process. Noting the knowledge gap in relation to the existence of a sound theory for SSCs, this chapter introduced a novel linkage between the ToC and SSCs. Based on this, a novel theoretical logic model for the transformation towards SSCs is introduced. The theoretical model highlights the minimum essential elements and components to be considered throughout a transformation process, thereby providing a holistic insight to city planners on how to transform their cities into SSCs.

In the next chapter, new definitions of the concepts of transformation, roadmap, and framework in the context of SSCs are presented.

CHAPTER FIVE: A NEW PERSPECTIVE ON TRANSFORMATION, ROADMAP AND FRAMEWORK CONCEPTS

5.1 Introduction

The main objectives of a SSC are to improve the quality of life of citizens, urban efficiency, and competitiveness, while taking into consideration the sustainability aspects of a city at all levels. The ICTs are used as a crosscutting enabler that can provide viable and environmentally friendly solutions. Transformation of a city into a SSC can be realize though a robust, systematic transformation process that considers all objectives of a SSC to be achieved (Ibrahim et al., 2015b, Ibrahim et al., 2015c).

A SSC transformation process, as illustrated in Figure 5.1 (Ibrahim et al., 2016), is often represented by two types of diagrammatic forms, namely, the transformation (1) roadmap and (2) framework. These forms can be used by a SSC team and key stakeholders to facilitate following up the different phases of a SSC transformation process as well as provide the tools needed to realize these phases.

To start with, the roadmap provides a diagrammatic illustration of the general directions (i.e. phases) and priorities of a transformation process (Withers et al., 2012) (e.g., outline the need for identifying a transformation plan). It guides a SSC team and key stakeholders to critical decision points throughout a transformation journey. Therefore, a generic SSC roadmap must be clear, understandable, achievable, and comprehensive as possible. It also should take into consideration the specificity of each city, its context, attributes, and characteristics.

The framework, in turn, in a diagrammatic form provides the tools needed to turn the transformation roadmap phases and components of each phase into actions (Di Biase, 2014; Borowik et al., 2015). It provides answers to the question of *how* to realize a SSC vision and objectives and its created transformation roadmap.

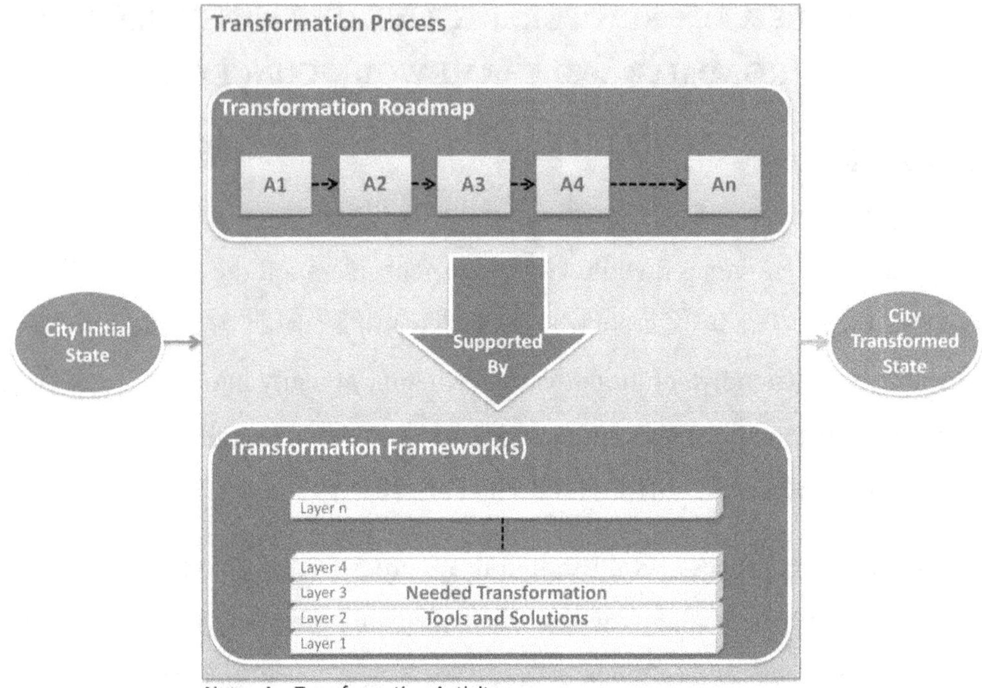

Figure 5.1: A Smart Sustainable City Transformation, Roadmap and Framework Concepts

Different definitions of the concepts of SSC transformation, SSC roadmap, and SSC framework exist in the literature. The majority of these definitions do not consider the specificity of a SSC as a solution that ensures the sustainability of a city at all levels while providing a high quality of life for its citizens using ICTs and other means.

Using definitions that do not take into account all aspects of a SSC leads to an incomplete city transformation from one state to another. Without clear definitions of a SSC transformation, SSC roadmap, and SSC framework, city planners, policy makers, and key stakeholders will not have a concrete base to follow in designing their transformation roadmaps and frameworks. Consequently, the possibility of neglecting essential aspects while transforming a city into a SSC becomes high. Therefore, a comprehensive definition for each of these three concepts is needed.

The aim of this chapter is to study and analyze existing definitions of SSC transformation, SSC roadmap, and SSC framework in the literature, highlight their weaknesses and deficiencies, and introduce new comprehensive definitions for these concepts. The proposed definitions could assist city policy makers and key stakeholders in developing and designing smart and sustainable initiatives that meet the objectives of a SSC. This part follows the literature-based method approach, or desktop research technique, through which a gap in knowledge in relation to the definitions of these three concepts in the contexts of SSCs is identified. On a final note, the proposed definitions along with the related analysis were published in the International Conference on Smart Cities, Systems, Devices and Technologies under the paper titled: "Smart Sustainable Cities: A New Perspective on Transformation, Roadmap and Framework Concepts" (Ibrahim et al., 2016).

The rest of this chapter is as follows. A review of the concepts of transformation, roadmap, and framework in the literature is presented in Sections 5.2, 5.3, and 5.4 respectively. Section 5.5 is devoted to the newly proposed definitions of these concepts in the context of SSCs. The chapter concludes in Section 5.6.

5.2 Transformation Concept in SSCs

The rapid urbanization is a significant challenge facing cities around the globe. City leaders need to address this phenomenon by increasing the efficiency of existing city's systems, services and infrastructures to a level that have never been achieved before. This is realizable through a holistic transformation process to enhance the sustainability of a city at all levels and improve the high quality of life of citizens, such as the case of the transformation towards SSCs. For this transformation to be consistent with the objectives of a SSC, a comprehensive definition of a transformation concept is needed.

In the development context, various definitions of transformational change exit in the literature. This concept encompasses a wide range of approaches and there is no agreement yet on what could be and what could not be considered as a transformation (Asefeso et al., 2013). To start with, in the "Transformation Theory", proposed by Daszko and Sheinberg (2005), a transformation is a "change" aims at creating something new that has never been existed before. This change is not predictable from the past and it leads to a change in the whole system structure, function or form. Geels and Kemp (2007) define a transformation as a continuous process (i.e., it is difficult to tell when a transformation process will end) that leads to changes in a direction of trajectories. During this process, a new system may be created from the old one, through changes that are being taken in a new direction.

The United Nations Development Program (UNDP, 2011) defines a transformational change as a process through which positive development results are achieved and sustained over time through institutionalizing policies, projects and programmes within national strategies. It ensures the consistency of achievements over time, and does not include short-term transitory impacts. For Satterthwaite and Dodman (2013) a transformation is used to represent both the substantial activities and the fundamental changes that affect the economic, social and political systems. This requires adaptation of policies and investments that could be integrated with the development process of a city to meet its needs and to address the massive ecological footprint.

Asefeso et al. (2013) define a transformation as *"an approach, a philosophy and a methodology. It is a profound, fundamental and irreversible. It is a metamorphosis, a radical change from one form to another"*. Finally, Harrington (2001) proposed a definition, which reads as follows: *"a transformational change helps to break the scope of change into manageable segments, identify the key behaviors necessary to sustain the change, then modify and reinforce positive behaviors by changing the structure of rewards and consequences while measuring progress toward the stated goals"*.

In the context of SSCs, a transformation occurs at every level of a city, ranging from the economic, social, and environmental structures to the ways that form citizens' everyday lives. As in the case of a transformational change concept, there is no agreement on the definition of the concept of transformation in the context of SSCs. The Department of Business, Innovation and Skills (BIS, 2013) does not provide a clear definition for a SSC transformation process; however; it shows a lack of absolute definition for a SSC that could be seen as a series of steps through which cities will be able to become more resilient and livable, hence, being able to respond quicker to new challenges. A SSC Transformation in De Santis et al. (2014) is a complex multidimensional process that changes over time as all involved stakeholders will work to achieve more and better results. The transformation will affect many aspects of city operations including government, mobility, energy, services, buildings, and environment.

The ITU-T FG-SSC (2015a) defines a SSC transformation as a long-term process that consists of a series of generic steps. These steps are defined to allow compatibility and promote sustainability of a city as time passes. Finally, Smart Dubai (Monitor Deloitte, 2015), defines a transformation as a process that focuses on four main issues: (1) efficiency through optimizing the use of city resources; (2) safety through protection of information and people and anticipating risks; (3) seamlessness through integrating daily services of life; and (4) impact through enriching business and life experiences.

In Section 5.5, a new comprehensive definition of a SSC transformation concept along with the required related discussion is provided.

5.3   Roadmap Concept in SSCs

Generally, a transformation roadmap is a high-level view of key activities needed to change a situation from one state to another by defining a set of milestones required to close a gap between the current and desired future situation (Withers et al., 2010). A transformation roadmap in SSCs has almost the same meaning; with some specificity related to the nature and complexity of a transformation process in the context of SSCs.

With no agreement on its definition, Schaffers (2010) indicates that a transformation roadmap is required to realize the aspiration of SSCs as innovation ecosystems. It presents the state of the art, trends, and developments as well as identifies gaps, challenges and obstacles related to the transformation towards SSCs. It reflects the vision of a SSC's socio-economic and cultural development. Komnison et al. (2011) define a SSC roadmap as a blueprint that provides recommendations for urban development by using of future technologies. It allows formulating of some policy recommendations to city authorities for mastering the new interdisciplinary planning for SSCs. A transformation roadmap's main purpose is to show how to control the interlinked city layers of infrastructure, digital technology, people-driven innovations ecosystems, and urban activities.

For the European Platform for Intelligent Cities (EPIC, 2013), a transformation roadmap supports cities in their transformation towards SSCs operating environments. It includes various aspects of the transformation process including strategy development, program management, business case creation, and implementing and operating SSC services. The British Standards Institution (BSI, 2014) does not provide a specific definition for a transformation roadmap. It indicates that a SSC roadmap could be seen as a realistic framework that aims to deliver clearly identified results in achievable stages. From their point of view, each city in the United Kingdom (UK) should develop its own transformation roadmap based on its vision and goals. A roadmap is not a master plan and it should be deliverable. To be effective, a roadmap should take a phased and incremental approach and there is no need to over-plan at the beginning but instead provides a framework to support the transformation process to deliver the city vision over time.

The ITU-T FG-SSC (2015b) defines a SSC roadmap as a process that can be followed by city leaders and managers to transform their city into a SSC. It provides a framework to guide the transformation process, identify a set of SSC services, and focus on different ICT infrastructures. It also consists of a security framework to protect citizens, and provides monitoring techniques and ways to include citizens in the transformation process. Finally, the Smart Cities Council (SCC, 2015) defines a transformation roadmap as a bridge between ideas and actions. It is linked directly to the city vision document and/or development plan; therefore; it is neither a vision document nor a master plan. A transformation roadmap is a simplified outline that shows the major steps of how to become a SSC and how to overcome the obstacles of a SSC transformation. The benefits of a SSC transformation roadmap include identifying the best place to start from, enabling cities to build in stages, maximizing synergies and minimizing cost, increasing public support, and attracting talent and businesses.

In Section 5.5, a new comprehensive definition of a SSC transformation roadmap concept along with the required related discussion is provided.

5.4 Framework Concept in SSCs

Transforming a city into a SSC requires a comprehensive framework to guide the transformation process. While a transformation roadmap provides a high-level view of changes that are needed to shift a situation from one state to another, a framework provides a set of tools that can be used to get there (Withers et al., 2010). A transformation framework, in general, is a structure that can be used as a guide to build systems from scratch or modify existing ones into something useful.

Although there is frequent use of the term "Smart Sustainable City" in the literature recently, there are still few attempts to provide a definition for its framework concept. To start with, a SSC framework has been defined by CISCO (2012) as a process that helps city key stakeholders and participants to understand how cities operate, define city objectives, understand the role of ICTs within the city physical assets, and define the role of stakeholders within a city. It is a step-by-step process of how to implement the SSC initiatives. It allows cities to create a standard index system to record, collect, and measure city data that could be used to manage and implement SSC solutions for the purpose of economic, social, and environmental gains.

Chourabi et al. (2012) define a SSC framework as an integrative framework that can be used to assist government professionals on how to establish SSC initiatives. From their point of view, a SSC framework should be based on eight critical factors, which are: economy, governance, policy context, technology, built infrastructure, management and organization, natural environment, and people and communities. A SSC framework should clarify the influences and relationships between any suggested SSC initiative and these eight factors. Lee and Hancock (2012) define a SSC framework as a conceptual framework that provides a holistic view of a SSC development. It is a tool that can be used to classify different initiatives and implementation practices.

The British Standards Institute (BSI, 2014) defines a SSC framework as a guide used by the UK city leaders of SSC programs, at all levels and from all sectors. The focus of a SSC framework is to enable processes by which new smart technologies could be coupled with organizational change to help deliver the different visions of UK future cities efficiently, effectively, and sustainably. It captures the current good practices and provides "how-to" advices to help city leaders in developing and delivering their own SSC strategies.

The International Organization for Standardization (ISO) and the International Electrotechnical Commission (IEC) indicate that a SSC framework could be seen as a layered structure that captures different cross-city governance processes aiming to deliver benefits based on core guiding principles while taking into account the critical success factors. It provides a valuable set of tools for scenario building to guide the transformation process through participative decision-making (ISO/IEC, 2015). Finally, the Smart Cities Council (SCC, 2015) defines a SSC framework as a guide through which cities can plan and implement their SSCs. It captures the relationship between city responsibilities (i.e., what should be accomplished for citizens) and its enablers (i.e., the use of smart technologies to make these tasks easier). A SSC framework could transform a city into a SSC while ensuring that individual projects are compatible with each other even if they are being developed separately and at different times.

In Section 5.5, a new comprehensive definition of a SSC transformation roadmap concept along with the required related discussion is provided.

5.5   Newly Proposed Definitions

The objectives of a SSC are to improve the quality of life of citizens, urban efficiency, and competitiveness, while ensuring the sustainability aspects of a city at the economic, social (i.e. including cultural aspects) and environmental levels (ITU-T, 2016). This could be achieved through providing innovative solutions, using ICTs and other means, on the dimensions of Smart Economy, Smart Environment, Smart, Governance, Smart Living, Smart Mobility, and Smart People (Giffinger et al., 2007), as illustrated in Figure 5.2.

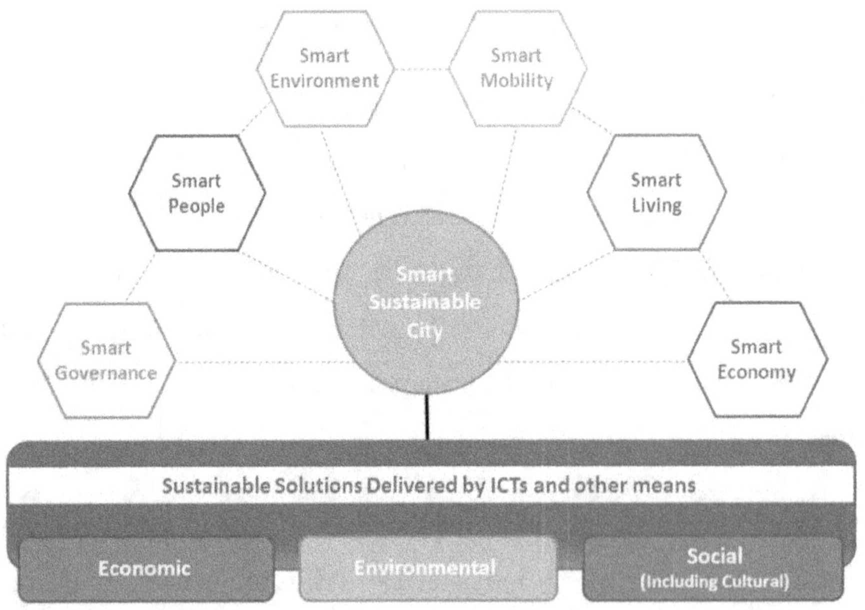

Figure 5.2: Overview of a Relationship between a SSC and City's Sustainability

Any attempt to design and develop a transformation process towards SSCs should take into consideration the objectives of a SSC and explicitly reflected in the definitions of a SSC transformation, SSC roadmap, and SSC framework concepts. In the following sub-sections, new comprehensive definitions for these concepts capturing the objectives of SSC are introduced (Ibrahim et al., 2016).

5.5.1   Proposed Definition of a SSC Transformation

The analysis of existing definitions of a SSC transformation concept in the literature shows that there is no standardized, commonly accepted set of terminologies to describe and define a SSC transformation. Depending upon the lens with which it is viewed, there are different definitions of the concept in the literature. None of the studied definitions takes into account all aspects of a SSC. For example, some of the listed definitions consider the quality of life as important objective of a SSC while others do not. Some definitions indicate the significance of improving the sustainability of a city while others neglect this issue. In addition, as shown through the analysis of the listed definitions and keywords used, the use of ICTs as an enabler to reach the SSC objectives is not highlighted. The list of extracted keywords used to define or describe a SSC transformation in the studied definitions is as below:

- Process
- Series of steps
- Series of generic steps
- Complex
- Multidimensional
- Change over time
- Compatibility

- Sustainability
- Resilient
- Livable
- Efficiency
- City resources
- Safety
- Seamlessness

Analyzing the above listed definitions shows that the objectives of a SSC are not properly considered. The role of ICTs, as an enabler to SSCs, is also not highlighted. Therefore, believing in the need to highlight these elements, this book defines the transformation towards a SSC as *"a complex multidimensional process through which changes are applied at all city levels; aiming to enhance the sustainability of a city and provide a high quality of life for its citizens through the use of ICTs and other means"*.

5.5.2   Proposed Definition of a SSC Roadmap

The existing definitions available in the literature of a SSC roadmap have been studied and analyzed. As in the case of a SSC transformation, the results show that there are no common set of terminologies to describe and define a SSC roadmap. Each definition defines the concept from its point of view. None of the studied definitions takes into account the objectives of a SSC. For instance, the sustainability of a city, which is one of the important objectives of the transformation towards SSCs, is not considered in any of the studied definitions. The list of keywords used to define or describe a SSC roadmap in the studied definitions is as below:

- Outline
- Process
- Blueprint
- Phased and incremental
- Realistic framework
- Show how
- Support transformation
- Provide recommendations

- Technology
- Not a vision
- Not a master plan
- City layers
- Urban development
- Cultural development
- Socio-economic development

Stemming from the above, this book introduces a new definition for the concept of a SSC roadmap, which reads as follows: *"A SSC roadmap provides a high-level view of the objectives and goals of the transformation process and identifies the transformation activities and milestones in order to realize the city's vision for being smart and sustainable"*.

5.5.3   Proposed Definition of a SSC Framework

The studied definitions of a SSC framework concept in the literature do not follow a standardized, commonly accepted set of terminologies to define and describe the concept. Each study defines a SSC framework from its perspective or depending on the needs of a city over which a framework will be applied. None of the listed definitions takes into account all aspects of the objectives of a SSC. For example, the quality of life of citizens is not highlighted in any of the listed definitions. The list of extracted keywords used to define or describe a SSC framework in the studied definitions is as below:

- Process
- Integrated
- Conceptual
- Layered structure
- Provide tools
- How-to
- Plan and implement
- Government professionals
- Stakeholders
- Change
- Services
- Deliver vision
- Strategies
- Initiatives
- Sustainability
- ICTs

Examining the readiness of a city for a change is essential before starting a transformation process. Any change programs or initiatives are likely to lead to only failure if they start before ensuring the readiness of a city for a change (Edwards et al., 2000). According to the Community Tool Box of the University of Kansas, the readiness for change differs from one city to another depending on its context and varies across city levels as well (KU, 2016). Some cities may be more than ready for the desired change while others being at a very early stage of readiness for that change. Therefore, any transformation process should take into consideration the city capacities and adapt the transformation framework accordingly.

The analysis of studied definitions of a SSC framework shows that the readiness of a city for a transformation process, which is assessed using tools identified by a transformation framework, is not taken into account in any of the listed definitions.

Accordingly, a new comprehensive definition of a SSC framework that takes into account all aspects of a SSC and the need for assessing the readiness of a city for a transformation process is introduced. This book considers a SSC framework as "*a layered structure that leads city planners and relevant stakeholders throughout a transformation process by providing guidance on city readiness for change and the innovative solutions needed to grant urban sustainability and high quality of life for citizens".*

5.6 Conclusion

The transformation from traditional cities into SSCs requires a comprehensive transformation process. This could be realized through a solid, systematic transformation roadmap and framework. Developing such a roadmap and framework requires complete understanding of the concepts of transformation, roadmap, and framework in the context of SSCs. Therefore, the main objectives of a SSC should be explicitly reflected in the definitions of these concepts definitions to avoid neglecting any essential aspects while transforming a city into a SSC. Results of reviewing the literature show the negligence of essential objectives in existing definitions, which constitutes a gap in knowledge. This research book bridges this gap by introducing new comprehensive definitions for the concepts of SSC transformation, SSC roadmap, and SSC framework, while ensuring that they are consistent with the main objectives of a SSC. The proposed definitions aim at guiding city planners, policy makers, and key stakeholders in understanding the meaning of these concepts in a SSC context, guiding them while developing and designing the SSC projects.

In the next Chapter, the proposed SSC transformation roadmap is presented.

CHAPTER SIX: THE INNOVATIVE SSC TRANSFORMATION ROADMAP

6.1   Introduction

Transforming a city into a SSC or developing a new one requires a transformation roadmap that considers all dimensions of a SSC. This roadmap should highlight the changes needed at all city levels based on the city context and needs. The necessity of checking the city readiness for change and identifying a set of activities that may lead to the desired change should be considered as well. While a transformation process varies from one city to another depending on the specificities of each city, a comprehensive and generic roadmap and framework that could be contextualized to meet the needs of each city are needed.

As discussed in Chapter 4, the fifth element of the ToC and ToSSC requires representing a transformation process using a diagrammatic form, i.e. a roadmap. The latter aims at capturing the discussion on the change process diagrammatically. The roadmap provides a high-level view of the bold lines to be considered by the city planners, policy makers, and key stakeholders throughout a transformation process.

This chapter focuses on the innovative roadmap, its phases and components under each phase. It is worth noting that than n initial version of the novel roadmap proposed here was published in the Sustainable Cities and Society Journal, the published article titled "Smart Sustainable Cities Roadmap: Readiness for Transformation towards Urban Sustainability".

The structure of this chapter is as follows. The proposed novel transformation roadmap is provided in Section 6.2. Section 6.3 is devoted to the discussion on the proposed roadmap. The chapter concludes in Section 0.

6.2   Transformation towards SSCs: The Innovative Roadmap

The SSC roadmap provides a high-level view of a transformation process. It identifies the transformation activities and milestones needed to realize the city's vision of being smart and sustainable (Ibrahim et al., 2016). A roadmap offers an overview of a transformation process, identifying the main phases and components under each phase to be realized during a transformation journey. It summarizes the change process and therefore; it should be clear, understandable, and comprehensive as possible.

Different attempts exist in the literature (Section 2.3) to develop such a roadmap. This includes EPIC (2013) roadmap, BSI (2014) roadmap, Huawei (2014) roadmap, Masdar (2014) city development process, SCC (2015) roadmap, and ITU-T FG-SSC (2015b) roadmap. Each approach tackles a transformation process from its point of view with a lack of strong basis for suggested stages and activities with missing of some important components that should be considered during a transformation process. None of the developed roadmaps takes into consideration checking the city readiness for change neither considering the SSC six dimensions. Only EPIC (2013) indicates that their roadmap is based on the six dimensions; however; EPIC provides all SSC services over EPIC platform based on cloud computing techniques using PaaS and SaaS delivery models. All suggested services are web-based services and controlled by EPIC team. With the different shortages of cloud computing (Apostu et al., 2013), developing a city into a SSC based only on this technology is insufficient. Moreover, there are many other solutions that have nothing to do with ICTs.

The innovative roadmap consists of six phases, namely, (1) City Vision, (2) City Readiness, (3) City Plan, (4) City Transformation, (5) Monitoring and Evaluation, and (6) Sustain Change. Dividing a roadmap into phases makes it possible to lead it in the best possible way. Each phase has a list of components to be carried out at a certain level of a transformation process. Dividing each phase into smaller components makes it easier to understand, implement, and monitor. Figure 6.1 illustrates the proposed innovative SSC transformation roadmap; noting that the returned arrows from the "Sustain Change" phase to "City Vision" phase and "City Transformation" phase indicate the continuity of a transformation process. Each phase and its associated components are to be further discussed in the next subsections.

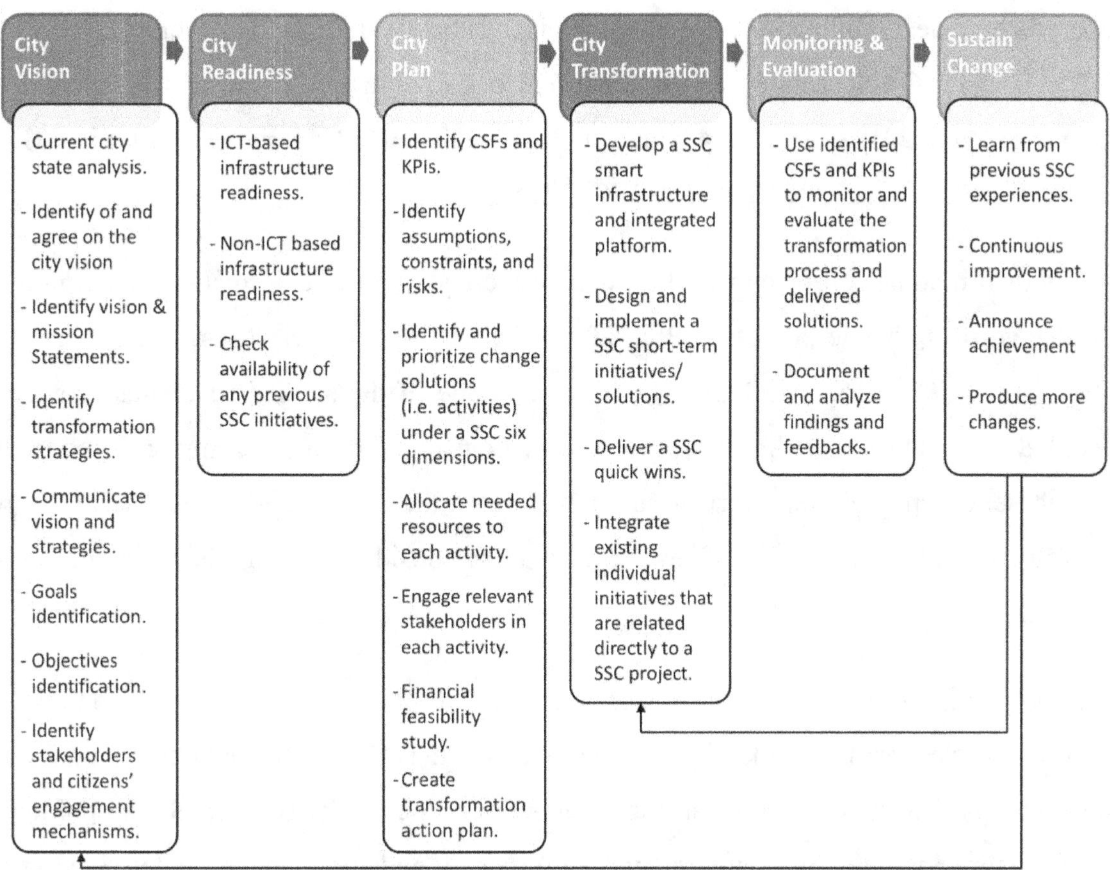

Figure 6.1: Proposed Innovative Smart Sustainable City Transformation Roadmap

It is worth noting that, as the engagement of different types of stakeholders is very important in a SSC transformation process, they are considered to be involved in most of the roadmap phases and components starting from the "City Vision" phase. To ensure an effective and efficient engagement process, this book proposes a stakeholders' engagement model under the proposed transformation framework (Section 7.2.1).

6.2.1   City Vision Phase

The first phase of the novel SSC transformation roadmap is the "City Vision" phase. In a transformational change, there is a need to develop a picture of a future that is clear, easy to communicate. This is achievable through a transformation vision. The purpose of a vision is to say something that helps in clarifying the direction in which a city, in this book's case, needs to move. Without a sensible vision, a transformational change effort could easily lead to a list of confusing and incompatible change activities and projects that could take the city in a wrong direction or even worst to nowhere at all (Kotter, 1995).

Therefore; a clear, competitive and holistic city vision (BSI, 2014; Huawei, 2014; SCC, 2015; ITU-T FG-SSC, 2016) that is identified based on a city context is essential for success (Vogel, 2012a, BSI, 2014; Huawei, 2014; KU, 2015; Government Summit, 2015; ITU-T FG-SSC, 2015b; PwC, 2015a; SCC, 2015).

All studied roadmaps in Section 2.3 agreed on the need of a transformation vision in the first stage of a change process (EPIC, 2013; BSI, 2014; Huawei, 2014; Masdar, 2014; ITU-T FG-SSC, 2015b, SCC, 2015). However, none of the studied roadmaps provides detailed information regarding the aspects to be considered during the implementation of this phase, except the brief information pointed out in the ITU-T FG-SSC technical report (2015b). Therefore, a clear list of key elements to be considered during the vision phase is needed.

On one hand, the first element (i.e. stage) of the ToC (i.e. Section 4.2.2) and proposed ToSSC (i.e. Section 4.5) is identifying the city context. This include analyzing the current state and challenges of a city regarding its economic, social, environmental, and political aspects; agreeing on appropriate transformation vision and strategies to be delivered as a result of a transformation process; and identifying the key stakeholders to be involved in a transformation process. On the other hand, and based on many practices on organizational change and community change in the literature, a transformational change vision phase purpose is to identify and agree on a vision statement, mission statement, transformation strategies, transformation goals and transformation objectives (DiNapoli, 2003; Carpenter et al., 2012; ACCS, 2012; Thompson et al., 2015; KU, 2015; Neumann, 2016; Hofstrand, 2016; Kohel, 2016). Comparing the latter to the ToC shows that the organizational change and community change practices merges the first and second stages of a ToC, named project context and long-term change respectively, into one stage named "vision phase". As both stages are interrelated (ACCS, 2012; KU, 2015; Hofstrand, 2016) and prerequisite for the identification of change activities (Vogel, 2012a), they are tackled as one phase in the innovative transformation roadmap.

Putting it all together, the proposed "City Vision" phase consists of a set of components to be considered during its implementation. The latter includes:

1. **Current City State Analysis**: this includes assessment of the current economic, social, environmental, and political state of a city (Vogel, 2012a). The latter includes clarifying the reasons for the change by identifying the challenges that are being faced by the city, needed to be reduced or eliminated. Getting the required political approvals by local government to ensure the continuity of a SSC transformation process are needed as well (ITU FG-SSC, 2015b).

2. **City Vision**: this aims at identifying a strong, clear change vision for the city. The change vision provides a picture for locals about what the city will look like in the future after applying a series of significant changes at all city levels. It also shows them the advantages and opportunities they can get once this vision is achieved. It serves to motivate all types of city citizens (e.g. locals, public and private sector organizations, civic organizations, and others) and it is essential for the success of a SSC transformation process. The city vision should be in-line with the city's identity and desired long-term change of transforming the city into a SSC, easy to understand, achievable, and measurable (BSI, 2014; ITU-T FG-SSC, 2015b).

3. **Vision and Mission Statements:** a vision statement is a one-sentence statement describing a desired future picture of a city resulting from a transformation process (DiNapoli, 2003; KU, 2015; Hofstrand, 2016). It should be a clear, inspirational and understandable by the broad range of people, thus encouraging several city locals and organizations to work hard towards achieving it. A mission statement, in turn, is a general statement describing how to achieve a vision statement (KU, 2015; Hofstrand, 2016). It is more concrete and action-oriented than a vision statement (KU, 2015; Hofstrand, 2016) and should be concise, outcome-oriented and inclusive (KU, 2015). Often this step includes also identifying a list of core change values that describe the principles and values to be followed in carrying out the transformation activities; for instance, focus of improving citizens' quality of life, protect the environment, encourage innovative business ideas, and others (Hofstrand, 2016).

4. **Transformation Strategies:** a mission statement could be represented by one or more strategies with the aim of achieving a vision statement. Even though a transformation process should have only one vision statement and one mission

statement, it may have several strategies that range from the very broad to the very specific ones (Thompson et al., 2015; KU, 2015; Hofstrand, 2016).

5. **Communicate Vision and Strategies:** one of the important issues to be considered before start planning a transformational change is to communicate a city new vision, mission, and strategies using all possible communication channels with locals (Kotter, 1995; Carpenter et al., 2012). If communicated properly, city citizens, key stakeholders, and organizations (i.e. in both public and private sectors) will get a city vision in a right way and will participate into it (Kotter and Cohen, 2012).

6. **Transformation Goals:** these are general statements used to support the vision and mission statements. They are identified in a way describing what is needed to be accomplished to implement the transformation strategies (ACCS, 2012; Hofstrand, 2016). Often each strategy is represented by one or more goals that could be achieved either in short-term or long-term period.

7. **Transformation Objectives:** objectives are statements that are specific, achievable and measurable (ACCS, 2012). They provide specific milestones with a designated timeline for achieving each goal and are typically achieved through activities identified in the action plan - to be discussed in the proposed "City Plan" phase (ACCS, 2012; KU, 2015; Hofstrand, 2016). A city objective usually clarifies how much of what needs to be accomplished and by when (KU, 2015). For example, one of the objectives of the community initiatives to promote healthcare for older adults might be "Increase elderly care services by 20% (how much) for those who suffer from Alzheimer's disease (of what) by 2020 (by when)".

8. **Identify Stakeholders and Citizen Engagement Mechanisms:** during this step, the mechanisms for key stakeholder involvement and citizen engagement in a transformation process are identified (Vogel, 2012a; Carpenter et al., 2012; BSI, 2014; Government Summit, 2015; ITU-T FG-SSC, 2015b). This also includes identifying communication types and information sharing techniques through a SSC transformation process (ITU-T FG-SSC, 2015b). More details regarding the types of stakeholders to be engaged in the transformation process are provided in Chapter 7.

Many books and studies in the literature based the earlier stages of their change process on the "VMOSA" concept; that is, Vision, Mission, Objectives, Strategies, and Action plan (i.e. action plan will be discussed in the proposed "City Plan" phase). Some prefer to first define the change vision and mission and then identify its goals, objectives, strategies and action plan (DiNapoli, 2003; ACCS, 2012; Thompson et al., 2015; KU, 2015; Neumann, 2016; Kohel, 2016). Others prefer to follow the order of vision, mission, strategies, goals, objectives, and action plan (Carpenter et al., 2012; Hofstrand, 2016). This book leaves this to city's decision makers to select the appropriate technique to follow based on the city context, needs, and local experiences.

6.2.2 City Readiness Phase

One of the aspects to be accomplished during the first stage of the ToC and ToSSC is to check the availability of resources that are needed to enable and support a change process as well as identify the gap and work towards closing this gap (Sections 4.2.2 and 4.5). The organizational change theory also demonstrates the necessity to assess the readiness for change before start planning a transformation process (PMI, 2013; Harrington et al., 2015; Kohl, 2016).

As transforming a city into a SSC is a complex process that requires changes at all city levels (BSI, 2014; ISO/IEC, 2015; ITU-T FG-SSC, 2016) with a need to check the city readiness for change before planning a transformation process (Edwards et al., 2000; PMI, 2013; Harrington et al., 2015; KU, 2015; Kohl, 2016), this research tackles the city readiness for change as a stand-alone phase due to its importance and effect on the whole transformation process. Accordingly, the next phase to be implemented after the "City Vision" phase is the "City Readiness" phase.

Different types of resources are required in a SSC transformation process that are classified as the ICT-based infrastructure (Nam and Pardo, 2011; ITU-T FG-SSC, 2014a; ISO/IEC, 2015) and non-ICT based infrastructure (ITU-T FG-SSC, 2016). Analysis of existing roadmaps in the literature shows the lack of checking the city readiness for change in any of the studied roadmaps (Section 2.3). Only the ITU-FG-SSC and SCC provide some kind of city assessment in their developed roadmaps. Although one of the aspects of the earliest stage of the ITU-T FG-SSC (2015b) roadmap is collecting the relevant data in relation to the city's ICT infrastructure status and its usage at a city-level, the ICT infrastructure is not the only resources that are needed in a transformation process (Rubel, 2014; Vogel, 2012a; Kohel, 2016). Existing non-ICT based infrastructure; such as policies and government systems; are essential and should be assessed as well. The SCC (2015) roadmap includes an assessment phase focusing on assessing the current state of a city in relation to available SSC initiatives and goals, which is also not adequate.

The aim of the "City Readiness" phase is to help city planners, decision makers and relevant stakeholders to assess where their city is, identify the gap, and plan a transformation process accordingly. After checking the city readiness for change, the list of change activities could be designed to help close this gap through smart solutions that are relevant to the objectives of a SSC. The "City Readiness" phase focuses on assessing the city assets in relation to the following:

1. **ICT-based infrastructure**: this includes assessing the availability of the ICT's hardware and software components at a city-level (Nam and Pardo, 2011; ISO/IEC, 2015), such as the network infrastructure, access devices, social applications, and others.

2. **Non-ICT based infrastructure**: this stage focuses on assessing the quality and effectiveness of all urban features that have been created by human activities and that are necessary for the operation of a city. There are two types of the non-ICT based infrastructure known as the hard infrastructure (Rubel, 2014), such as buildings, roads and bridges; and soft infrastructure (Rubel, 2014; Vedashree and Bose, 2015), such as existing financial systems, laws, and regulations.

3. **Available SSC initiatives**: this includes checking the availability of any previously implemented SSC initiatives all city levels (SCC, 2015) and examine the possibilities of how to integrate them with the whole transformation process. The aim of this step is to benefit from previously planned and implemented urban development initiatives and avoid the duplication of efforts as well as learn from existing experiences.

A transformation roadmap often provides a high-level view of a transformation process. A transformation framework, in turn, provides more detailed information and tools of how to realize the roadmap identified stages and elements. Accordingly, the minimum set of components to be checked during the "City Readiness" phase will be discussed in more details in Section 7.2.3.

6.2.3 City Plan Phase

The studied solutions in Sections 2.3 indicate the necessity of planning a SSC transformation process before implementing the change activities (EPIC, 2013; BSI, 2014; Huawei, 2014; Masdar, 2014; ITU-T FG-SSC, 2015b). All studied solutions name this phase as a "Plan" phase, except the ITU-T FG-SSC (2015b), which mixes the concept of planning with the concept of building a SSC. The second phase of the ITU-T FG-SSC roadmap is named as "Identify SSC Targets" which involves identifying and developing of the SSC services; developing a SSC infrastructure; and defining a SSC Key Performance Indicators (KPIs), while a SSC master plan is developed in their roadmap's fourth phase, the "Build the SSC" phase (ITU-T FG-SSC, 2015b). The results of analyzing the proposed SSC roadmaps in the literature show that each roadmap tackles the planning phase from its point of view with no agreement on the aspects to be considered during the implementation of the planning phase.

Based on the ToC and ToSSC (Sections 4.2.2 and 4.5 respectively), the third stage of a change process involves identifying and prioritizing the sequence of change activities, engaging relevant stakeholders in each change activity along with their responsibilities, allocating predefined strategies to the appropriate change activities, and allocating the required resources to each change activity. The third stage also requires identifying a set of assumptions (ToC, Section 4.2.2) and constraints (ToSSC, Section 4.5) for the change activities. The set of assumptions suggest different pathways to the change process and are useful to create a risk management plan. The constraints specify the barriers that may affect the change process and the ways of dealing with them. Based on the urban development discipline (UN-HABITAT, 1997; WHO, 1999; Polat; 2009; Wikström, 2013), urban planning (i.e. such as developing a city into a SSC) should take into consideration the financial feasibility analysis of the required change solutions, this step often takes place in the planning phase of a change process. Identifying the Key Performance Indicators (KPIs) (EPIC, 2013; SCC, 2015; ISO/IEC, 2015; PwC, 2015b; ITU-T FG-SSC, 2016) and Critical Success Factors (CSF) (BSI, 2014), that are used to monitor and evaluate a SSC performance and success, are required as well. Lastly, all required aspects of the planning phase should be documented in a will structured action plan (UN-HABITAT, 1997; Polat, 2009; Wikström, 2013; KU, 2015).

The SSC project planners should always keep in mind the main objectives of developing their city into a SSC while working on the "City Plan" phase. The latter could be achieved through designing change activities (i.e. initiatives) with a focus on preserving the city sustainability; economic, social and environmental sustainability; meeting the city's local needs, interests, and aspirations, and improving the citizen' quality of life as a crosscutting issue at all city-levels. The ICT-based solutions are used as an enabler to enhance the smartness level of a city, opening the door for local innovations. Finally yet importantly, based on urban development planning, the "City Plan" phase should be embedded within the city's national plan (WHO, 1999; Polat, 2009; BSI, 2014).

The proposed "City Plan" phase consists of seven steps; recommended but not mandatory to be implemented in sequence; as below:

1. **Identify Critical Success Factors (CSF) and KPIs**: the first step in the planning phase is identifying the CSFs and KPIs. The CSFs are identified from a SSC predefined goals and objectives. They are the elements that must go right for a SSC transformation process to meet its objectives and success (BSI, 2014). The KPIs, in turn, are used to measure the performance of a SSC transformation process and activities (EPIC, 2013; Masdar, 2014; SCC, 2015; ISO/IEC, 2015; ITU-T FG-SSC, 2016). The CSFs and KPIs are not only used to monitor and assess the change activities' results, they are also used to assess the transformation process as a whole (Booher, 2003). Therefore, the identified measures should be used all along a change process. The team responsible for developing the city measures needs to be aware of the difference between measuring a change process and activities results. Change process relatively is easier to capture. The change activities' results are more difficult but more important to document (Booher, 2003) as they are used to evaluate the success of the change process. It is worth noting that, the assessment measures that are appropriate for one city (i.e. context) many not be appropriate for others (ISO/IEC, 2015). Thereby, each city needs to either identify its own related CSFs and

KPIs or adopt appropriate ones from international standards bodies, such as ISO/IEC, ITU, IEEE (Institute of Electrical and Electronics Engineers), ETSI (European Telecommunications Standards Institute) or others. On a final note, all relevant stakeholders (e.g. citizens, NGOs, businesses, government institutions) should be involved in identifying the change measures (Booher, 2003); aiming to ensure transparency and improve their buy-in (SCC, 2015).

2. **Identify Assumptions, Constraints, and Risks**: during this stage, a list of assumptions about how the transformation process might happen in a way that may lead to the desired goal of transforming a city into a SSC is identified. Assumptions are frequently related to the CSFs. They define a list of states that must exist if the identified CSF is to be achieved (Tayntor, 2002). In large projects, such as SSC projects, there will be a large number of CSFs and related assumptions; therefore; the recommendation is to develop a CSF/Assumptions matrix to simplify the monitoring process. It is also useful to add this matrix to the feasibility study or action plan of the project (Tayntor, 2002). In addition, all possible constraints/barriers that may face the implementation of each activity and the possible ways of handling them must be identified as well (Tayntor, 2002; EPIC, 2013). Each project may also face different types of risks. Therefore; a SSC transformation project should take into consideration a series of possible risks and develop a risk management strategy to mitigate them (Tayntor, 2002; Usmani, 2013; EBIC, 2013; BSI, 2014; Huawei, 2014).

3. **Identify and Prioritize Change Activities**: this includes identifying a list of short-term, medium-term, and long-term change activities (or change initiatives) to be prioritized based on the city needs and local interests and aspirations. The change activities should be aligned with the predefined CSFs and long-term goal of developing a city into a SSC (EPIC, 2013; BSI, 2014; ITU-T FG-SSC, 2015b). They should be designed in a way that ensures the consideration of the SSC six dimensions and sustainability of a city over its three main pillars, namely, economic sustainability, environmental sustainability, and social sustainability. It is the responsibility of the SSC project planners to link each identified change activity to the previously identified related assumptions, constraints, and risks. It is also highly recommended to consider the list of previously implemented SSC activities, resulted

from the "City Readiness" phase, and compare it with the list of identified change activities for the purpose of avoiding the duplication of work and efforts. Any identified gap in resources should be closed by a series of relevant solutions. More detailed information about the minimum list of areas and change activities that should be considered by a SSC project team is available in Section 7.2.3.

4. **Allocate Resources**: during this step, available resources are allocated for each identified activity. This includes the required set of ICT-based and non-ICT based infrastructures as well as a list of people that are responsible to carry out, execute, and implement each change activity.

5. **Engage Stakeholders**: this includes the involvement of all relevant pre-identified stakeholders; e.g. citizens, private and public sectors, NGOs; in each change activity, along with their roles and responsibilities within it (EPIC, 2013; BSI, 2014; SCC, 2015; ITU-T FG-SSC, 2015b). The latter should include everyone whose interests might be affected by the change activity (Polat, 2009).

6. **Financial Feasibility Study**: urban plans should take into consideration the financial implications of the proposed change activities (i.e. solutions) (UN-HABITAT, 1997; WHO, 1999; Polat, 2009). Therefore; the required budget, funding mechanisms and other related financial issues that are needed to support each change activity should be defined (EPIC, 2013; SCC, 2014; Masdar, 2014; ITU-T FG-SSC, 2016). The latter, for instance, includes the required cost for capital and maintenance and cost-recovery mechanisms, such as taxes and intergovernmental transfers (UN-HABITAT, 1997; WHO, 1999; Polat, 2009). This could be achieved through innovative financial mechanisms, bearing in mind that the financial base of municipal governments is typically fragile (UN-HABITAT, 1997).

7. **Create Transformation Action Plan**: the final step of the "City Plan" phase is to put together the outputs of previous six steps in a single document named as the transformation process action plan (Polat, 2009; EPIC, 2013; Masdar, 2014; Huawei, 2014) or master plan (SCC, 2015; ITU-T FG-SSC, 2016). The action plan could be used to assess city planners, policy and decision makers, and key stakeholders in following up and monitoring a transformational change process of their city into a SSC.

City urban planning differs from one city to another and it is highly dependent on the city context and needs (EPIC, 2013; BSI, 2014; SCC, 2015; ISO/IEC, 2015; PwC, 2015a; ITU-T FG-SSC, 2016). The identified activities should provide opportunities to solve the city urbanization challenges as well as provide a high quality of life for citizens. Therefore; the city leaders, decision makers and relevant stakeholders should take into consideration their local needs and interests while planning a SSC initiatives and activities.

6.2.4 City Transformation Phase

Once the change activities are approved and the "City Plan" is completed, a SSC project team can cross the gate to the next phase named, by this book, as the "City Transformation" phase. The aim of this phase is to put the city plan into motion and perform the actual work on a SSC project. The design and implementation of change activities take place during this phase and some of the most significant activities' outcomes start coming on stream.

Various studies in a SSC discipline show the necessity of developing both a smart infrastructure (Al-Hader and Rodzi, 2009; IEC, 2014; Escher Group, 2015; ISO/IEC, 2015; KPMG, 2015b; ITUT FG-SSC, 2016; UNCTAD, 2016) and integrated platform during the "City Transformation" phase (BSI, 2014; IEC, 2014; ISO/IEC, 2015; EIP-SCC, 2015; ITU-T FG-SSC, 2016, UNCTAD, 2016). The aim of a SSC's smart infrastructure is to response intelligently to business and public-sector needs (ISO/IEC, 2015), user demands and other infrastructures (UNCTAD, 2016). It connects the city's physical infrastructure, social infrastructure, business infrastructure, and ICT infrastructure (digital infrastructure) in a way that allow the city to integrate, analyze, gather, optimize, and make decisions based on detailed operational data (Harrison et al., 2010). A smart infrastructure provides the needed foundation to the six dimensions of a SSC and its components are context-specific, depending on the developing level of a city (UNCTAD, 2016). While developing a smart infrastructure, the recommendation is to reuse existing infrastructures, enhance them if possible, and add new ones that are resulted from emerged technologies (BSI, 2014; ISO/IEC, 2015; KPMH, 2015b; ITU-T FG-SSC, 2015; UNCTAD, 2016).

A SSC's integrated platform is a technology architecture, available across the city to all its members and community. It is a digital platform from which all needed information and knowledge could be created. Such a platform should be designed in a way not only to facilitate the aggregation of city data and information analysis, but also to facilitate collaboration between different city levels and to better understand how the city is functioning in terms of services, resource consumption, and lifestyle. City administrators and relevant stakeholders can use the information made available by a SSC integrated platform to take actions and create policy and regulation directions that would help in improving the quality of life of citizens and society as a whole (Escher Group, 2015; ITUT FG-SSC, 2016; UNCTAD, 2016).

One of the required steps during the "City Readiness" phase is to check the availability of any previously implemented SSC activities (i.e. initiative) at all city levels aiming to benefit from them and integrate them with the whole transformation process as well as to avoid repeating the same work twice. Previous projects often provide experiences either to follow or to avoid during a change process. Therefore, the "City Transformation" phase takes into consideration the integration of previously implemented activities that meet the SSC objectives, city needs, and local interests and aspirations.

The proposed "City Transformation" phase focuses not only on designing and implementing the identified set of SSC solutions, but also developing a SSC smart infrastructure and integrated platform and integrating the appropriate previous initiatives into the transformation process. One way of doing this is by considering them while developing the smart infrastructure and integrated platform.

While carrying out the "City Transformation" phase, a recommendation to a SSC project team is to focus on implementing the change activities from which they can deliver quick-wins, to show tangible benefits of a transformation process and to get the needed support to the success of SSC change activities (i.e. initiatives) from locals and community (BSI, 2014; ITU-T FG-SSC, 2016). The components to be considered while developing a SSC smart infrastructure and integrated platform are to be more explained in Section 7.2.3.

6.2.5 Monitoring & Evaluation Phase

Based on existing practices and ToC, there is a necessity to monitor and evaluate large-scale transformation changes by measuring their performance or they would be more likely to fail (Booher, 2003; Jayashree and Hussain, 2010; BAH, 2012; BSI, 2014; SCC, 2015). Performance measures helps in reducing the risks associated with the large-scale change, while resulted performance data used to inform a SSC project team about the impact of the performed change, reinforce positive change outcomes (Jayashree and Hussain, 2010) and learn from experiences (ITU-T FG-SSC, 2016).

The proposed "Monitoring & Evaluation" phase aims at assessing the overall performance of the change process towards achieving the agreed-upon goals and generating the required feedback needed to improve a transformation process. During the change process, adequate performance measurement metrics should be available to track the process and measure its outputs as well as document and analyze findings and feedbacks. This is achievable using a well-defined list of CSFs and KPIs, identified or selected during the "City Plan" phase. The team responsible for city measures should be aware of the great difference between documenting efficiency and effectiveness. Efficiency aims at measuring the implementation of a change activity (i.e. monitoring), while effectiveness focuses on measuring the quality of activity's output(s) (i.e. evaluation) (UNICEF, 1990; Booher, 2003).

As a result, the proposed "Monitoring & Evaluation" phase focuses on the (1) use of the identified CSFs and KPIs to monitor and evaluate the change process and its related activities, and (2) analyze and document findings and feedbacks (e.g. citizens' feedback), with the aim of enhancing the future developments. As the concept of developing cities into SSCs is recent, few attempts exist in the literature to create such a metric.

6.2.6 Sustain Change Phase

Once the initially set goals are met and the outcomes and impact of a transformation process became tangible, it becomes necessary to publically announce achievements to increase the stakeholders and citizens buy-in. Developing cities into SSCs is a journey, not a destination, which is realized through continuous learning, improvements, and producing of more changes. This transformation should be a long-term process, extending into the following generation (Kotter and Cohen, 2012). Therefore, a project team should learn from the documented findings and feedbacks of the "Monitoring & Evaluation" phase. This is done either by updating a SSC vision's strategies, goals, and objectives, if documentations show that critical issues have been neglected during the "City Vision" phase, or by improving implemented change solutions and producing others, and repeating the loop (Kotter, 1995; Harrington et al., 2015; Vedashree, and Bose, 2015).

The proposed "Sustain Change" phase aims at sustaining a transformation process through three interrelated steps that are:

1. **Learn from previous SSC experience**, by studying introduced documentations of findings and feedback an avoid repeating the same previous mistakes (Daszko and Sheinberg, 2005; BSI, 2014; Huawei, 2014; ITU-T FG-SSC, 2015b).

2. **Continuous improvement** by considering lessons learned from the past experiences to continuously update the vision's strategies, goals and objectives if needed; improve the ability to maintain implemented solutions; and introduce best practices concerning a SSC (Kotter, 1995; BSI, 2014; Huawei, 2014; Vedashree and Bose, 2015; ITU-FG-SSC, 2016).

3. **Announce achievements and produce more changes**, by proclaiming the advent of a new era and sharing achievements' news with locals and community (Kotter, 1995; Daszko and Sheinberg, 2005). This also includes not letting-up before completing the transformation by stimulating the change process by new change activities, aiming to achieve the long-term goal of developing a city into a SSC (Kotter, 1995; Daszko and Sheinberg, 2005; BSI, 2014; SCC, 2015; ITU-T FG-SSC, 2015b).

6.3   Discussion

This chapter provides an insight into what are the aspects to consider before and during the process of developing cities into SSCs, introducing an easy to follow transformation roadmap. The latter is a result of three years of research of studying and analyzing hundreds of technical reports and publications related to the subject matter in the literature and applying an in-depth analysis on these studies that provide detailed information about the required stages for the SSC transformation process. The results show a gap in knowledge in relation to the required aspects that should be taken into consideration throughout a transformation process. For instance, none of the studies mentions the necessity of checking the city readiness for change before planning the needed transformation activities, which has a critical effect on the success of a transformation process that may only lead to failure. On another note, the introduced roadmap is developed as a context-based roadmap, to be customized by any SSC team project. It is not designed to a specific city, neither applicable on a particular context. The first phase of the innovative roadmap is checking the city context in relation to its economic, environmental, social and political state before agreeing on a city transformation vision and its related strategies, goals and objectives. After checking the city context and readiness for change, a SSC project team can plan a transformation process based on its city context, needs, and local interests and aspirations taking into consideration a SSC objectives and dimensions.

On a final note, Table 6.1 provides an overview comparison of differences and similarities between the proposed innovative roadmap and other roadmaps in the literature (Section 2.3). Noting that it is focusing on highlighting the neglected phases and components in other studied proposed solutions.

Table 6.1: Comparison of the Proposed Innovative Roadmap to others in the Literature

Roadmap	Consider the SSC six dimensions*	City governs solutions	Check current city state	City Readiness			Identify assumptions /constraints/ Risks
				ICT Infrastructure	Non-ICT Infrastructure	Previous initiatives	
Innovative roadmap	YES	YES	YES	YES	YES	YES	YES
BSI	NO	YES	NO	NO	NO	NO	YES (Constraints/ Risks)
Huawei	NO	YES	NO	NO	NO	NO	NO
EPIC	YES	NO	NO	NO	NO	NO	YES
ITU-T	NO	YES	NO	YES	NO	NO	NO
SCC	NO	YES	YES	NO	NO	YES	NO

Source: This book, page 57

6.4   Conclusion

Different attempts exist in the literature to develop a SSC transformation roadmap; each focuses on a selected lens without considering all aspects of SSCs, which denotes a gap in knowledge. This chapter focused on introducing an innovative roadmap that could be customized based on the city context, needs, and local interests. The roadmap provides an overview of the general directions of a transformation process, identifying the main phases and components that should be realized during a transformation journey. It is being developed while taking into consideration the six dimensions of SSCs, city readiness for change, and sustainability of a city over its dimensions.

The innovative roadmap lays the foundation stone for developing a SSC transformation framework. The latter aims at providing the necessary tools to deliver and manage the identified changed activities as well as identifying the minimum list of activities that are needed to be accomplished under the six dimensions of a SSC.

In the next Chapter, the proposed innovative SSC transformation framework is presented.

CHAPTER SEVEN: THE INNOVATIVE SSC TRANSFORMATION FRAMEWORK

7.1   Introduction

A transformation roadmap is a high-level view of a change process. It provides information about the general directions without indicating the mechanisms of how to turn the identified transformation strategies into actions, what tools and solutions are needed under each of its components, and how they are interrelated. This is often detailed in the transformation framework.

As defined in (Ibrahim et al., 2016), a SSC transformation framework is *"a layered structure that leads city planners and relevant stakeholders throughout a transformation process by providing guidance on city readiness for change and the innovative solutions needed to grant urban sustainability and high quality of life for citizens"*. Based on its definition, a SSC transformation framework serves as a guide, clarifying how to apply the transformation roadmap in a way that allows a SSC team to achieve the transformation vision, objectives, and goals. It enables the implementation of the transformation strategies on existing city's systems that need to be transformed.

The aim of this chapter is to introducing a novel framework used to provide the tools needed to realize the SSC transformation roadmap phases and components (Ibrahim et al., 2017a, 2018; Ibrahim, 2019). The structure of this chapter is as follows. The proposed innovative transformation framework is provided in Section 7.2. Discussion on the proposed framework and its comparison to others in the literature are presented in Section 7.3. The chapter concludes in Section 7.4.

7.2   Transformation towards SSCs: Innovative Framework

Few attempts exist in the literature for developing a SSC framework. The latter includes CISCO (2012) framework, EPIC (2013) framework, BSI (2014) framework, Deloitte (2015b) framework, and PwC (2015a) framework. Each framework tackles a transformation process from its point of view based on cities over which a transformation framework is to be applied. For instance, BSI proposed a framework that fits the needs of the United Kingdom cities. Both Deloitte and PwC proposed two different frameworks for the 100 SCs initiative in India. In turn, CISCO proposed undetailed framework, suggesting only a logical flow of a transformation process that may enable key stakeholders to push through and test SSC initiatives. EPIC framework provides six strategic domains (i.e. same as the six dimensions of a SSC) and six strategic characteristics to be used to describe the goals and initiatives that are needed for a city to become a SSC. It only focuses on the six dimensions of SSCs, without highlighting the minimum required initiatives to be delivered under each domain, noting that all proposed solutions are controlled by EPIC team and delivered to city locals using cloud computing techniques.

The results of studying and analyzing existing frameworks show that none of the developed frameworks takes into consideration checking the city readiness for change neither considering all needed requirements of developing cities into SSCs. None highlights the mechanisms of how to contextualize their proposed framework based on current city resources, needs, and local interest while taking into consideration the objectives of a SSC and city sustainability. The latter should be the basis of any change activity to be planned, developed, implemented, and delivered.

This book proposes a novel SSC transformation framework that takes into consideration all above mentioned aspects. The framework aims at providing the tools needed to realize the proposed transformation roadmap. It focuses on the techniques that could be used to achieve the roadmap phases and components. As a result, to ensure the consideration of the findings of other researches and studies in the literature as well as closing the identified gap in knowledge in relation to the tools needed to realize the innovative roadmap, the innovative framework is proposed by undertaking the following steps:

a. The main layers and tools constituting each studied framework were extracted and tabulated.
b. Common layers and tools were tabulated, creating a list of essential layers and tools to consider and use in the innovative framework.
c. Overlooked components and tools in existing frameworks were either adopted for adequate studies in the literature or proposed.

d. As the aim of a framework is to realize a transformation roadmap and put its stages into action, this research book has identified the layers and tools needed to realize the added phases and components of the proposed novel roadmap.

Stemming from the above, the innovative framework consists of five layers at its top-level, as illustrated in

Figure 7.1, one preparation and four main layers as summarized below:

[P] Preparation Activities: this is the only preparation layer of the proposed framework. To differentiate it from main layers, the "Preparation Activities" is numbered using the "[P]" symbol, as the letter "P" is one of the abbreviations used to denote the word "Preparation". The layer includes all activities related to the "City Vision" phase of the proposed roadmap. The latter includes the current city state analysis regarding its economic, social, environmental, and political challenges, agree on the city vision and vision and mission statements, identify transformation strategies, communicate the city vision and strategies with locals, identify transformation goals and objectives, and identify stakeholder and citizen engagement mechanism. The outputs of this phase are highly dependent on the city context and local experiences. Therefore, this book provides only the tools needed to identify the stakeholders and citizen engagement mechanisms (i.e. [P6] activity), as they are often identified using a generic model. This model is presented in Section 7.2.1.

[A] Check City Readiness and Gap Analysis: the aim of this layer is to check the status of the current city assets, including its hard, soft, and digital infrastructures along with the level of its digital literacy. It provides the needed tools to realize the "City Readiness" phase of the proposed roadmap. More details available at Section 7.2.2

[B] Develop, Implement, and Deliver Transformation Solutions: during which a SSC project team work together with the relevant stakeholder in identifying a set of SSC services and deliverables to be implemented. This includes prioritizing the change solutions based on urgency, cost, and city needs. One suggestion for prioritization is to focus on change solutions that can be delivered quickly, at low risk and low cost (BSI, 2014). This will give a SSC project more trust and attention from locals as they are seeing its real outputs and benefits as well as increase their buy-in the project as a whole. This layer is related directly to the "City Plan" and "City Transformation" phases of the proposed roadmap. It consists of two main sub-layers, namely, the development of the SSC [B1] Smart Infrastructure and Integrated Platform and [B2] Innovative Smart Solutions. It is worth noting that the implementation and delivery of services under the [B1] and [B2] could be accomplished in parallel. As to be discussed in sub-Sections 7.2.3.1 and 7.2.3.1, the infrastructure and integrated platform should be developed in a way that enables future capacities and solutions to be easily added to the overall system. Moreover, although the development of some SSC solutions may be dependent on one another, many solutions are integrated. Meaning that, the development of a solution may have a positive effect on more than one dimension of a SSC. For example, well-educated people (i.e. a smart living dimension solution) are one of the corner stones for improving the economic level of a city through their work productivities (i.e. smart economic factor). These educated people may be later on experts in transportation engineering and work on projects for building new smart bridges within a city to improve the mobility quality of a city (i.e. a smart mobility dimension solution). In case of interdependencies between transformation stages, the independent stage should be implemented first. Dependent stages would follow. Section 7.2.3 provides more details regarding this layer.

[C] **Monitoring and Evaluation**: this includes the techniques that can be used to monitor and evaluate the performance of a transformation process and its outputs (i.e. delivered solutions) and their impacts. It provides the tools needed to realize the "Monitoring & Evaluation" phase of the proposed roadmap. Sub-Section 7.2.4 sheds light on existing solutions to be either fully or partially adopted by a SSC project team.

[D] **Sustain Transformation and Produce More Changes**: the aim of this layer is to ensure the sustainability and continuity of a SSC transformation process through learnings, improvements, and additional changes. It is related to the "Sustain Change" phase of the proposed roadmap and to be discussed in sub-Section 7.2.5.

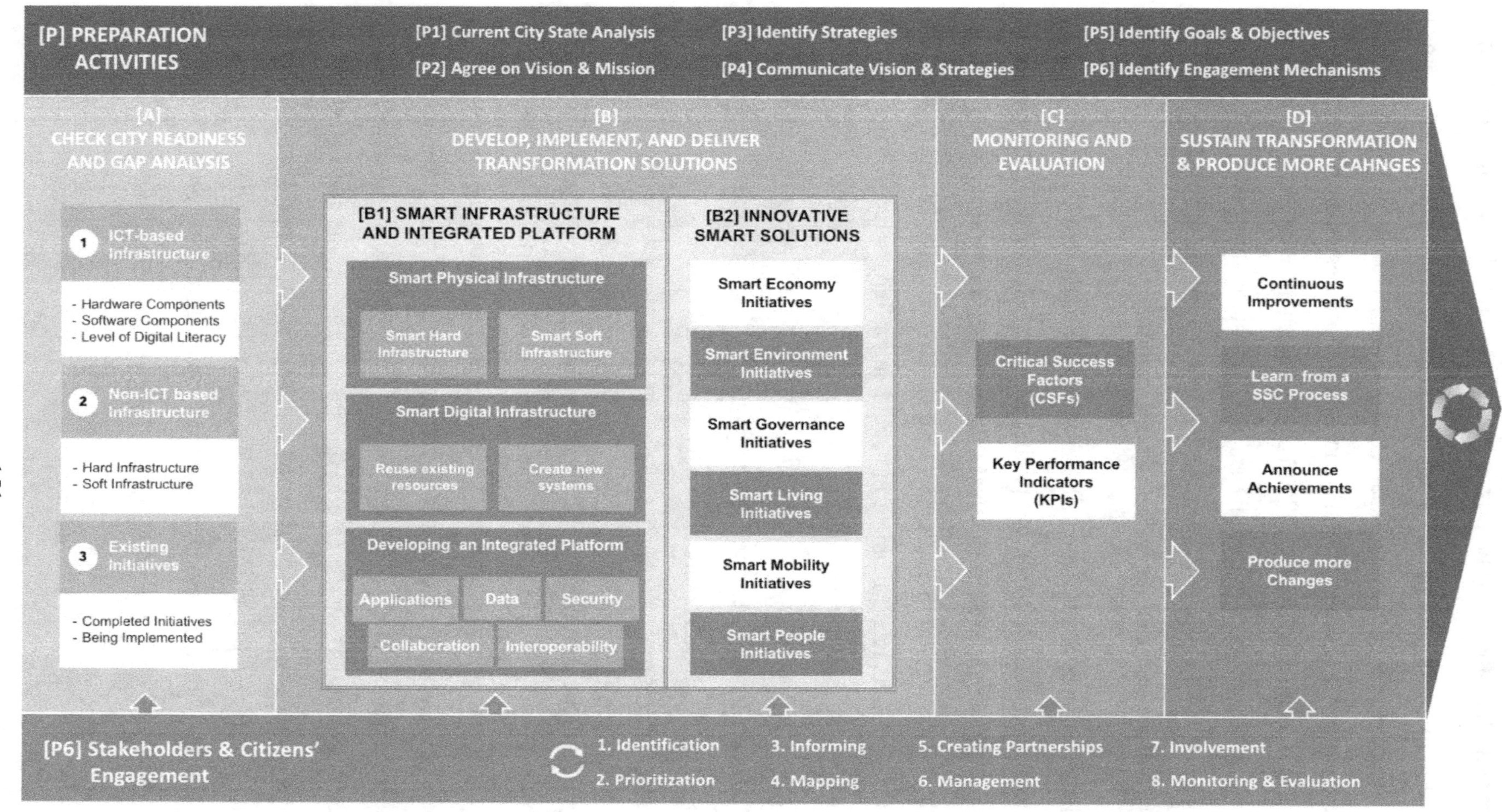

Figure 7.1: The Innovative Smart Sustainable City Transformation Framework

7.2.1 [P6] Stakeholders and Citizens Engagement in Smart SSCs: Proposed Model

Cities are dynamic living organisms that are continuously changing and evolving over time aiming to enhance their economic, social, environmental, and physical structures. At the heart of these structures, there are the stakeholders that are treated as end users of city services. A SSC transformation process will affect city stakeholders, directly or indirectly, in different ways based on the context of each SSC transformation activity. This sub-section is focusing on the concept of stakeholders, their engagement in a SSC project, and introducing a systematic approach for this engagement process.

The term 'Stakeholder' was firstly invented in 1963 by the Stanford Research Institute, where the term meant to refer to those groups that without their support the organization may cease to exist (Freeman, 1984). In 1984, Edward Freeman published the *"Strategic Management: A Stakeholder Approach"* book in which a Stakeholder Theory was detailed and invented, forming a landmark moment in developing a Stakeholder Theory (Raffay, 2007). Freeman (1984) define a stakeholder as *"any group or individual who can affect or is affected by the achievement of the organization's objectives."* From that time on, the importance of stakeholder engagement, including citizens, has emerged in at least three different areas of studies: organizational management, public policy, and (national and international) development projects (Mathur et al., 2007).

In the context of development projects, the term 'Stakeholder' refers to those who affect or could be affected by the proposed development initiative (World Bank, 1996). Urban development, which is the main constituent of cities' vision, particularly SSCs' vision, is one type of these development projects. In this context and in-line with Freeman's (1984) definition, the term 'Stakeholder' could refer to those who can affect or are affected by the urban development project. In the case of this research book, the concept of SSCs is emerging as a new approach to make urban development more sustainable (Alawadhi et al. 2012). Thereby, the term 'Stakeholder' in SSCs projects would have the same meaning related to that used by urban development projects; meaning that *"a Smart Sustainable City's stakeholder is any individual or group of individuals who can affect or is affected by the SSC initiative"*.

There is not much disagreement in literature on what kind of entity can be a stakeholder (Mitchell et al., 1997). A stakeholder can take many forms; including persons, groups of people, citizens, institutions, public/private organizations, neighborhoods, societies, natural environment (Mitchell et al., 1997), government, local community organizations, advocates, media, consumers, unions, environmentalists, associations, political groups, employees, financial community, suppliers and others (Freeman, 1984). The selection of stakeholders is determined based on those who have stake in the project. To clarify the term stake, a SSC project team should differentiate between those that have direct influence on a SSC transformation process and its outcomes and those who have interest with no power but are important and should be involved in a transformation process.

Mitchell et al. (1997) divide stakeholder typology into three classes of attributes that are: (1) Power, (2) Legitimacy, and (3) Urgency. The Power attribute refers to the ability of influencing the actions of other stakeholders and achieving the desired outcomes. Legitimacy attribute means the normative appropriateness through identifying the stakeholder's relationship with the project. Urgency attribute refers to the degree of stakeholder's claim for immediate actions, which is often related to goals that are time-sensitive and any delay in achieving them is unacceptable and/or costly (e.g. the urgency of taking immediate actions on climate change phenomenon around the globe). This classification also used to identify stakeholders into eight categories, as illustrated in Figure 7.2, based on their salience in the project, namely:

1. **Dormant Stakeholders**: refer to those who have the power to impose their will on the project but not having the legitimacy and urgency attributes, this power remains unused.
2. **Discretionary Stakeholders**: refer to those who possess the legitimacy attribute but not having the power to influence the project nor having urgent claims.
3. **Demanding Stakeholders**: are those who have urgent claims but not having the power and legitimacy to enforce them.
4. **Dominant Stakeholders:** refer to those who are powerful and legitimate and have a strong influence on the project.

5. **Dangerous Stakeholders:** are those who have power and urgency but lacking the attribute of legitimacy. They are coercive or even possibly violent, which make them dangerous to the project.

6. **Dependent Stakeholders:** refer to those who lack the attribute of power but having both the urgent and legitimacy attributes.

7. **Definitive Stakeholders:** are those who have the three attributes of power, legitimacy, and urgency.

8. **Non-stakeholders:** refer to those who are not possessing any of the attributes of power, legitimacy, and urgency.

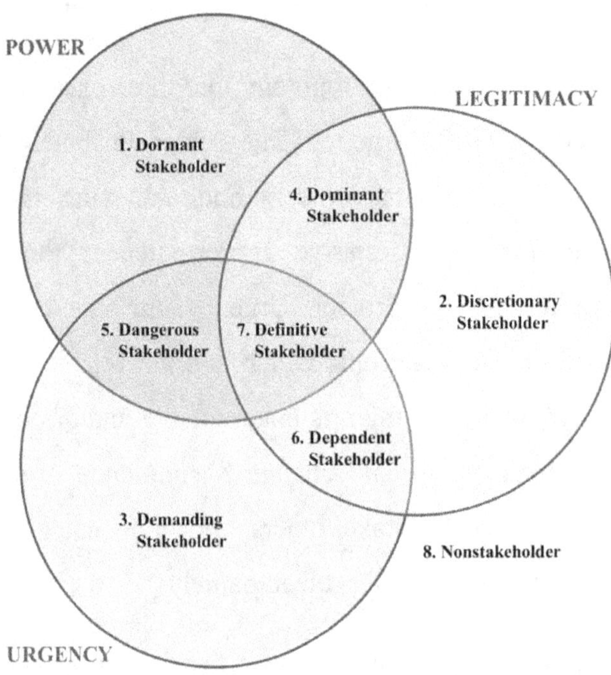

Figure 7.2: Stakeholder Topology (Mitchell et al., 1997)

From this research point of view, the stakeholder typology presented by Mitchell et al. (1997) should not be used as a static instrument for categorizing and mapping stakeholders, rather, it should be used as an approach to understand how interests are stakeholders along with their relationships evolve and change over time. In large-scale projects such as SSCs and urban development projects there are various activities to be designed and achieved and there are different stakeholders to be involved. Thus, stakeholders' salience will change over time based on changes in a SSC project's strategies and activities.

In 2010, Futaki Károly provided a study on *Stakeholder Selection Strategy* for *Danube FloodRisk Project* in which he described how to link the eight categories of Mitchell et al. (1997) to the benefit of public participation in development projects (Futaki, 2010). This linkage gives a lens for this research book to understand how to link Mitchell et al.'s eight categories to the SSC projects. For stakeholders and citizens engagement is SSCs projects, dominant and definitive stakeholders could be seen as the groups a project needs to cooperate with (e.g. local unions' representatives are dominant stakeholders, companies are definitive stakeholders while government organizations are both dominant and definitive stakeholders). In relation to the discretionary and dependent stakeholders, there is a need to enhance their capabilities to participate in a project (e.g., schools and nonprofit organizations that receive donations are examples of discretionary stakeholders; citizens with lack of resources, such as technical experience, to properly participate in a project are dependent stakeholders). The participation of demanding stakeholders should be monitored and motivated (e.g., protestors are demanding stakeholders) while dangerous stakeholders' participation should be only monitored (e.g. computer criminals are dangerous stakeholders). The dormant stakeholders should be monitored because they may harm the whole project (e.g. a person or group that are able to manipulate media attention in a wrong way is a dormant stakeholder). Finally, non-stakeholders are to be considered outside the project process (e.g., newly or recently born children are non-stakeholders; however; there are other stakeholders to care about their rights and needs).

In his book titled *"The Stakeholder Theory: The State of the Art"*, Freeman et al. (2010) shows how the stakes of each stakeholder and/or stakeholder group could contribute, either positively or negatively, to the value creation process of the project activities. The book clarifies that the seven categories of stakeholders, after excluding non-stakeholders from the list, could be classified into two types of groups:

- **Primary Stakeholders**: include all stakeholder groups that without their support the project may cease to exist. These are known as 'Key Stakeholders'.

- **Secondary Stakeholders**: include all stakeholder groups who can affect or being affected by the project activities.

In the context of SSCs, stakeholders and citizens' engagement in a SSC project is important due to the benefits they may provide to the whole transformation process. An effective management of their involvement is crucial for the following reasons:

- Stakeholders and citizens provide a wide range of knowledge, skills, and experiences to the project. If well managed, this could increase the successfulness of the project.
- Stakeholders and citizens can play a significant role in the project process. They could improve the quality of decision-making and designed activities if they have a good understanding of the project goals and objectives.
- Involvement of stakeholders and citizens in the project process boosts transparency and improves citizens' buy-in, reducing oppositions and ensuring that opinions are for the benefits of the projects.
- The establishment of good relationships with stakeholders and citizens' various groups ensures that complains and issues could be addressed at an early stage of the project design.
- Stakeholders and citizen engagement helps in avoiding potential problems during the transformation process, such as neglecting of essential local needs and aspirations.
- Stakeholders and citizens can facilitate the implementation of process activities as well as help in monitoring and evaluating outcomes. Their feedbacks are crucial for continuous improvements and sustainability of a transformation process.

Various SSC studies in the literature indicate the necessity of stakeholders and citizens' engagement in the process of transforming cities into SSCs (EPIC, 2013; BSI, 2014; IEC, 2014; Deloitte, 2015b; ISO/IEC, 2015; PwC & CII, 2015; ITU-T FG-SSC, 2016; Ericsson, 2016). However, none provides a systematic model that ensures an effective and efficient stakeholders and citizens' engagement in a SSC transformation process, which sheds light on a gap in knowledge. The ITU-T FG-SCC in their *"Setting the Stage for Stakeholders' Engagement in SSCs"* technical report provides only recommendations regarding stakeholders' engagement in a SSC project based on a set of steps proposed by the World Bank and Logical Framework Approach, which are (1) Identification, (2) Categorization, and (3) Engagement (ITU-T FG-SSC, 2016).

After studying the Stakeholder Theory and different related studies regarding the required stages for stakeholder and citizens' engagement in development projects, this reach study takes a step forward in closing a knowledge gap in relation to the process of stakeholders and citizens' engagement in SSC projects. In this regard, it introduces a novel systematic model to be fully or partially adopted for this purpose.

Based on Stakeholder Theory (Freeman, 1984), any stakeholder engagement tool should take into consideration three essential aspects these are (1) stakeholder identification and analysis, (2) stakeholder relationship with the project, and (3) stakeholder mapping to the project activities. This includes understanding of when to communicate with stakeholders, which information to share with them, what type of communication channels are needed, what are the benefits of partnership with them, and what type of feedback they can provide while monitoring and evaluating the project activities. After identifying these three aspects, various stakeholder engagement tools start coming out in the literature based on them.

The International Financial Corporation (IFC) proposes a stakeholder engagement handbook that is being used by some sustainable development projects. The IFC indicates that the term 'stakeholder engagement' encompasses a range of activities and interactions throughout the lifecycle of the project (IFC, 2007), and divides them into eight components. The latter includes (1) stakeholder identification and analysis, (2) information disclosure, (3) stakeholder consultation, (4) negotiation and participation, (5) grievance management, (6) stakeholder involvement in project monitoring, (7) reporting to stakeholders, and (8) management functions. Another interesting stakeholder engagement model for sustainable development projects is that one proposed by Bal et al. (2013). The model was developed based on face-to-face interviews with different UK-based organizations that show interest on sustainable development projects in the United Kingdom, specifically, sustainable construction projects. The suggested model of stakeholders' engagement in sustainability projects has been divided into six phases namely (1) Identifying all key stakeholders, (2) relating the stakeholders with sustainability targets, (3) prioritizing the stakeholders, (4) managing stakeholders, (5) Measuring their performance, and (6) putting targets into action (Bal et al., 2013).

Putting these all together; the "Stakeholder Theory" engagement essential aspects (Freeman, 1984, Freeman et al., 2010), the IFC (2007) stakeholder engagement components, Bal et al. (2013) model phases, and ITU-T FG-SSC (2016) recommendations; a novel stakeholder and citizens' engagement model to be fully or partially adopted by various SSC project teams has been introduced. This model provides detailed information needed during the identification of stakeholders and citizens' engagement mechanism task of the 'City Vision' phase of the innovative roadmap. It also helps in mapping and engaging relevant stakeholders to different SSC change activities related to the "City Plan" phase as well as involving them in the 'City Transformation', 'Measure Transformation', and 'Sustain Change' phases. The term 'Stakeholder' in the proposed model is an abbreviation for the term 'Stakeholder and citizen'. Figure 7.3 illustrates this model followed by descriptions about each of its stages.

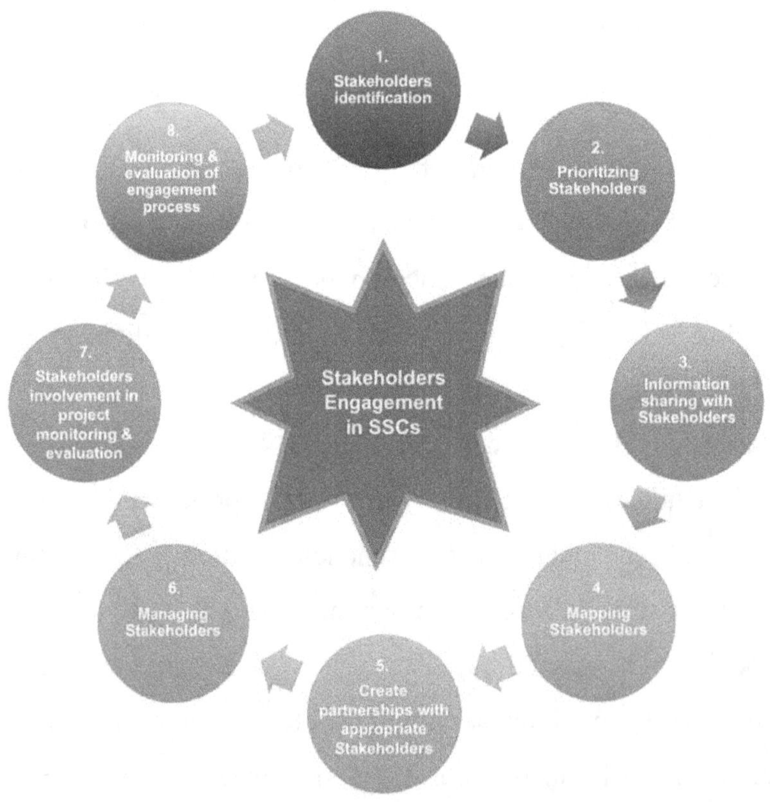

Figure 7.3: Smart Sustainable Cities Stakeholder Engagement Proposed Model

1. Stakeholders Identification

During this stage, all stakeholders that can affect or may be affected, directly or indirectly, by a SSC project along with the stakes of each should be identified. Based on the identified objectives and goals related to a SSC vision and mission, the identified stakeholders are classified into key stakeholders and secondary stakeholders. Freeman (1984) indicates that identifying stakeholders and their stakes is not an easy task. To simplify this process, a project team should answer a list of questions, helping them in identifying these stakeholders. For instance, the latter may include the following questions (Futaki, 2010):

- Who are the individuals, groups, institutions, and organization that are interested in the SSC change activity/activities?
- What is the expected stake (i.e. role) of each?
- Who are the potential beneficiaries of these activities?
- Who has the power to influence each activity?
- Who might have constraints about activities and why?
- Who would be affected by the changes expected from the project implementation?

To simplify the identification process, Mathur (2007) suggests a generic stakeholder categorization technique in which stakeholders are divided into three main categories. These are (1) those who affect the project, (2) those who are affected by the project, and (3) those who may be interested in the project; noting that a stakeholder may be belonging to more than one category at the same time. For instance, the local ICT companies could affect a SSC project by providing new technical solutions to enhance the city's ICT infrastructure, and may be affected by the project after announcing new trade legislations from the government side. This categorization technique deemed applicable to the context of SSCs, as it simplifies the process of identifying a SSC project's stakeholders who should be considered for engagement. Table 7.1 illustrates an example, provided by this book research, on how the SSC stakeholders can be categories based on Mathur (2007) categorization technique.

Table 7.1: Generic Stakeholder Categorization* (Hypothetical Example)

Category	Sub-Category	Examples of Stakeholders
Those who affect a SSC project	Those who are involved in the delivery of a SSC project	Developers
		Government organizations
		Investors
		ICT companies
		Designers
		Banks
		Fund bodies
		Professional consultants; e.g. structural, architectural, engineers, financial, etc.
	Those who determine the context of the activity	Municipalities such as planning department
		Central government departments
		Non-governmental bodies; e.g. environment agencies, women's right bodies, etc.
Those who are affected by a SSC	Directly affected by a SSC project	Users of public transformations, buildings, facilities, parks, spaces, etc.
	May or may not be directly or indirectly affected by a SSC project depending on the context of the activity	Citizens
		Local/surrounding community members
		Local community groups; e.g. child care group, residents' groups or societies, advocacy group, etc.
		Specific demographic groups; e.g. those based on gender, economic, age, education, etc.
Those who may be interested in a SSC project		Academia – researchers
		Social/Environmental campaigning organizations
		Media
		Potential users of services

** Source: adopt the concept from Mathur (2007), and modified to be used in a SSC context*

Different types of stakeholders can be engaged in a SSC project. This includes but not limited to municipalities, city administrators, and city council; city services companies; ICT companies; utilities providers; NGOs; industry organizations; regional, international and multilateral organizations such as UN agencies and the World Bank; citizens; urban planners; research organizations and academia; standardization bodies (ITU FG-SSC, 2016), local government organizations; civil society organizations; local, regional and international businesses; other governments such as the national digital agenda drivers and national broadband and telecommunication regulatory authorities; and city departments including those interest in innovations, public safety, education, health care, environment, waste management, and transportation (Ericsson, 2016).

2. Prioritizing Stakeholders

This stage aims at ranking stakeholders' degree of importance based on their potential impact (i.e. influence) on the success of a SSC project. All stakeholders are important to the project; however; they should be prioritized according to their characteristics and the needs of a SSC project, such as their ability to influence the project, bring integrity and legitimacy. The prioritization task should consider those who have the power for decision-making; who can economically, socially, environmentally, and politically contribute to the project; and who are not directly linked to the project but they are interested in its smart and sustainable solutions to be developed and delivered. Freeman (1984) suggests creating a matrix to show the importance of each class of stakeholders, as illustrated in Table 7.2, to achieve success in each transformation activity.

Table 7.2: Stakeholders/Activities Prioritization Matrix (Hypothetical Example)

Stakeholder	Activity A	Activity B	Activity C	...	Activity X
Government	5	4	4		3
Unions	3	3	NA		4
Schools	NA	5	1		NA
Banks	5	5	3		4
Universities	1	5	5		NA
Private Organization	4	4	2		5

1 = Not important to achieve activity success
3 = Moderately important to achieve activity success
5 = Critically important to achieve activity success
NA = not a stakeholder in this activity

In this table, the degree of importance of each stakeholder is selected from a set of values {1,2,3,4,5}, which is a ranking scale used to represents "Not Important", "Slightly Important", "Moderately Important", "Important", and "Critically Important" respectively. The set of abbreviation values {"Activity A", "Activity B", "Activity C", …, "Activity X"} is used to represent different types of transformation activities. In this case, the first activity is given the name "Activity A" while the last activity is named as

"Activity X", where "X" is a placeholder variable (i.e. the value of X could be any alphanumeric value). Another type of abbreviations can be used as well in place of the alphanumeric one.

The following example simplify the understanding of the concept. Assume the set of abbreviation values {"Activity A", "Activity B"} is used to represent the transformation activities: (1) "Reducing Local Unemployment Rate" and (2) "Enhancing Healthcare Services" respectively and one of the stakeholders to be engaged in these activities is the local government. To identify the degree of importance of the local government in each activity, there is a need first to identify its potential role and level of impact in each activity. The latter is selected based on the judgment and foresight of a SSC decision-making team. Accordingly, the degree of importance is then identified, using a rank value from 1 to 5 in the periodization matrix. Table 7.3 summarizes this example, noting that "No Impact", "Minor Impact", "Moderate Impact", "Major Impact", or "Critical Impact" represents the impact level of engaging a specific stakeholder in an activity.

Table 7.3: Hypothesis Example of the Stakeholders/Activities Prioritization Matrix

Activities	Expected Roles of Local Government	Level of Impact	Degree of Importance
Activity A: Reducing Local Unemployment Rate	• Encouraging local businesses to increase their work capacities through Tax breaks. • Encouraging the establishment of small and medium sized businesses by enactment of new laws.	Critical Impact	Critically Important (value = 5)
Activity B: Enhancing Healthcare Services	• Regulating healthcare market to prevent inefficiency and unfairness. • Establishing partnerships among local government and healthcare private sector institutions to improve the quality of public healthcare services.	Major Impact	Important (value = 4)

The Stakeholders/Activities prioritization matrix allows the project team to determine the impact of each stakeholder in a transformation process. It also simplifies the mapping of stakeholders to change activities in the 'Mapping Stakeholder' stage of this model.

3. Information Sharing with Stakeholders

During this stage, a SSC project team share with stakeholders all needed information regarding a SSC transformation process activities and how they can contribute to activities' success. This stage provides a SSC project team with the needed information about the level of interest of each class of stakeholders in the proposed activities as well as their insights and complains about these activities. Thereby, it is recommended to communicate with stakeholders at an early stage of decision-making to plan the mapping of stakeholders effectively (IFC, 2007). This communication should also continue throughout a SSC transformation process lifecycle. Freeman (1984) suggests to create another matrix, as illustrated in Table 7.4, focusing on the level of interest of each class of stakeholders in each transformation activity.

Table 7.4: Stakeholders/Activities Interests Matrix (Hypothetical Example)

Stakeholder / Activity	Government	Unions	Banks	Private Organization	...
Activity A	5	NA	2	5	
Activity B	4	3	NA	2	
Activity C	NA	1	5	NA	
...					
Activity N	2	5	1	NA	

1 = Not important to stakeholder
3 = Moderately important to stakeholder
5 = Critically important to stakeholder
NA = not of interest to stakeholder

This matrix along with the prioritizing matrix allow the project team to take the appropriate actions regarding stakeholders mapping to activities. They give them an indication about those who are critical to the project but are not interested into it, thus try to negotiate with them and persuade them to be part in this process. The stakeholder/activities interests' matrix is then updated based on the results of these negotiations.

4. Mapping Stakeholders

Stages 1, 2 and 3 create an external view of the transformation process by identifying and analyzing stakeholders and key interests of each. The aim of stage 4 is to identify how a SSC project team can map each stakeholder or group of stakeholders onto a transformation process's strategies and activities (Freeman, 1984). This also includes highlighting the effectiveness (i.e. impact) level of each stakeholder in achieving each transformation activity and its related objectives and goals. Following the same logic used in stages 3 and 4, this book research recommends to create a new matrix in which each row is dedicated to each stakeholder while columns are dedicated to the transformation activities, as illustrated in Table 7.5. Each cell in the matrix show the desired impact of a particular stakeholder on a specific activity. The last column is used to highlight the desired impact level, from 1: no impact to 5: critical impact, of each stakeholder on achieving each activity.

Table 7.5: Stakeholders/Activities Mapping and Impact Matrix (Hypothetical Example)

Activity Stakeholder	Activity A	Activity B	...	Activity X	Impact[*]
Government	Increase online services by 65%	Increase women's participation in political decisions by 25%		Decrease taxes on new established firms by 10% for the first year of establishment	A=5, B=4, ..., N=5
Local ICT Companies	Increase investment in smart infrastructure	Employment equity		Currently ignoring stakeholder	A=5, B=4, ...
Universities	Currently ignoring stakeholder	Increase research on the importance of gender equality at all city levels		Provide workshops for students regarding entrepreneurships and startups	B=3, ..., N=4

* 1 = No Impact, 2 = Minor Impact, 3 = Moderate Impact, 4 = Major Impact, 5 = Critical Impact

For instance, if one of the transformation activities is to improve the gender equality at all city levels, then one of possible desired impact from universities may be to increase the awareness about the issue by providing different research studies on the importance of gender equality and its impact on the economic, social, environmental, and political levels of a city. This desired impact could be assigned to a 'low impact' level on achieving the activity, not because it is not important, but because universities in this case are classified as secondary stakeholders with legitimacy and urgency attitude but with no power. They could not influence decision-makers regarding the issue; they can only provide recommendations based on national, regional, and international trends and show the disadvantages of not considering this gender equality at all city levels. In turn, decision-makers may or may not consider these recommendations.

5. Create Partnerships with appropriate Stakeholders

After mapping stakeholders to SSC transformation activities, seeking partnerships with relevant stakeholders is a need (Freeman, 1984; IFC, 2007). Developing cities into SSCs is a large-scale transformation process that leads to various changes at all city levels. To be realized, these changes need massive investments, such as improving current infrastructure or building of new ones, building labs for innovative and smart solutions, providing technical trainings for citizens, promoting tourism through the development of attractive tourism projects, developing of an index to measure and evaluate a SSC project performance, and others. A SSC project, therefore, needs real partnerships at national and international levels to succeed (ITU-T FG-SSC, 2016). These partnerships aim at achieving the desired large-scale transformation.

Depending on the type of the transformation activity, a SSC project team could seek to collaborate with different types of stakeholders, such as private sector, universities, NGOs, banks, fund institutions, local government organizations, unions, schools, environmental protection agencies, and others. Building such collaboration leads to achieving a SSC vision and building of social capital (IFC, 2007).

6. Managing Stakeholders

The purpose of this stage is to manage stakeholders through managing their relationships with a SSC project. In Freeman (1984), a 'Stakeholder Management' concept refers to *"the necessity for an organization to manage the relationships with its specific stakeholder groups in an action-oriented way"*. By adopting this definition, a 'Stakeholder Management' concept in the context of SSCs can be used to refer to *"the necessity for a SSC project team to manage the relationships with its relevant selected stakeholder groups in an action-oriented way"*. The term 'action-oriented' indicates that the relationships to be built by a SSC project team should be capable of yielding concrete actions with specific stakeholder groups and individuals (Freeman, 1984).

The aim of managing the relationships with shareholders is to help raising the awareness about a SSC project and make it more prepared to deal with stakeholders' needs that are changing throughout the lifecycle of a transformation process. It also makes a SSC project more capable to response effectively and efficiently to the issues that need to be resolved or difficulties that may arise throughout a transformation process (Bal et al., 2013). It is a non-ending task of integrating and balancing of multiple types of relationships and objectives.

7. Stakeholders Involvement in Project Monitoring and Evaluation

Once the SSC transformation activities are implemented and delivered, the outputs must be monitored and evaluated (BSI, 2014; ISO/IEC, 2015; SCC, 2015; ITU-T FG-SSC, 2016). This stage ensures that the monitoring and evaluation tasks are taking place with a full coordination and collaboration with relevant stakeholders. It aims at involving directly affected stakeholders to assess each transformation activity impact for the benefit of enhancing a SSC project transparency and accountability (Freeman, 1984; IFC, 2007).

Stakeholder can be a useful instrument to monitor, evaluate, and manage a change. They can help in identifying new and emerging issues resulted from their evaluation and monitoring process (Futaki, 2010) as well as quantify efficiency improvements in city services (ITU-T FG-SSC, 2016). From the management side of a SSC project, the results of these evaluations should be reported for future learning that may lead to either re-review of a SSC vision' objectives, goals, and strategies or to make modifications on previously implemented activities and produce new ones, as stated in the proposed SSC transformation roadmap (Sections 6.2.5).

During this stage, different types of matrixes are created to reflect the outputs of this stage, as to be introduced by this research. For instance, a new matrix to highlight the feedback of stakeholders regarding issues that should be resolved on the implemented SSC activities is created. The matrix rows and columns are dedicated to the involved stakeholders and related SSC activities respectively, as illustrated in Table 7.6. The intersection cells are used to highlight the issues that must be resolved. The last column is used to highlight the urgency level of making an action to resolve each issue.

**Table 7.6: Stakeholders/Activities Feedback on Issues to be Resolved Matrix
(Hypothetical Example)**

Activity / Stakeholder	Activity A	Activity B	…	Activity X	Urgency[6]
Government	A need for skilled people to manage the government portal	A need for consultation on Women's political participation framework		Urge big companies to create partnerships with government	A=5, B=5, … N=3
Local ICT Companies	Urge the government to ease the process of establishing new cell sites	Some companies refuse employment equity		NA	A=2, B=3
Universities	NA	No urgent issues to handle		A need to increase citizens' awareness about the project	N=5

1 = Not important to handle
3 = Moderately important to handle
5 = Critically important to handle
NA = This stakeholder is not part of this activity

8. Monitoring and Evaluation of Engagement Process

This stage sheds lights on the importance of the monitoring and evaluation of stakeholders' engagement in a SSC transformation process. Monitoring and evaluation (i.e. named as 'Measuring Stakeholder Performance' in (Bal et al., 2013)) need to be a two-way process. From one side, it allows stakeholders to provide their feedbacks, identify problems, and express concerns on a SSC transformation process outputs and outcomes, as in stage 7 of this model (Larson and Williams, 2009; Bal et al., 2013). From another side, it helps in looking into the quality of stakeholders' engagement in a SSC project (Larson and Williams, 2009), which is the core objective of this stage. For instance, the monitoring and evaluation report might illustrate the number of meetings being held with public, and assess the quality of stakeholders' participation and engagement in these meetings.

Monitoring and evaluation of stakeholders' engagement refers to both, the efforts needed to monitor the development of stakeholders' and people's participation within the SSC project's activities and the evaluation of the effects and outcomes of stakeholders' engagement in the SSC project's process as well as the development of people's skills, knowledge, and understanding (Larson and Williams, 2009). There is a large body of literature deals with different aspects of stakeholders' engagement in the development projects. This includes covering of stakeholders' engagement in implementing the projects' activities, monitoring of stakeholders' engagement related to achieving project outcomes, and monitoring of participation (Larson and Williams, 2009). In the context of SSCs, various publications indicate the necessity of engaging different types of stakeholders in the implementation of SSC project's activities. However, none considers monitoring and evaluation of stakeholders' engagement in achieving the SSC project's outcomes or quality and level of their participation.

Despite the availability of various studies that cover different aspects of stakeholders' engagement in development projects that are summaries in Larson and Williams (2009) research study, this book research sheds some light on one technique that could be used for this purpose. As in stage 7, a SSC project's team can create a number of matrices to monitor and evaluate stakeholders' engagement in a SSC project. For example, a matrix to reflect the quality of stakeholders' participation and effect in achieving the SSC activities is created, as illustrated in Table 7.7. The last column of this matrix is dedicated to the recommendations to be taken in the future regarding the stakeholder engagement in a SSC related activity.

Table 7.7: Stakeholders/Activities Quality of Participation and Effect Matrix (Hypothetical Example)

Activity / Stakeholder	Activity A	Activity B	...	Activity X	Recommendations
Government organization 'XYZ'	2	3		5	ACTIVITY A: Try to increase the organization interest in this activity or ignore this stakeholder in future
Organization 'XYZ'	1	1		1	Ignore this stakeholder in future activities
Union 'XYZ'	4	5		4	Keep this stakeholder

1 = Not very good quality of participation and effect
3 = Somewhat good quality of participation and effect
5 = High quality of participation and effect
NA = This stakeholder is not part of this activity

The resulted data from all matrices should be collected and documented in a single report, forming a recommendation document that can be used for future decisions. This report helps in improving a SSC project's process, enhancing the decision-making, and avoiding repeating the same mistakes in future activities.

7.2.2   [A] City Readiness for Change and Gap Analysis

The definition of a SSC introduced by the ITU-T FG-SSC (2014b) states that *"a SSC is an innovative city that uses ICTs and other means to improve quality of life, efficiency of urban operations and services, and competiveness, …"*. It is clear from the definition that developing cities into SSCs relies on the ICT capacities of these cities and the use of other means, such as establishing of new policies, laws, and regulations, throughout a transformation process. As discussed in Section 2.4, the ICTs are used as an enabler in a SSC transformation process by providing the required infrastructure to connect different city systems and services and provide solutions that are smart, sustainable and environmentally viable (ITU-T FG-SSC, 2014a). A SSC also should provide at least one smart solution initiative for each dimension of its six dimensions by the use of ICTs as a key medium to ensure city's sustainability (EP, 2014). Therefore, the basic ICT infrastructure and knowledge of ICTs usage are necessary before transforming a city into a SSC (Lorenz et al., 2013).

On another note, cities are the result of agglomeration of hard and soft infrastructures in addition to its ICT or digital infrastructure. These infrastructures are urban features that have been installed by human activities and are essential for a city to operate. The hard infrastructure refers to tangible (i.e. physical) structures such as buildings, roads, pipes, wires, shared spaces, bridges, ports, among others. The soft infrastructure, in turn, refers to intangible structures such as laws, regulations, rules, conventions, financial systems, government systems, healthcare systems, education systems, human capital, business environments, and others (Pincetl, 2015; Anderton, 2016). These two structures are completing each other, for instance, an airport as a hard infrastructure of a city cannot function without a set of soft infrastructures that provides a list of rules about the minimum acceptable size of runways, required distance between landing and taking off planes, conventions regarding passenger loading and unloading, and others (Pincetl, 2015). The hard and soft infrastructures are also increasingly becoming interlinked with and operated using new technologies, such as sensor devices, online services, GPS takers, and computing systems. This interlink offers opportunities for improving existing city services and systems and creating new sustainable ones.

Developing a city into a SSC aims at enhancing existing systems and services and providing new smart and sustainable ones, as the case in Brownfield cities, or building a SSC from scratch, as the case of Greenfield cities. In the case of existing cities, one of the challenges is how to identify a list of change activities during a transformation process. Another challenge is to ensure that these identified activities increase the smartness of a city while maintaining its sustainability at all levels and are based on the city context, needs and local interests. Checking the city state (Section 6.2) and its readiness for change would facilitate this task. This requires examining the current state of a city regarding its hard, soft and digital infrastructures. Checking the city readiness differs from checking the current city-state regarding its economic, social, environmental, and political conditions. The former focuses on examining the capacities of the current city's infrastructures and existing skills of ICTs usage, while the latter refers to the challenges the city is being facing under each of its pillars that boost the initiation of a SSC project.

As discussed in Chapter 4, examining the readiness of a city for a change is an essential step in any SSC transformation process; if not considered well, the desired outcomes and benefits from a transformation process may not be achieved properly or even worst, the whole process may fail. Based on the ToC and proposed ToSSC, the city readiness for change and the identification of the gap should take place before planning the transformation solutions. The aim of this phase is to study and analyze existing city' hard, soft, and digital infrastructures in addition to the level of existing digital literacy, and identify the shortages of each one if exists. The results of these analyses form the basis for planning the transformation solutions regarding the city infrastructures and digital skills, needed for or resulted from a transformation process.

None of existing SSC transformation roadmaps and frameworks in the literature takes into consideration the necessity of checking the city readiness for a transformation process. As a result, this book introduces a roadmap considers checking the city readiness for change as a stand-alone phase and provide a high-level view of the components to be examined during it. The needed information about each of these components is to be detailed along with the tools that could be used for this purpose. To eliminate the possible confusion between the different types of the city infrastructures, this book research divides the hard, soft, and digital infrastructures and the level of digital literacy of a city into two groups. These are the (1) ICT-based infrastructure that refers to all digital components of a city in addition to the level of the digital literacy, and (2) Non-ICT base infrastructure that refers to the hard and soft infrastructures. Finally, the third component to be examined during this phase is checking the availability of existing smart and sustainable initiatives at all city levels.

(1) City Readiness: ICT-based Infrastructure

Checking the ICT capacities of a city is not an easy process due the diversity of existing technical solutions, various technological routes, and the continuous advancement in technologies (Yasser, 2007). It should be examined to decide whether the current ICT resources and skills of a city are adequate to achieve the objectives of a SSC project or not and take the appropriate actions accordingly. The current ICT capacities should be conducted using a thorough assessment model to generate trustful results to be used in the future analysis to identify the city's ICT readiness gap and opportunities for improvements.

The ICT-based infrastructure of a city consists of three main components, namely: (1) hardware infrastructure, (2) software infrastructure (Nam and Pardo, 2011; ISO/IEC, 2015; ITU-T FG-SSC, 2016), and (3) level of digital literacy (Kirkman, et al., 2002; Baller et al., 2016). The hardware infrastructure includes various types of components, such as network infrastructure, access devices, sensor devices, wireless networks, GPS trackers, safety and security devices, data storage devices, among others. The software infrastructure includes different types of components, such as social, businesses, and government applications; safety and security systems and standards; computing systems; communication standards; data access systems; data storage systems, among others. For both, hardware and software infrastructures, another factor that should be taken into consideration while checking the city's ICT readiness for change is people knowledge and skills for using both, which is related to the third component of the ICT-based infrastructure, the digital literacy (Kirkman, et al., 2002; Baller et al., 2016). The digital literacy refers to the knowledge and skills of using traditional computers, smart devices, software applications, networks, and elements of digital technology (ETS, 2007). It also compromises a set of basic skills related to the participation in social media for the aim of knowledge sharing and gaining, information processing and retrieval, and production of digital media (UNESCO, 2011). Checking the current level of digital literacy requires examining a set of skills that are interdisciplinary in nature. The latter includes, but not limited to, checking the level of current ICT skills, information skills, media skills, learning to learn skills, and civic skills (UNESCO, 2011).

The examination of ICT readiness of a city reflects its technical resources and existing ICT infrastructure as well as the digital literacy level. To check the ICT readiness, a SSC project's teams needs to either create their own KPIs or use existing index for this purpose. One of the international indexes used by many countries around the globe is the Networked Readiness Index (NRI), also known as Technology Readiness. The Information Technology group originally developed the index at Harvard University's Center for Development. This group was using it until 2002, and then, the World Economic Forum adopted this index and modified and used it as a tool for publishing 'The Global Information Technology Report' annually. The index consists of four subindexes (i.e. indicators) and 54 variables, as illustrated in Figure 7.4 (Baller et al., 2016). The aim of the NRI is to assess countries based on four subindexes that are (Baller et al., 2016):

1. *Environment Subindex (consists of 18 variable)*: to assess the overall environment for technology use and creation. It consists of two main pillars namely: the political and regulatory environment pillar and business and innovation environment pillar.
2. *Readiness Subindex (consists of 12 variable)*: to assess the digital infrastructure readiness and capabilities of citizens for using related digital services and devices. It consists of three main pillars; the digital content pillar to assess the ICT infrastructure such as hardware and software infrastructures; affordability pillar to measure the cost of accessing ICTs, and skills pillar to assess the quality of the basic educational technical skills.

3. *Usage Subindex (consists of 16 variable)*: to assess the technology adoption and usage by the three groups of stakeholders namely the individuals, business (private sector), and government (public sector) as well as their efforts to increase their capability to use ICTs in their day-to-day activities with other agents. It consists of three main pillars, namely, the individual usage pillar, business usage pillar, and government usage pillar.

4. *Impact Subindex (consists of 8 variable)*: to assess the broad economic and social impacts accruing from the ICTs to boost competitiveness and well-being (i.e. quality of life). The subindex also finds out what the different stakeholders of society can do to contribute to their country-networked readiness. The main two pillars of this subindex are the economic impacts pillar and social impacts pillar.

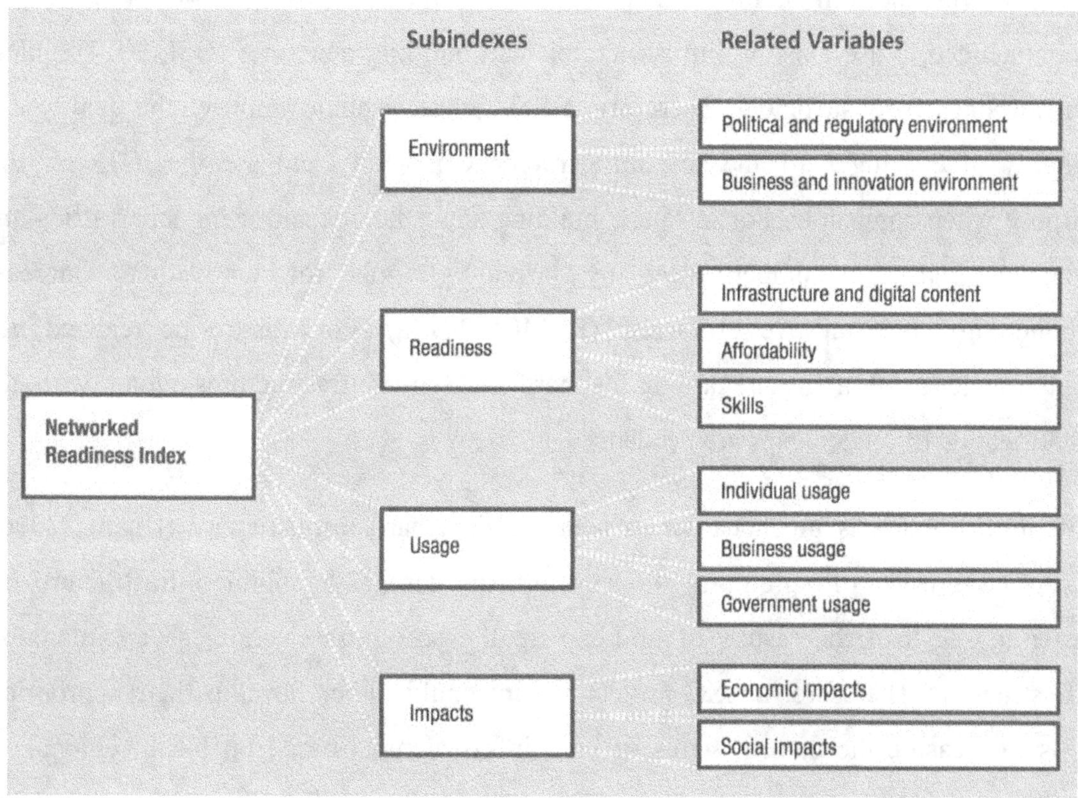

Figure 7.4: The Network Readiness Index (NRI)

(2) City Readiness: Non-ICT based Infrastructure (Hard and Soft)

The main objectives of a SSC in to improve the quality of life, efficiency of urban operations and services, and competitiveness (ITU-T FG-SSC, 2016). The ICT solutions aims at improving existing systems and services of a city or providing new smart and sustainable ones to improve the quality of life of a city. Despite its essential usage in SSC projects, various studies in the literature are classifying the ICTs as an enabler only to the transformation process (EPIC, 2013; SCC, 2015; BSI, 2014; ISO/IEC, 2015; PwC, 2015b; ITU-T FG-SSC, 2016). This opens a door for a question of how a SSC project then could improve the urban operations and competitiveness of a city. After conducting as extensive literature review on a subject matter, this book research founds that the competitiveness level of a city and its economic growth is highly dependent on the quality and quantity of the city's hard and soft infrastructures (Huang, 2006). Also, the urban operations; that refer to the city operating systems, such as water, energy and transportation systems; are related directly to the hard and soft infrastructures of a city as well (Aoun, 2013). In SSC projects, with the aim of minimizing the total cost of a transformation process, it is recommended to use existing infrastructures than building new ones (BSI, 2014), unless existing ones are insufficient. Therefore, a SSC project should improve the quality and quantity of existing hard and soft infrastructures of a city and use the ICTs for this purpose when applicable. For instance, building smart homes and using smart grids and enhancing national competiveness by providing tools for innovations, increase productivity, and improve efficiency (KPMG, 2015a). For this to be realized, the readiness level of a city regarding its hard and soft infrastructures along with the identification of related gaps are needed.

Soft infrastructure is much harder to measure than hard infrastructure (Huang, 2006), because the results of building up the hard infrastructure, as a tangible infrastructure, are easier to see than the results of building up the soft infrastructure, as an intangible infrastructure. Therefore; a SSC project's team could either develop their appropriate KPIs to measure the current status of both infrastructures based on local, regional, or international expertise or adopt an existing international index for this purpose and rely on its analytical results. However, there is no international index that is directly dedicated to measure the hard and soft infrastructures status and performance of a country or a city. These measures are often divided into a number of pillars under which a list of sub-indices may be used to measure these infrastructures. For instance, the international Change Readiness Index (CRI) proposed by the KPMG and Oxford Economics, discussed in Chapter 4, measures the readiness of a country for a change based on three main pillars related to its Enterprise, Government, and People and Civil Society capabilities. Each pillar is divided into a set of sub-indices, as illustrated in Figure 7.5 (KPMG, 2015a), from which each country or city could select the appropriate sub-indices to measure its hard and soft infrastructures. It is worth mentioning that despite the availability of a 'Technology Infrastructure' sub-index under the 'Enterprise Capability' pillar of the CRI; it is recommended to use an index, such as the NRI, that focuses only on the ICT infrastructure and its impact on community than selecting a sub-index of an index that may provide limited information about the issue.

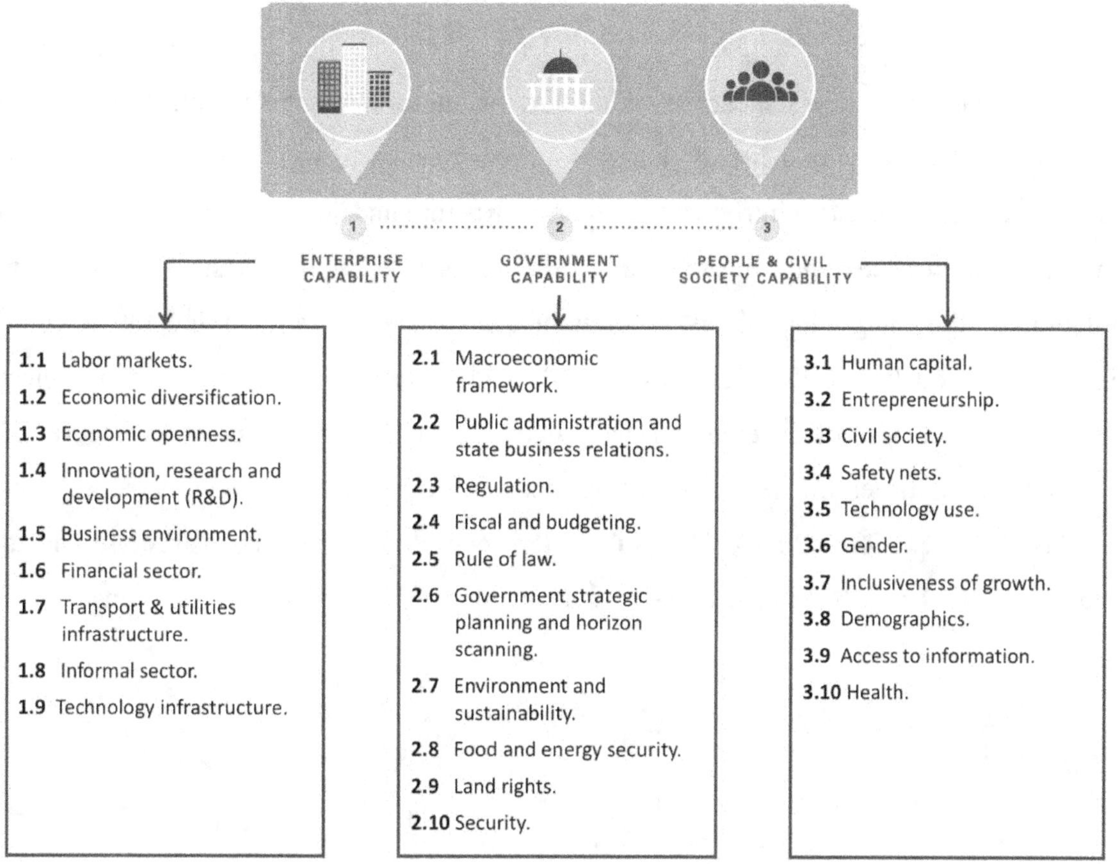

Figure 7.5: Change Readiness Index Pillars and Sub-indices

(3) City Readiness: Existing Initiatives

This stage aims at checking the availability of any existing smart and sustainable initiatives at all city levels and examine the possibilities of integrating them into a transformation process. By doing so, a SSC project's team would be able to learn from previous experiences and outcomes as well as avoid the duplication of efforts. There is no specific tool that can be used for this examination; however; national statistical reports and studies could be used for this purpose. Establishing a strong collaboration between public and private sectors and statistical bodies in the city open the door for a SSC project to find out a list of previously or currently implemented initiatives that are related to the project.

7.2.3   [B] Develop, Implement, and Deliver Transformation Solutions

7.2.3.1   [B1] Develop a SSC Smart Infrastructure and Integrated Platform

Once the level of city readiness for change measured and the gap identified, a SSC project's team with key stakeholders can start planning a transformation process. The latter aims at identifying a list of change solutions needed to increase the efficiency of existing infrastructure and introducing new infrastructure and services that can respond to the community needs and objectives of a SSC. This also requires a step of change in relation to the integration of city's infrastructure and services to a level that could influence the quality of life of city residents through maximizing the degree of smartness and user-friendliness of different services that a city is looking to provide. Figure 7.6 illustrates a multi-tier architecture of a SSC smart infrastructure within a city as proposed by the ITU-T FG-SSC (2016). This Subsection focuses on a SSC infrastructure and its integrated platform while the next one is dedicated to a SSC services and solutions.

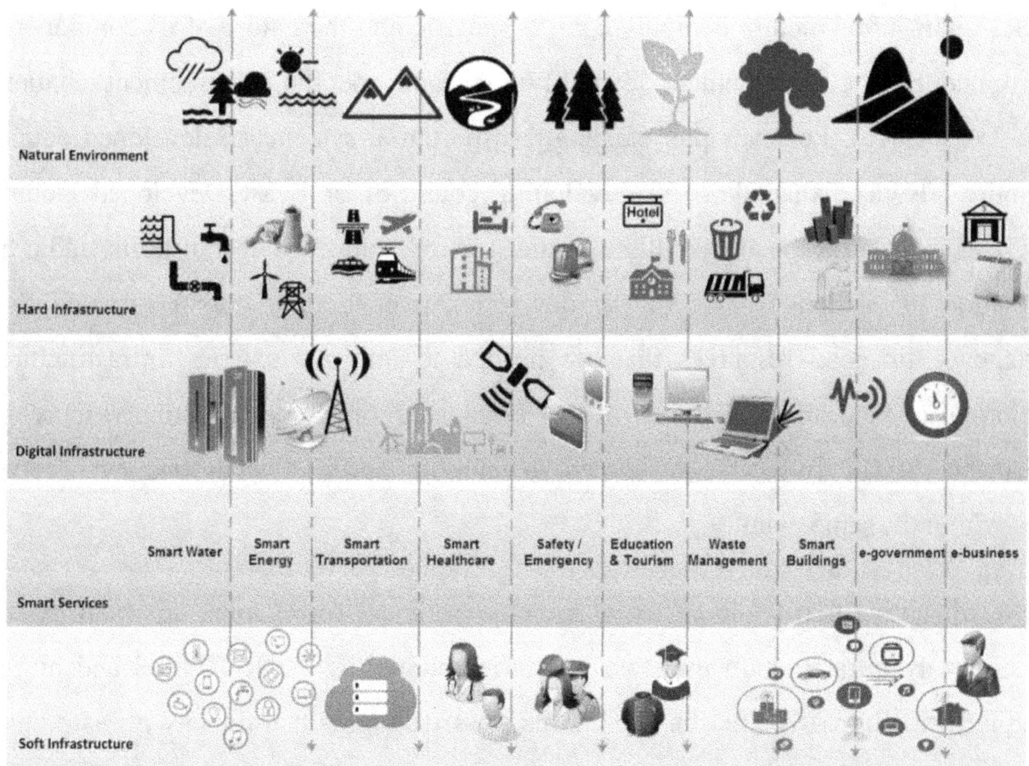

Figure 7.6: A Smart Sustainable City Multi-tier Smart Infrastructure

Various studies in the literature agree on the necessity of developing the SSC smart infrastructure and integrated platform. The former forms the foundation of the services to be provided under each of the six dimensions of a SSC. The latter, in turn, facilitates the aggregation and sharing of data between various SSC services (Al-Hader and Rodzi, 2009; BSI, 2014; IEC, 2014; EIP-SCC, 2015; Escher Group, 2015; KPMG, 2015b; ISO/IEC, 2015; ITU-T FG-SSC, 2016; UNCTAD, 2016).   This also includes the deployment of smart services in a real city environment (Atzori et al., 2010; ISO/IEC, 2015; Li et al., 2015; ZTE, 2015).

(1) Developing of a SSC Smart Infrastructure

A SSC smart infrastructure allows new innovative services and solutions to be implemented to address urbanization challenges at all city levels and to respond to the sustainable development needs of the society. For example, the data collected from the smart mobility infrastructure could be used to generate information to redesign the transportation networks of a city and to build new smart mobility applications for the benefit of citizens.

A SSC smart infrastructure is highly context specific and the nature of its components is determined by the development level of cities and specific development challenges (UNCTAD, 2016). For example, existing transportation systems in developed countries are more advanced than those in developing countries or Least Developed Countries (LDC). This includes the availability of trains, metros, trams, water transports, and others. In relation to challenges, one of the development challenges may be related to the shortage of financial resources that are needed to improve existing infrastructure or developing of new ones. The level of this financial shortage and existing resources for securing it varies between the developed, developing, and LDC countries, even between cities within the same country.

It is worth noting that while checking the city readiness for change, this book research divides a city infrastructure into two categories named as the ICT-based and non-ICT based infrastructures. The reason behind this classification is that the city infrastructure is often categorized into the digital infrastructure (named as ICT-based Infrastructure) and the hard and soft infrastructures (named as non-ICT based infrastructure) as discussed in Subsection 7.2.2. The combination of these infrastructures is known as a traditional city infrastructure (UNCTAD, 2016), where its components often are rarely connected to each other and have very limited operational functionalities for controlling and monitoring them (Al-Hader and Rodzi, 2009). This traditional infrastructure must be improved to a level never previously achieved (KPMG, 2015b), where the ICT infrastructure and capacities are used as an enabler to increase its smartness level. Thereby, to differentiate it from the traditional infrastructure, the SSC smart infrastructure, as the foundation of the development of SSCs, is broadly divided into two categories named: (1) Smart Physical Infrastructure and (2) Smart Digital Infrastructure (IEC, 2014; Escher Group, 2015; KPMG, 2015b; ISO/IEC, 2015; ITU-T FG-SSC, 2016; UNCTAD, 2016).

1. Smart Physical Infrastructure

Smart physical infrastructure refers to the SSC assets of the hard and soft infrastructures and the use of the city's digital infrastructure (i.e. ICT networks and systems) to improve these assets (ISO/IEC, 2015; ITU-T FG-SSC, 2016). For the hard infrastructure, a list of innovative change activities should be planned and implemented to efficiently improve the current city's hard infrastructure systems through the use of appropriate technologies (ISO/IEC, 2015; Vedashree and Bose, 2015; ITU-FG SSC, 2016). This includes the development and use of the smart water management systems, smart grids for smart energy, smart waste management systems, smart healthcare systems, Intelligent Transportation Systems (ITS), e-government solutions and services, smart safety and security management systems, e-business solutions and services, smart buildings and homes, and smart systems for education and tourism management (ITU-T, FG-SSC; 2016; UNCTAD, 2016). Table 7.8 provides examples of some of SSC hard infrastructure solutions and how they could be used to address some urbanization challenges aiming to enhance the sustainable development of a city and provide a high quality of life for its citizens (Soom, 2009; ITU-T FG-SSC, 2016; UNCTAD, 2016).

Table 7.8: Use of SSC Smart Infrastructure to Meet Challenges of Urbanization

Sustainability Need/Challenge	Example of SSC Smart Infrastructure Solution	Description
Improve Energy and Utility infrastructure	Smart Grids	Use of the digital technology to improve flexibility, resiliency, efficiency, and reliability of the electric delivery system through applications of smart appliances, smart meters, and renewable energy resources.
	Smart Meters	Real-time electric devices to measure electricity, water, and natural gas consumption.
Buildings, parking, and streets	Smart buildings	Use of technologies and sensors to improve security, safety, usability, and energy efficiency.
	Smart Parking	Use of technologies and sensors to provide real-time information about car parking capacities and locations to citizens.
	Smart traffic lights	Use of technologies and sensors to manage vehicle and pedestrian traffic.
Improve Environment Performance	Environmental Sensor Network	Use of technologies and sensors to continuously collect data about the condition and level of pollutants of water, air, and soil.
	Smart waste management	Use of technologies and sensors to continuously monitor the efficiency and performance of waste collection. Appropriate technologies can be used to provide waste recycling and disposal solutions.
Improve Education and Health Services	Online education and remote healthcare	Use of technologies to facilitate the remote access to education and health services.
Increase efficiency of City Management	SSC operation centers	To monitor and manage a range of transport, government, environmental, and emergency services.

Sustainability Need/Challenge	Example of SSC Smart Infrastructure Solution	Description
Ensure Public Safety and Security	Video security	Use of sensors and cameras networks for crowd management, public safety and people counting.
Improve government services	e-Government solutions	Use of ICTs to improve public sector organizations processes and provide public services to citizens, for example, through online portals.

The soft infrastructure is an intangible infrastructure that refers to different types of human institutions that maintain the country, thereby the city, core social and economic standards. This includes laws, regulations, rules, conventions, financial systems, government systems, healthcare systems, education systems, human capital, business environments, and others (Pincetl, 2015; Anderton, 2016). These standards should be improved in a way to allow achieving the SSC objectives and goals. Without improving a city's soft infrastructure throughout a SSC transformation process, the hard infrastructure of a city will not be able to communicate probably (Government Offices of Sweden, 2011). For instance, the soft infrastructure forms a foundation on which to achieve interoperability, i.e. make SSC systems operate together and communicate with each other following agreed rules. Improving existing interoperability standards or creating new ones would ensure smooth and secure interactions between various SSC systems.

A SSC soft infrastructure is also affected by the use of ICTs as an enabler to various solutions to be provided by a SSC project. With this numerous use of ICTs, creating and agreeing on the standards to control the usage of vital public services and critical components of a SSC smart infrastructure created by the ICTs becomes highly important. Central government should ensure that the local needs to be realized through ICT solutions are met by relevant standards (Government Offices of Sweden, 2011). For example, a SSC allows different types of data sharing between various city systems including citizens' information. A SSC soft infrastructure should have special standardizations to guarantee information sharing security. In addition, using of cloud computing techniques should be managed using special standards for data exchange, security issues, and type of contracts to establish (Government Offices of Sweden, 2011).

Categorizing all city soft infrastructure is not a simple task due to the huge number of standards and systems at all city levels. Therefore; it is recommended for each SSC project's team to benefit from the information and data analysis collected during the 'City Readiness' phase of proposed innovative roadmap and framework regarding the current status of the city soft infrastructure and use it as a base to either enhance existing standards and systems or introduce new innovative ones.

2. Smart Digital Infrastructure

The ICTs play a crucial role in developing cities into SSCs. They provide the needed tools to improve the smartness level of a city through smart services over each dimension of a SSC (Section 7.2.3.2). The ICTs also allow various SSC systems to capture and share information in a timely manner. Without the ability of providing and sharing an accurate information quickly on real-time, the city would not be able to take potential actions to solve specific problems, such as the traffic congestion, rapidly and before the problem begins to escalate (UNCTAD, 2016). This in turn improve the quality of life of citizens as it allows them to be more informed about different local situations and make decisions about next actions easier. Moreover, the digital infrastructure has a great impact on a SSC soft infrastructure. The digital integrated platform of a SSC is used to create information and knowledge network, which can be used to better understanding how the city is functioning (Geyer, 2009). City administrators and relevant stakeholders can use this information to upgrade existing soft infrastructure to improve the quality of life of citizens. The smart digital infrastructure, as a result, should be designed in a way to facilitate the development of different SSC services and solutions.

In SSC projects, the main issue that should be taken into consideration during a transformation process is to maximize the potential for the reuse of existing digital resources of a city before developing of new ones (BSI, 2014, KPMG, 2015). Existing digital assets should be measured during the "City Readiness" phase of the proposed roadmap using the suggested framework tools highlighted in Section 7.2.2. These resources are then prioritized based on the planned transformation change solutions with the greatest potential of reuse; including establishing of usage policies and governance processes to ensure a more efficient use of these resources.

A SSC smart digital infrastructure consists of four main layers that are (1) sensing layer, (2) network communication layer, (3) platform layer (data and support layer), and (4) (smart) application layer (ISO/IEC, 2015; Vedashree and Bose, 2015; ITU-T FG-SSC, 2016; UNCTAD, 2016). The first three layers form the hardware infrastructure of a SSC smart digital infrastructure, while the smart application layer contains the software applications developed to realize different types of SSC services. These four layers in turn are connected to a SSC smart physical infrastructure, providing the needed services and solutions to its hard and soft components.

This book adopted the ITU-T FG-SSC (2016) architecture design of a SSC digital infrastructure, as it is the only architecture related to SSCs with a clear design that is being referenced by some related studies in the literature. This architecture design has been upgraded based either on recommendations from various studies in the literature or on this research point of view, aiming to provide a holistic view of a SSC smart digital infrastructure. The latter includes making the smart application layer focusing on all smart solutions to be implemented under the six dimensions of a SSC without limiting it into a specific list of solutions. The list of minimal required smart solutions to be implemented under each dimension is to be clarified in the next Subsection. This layer is named as a 'smart application layer' instead of 'application layer' to differentiate it from the one being used in a city traditional infrastructure design and to highlight the term 'smart' as a concept to be considered while developing cities into SSCs.

Moreover, based on the ISO/IEC smart cities preliminary report (2015), the network communication layer is divided into two main types namely the public networks and private networks to make sure that all types of networks in a SSC are connected into its smart digital infrastructure. The communication protocols for each network determine the type of communication channels to be established with these networks and the type of data to be shared taking into consideration the security issues.

On another note, after doing a wide research on the role of the integrated platform in SSCs and how and where it should be illustrated in the smart digital infrastructure architecture design, the "Data and Support Layer" proposed by the ITU-T FG-SSC (2016) has been renamed into the "Platform Layer". Despite that one of the main roles of the integrated platform is to deal with the city big data collected from various systems and applications (ITU-T FG-SSC, 2016), the holistic roles go far beyond this particular role (Atzori et al., 2010; ISO/IEC, 2015; Li et al., 2015; ZTE, 2015). The roles of the integrated platform are to be discussed later.

Finally, the 'Operation and Maintenance Systems' along with the three types of end users that would be able to access SSC services are adopted from ISO/IEC (2015). This includes the public citizens, enterprises and other institutions, and public sector. Figure 7.7 provides an illustration regarding the SSC smart digital infrastructure architecture design.

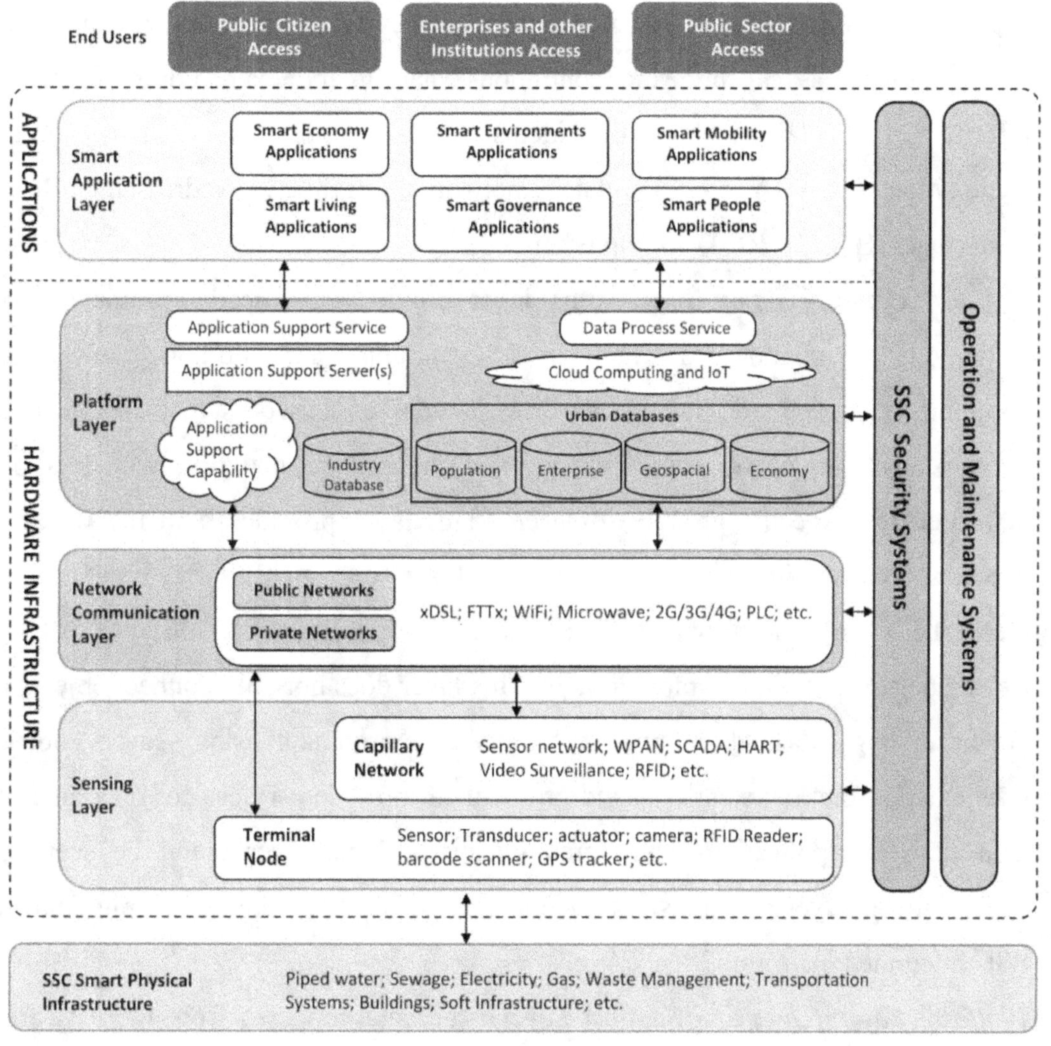

Figure 7.7: Smart Sustainable Cities Smart Digital Infrastructure Architecture Design

The purpose and functionality of each layer in a smart digital infrastructure are summarized below (Vedashree and Bose, 2015; ITU-T FG-SSC, 2016; UNCTAD, 2016):

1. *Sensing Layer*: contains smart devices that are used to monitor and measure different types of parameters related to water, air quality, humidity, energy, temperature, occupancy, solar flux, state of equipment among others. This layer consists of two types of components that are the Terminal Node and Capillary Network. The terminal node, such as the Radio-Frequency Identification (RFID) readers, cameras, actuators, barcode symbols, transducers, Global Positioning System (GPS) trackers, etc., are used for sensing the hard-physical infrastructure of a city. They have the ability to detect, monitor and control the environment of this infrastructure intelligently. The capillary network connects various terminal nodes to the network communication layer, allowing a real-time and continuous sharing and exchanging of data and information. This layer includes the video surveillance, Supervisory Control and Data Acquisition (SCADA), GPS related networks, Highway Addressable Remote Transducer (HART), RFID among others.

2. *Network Communication Layer*: this layer provides the needed framework and technology foundation for managing, designing, and building of a SSC communication network. It consists of two types of networks that are the public network with an open access feature; and the private network, which is often dedicated to a specific group(s) of users. This layer provides both the wired and wireless connectivity via different types of services such as 2G/3G/4G, Wi-Fi, General Packet Radio Service (GPRS), fibers (FFTx), Ethernets, all types of Digital Subscriber Lines (xDSL) among others. This layer does not only connect objects that are harvesting data and information form the environment using sensors, but also uses existing Internet standards and protocols to provide services for data analytics, data transfer, applications and communications. This layer could be seen as a superhighway layer that transfers huge amount of data (i.e. known as big data) to a SSC integrated platform.

3. *Platform Layer (Data and Support Layer)*: the data collected from the network of interlinked objects, such as energy, water, transport, public areas, etc., is made accessible to various services and applications at all city levels throughout this layer.

The aim of this layer is to provide the needed tools for big data analysis and management as well as to ensure the support capacities for different city-level services and applications. It contains different types of data centers and databases from enterprises, industries, institutions, and government and/or municipal(s). It also includes huge amount of data collected from the clouds and Internet of Things (IoT) objects, such as smart devices, vehicles, buildings, heart monitors, among others. It includes data warehousing that are established for the realization of data processing, such as the use of analytical tools and application support systems. The available analytical tools facilitate the analysis of large structured and unstructured data (i.e. big data) to generate insights about what type of data to be used for each service and application at all city levels, such as classifying this data to be used for public safety, transportation planning, water management systems, and others. The management of data enables the citywide consolidation and exchanging of these data across different sectors and owners. The latter includes citizens, public sector, private sector, international organizations, NGOs, among others.

4. *Smart Application Layer*: this layer comprises of smart applications to enable the six dimensions of a SSC and their related domains such as energy, water, transportation, buildings, healthcare, and education. It also includes the core enterprise applications such as the Enterprise Resources Planning (ERP), Business Process Management (BPM), and performance management. In a SSC, these services should be designed to be used across different types of delivery channels (i.e. through mobiles, kiosks, websites, call centers, interactive voice responses, points-of-sale, etc.). It aims at increasing both the speed of services delivery and cost saving as well as improving the quality of life of citizens, efficiency of urban operations and services, and competitiveness.

A SSC smart digital infrastructure should be designed as a fully integrated service based architecture that enables future capacities and solutions to be easily added to the overall system as well as collects, manipulates, and exchanges data in an efficient way. With this architecture design, the newly designed and implemented services can quickly be added and interlinked to other services, creating composite services and enhancing the city processes. In addition, the data collected could be used to make better decisions, improve economic competitiveness, provide green and sustainable environment, and facilitate social inclusiveness and citizen's engagement. The core components of this desired architecture is the integrated platform, which is responsible about interlinking various components of a SSC smart infrastructure and to collect data and information from different parties of a city. Due to its importance, the integrated platform, that has been represented as the "Platform Layer" in the introduced SSC smart digital infrastructure architecture design, is to be discussed further below.

(2) Developing of a SSC Integrated Platform

A city traditional operating model is often based around functionally oriented service providers. These services operate as unconnected and isolated silos and often built without considering the end user needs (BSI, 2014, ITU-T FG-SSC, 2016). A SSC, in turn, aims at developing new operating model to support collaboration and innovation across these silos. Based on the discussions provided by the BSI (2014) and ITU-T FG-SSC (2016), this research introduces a graphical representation of the operating model of a traditional city and a SSC. Figure 7.8 illustrates how traditional city operating model systems are not interlinked with each other and how each system controls and exchanges its data and applications in an isolated silo. It is clear from the illustration that individual citizens, businesses and public-sector institutions must be engaged in each service separately. The potential for collaboration and innovation across a city is limited as the data and information are often locked within these silos. Adopting this type of models also limits the ability to drive city-scale change at speed (BSI, 2014).

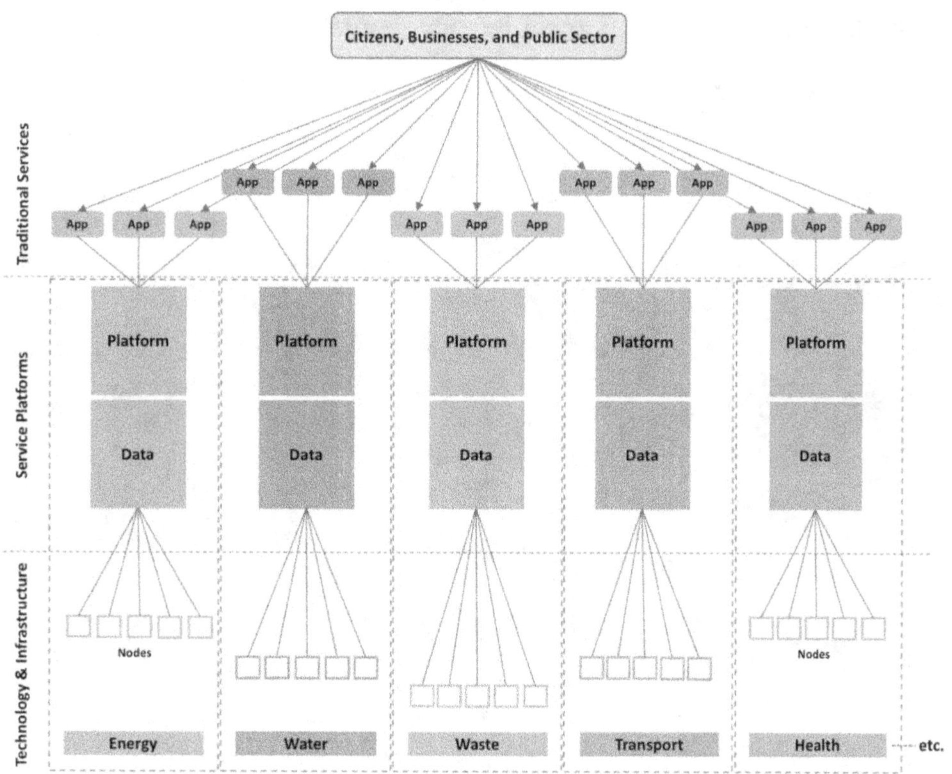

Figure 7.8: The Traditional Operating Model of a City

On the other hand, a SSC operating model allows the city data to be unlocked from individual silos, ensuring that the digital assets (i.e. digital data, applications and services) of a city are available in real time and on an open and interoperable basis. This enables a real-time integration and optimization of city resources. Instead of having a complete separation between different silos of a city, a logical separation between data, services, and users is used, which represented as separated layers in a SSC operation model as illustrated in Figure 7.9. In this Figure, the blended application refers to an application that uses data from more than one resource. This model allows both, externally-driven and internally-driven innovations within a city. The former enables new and centralized marketplace for city information and data and enables residents, such as citizens, social entrepreneurs, and small and medium size enterprises, to co-create public services and create new values using city's data. The internally-driven innovation aims at improving and integrating delivery of services and optimization of resources. It provides the end users with public services that are accessible in one stop, over multiple channels. This allows end users to be directly engaged in the creation of services based on their needs instead of building these services around the city's organizational structure. This type of models also has the ability to drive city-scale change at speed (BSI, 2014).

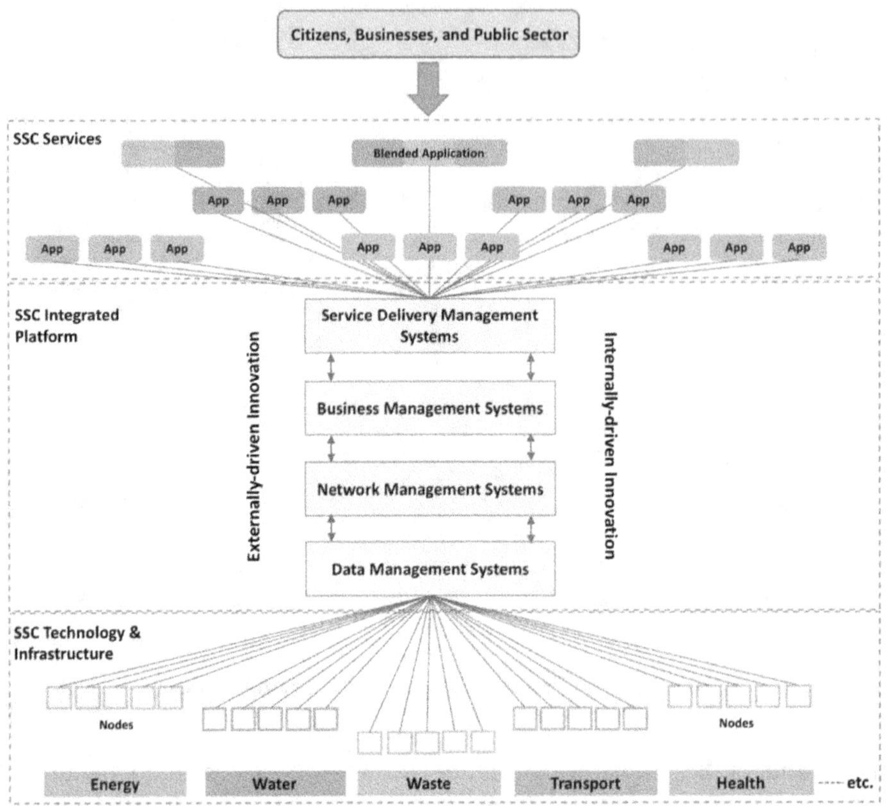

Figure 7.9: A SSC Operating Model

A SSC integrated platform forms the heart of a SSC operating model. It allows different systems of a city to be connected together and enables new applications and services to be developed across these systems, forming a true representation of a SSC as a "system of systems". It is responsible about various functions, such as management, coordination, storage, mining, computing, analysis, and providing public services to end users. This includes data management and processing systems, network management systems, business management systems, and services delivery management systems (BSI, 2014; ZTE, 2014; Li et al., 2015). Using these functions, a SSC integrated platform can combine data from different and large number of resources, distributed around a city. It can generate new insights on how to create new services based on the city needs and local interests and enhance existing ones, resulting in improving the society quality of life.

7.2.3.2   [B2] Develop the Innovative Smart Solutions: Proposed List

Even though various types of smart solutions have been proposed by different studies in the literature, none of existing studies provides a list of minimum requirements to consider by a SSC project's team to be used as a reference while planning their transformation process solutions. For example, the ITU-T FG-SSC (2016) indicates that the common smart solutions that are found in the literature are related to the smart energy, smart transportation, smart waste, smart water, smart buildings, smart healthcare, smart physical safety and security, and smart education. However, the need for implementing such initiatives varies from one city to another based on the city context and local needs, interests, and aspirations. Moreover, there are many solutions that are neglected from this suggested list related to the physical, either hard or soft, infrastructure of a city, such as legislations to ensure transparency, social inclusion activities, and increase of green areas. Finally, the selection of these solutions is not based on a logical correlative study or research. They are selected based on the lens through which each study is viewing the objectives of a SSC transformation process. Thereby, a generic list of minimum areas that need a set of smart solutions to be considered by every SSC project's team must be identified, through logical and coherent analysis. It is worth noting that each dimension of a SSC consists of more than one area (i.e. factor) to focus on according to Giffinger et al. (2007). This list aims at highlighting the minimum areas under each dimension of a SSC that should be enhanced through change solutions during a transformation process, leading to innovative changes at all city levels using ICTs and other means. A SSC project team can then prioritize a transformation solutions based on necessity, urgency, and local interests.

To start with, a SSC definition explains that developing cities into SSCs aims at improving the quality of life of citizens, urban operations and services, and competitiveness while ensuring the sustainability of a city at all levels. The transformation as well varies from one city to another based on the city context and needs (BSI, 2014; ITU-T FG-SSC, 2016). Therefore, a SSC project team should keep in mind the following main issues while planning the innovative change activities and smart solutions:

1. Ensure the sustainability of a city over its economic, social, and environmental pillars.

2. Meet urban needs through improving urban operations and services.

3. Improve quality of life of citizens.

4. Consider the six dimensions of a SSC, namely, smart economy, smart environment, smart governance, smart living, smart mobility, and smart people.

5. Consider the city context and the use of ICTs as an enabler to provide solutions that are viable and environmentally friendly.

This part of the research is carried out following the "Intersection Research Method" to estimate the minimum set of areas under each dimension of a SSC that need smart solutions to be developed by a SSC project team, allowing them to count their city as a SSC after then. The methodology that was followed in developing such a list is as below:

1. Identify and tabulate the areas of interest under each pillar/dimension of the (a) sustainable development, (b) city urban life and needs, (c) Quality of Life (QoL), and (d) SSC.

2. Apply the Intersection Method, as illustrated in Figure 7.10, on the identified areas. The results of this intersection are tabulated and examples of initiatives under each dimension are provided.

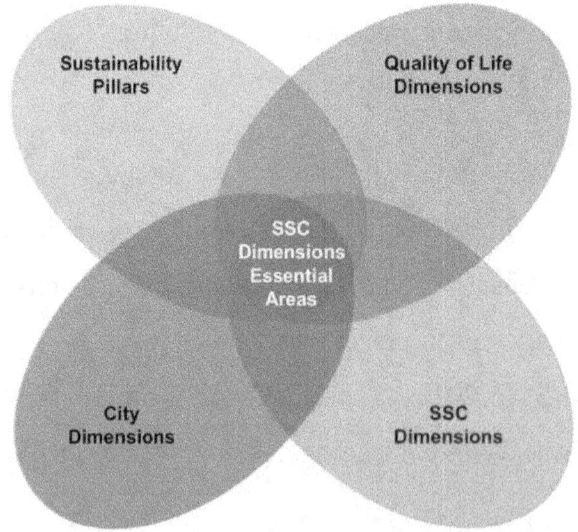

Figure 7.10: A SSC Dimensions Essential Areas using the Intersection Method

(1) Ensure the Sustainability of a City

Sustainable development theory demonstrates that a city sustainability should be achieved over three main pillars, namely, economic sustainability, social sustainability, and environmental sustainability, as illustrated in Figure 7.11 (Kahn, 1995; Basiago, 1999; Rodriguez et al., 2002; Kates et. al, 2005; OECD, 2016). Sustainability is a tripartite complex concept that aims at achieving economic stability, social equity, and environmental quality at all city levels. Its pillars are integrated and interlinked and should not be treated as an isolated silo. Sustainability

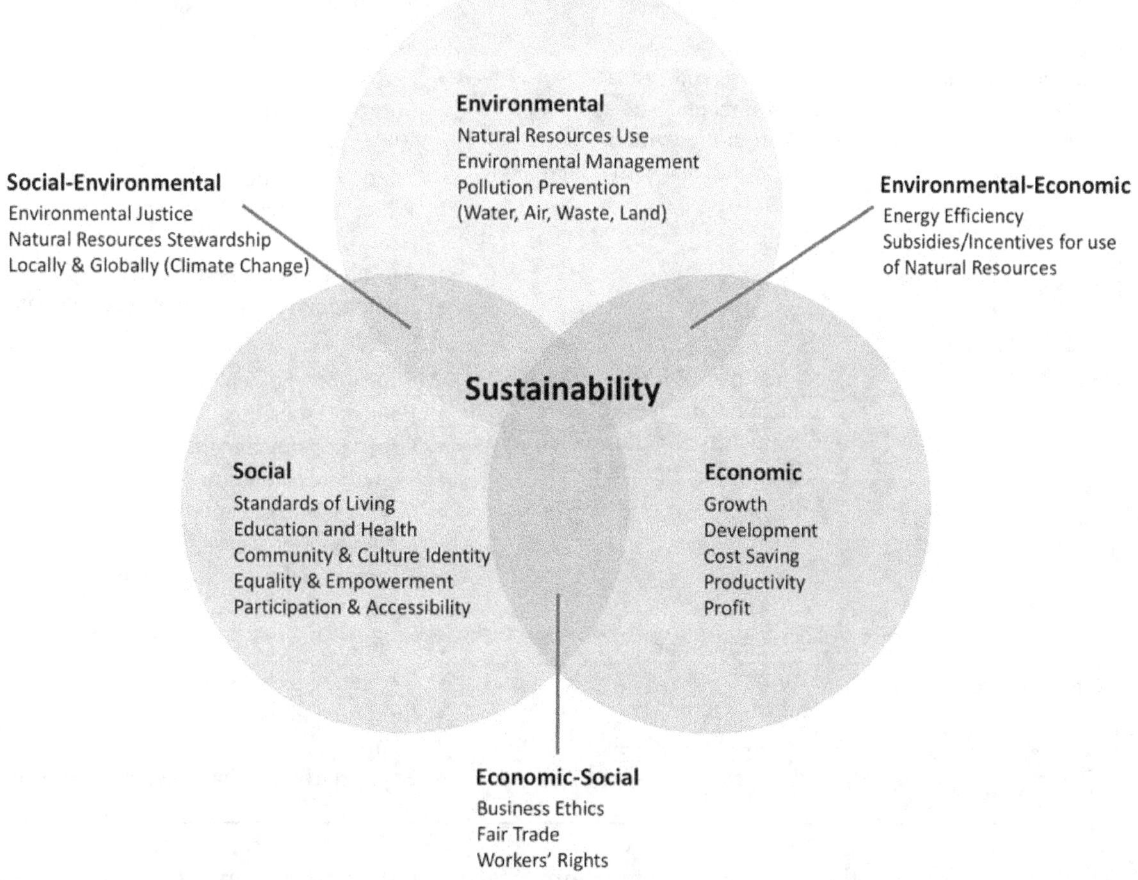

Figure 7.11: Sustainable Development Pillars and their Interlinks

The Department of Economic and Social Affairs (DESA) of the United Nations Secretariat and the European Commission highlights the need of considering urban governance while working on achieving the three main pillars of sustainability (DESA, 2013; EC, 2015). Introducing sustainable initiatives under each pillar of the sustainable development in addition to initiatives to support the urban governance would improve and enhance the sustainability of a city at all levels. Different areas of improvements under the sustainability pillars and urban governance are summarized in Table 7.9 (Kahn, 1995; Basiago, 1999; DESA, 2013).

Table 7.9: Sustainable Development Pillars, Factors, and Areas to Improve

Sustainability Pillar	Factor	Area to Improve
Economic	- Growth - Development - Cost Saving - Productivity - Profit	• Green productive growth • Creation of decent employment • Production and distribution of renewable energy • Technology and innovation (R&D = Research & Development)
Environmental	- Natural Resources Use - Environmental Management - Pollution Prevention (e.g. water, air, waste, land)	• Eco-system integrity • Forest and soil management • Waste and recycling management • Energy efficiency • Water management (including freshwater) • Air quality conservation • Adaptation to and mitigation of climate change
Social	- Standards of Living - Education and Health - Community & Culture Identity - Equality & Empowerment - Participation & Accessibility	• Education and health • Food and nutrition • Green housing and buildings • Water and sanitation • Green public transportation • Green energy access • Recreation areas and community support
Urban Governance	- Decentralization - Equity - Human Rights - Local, national, regional, global links	• Planning and decentralization • Reduction of inequities • Strengthening of civil and political rights • Support of local, national, regional and global links

The integration of the economic, environmental, social, and urban governance can generate synergies. For example, the integration could be between access to water and sanitation (social development) and waste and recycling management (environmental management). Between green public transportation (social development) and air quality conservation (environmental management). Between ensuring adequate access to education, green housing, and health (social development) and goal of reducing inequities (urban governance); and between distribution and production of renewable energy sources (Economic development), adaptation and mitigation of climate change (Environmental Management), and green energy access (Social development). Investment is the catalyst behind the realization of each component goals of urban sustainability (DESA, 2013).

(2) Meet Urban Needs: Improve Urban Operations and Services

Cities are complex artifacts with dynamic and powerful systems that attracted very large number of people to live in. They are centers of the urbanization growth that is so far reaching unprecedented level and expected to rise more. This, in turn, increases the necessity of providing improved urban operations and services that meet the local needs through enhancing the urban development of cities over their dimensions.

Cities are intrinsically multidimensional in character. These dimensions are directly related to the primary dimensions of the urban development of urban life, which are essential to the functioning of cities, and are classified into five major dimensions, namely, urban economic, urban environmental, city and society, urban governance, and urban infrastructure, services, and management (Friedmann, 2000; Safier, 2001; IESE, 2015). Each dimension represents areas for innovative solutions, both for hard and soft initiatives, to be developed to improve the city urban services and operations, as illustrated in Table 7.10 (Safier, 2001; IESE, 2015).

Table 7.10: Urban Life Dimensions and Areas to Improve

Urban Life Dimension	Area to Improve
Urban Economy	• Responses to globalization and structural adjustment programmes: including new policy analyses of urban economies and new initiatives. • Macro-economic development and finance: including new analyses of relationships between urban economic growth and urban poverty, new assessments of urban competitiveness, and new guidelines for urban development strategies, urban taxation, and financial improvements. • Employment and labor markets: including small and medium enterprise development, skills enhancement, and new directions in labor market segmentation. • Informal economy: including measures to provide improved provisions for legal recognition, regularization of land and housing developments, street trading, and energy consumption. • Fostering innovative financial mechanisms: including new practices in savings and loan schemes, microfinance, community asset management, and community finance facilities.

Urban Life Dimension	Area to Improve
Urban Environment	<ul><li>Combating environmental degradation, health hazards, and pollution.</li><li>Environmental planning.</li><li>Natural resource conservation.</li><li>Supporting Sustainability.</li></ul>
City & Society	<ul><li>Sustaining urban livelihood.</li><li>Improving health and education for all.</li><li>Promoting social inclusion (and cohesion).</li><li>Enhancing culture and identity.</li><li>Supporting gender equality and empowerment.</li><li>Reducing violence and advancing human rights.</li><li>Provide different types of services and facilities based on citizens' needs, which are accessible by all citizen types including elderly, women, people with special needs, etc.</li></ul>
Urban Governance	<ul><li>Participatory urban management and budgeting.</li><li>Capacity building.</li><li>Accountability and transparency.</li><li>Community action, organization, and assets management.</li><li>Participatory processes and tools for poor community.</li><li>Democracy and empowerment.</li></ul>
Urban Infrastructure, Services, and Management (Physical)	<ul><li>Enhancing shelter and settlement.</li><li>Enhancing strategic, participative, and responsive urban planning (i.e. represented as urban planning in IESE (2015)).</li><li>Securing land tenure.</li><li>Improving urban mobility and transportation (i.e. represented as mobility and transportation in IESE (2015)).</li><li>Promoting public-private-community partnerships for urban service delivery.</li><li>Basic Infrastructure.</li><li>Promoting the use of appropriate technology (i.e. represented as technology in IESE (2015)).</li></ul>

The IESE (2015) uses the same dimensions mentioned in Table 7.10 to develop the City in Motion Index (CIMI), in addition to two dimensions named as Human Capital and International Outreach. The former focuses on creating plans to improve education, attracting and retaining talent, and promoting creativity and research. The latter focuses on improving the city's brand name and its international recognition through attracting foreign investment, strategic tourism plans, and having representation abroad.

(3) Improve Quality of Life

Quality of Life (QoL) is a complex, multidimensional construct with many attempts in the literature to define its concept as well as define what constitutes it in different disciplines. It is a concept that encompasses how an individual measure the goodness of his or her multiple aspects of life, the satisfaction that comes from having comfort, good living conditions, good health, among others (El Din et. al, 2013; Theofilou, 2013). QoL refers to the daily living constituents that are enhanced by the clean air, food, and water, personal security and safety, unfettered enjoyment in open spaces and bodies of water, protection from toxic and radiation substances, and conservation of natural resources and wildlife. It may also refer to the measurement of the power and energy an individual is endowed to enjoy the life and overcome the life's challenges irrespective of the barriers he or she may face (El Din et. al, 2013). In turn, the community QoL is often related to the community resources, services, and factors that the community members observe as factors to influence their quality of life or to help them to cope with each other (Sun, 2005, El Din et al., 2013).

In his paper "A Theory of Human Motivation" published in 1943, Abraham Maslow proposed a hierarchy of needs theory that formed a corner stone in developing a theory of QoL, which has been established later in his book "Towards a Psychology of Being" published in 1962 (Sirgy, 1986; Ventegodt et al., 2003). Maslow's hierarchy of needs is often represented as a pyramid of five needs (Maslow, 1943) or eight needs (Maslow, 1962), providing a roadmap of personal development towards happiness and satisfaction (Maslow, 1943; Maslow, 1962; Ventegodt et al., 2003). Figure 7.12 illustrates the eight levels pyramid of Maslow's hierarchy of needs (Maslow, 1962).

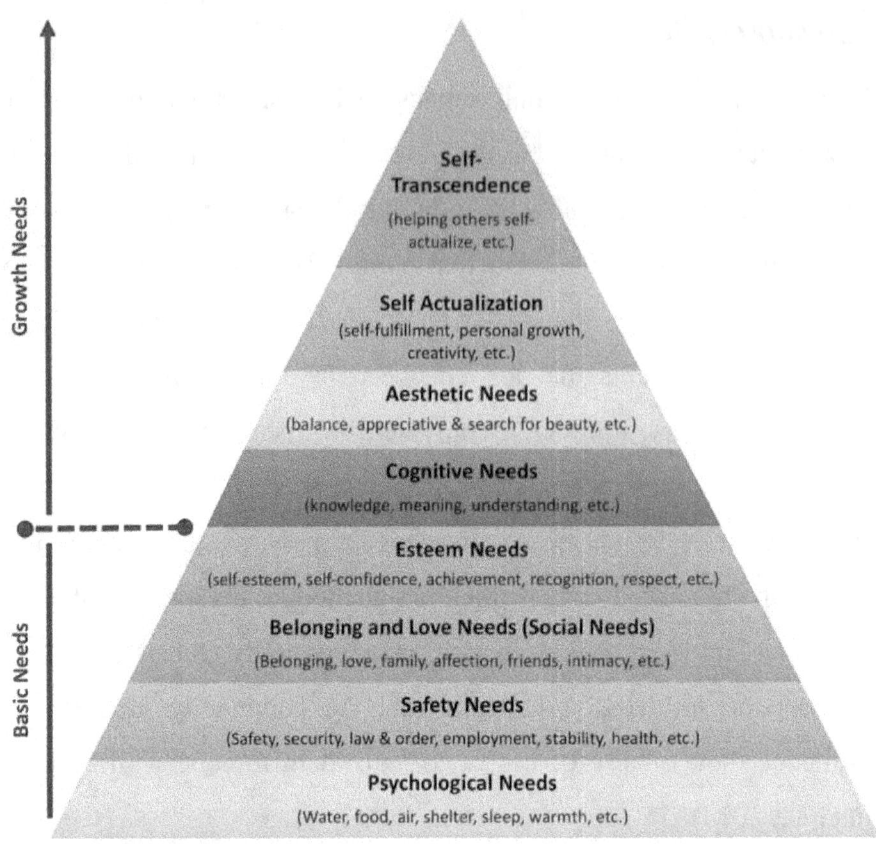

Figure 7.12: Maslow's Hierarchy of Need – Eight Levels

After studying the literature, Massam (2002) clarified the existence of a general agreement between many researchers that the QoL must be recognized by two interlinked aspects, namely, psychological and environmental aspects. These two aspects are divided into a set of dimensions based on the discipline over which a QoL is being studied. With respect to the psychological (i.e. endogenous) aspect, other terms were used, such as individual/personal QoL, life satisfaction and happiness, or subjective well-being. For the environmental (i.e. exogenous) aspect there are different levels and terms used, such as community QoL, urban QoL, environmental QoL, quality of place, or objective well-being (Massam, 2009; Lotfi and Solaimani, 2009; Theofilou, 2013). An individual's QoL depends on the objective (exogenous) factors, such as income, employment, and education, of his or her life, and the subjective (endogenous) perceptions of these factors and of himself and herself (Massam, 2002). The interlinks among the objective and subjective aspects form the basis of measuring the satisfaction level of an individual within a community in term of education, health, economic prosperity, social needs, capacity to cope, outcome levels, happiness, take control of life chances and opportunities, and others. The latter were explored and studied by researchers in different disciplines (Massam, 2002). This includes urban development discipline (El Din et al., 2013), which is the main constituent of cities' vision, particularly SSCs' vision.

The objective and subjective aspects of the QoL were divided into different sets of dimensions that varies from one area of research to another. In relation to the improvement of sustainability of cities, the literature shows that the QoL is measured by a common set of dimensions, namely, environmental, social, economic, psychological and physical ones (Hancock and Labonté, 1999; Massam, 2002; Olfert, 2003; Lotfi and Solaimani, 2009; Conrad et al., 2014). El Din et al. (2013) add two other dimensions, namely, Mobility QoL and Political QoL based on extensive research on urban development theories and approaches. These dimensions are interrelated and depend on each other as illustrated in Figure 7.13 (El Din et al., 2013).

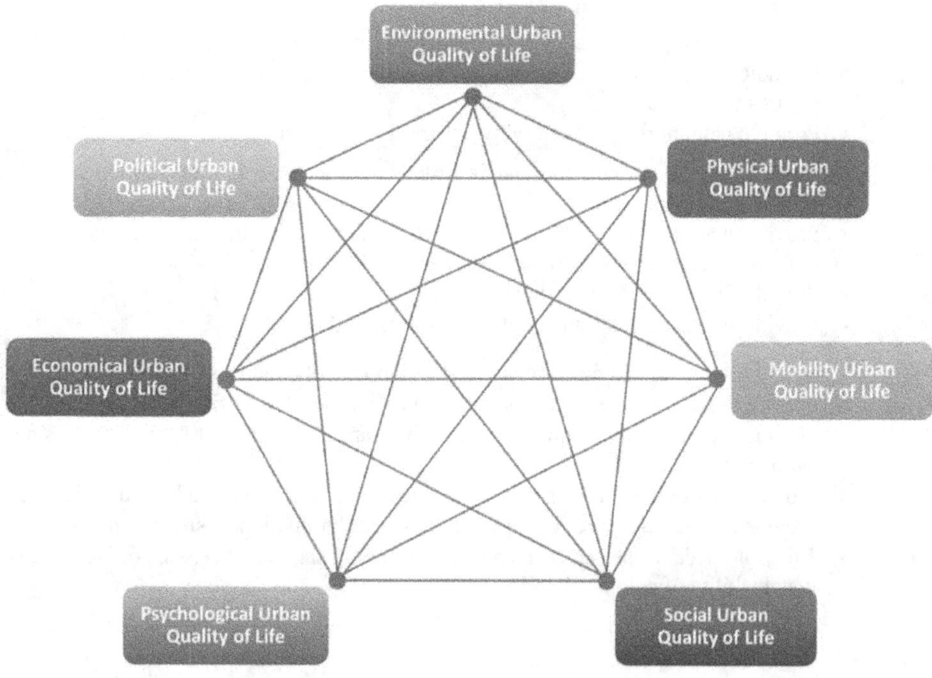

Figure 7.13: Quality of Life Interlinked Dimensions

QoL dimensions are divided into various principles that can be applied in various combinations to achieve QoL for societies. These principles form areas for innovative solutions, as illustrated in Table 7.11, to be developed to improve the QoL of a city.

Table 7.11: Quality of Life Dimensions and Areas to Improve

QoL Dimension	Principle/Area to Improve
Economy	• Provide job opportunities and promote local business by supporting locally owned stores and business as well as by encouraging mixed-use development. • Minimize cost of living by promoting the access to affordable housing, services and facilities
Environment	• Promote the access to clean air, water, land and non-toxic materials; in order to protect people and maintain biodiversity. • Preserve resources and minimize energy demand by taking energy saving technologies. • Give the ability to enjoy natural landscape by providing a range of green areas distributed within the neighborhood. • Provide appropriate ways to control and manage wastes.
Society	• Promote social justice and equity by providing equal access to affordable housing, economic activities, services and facilities (healthcare, education, physical safety and security, etc.). • Remove all barriers that reduce the participation in daily life of certain social groups, such as those with disabilities, women, children and elderly. • Design of streets and buildings should reinforce safe environments. • Promote social integration by providing a broad range of housing types, tenure types and prices levels. • Promote good relationships and daily interaction between people by providing civic buildings and public gathering places. • Promote social participation in all the project processes. • Promote the liveablilty of streets by providing safe, comfortable, interesting streets and squares to the pedestrian. • Promote neighborhood stability by ensuring secure tenure.
Mobility	• Provide alternatives to using car in order to reduce traffic load, minimize air pollution and conserve energy. • Provide activities of daily living and transit stops within walking distance to allow independence to elderly, young and who do not drive. • Provide fine network interconnecting streets to encourage walking. • Provide streets friendly with pedestrian, cycle and vehicle.
Physical	• Neighborhood should be compact, pedestrian friendly and mixed use. • Provide the access to adequate services and facilities that fulfill people's needs. • Provide the access to adequate eco-buildings and housings that fulfill people's needs and national building code. • Provide well-defined streets and open spaces by a well-structured building layout. • Provide a hierarchy of complete street networks based on pedestrian and vehicle load. • Take into account projected management, maintenance and repair policies to ensure the sustainability of neighborhood.
Political (Governance)	• Promote integrated urban governance. • Provide codes and legislation to control evolution. • Promote the community involvement in council decision-making.
Psychological	• Promote community identity by preserving heritage and historic remains, making architecture and landscape responding to their context. • Given the opportunity for people to have a place of their own by giving the ability to personalize the space. • Promote a pleasing milieu by enhancing urban-esthetic character of the built environment.

(4) Consider the Six Dimensions of a SSC

The six dimensions of SSCs should be taken into consideration while transforming cities into SSCs. For the comparison purposes, these dimensions along with their related factors are illustrated again in Table 7.12.

Table 7.12: Smart Sustainable Cities Dimensions and Areas to Improve

SSC Dimension	Factors/Area to Improve
Smart Economy	• Innovative spirit • Entrepreneurship • Economic image and trademarks • Productivity • Flexibility of labour market • International embeddings • Ability to transform
Smart Environment	• Attractive natural conditions • Pollution • Environmental protection • Sustainable resource management
Smart Governance	• Participation in decision-making • Public and social services • Transport governance • Political strategies and perspective
Smart Living	• Cultural facilities • Health conditions • Individual safety • Housing quality • Education facilities • Touristic attractivity • Social cohesion
Smart Mobility	• Local accessibility • (Inter)-national accessibility • Availability of ICT infrastructure • Sustainable, innovative, safe transport systems
Smart People	• Level of qualification • Affinity for life-long learning • Social and ethic plurality • Creativity • Flexibility • Cosmopolitanism/open-mindedness • Participation in public life

COMPARISON: Generic List of Areas to be Improved by a SSC Project

The comparison aims at creating a generic, not a holistic, list of areas that should be improved by a SSC project. Although the city context is not taken consideration during this comparison, the city context will be used later on to customize this list. The "Intersection Research Method" is used for such a comparison. The followed methodology along with the results are summarized below:

1. Compare the Sustainable Development (SD) factors and areas of improvements in Table 7.9 to these in Table 7.10 related to Urban Life. Then, tabulate the common components as illustrated in Table 7.13. As the SD does not have a dimension specifically related to infrastructure and service, the areas to improve under the "urban infrastructure, services, and management" dimension of the Urban Life are compared to the areas under all dimensions of the SD to find possible intersections. Each intersection is then added to the appropriate dimension and highlighted.

Table 7.13: Sustainable Development and Urban Life Common Components

Dimension	SD factors and areas	Urban Life areas
Economic	Green productive growth.	Macro-economy development and finance: including new analyses of relationships between urban economic growth and urban poverty, new assessments of urban competitiveness, and new guidelines for urban development strategies, urban taxation and financial improvements.
	Creation of decent employment.	Employment and labor markets: including small and medium enterprise development, skills enhancement, and new directions in labor market segmentation.
	Production and distribution of renewable energy	Informal economy: including measures to provide improved provisions for legal recognition, regularization of land housing developments, street trading, and energy consumption.
	Technology and innovation (R&D)	Promote the use of appropriate technology. (From Infrastructure, Services, and Management dimension).
Environmental	Eco-system integrity • Waste and recycling management • Energy efficiency. • Water management. • Air quality conservation. • Adaptation to and mitigation of climate change. • Green housing and buildings (From social dimension). • Green public transportation (From social dimension).	Natural resource conservation • Combat environmental degradation, health hazards and pollution. • Environmental planning. • Supporting sustainability. • Securing land tenure.

Dimension	SD factors and areas	Urban Life areas
Social	Education and Health	Improve health and education for all.
	Green public Transportation.	Improving urban mobility and transportation. (From Infrastructure, Services, and Management dimension).
	Recreation areas and community support.	Enhance shelter and settlement (From Infrastructure, Services, and Management dimension).
	Participation and sharing.	Promote social inclusion and cohesion.
	Culture identity.	Enhance culture and identity
	Equity and empowerment.	• Support gender equality and empowerment. • Reduction of violence and advancing human rights.
	Accessibility.	• Provide different types of services and facilities based on citizens' needs, are accessible by all citizen types including elderly, women, people with special needs, etc. • Basic infrastructure that support accessibility issues. (From Infrastructure, Services, and Management dimension).
Governance	Planning and decentralization	• Enhance strategic, participative and responsive urban planning (From Infrastructure, Services, and Management dimension) • Participation urban management • Accountability and transparency • Participation processes • Democracy and empowerment
	Reduction of inequity	Support gender equality and empowerment (From Urban Social dimension)
	Strengthen of civil and political rights	Advancing human rights
	Support of local, national, regional and global links	• Social inclusion • International outreach, which means improving the city's "brand name" and its international recognition through strategic tourism plans, attracting foreign investment and having representation abroad (From IESE (2015))

2. Compare the components of Table 7.13 with the areas to improve of the QoL in Table 7.11 and SSC dimensions and factors/areas to improve of Table 7.12. Common components are tabulated and related SSC's factors are highlighted along with

suggested hypothesis examples of improvements. The results of this comparison, as illustrated in Table 7.14, provides a list of generic areas to improve through a series of transformation solutions by a SSC project. It is worth mentioning that Table 7.13 does not have specific dimensions related to smart mobility, smart living, and smart people of a SSC. The components of these three dimensions are embedded in other dimensions. For SSC smart mobility, all components of the QoL mobility dimension have been considered and linked to appropriate components from other dimensions in Table 7.13. In relation to SSC smart living and smart people dimensions, the analysis of the QoL dimension shows intersections between the components of the physical, psychological, and social dimensions of QoL and the factors of smart living and smart people dimensions of SSCs. Each intersection has been noticed and compared to appropriate components in Table 7.13.

Table 7.14: Generic List of Areas for Improvements by SSC Projects

SSC Dimension	QoL Components	SD & Urban Life Components	SSC Factors	Hypothesis Examples/Initiatives
Smart Economy	*Economic dimension:* Provide job opportunities and promote local business by supporting locally owned stores and business as well as by encouraging mixed-use development.	• Employment and labor markets: including small and medium enterprise development, skills enhancement, and new directions in labor market segmentation. • Informal economy: including measures to provide improved provisions for legal recognition, regularization of land housing developments, street trading, and energy consumption	• Innovation. • Entrepreneurship. • Productivity. • Flexibility of labor market.	• High-tech industry. • Ease of establishing businesses. • Innovation & entrepreneurship culture. • Flexible laws for new businesses.
	Economic dimension: Minimize cost of living by promoting the access to affordable housing, services and facilities.	Macro-economy development and finance: including new analyses of relationships between urban economic growth and urban poverty, new assessments of urban competitiveness, and new guidelines for urban development strategies, urban taxation and financial improvements.		
Smart Environment	*Environment dimension:* Promote the access to clean air, water, land and non-toxic materials; in order to protect people and maintain biodiversity.	• Waste and recycling management. • Water management. • Air quality conservation. • Adaptation to and mitigation on climate change.	• Attractive natural conditions. • Pollution. • Environmental protection. • Sustainable resource management.	• Smart buildings. • Smart waste and smart water management, e.g. using of real-time data & information. • Smart transportation, such as using of eco-cars • Increase green areas • Smart energy, e.g. use of smart grids.
	Environment dimension: Preserve resources and minimize energy demand by taking energy saving	• Energy efficiency. • Green housing and buildings. • Green public transportation.		

SSC Dimension	QoL Components	SD & Urban Life Components	SSC Factors	Hypothesis Examples/Initiatives
	technologies.			
	Environment dimension: Give the ability to enjoy natural landscape by providing a range of green areas distributed within the neighborhood.	• Eco-system integrity. (i.e. such as increasing of green areas.)		
	Environment dimension: Provide appropriate ways to control and manage wastes.	• Waste and recycling management		
Smart Governance	*Governance dimension:* Promote integrated urban governance.	• Planning and decentralization: - Enhance strategic, participative and responsive urban planning - Accountability and transparency - Democracy and empowerment • Strengthen of civil and political rights	• Participation in decision-making. • Public and social services. • Transport governance. • Political strategies.	• E-Government services. • Open data platforms. • Legislations to support transparency.
	Governance dimension: Provide codes and legislation to control evolution.	• Reduction of inequity (i.e. support gender equality and empowerment). • Strengthen of civil and political rights (i.e. advancing human rights). • Support of local, national, regional and global links (i.e. advance human rights).		
	Governance dimension: Promote the community involvement in council decision-making.	• Planning and decentralization: - Participation urban management. - Participation processes. • From Social:		

SSC Dimension	QoL Components	SD & Urban Life Components	SSC Factors	Hypothesis Examples/Initiatives
		participation and sharing (i.e. promote social inclusion).		
Smart Living	*Physiological dimension:* • Promote community identity by preserving heritage and historic remains, making architecture and landscape responding to their context. • Promote a pleasing milieu by enhancing urban-esthetic character of the built environment.	• Culture identity (i.e. enhance culture and identity) • From Governance: improve the city's "brand name" and its international recognition through strategic tourism plans, attracting foreign investment, and having representation abroad (i.e. International outreach).	• Culture facilities. • Health conditions. • Individual safety. • Housing quality. • Education facilities. • Touristic attractively. • Social cohesion.	• Smart healthcare, e.g. e-health services. • Smart physical safety and security. • Intermodal transport systems. • Smart education, e.g. e-learning and capacity building services.
	Physical dimension: Provide the access to adequate services and facilities that fulfill people's needs.	• Education and Health (i.e. improve health and education for all) • Accessibility: provide different types of services and facilities based on citizens' needs, which are accessible by all citizen types including elderly, women, people with special needs, etc.		
	Physical dimension: Provide the access to adequate eco-buildings and housings that fulfill people's needs and national building code.	• Accessibility: provide different types of services and facilities based on citizens' needs, which are accessible by all citizen types including elderly, women, people with special needs, etc.		

SSC Dimension	QoL Components	SD & Urban Life Components	SSC Factors	Hypothesis Examples/Initiatives
	Physical dimension: Provide well-defined streets and open spaces by a well-structured building layout.	• Accessibility: provide different types of services and facilities based on citizens' needs, which are accessible by all citizen types including elderly, women, people with special needs, etc. • Green public transportation (i.e. improving urban mobility and transportation). • Recreation areas and community support (i.e. enhance shelter and settlement).		
	Physical dimension: Provide a hierarchy of complete street networks based on pedestrian and vehicle load. _Social dimension:_ • Promote the livability of streets by providing safe, comfortable, interesting streets and squares to the pedestrian. • Design of streets and buildings should reinforce safe environment.	• Accessibility: provide different types of services and facilities based on citizens' needs, which are accessible by all citizen types including elderly, women, people with special needs, etc. • Green public transportation (i.e. improving urban mobility and transportation). • Recreation areas and community support (i.e. enhance shelter and settlement).		

SSC Dimension	QoL Components	SD & Urban Life Components	SSC Factors	Hypothesis Examples/Initiatives
	Social dimension: • Promote good relationships and daily interaction between people by providing civic buildings and public gathering places.	• Culture identity (i.e. enhance culture and identity). • Participation and sharing (i.e. promote social inclusion and cohesion). • Equity and empowerment (i.e. support gender equality and empowerment).		
Smart Mobility	_Mobility dimension:_ Provide alternatives to using car in order to reduce traffic load, minimize air pollution and conserve energy. _Mobility dimension:_ Provide activities of daily living and transit stops within walking distance to allow independence to elderly, young, and who do not drive. _Mobility dimension:_ Provide fine network interconnecting streets to encourage walking. _Mobility dimension:_ Provide streets friendly with pedestrian, cycle and vehicle.	_Mobility is embedded in Social dimension:_ • Green public transportation • Improve urban mobility and transportation	• Local mobility. • (inter)-national mobility. • Sustainable, innovative, safe transport systems.	• Smart transpiration, e.g.: - Public transport systems organized through information gathered by satellites. - Use of eco-cars. - Smart lighting systems.

SSC Dimension	QoL Components	SD & Urban Life Components	SSC Factors	Hypothesis Examples/Initiatives
Smart People	_Social dimension:_ Promote social justice and equity by providing equal access to affordable housing, economic activities, services and facilities (healthcare, education, physical safety and security, etc.).	• Equity and empowerment (i.e. support gender equality, empowerment, and reduction of violence and advancing human rights). • Accessibility: provide different types of services and facilities based on citizens' needs, which are accessible by all citizen types including elderly, women, people with special needs, etc.	• Social and ethic plurality. • Flexibility. • Participation in public life.	• Social inclusion activities, e.g. meetings with public to raise awareness about the government development initiatives. • Introduction of legislations to support equality and human rights.
	Social dimension: Remove all barriers that reduce the participation in daily life of certain social groups, such as those with disabilities, women, children and elderly.	• Equity and empowerment (i.e. support gender equality, empowerment, and reduction of violence and advancing human rights). • Accessibility: provide different types of services and facilities based on citizens' needs, which are accessible by all citizen types including elderly, women, people with special needs, etc.		
	Social dimension: • Promote social integration • Promote social participation	Participation and sharing (i.e. promote social inclusion and cohesion).		

(5) City Context and use of ICTs

Cities are different from one another. They perform different specializations and they are characterized by different functions. This gives each city a specific local context and makes its uniqueness. The city context is often shaped by its economic, social, cultural, environmental, and political (i.e. governance) contexts along with their related factors (Meikle et al., 2001; Rakodi and Lloyd-Jones, 2002; ESRC, 2007). The factors include financial market, civil society, physical infrastructure, local government, consecration culture, ability to open new businesses, global trends, social support mechanisms, national and local policies, among others (Rakodi and Lloyd-Jones, 2002; ESCR, 2007; UN-HABITAT, 2010).

Transforming cities into SSCs is a context-based process. The transformation starting point and the needed set of activities and initiatives differ from one city to another, depending on the city context, needs, and local interests (ITU-T FG-SSC, 2016). Determining the particular economic, environmental, governance, and social contexts of the city as well as its characteristics, history, and culture are crucial to determine the appropriate path to follow towards becoming smart and sustainable city. This also provides the needed knowledge about determining and prioritizing the required activities for a SSC transformation process. Using this knowledge, the list of areas under each of the SSC six dimensions introduced in Table 7.14 could be subdivided into sub-lists based on the city's context, needs and local interests and aspirations. These lists can then be used as a reference in a SSC transformation process.

Some cities may already have completed some of the required transformation activities during previous development programmes and projects. In this case, the "Checking City Readiness for Change and Gap Analysis" layer of the proposed framework, Section 7.2.2, helps in providing the needed knowledge about these activities. It also helps in determining and recognizing the city status in relation to its hard, soft and digital infrastructure. The relationship between the city context and the list of SSC areas to improve through transformation change activities is illustrated in Figure 7.14.

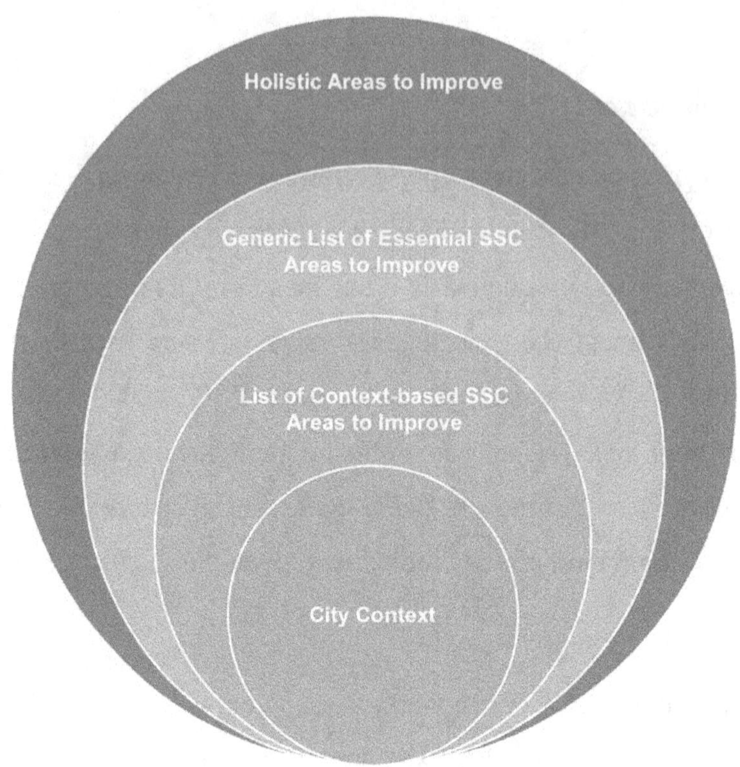

Figure 7.14: City Context and SSC Transformation Initiatives

Although improving the ICT infrastructure is not mentioned as a required activity under any of the dimensions of Table 7.14, checking the city ICT assets and improving them is a must. The ICT has an important role in SSCs as it acts as a digital platform to aggregate and exchange information and data between different city's services. The ICT tools also could provide eco-friendly and economically viable solutions for cities (ITU-T FG-SSC, 2016). For example, most of the e-government services are enabled and delivered using the ICT tools. As a result, checking the city's ICT assets would allow a city to determine its ICT deficiencies and work towards enhancing its ICT infrastructure, especially the physical one.

Each city should implement at least one activity under each of the SSC six dimensions to enhance its hard and soft infrastructures. The improvement of the city ICT infrastructure, as an enabler, should also be considered to ensure an effective transformation process. Figure 7.15 summarizes the findings of this Sub-section.

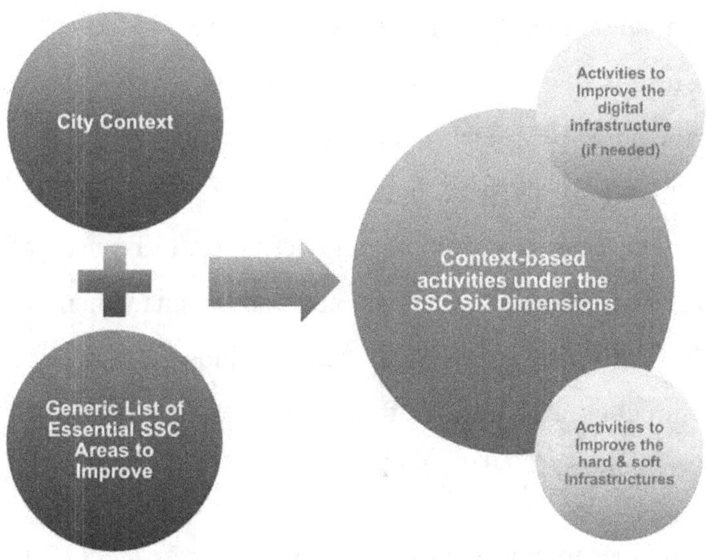

Figure 7.15: Overview of the SSC Transformation Process's Change Activities

It is worth mentioning that the SSC change solutions can be implemented in parallel unless some are dependent on another. For example, the economic productivity depends on healthy, happy citizens, who need easy access to education, healthcare, security, food, water, transport, clean air, and electricity. Therefore, improving the economic productivity of a city needs various types of activities related to other dimensions. For example, improving the education and health conditions of the Smart Living dimension and increasing the green areas that contribute in reducing the air pollution of the Smart Environment dimension.

7.2.4 [C] Monitor and Evaluate

The fifth step of the proposed innovative roadmap and framework aims at monitoring and evaluating a SSC transformation process required to achieve the targets. This includes checking the performance of a work process as a whole, such as the performance of identified goals and strategies, and its change activities' outputs and impacts, such as the performance of implemented services. Work process relatively is easier to capture while change activities' outputs and impacts are more difficult but more important to document (UNICEF, 2002; Booher, 2003) as they have a direct or indirect effect on the quality of life and overall performance of a city.

Monitoring and Evaluation (M&E) is a process that helps in improving the performance and achieving the results of a SSC project. Its main goal is to improve the current and future management of a SSC project outputs, outcomes, and impact. It establishes links between a SSC project past, present, and future actions and focuses on collecting and analyzing relevant data, from past and ongoing activities, to be used as a basis for fine-tuning, reorienting, and enhancing the planning and management of a SSC project. Without M&E, a SSC project team will not be able to judge if a transformation process is going in the right direction, how future efforts could be improved, and whether progress and success could be claimed (UNDP, 2002).

The UNDP (2002) defines monitoring as "*a continuous assessment that aims at providing the management and main stakeholders with early detailed information on the progress or delay in the achievement of results*". Monitoring is an oversight of the implementation stage(s) of the activity and the transformation process as a whole. Its main purpose is to determine if the planned outputs, deliveries, and schedules have been reached and take the appropriate actions to correct any deficiencies as quick as possible (UNDP, 2002).

The UNICEF Guide for Monitoring and Evaluation defines evaluation as "*a process which attempts to determine as systematically and objectively as possible the relevance, effectiveness, efficiency and impact of activities in the light of specified objectives. It is a learning and action-oriented management tool for improving both current activities and future planning, programming and decision-making*" (UNICEF, 1990). The main purpose of evaluation is to make sure not to repeat the same errors in future activities and to provide the needed successful mechanisms for current and future activities, initiatives, and projects. The evaluation recommendations and lessons could also be shared with other SSC projects, forming a basis for best practices sharing for future benefits.

Monitoring and evaluation are two different concepts and the only common ground between them is that they are both management tools. For monitoring, the collection of data and information for tracking progress is gathered periodically and regularly according to the terms of reference (i.e. criteria, success factors, constraints, and risks). Evaluation, unlike monitoring, is more episodic, where the collection of data and information takes place in view of or during the evaluation process. Monitoring does not take into consideration the outcomes and impact of change activities. It focuses only on the implementation process and progress towards achieving of the SSC project objectives. Evaluation focuses on specific questions related to the change activities' effectiveness and impacts. It measures how well the SSC change activities have met expected objectives (UNICEF, 1990).

The best way to understand the difference between these two concepts is through an example, which is about to be provided. For example, monitoring the stakeholder engagement in a transformation process often takes place from the time of selecting and engaging this stakeholder until completing the activity/activities he or she was assigned to. The data in relation to the stakeholder performance monitoring are collected based on a predefined set of success factors (e.g. each stakeholder should attend 90% of group meetings). During the evaluation of stakeholder engagement, which often takes place after monitoring, data and information that can be used to measure the output and impact of this stakeholder in each change activity is collected and analyzed (e.g. stakeholder attendance rate is 17% only). The results of both, the monitoring and evaluation, are reported and documented for future use. The appropriate actions to be taken in relation to the stakeholder future re-engagement often take place during the next phase, the "Sustain Transformation and Produce more Changes" phase.

A SSC process is a continuous long-term transformation process. This process is often divided into stages or cycles. Meaning that, the first stage may focus only on urgent set of change activities to be implemented and delivered. After monitoring and evaluating the first stage, the second stage may focus on improving previously implemented services, enhancing transformation strategies and objectives, producing more changes, and others. The transformation process then continues moving from one stage to another taking into consideration a set of recommendations about outputs, impacts, and performance analyzes of previous stages. Therefore, the monitoring and evaluation process is a continuous process that should happen throughout the life cycle of a SSC project, not just at the end. The results of each stage are analyzed and reported for future developments.

The performance measurement process would help cities in judging their strength and weaknesses regarding their transformation process. This give them a holistic view about how to improve their implemented services and previously identified strategies and objectives. For this purpose, cities need a well-defined list of Critical Success Factors (CSF) (BSI, 2014) and Key Performance Indicators (KPIs) (ISO/IEC, 2015; ITU-T FG-SSC, 2016). As the assessment measures that are appropriate for one city (i.e. context) many not be appropriate for others (ISO/IEC, 2015), cities can either adopt existing international indicators or create their own ones. Noting that existing indicators regarding SSC projects are still not consistent, standardized, or comparable across cities (ISO/IEC, 2015). Each city should identify its CSFs and KPIs that fit to its SSC transformation process vision, strategies, goals and objectives. This selection should ensure a transparent, comprehensive performance measurement process that helps a city in achieving its targets. This process should focus on linking the implemented services/solutions to targets and indicators that can be used to measure the performance of a SSC transformation process. The necessary information needed for monitoring and evaluation must be made available to realize each change activity and learn from experiences. The CSFs and KPIs use this information for performance measurement. The results are then registered, reported, and documented to be used as a reference for the next phase, namely, the "Sustain Transformation and Produce more Changes" phase.

This book does not seek to introduce any CSFs or KPIs for SSC projects, as this a massive and standalone research and highly dependent on the context of each city . This research, in turn, sheds some light on existing international attempts for identifying such CSFs and KPIs for SSCs. To start with, the BSI (2014) define CSFs as *"a checklist of issues which a city should regularly monitor to ensure that it is on track in the successful delivery of its SSC programme"*. Each city needs to identify its CSFs and track the transformation process against them. The BSI defined nine CSFs that could be adopted by cities or used as a reference while identify their specific ones. The nine CSFs are summaries in Figure 7.16 (BSI, 2014).

Strategic clarity	Leadership	User focus
• Clear vision • Strong business case • Focus on results	• Sustained support • Leadership skills • Collaborative governance	• A holistic view of the city's citizen and business customers • Citizen-centric delivery • Stakeholder empowerment
Stakeholder engagement	Skills	Supplier partnership
• Stakeholder communication • Cross-sectoral partnership • Engagement with other cities	• Skills mapping • Skills integration	• Smart supplier selection • Supplier integration
Achievable delivery	Future-proofing	Benefit realization
• Phased delivery • Continuous improvement • Risk management	• Interoperability • Web-centric delivery • Agility • Shared services • Support and maintenance	• Benefit mapping • Benefit tracking • Benefit delivery

Figure 7.16: The BSI Suggested SSC's Critical Success Factors

The ITU-T FG-SSC (2016) defines the KPIs as the indicators that are used to assist city leaders in evaluating their city services performance and measure the degree of success in achieving a SSC objectives and goals. The KPIs could also be used to compare the 'smartness' and 'sustainability' levels of cities in relation to facing of particular challenges. The ITU-T FG-SSC proposed a list of KPIs focusing specifically on a set of ICT-related indication for SSCs. This list of KPIs is not thorough and needs more additions to cover the six dimensions of a SSC from other perspectives not only from the ICT perspective (ITU-T FG-SSC, 2016). The list consists of 6 main dimensions, 37 sub-dimensions, and 62 ICT-related indicators that are divided into 39 core ICT-related indicators and 23 additional ICT-related indicators. Cities can adopt all these indicators, select the appropriate ones, and/or introduce new indicators (Appendix A). The six dimensions and the number of their related sub-dimensions and ICT-related indicators are illustrated in Table 7.15.

Table 7.15: ITU-T FG-SSC KPIs Dimensions, Sub-dimensions, and ICT-related Indicators

Dimension #	Dimension Name	No. of Sub-dimensions	No. of core Indicators	No. of additional indicators
D1	Information and Communication Technology	4	11	11
D2	Environmental Sustainability	5	3	0
D3	Productivity	9	8	3
D4	Quality of life	4	7	2
D5	Equity and social inclusion	4	6	2
D6	Physical infrastructure	11	13	5

In the planning phase of a SSC project, the CSFs are identified along with the KPIs. The transformation process is monitored against the CSFs while the KPIs are used to measure whether the CSFs are working or not, using predefined success criteria (DAFWA, 2016). To better understand the difference between the CSFs and KPIs, this book provides the following example. If one of the identified objectives of a SSC project is to increase the city's quality of life by increasing health services by 10% by the next 16 months, then by using the Table 10.1 in Appendix A, the CSF and KPIs could be defined as below:

CSF	KPI	Target
Improve health services	% of e-health services	10%
Patients satisfaction	% patients who are satisfied	95%
Services quality	% of bugs and system errors in online systems	2%

This means the following:

- To achieve this objective, it is critical to improve the city health services and maximize patients' satisfaction and quality of services (i.e. these are the CSFs).
- The indicator to measure whether the health services are improved will be how many e-health services have been developed and delivered for patients (i.e. this is the KPI).
- The transformation process is on track to the identified objective when the target of 10% is achieved (i.e. this is the success criterion).

The outputs generated during this phase are used as an input to the next phase of the transformation process, the "Sustain transformation and Produce more Changes" phase. These outputs aim at assisting a SSC project team in taking the appropriate decisions regarding the next actions in the transformation process.

7.2.5   [D] Sustain Transformation and Produce more Change

Developing cities into SSCs is a journey, not a destination. It is a transformation process of learning, where actions are taken based on continual new learnings (Daszko and Sheinberg, 2005; BSI, 2014). The feedbacks of these learnings may lead to essential or partial improvements of already implemented activities and produce of new ones. This may also lead to revisiting the transformation process strategies, goals, and objectives to be enhanced and/or updated. This ensures the continuity, efficiency, and effectiveness of a transformation process.

In continuous processes, the feedbacks generated during the performance measurement become part of the input for the next stage (Booher, 2003). Therefore, once the performance reports and documentations of the "Monitoring & Evaluation" phase become available, a SSC project team along with the relevant stakeholders can use them as a reference to plan the appropriate future actions to be taken.

This phase consists of four main tasks, namely, (1) learn from previous experience, (2) continuous improvements, (3) announce achievements to others, and (4) produce more changes. The aim of these tasks is to sustain a transformation process and ensure its continuity. It also forms the corner stone to start the next stage of a transformation process and moving forward, as illustrated in Figure 7.17. Learning from previous experiences ensures avoid repeating the same previous mistakes (Daszko and Sheinberg, 2005; BSI, 2014; Huawei, 2014; ITU-T FG-SSC, 2015b). The continuous improvements use the learnt lessons to update and/or improve the transformation strategies, objectives, and goals if needed as well as to improve and maintain implemented and delivered solutions (Kotter, 1995; BSI, 2014; Huawei, 2014; Vedashree and Bose, 2015; ITU-FG-SSC, 2016). It is also important to continuously share the transformation process achievements with citizens, key stakeholders, all types of local institutions, and other cities (Kotter, 1995; Daszko and Sheinberg, 2005). The latter aims at maintain the transparency of a SSC transformation process, share experiences with others to learn from, and increase citizens and stakeholders buy-in. Finally, the fourth task ensures the continuity of a transformation process by stimulating the change process through producing of new change activities, aiming to realize the long-term goal of developing a city into a SSC (Kotter, 1995; Daszko and Sheinberg, 2005; BSI, 2014; SCC, 2015; ITU-T FG-SSC, 2015b).

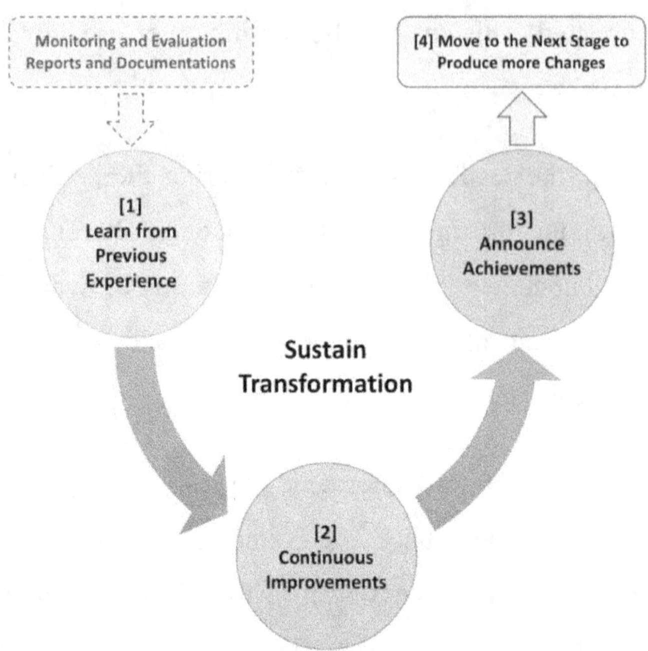

Figure 7.17: Sustain a SSC Transformation Process and Moving Forward

There is no one-size-fits-all mechanism to be followed during this phase. Each city, based on its previously identified strategies, objectives, and goals and implemented services, needs to find the appropriate mechanism to follow during this phase. However, each city should take into consideration the following aspects during this phase while referring to the performance reports and documentations of the previous phase:

1. Identify performance gaps and improvement areas regarding implemented and delivered services.

2. Identify improvement initiatives based on these gaps. The improvements should be in harmony with the economic, social, and environmental sustainability aspects of a city and the six dimensions of a SSC.

3. Identify the current stage strengths and weaknesses regarding the transformation strategies, objectives, and goals and the possibilities of improvements, if needed.

4. Take the appropriate decisions concerning stakeholders' engagement. The decisions may include avoiding of some inactive stakeholders, emphasizing active stakeholders, and engaging of new ones.

5. The new change activities to be produced should be identified in consistent with the whole transformation process vision.

7.3 Discussion

This book reaches its aim by introducing a novel conceptual framework for the transformation towards SSCs. The novel framework is designed to facilitate the transformation process by highlighting the essential components to be considered throughout a SSC transformation journey along with either adopted or introduced transformation tools.

To start with, the innovative framework takes into account checking the city context regarding its current economic, social, environmental, and political state and challenges. It also follows a theoretical logic model as a base to identify the city vision and its related objectives, goals, and transformation strategies. It highlights the necessity of engaging different types of stakeholders in a SSC transformation process from an early stage. To do so, it introduces a model that could be partially or fully adopted to ensure an effective stakeholders' engagement process. In additions, the proposed framework takes an unprecedented step by emphasizing the necessity of checking the current city assets, city readiness for change, before start planning the transformation process smart and sustainable solutions, aiming to consider the identified gap as part of the planned solutions. It highlights the international tools that could be used for this purpose as well. It also provides a list of minimum areas under which a SSC transformation process should provide a series of solutions and services. Based on the "Intersection Research Method", this list is built taking into consideration the sustainability of a city over its dimensions, urban needs, quality of life of citizens, six dimensions of a SSC, and city context through the use of ICTs as an enabler to provide solutions that are viable and environmentally friendly. Finally, it takes into consideration the importance of monitoring and evaluation of a SSC transformation process as a whole and its resulted and delivered solutions. The latter aims at ensuring the sustainability of a transformation process through continuous improvements and producing of more changes at all city levels.

On a final note, Table 7.16 provides an overview comparison of differences and similarities between the innovative SSC transformation framework and other frameworks in the literature (Section 2.3). Noting that it is focusing on highlighting the neglected phases and components in other studied proposed solutions.

FW	Consider the SSC six dimensions*	City governs solutions	Stakeholders engagement mechanism	City Readiness			Identify list of generic solutions
				ICT Infrastructure	Non-ICT Infrastructure	Previous initiatives	
Novel FW	YES	YES	YES	YES	YES	YES	YES
CISCO	NO	YES	NO	NO	YES (hard not soft)	NO	NO
BSI	NO	YES	NO	NO	NO	NO	NO
EPIC	YES	NO	NO	NO	NO	NO	NO
PwC	NO	YES	NO	NO	NO	YES	NO

Source: This book,, page 57, ". FW" = Framework

7.4   Conclusion

A SSC transformation framework provides the needed guidance and tools on how to realize a SSC vision and objectives. It highlights the areas over which the smart and sustainable solutions should be applied. Different attempts exist in the literature aiming at developing such a framework, each focuses on a selected lens. None of these models take into account all required aspects needed for a coherent transformation journey, which denotes a gap in knowledge. This book research closes this gap by introducing a holistic transformation framework that considers the city context, current state, readiness for the change, and local needs along with the SSC six dimensions and the necessity of sustaining a transformation process.

The next chapter presents the validation process of the proposed transformation roadmap and framework.

8.1 Introduction

In the previous chapters, the proposed SSC transformation roadmap and framework were explored. The roadmap is designed to provide a high-level overview of a SSC transformation process and its recommended essential phases with details on their components. These phases are introduced based on the elements and stages of the ToC, sustainable urban development core components, related urban studies structures, and common extracted phases and components from existing SSC roadmaps. One of the newly introduced components is a phase dedicated to examining the current city readiness for change before planning the desired smart and sustainable solutions of a transformation process. The roadmap is then used as a base to introduce a conceptual framework for the transformation towards SSCs. The latter aims at providing the guidance needed to realize the roadmap phases and components. It provides the tools needed to assist the transformation process. These tools are either adopted from existing international techniques or introduced through this book, such as the Stakeholders' engagement model and the list of basic areas of solutions under each of the SSC six dimensions.

As known, any newly proposed model needs to be validated prior to its usage. In this book, a new roadmap and framework providing a holistic guidance for the transformation towards SSCs are introduced. A trustful validation technique that captures the level of significance of the proposed approaches must be selected. According to the literature, numerous are the validation techniques that researchers may adopt to validate their work. These include examining the effectiveness of the proposed models via its application on real cases; conducting surveys, undertaking interviews with experts and others. Each technique has its advantages and disadvantages. Given that the novelty of this research is of conceptual nature, it becomes important to validate it via capturing the insights of experts in the field on the various components of the model and refine it accordingly prior to applying it to real cases. Therefore, this research uses the survey questionnaire method to validate the different components of the proposed roadmap and framework. It captures the insights of a group of experts from Europe, Americas, and Asia with a notable professional and/ or Academic expertise in SSCs, sustainable cities, urban development and ICT. The validation exercise mainly took place in the United Kingdom in collaboration with the University of Portsmouth. Most of the experts met face-to-face were available in the United Kingdom. Others were contacted online. More details on this process are provided in the remaining sections of this chapter.

It is worth noting that the findings of the validation process were published in three different papers. The first one related to the validation of the proposed roadmap, was published in the Sustainable Cities and Society Journal. The framework validation process and findings were published in the International Conference on Information Society and Smart Cities and the International Conference on Smart Applications, Communications and Networking.

The structure of this chapter is as follows. Section 8.2 presents an overview of the techniques available in the literature to validate conceptual models. Section 8.3 is dedicated to the design process of the used validation questionnaire. In Section 8.4, the validation structure of the questionnaire is explained. Section 8.5 is devoted to the questionnaire analysis and findings. The chapter concludes in Section 8.6.

8.2   Validation of Conceptual Models

Determining the accuracy of a proposed conceptual model (i.e. roadmap and/or framework) in representing a specific phenomenon requires going through a process called "Validation". It is necessary whenever a proposed model is designed to answer questions about real-world systems (Kleijnen, 1994). In 1981, Sargent proposed the "model development process", in which he highlighted the necessity of creating a conceptual model to be used as a guidance to facilitate achieving the final goal of a desired study. A general view of Sargent's model development process, specifically, the part related to the development of the conceptual model is illustrated in Figure 8.1 (Sargent, 1981; Sargent, 1992). In this paradigm, the *problem entity* is used to refer to an idea, system, policy, situation, or phenomenon to be modeled. The *conceptual model*, in turn, refers to the logical or verbal/mathematical representation of the problem entity created for a particular study to be realized. In the context of this book, the problem entity is considered as the phenomenon of transforming cities into SSCs while the conceptual model refers to the logical representation of a transformation process represented by both the SSC transformation roadmap and framework.

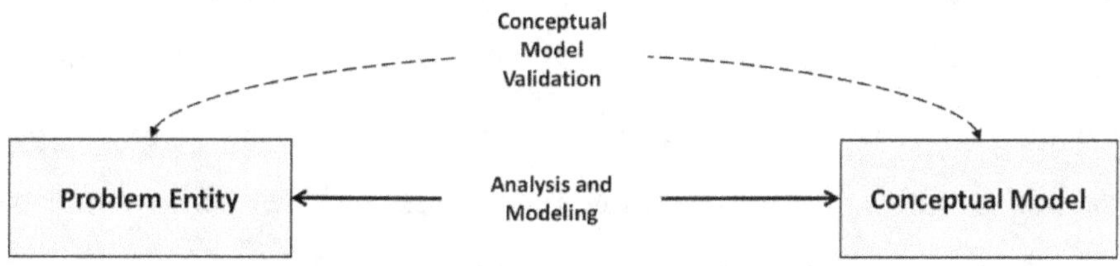

Figure 8.1: Conceptual Model Modeling Process by (Sargent 1981)

The validation of a conceptual model aims at determining its correctness and ensuring that its representation (e.g. its components) is reasonable for its intended purpose (Sargent, 1981; Sargent, 1992; Kleijnen, 1994; Robinson, 1997). However, there is no formal method or theory for validating a conceptual model (Kleijnen, 1994; Robinson, 1997). Instead; there are methods used based on the type of the problem entity to be modeled.

One of the widely used techniques to validate a conceptual roadmap and framework is based on asking individuals, who are experts or knowledgeable about the problem entity, to check the correctness of each of its components (Sargent, 1992; Robinson, 1997; Banks, 1998). Experts' feedbacks are then used to modify and update the model, if needed; either by adding the missing components or modifying existing ones. This aims at enhancing the credibility of the conceptual model to be used on real-world systems and case studies. To do so, a data collection instrument, such as a survey questionnaire, is developed with a series of questions for the purpose of collecting information from targeted experts. Each expert expresses his/her insight on the posed questions relating to the contributions of the research at hand by either agreeing or disagreeing with a specified issue and providing suggestions for improvements, if any. This technique is widely used to validate social and urban related proposed models especially when accessing information on real scenarios, cities in this case, is difficult (Sharp et al., 2002; Okoli and Pawlowski, 2003; FoF, 2012; Steenkamp and Kraft, 2012; Mureddu et al., 2014; Grafakos, 2015). Accordingly, this research will resort to the questionnaire method to validate the proposed SSC transformation roadmap and framework.

8.3   Validation Questionnaire Design Process

A questionnaire is a data collection instrument used by many researchers to gather information from the respondents about a specific study (Sharp et al., 2002; McDaniel and Gates, 2011; ACAPS, 2016). It consists of a series of questions, organized in a specific format to be answered by each respondent. There are various questionnaire design processes available in the literature. In this research, we follow one of the most commonly used design techniques for questionnaires; it is the one adopted from the process provided by (McDaniel and Gates, 2011; Felderer and Keckeis, 2014; ACAPS, 2016). The process consists of eight steps, namely, determining the objectives of the questionnaire and its limitations, determining the data collection method, determining the format of the questions, establishing the flow and layout of the questionnaire, evaluating the questionnaire, revising the questionnaire and obtaining the approvals needed to run it, preparing the final copy of the questionnaire and implementing it. These steps are illustrated in Figure 8.2.

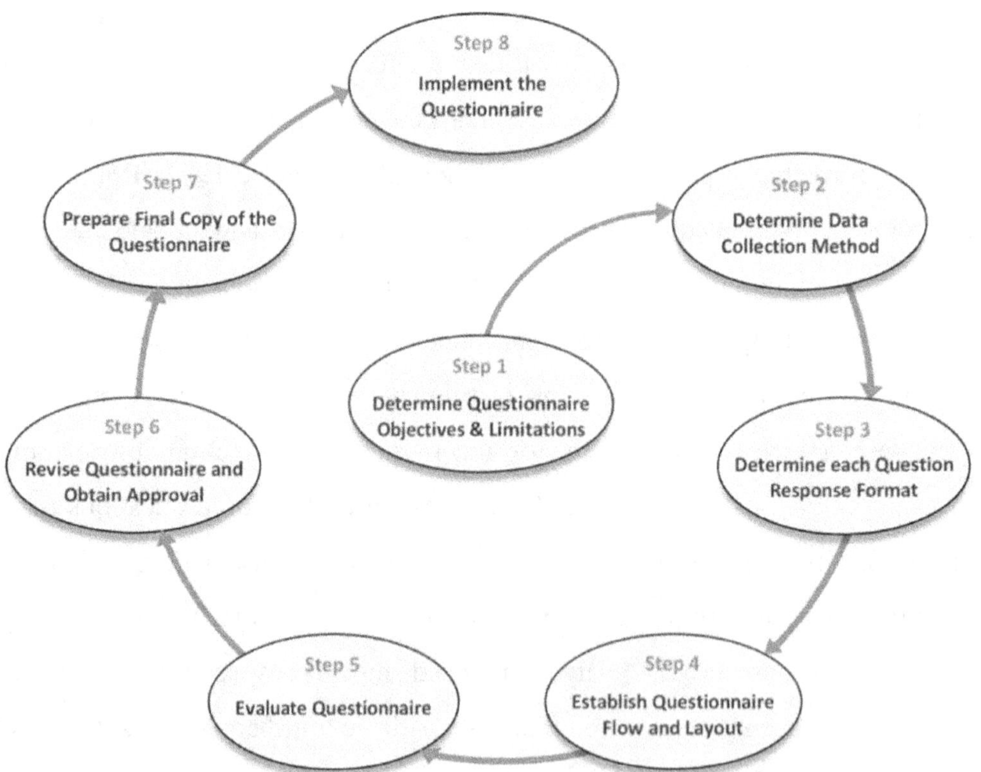

Figure 8.2: Questionnaire Design Process

8.3.1   Step 1: Determine Questionnaire Objectives and Limitations

The objectives of the validation questionnaire developed in relation to this research are numerous. These include collecting experts' insights on the proposed innovative transformation roadmap and framework (i.e. phases, components, and tools); highlighting the importance of each proposed items added to their strengths and/or weaknesses; and shedding light on neglected components and tools that should be considered during a transformation process, if any. Once the needed information is collected, an analysis of the results is undertaken using relevant statistical techniques mainly capturing the level of agreement or disagreement between respondents on each posed question.

The use of the survey questionnaire instrument in this research was faced by a set of limitations, which we shortly summarize here. To start with, the concept of SSCs is recent which limited the number of experts in this area of research, especially in the Arab region. As a result, it was challenging to find experts to contribute to the validation process of this research. In addition, although the experts participating in the validation exercise were mostly at the level of directors or managers of smart city projects in their respective countries, some refused to fill the questionnaire as they could not provide their responses without taking permissions from the responsible authorities at the city management level, which is a time-consuming bureaucratic process. Moreover, the targeted experts were of high profiles, thus, it was a challenge to secure appointments and/or convince them to take the time to fill the validation questionnaire. Lastly yet importantly, the limited number of experts in SSCs in the Arab region and the limitations in relation to information sharing limited the chances for inclusion of experts from the region.

8.3.2   Step 2: Determine Data Collection Method

The data collection process to validate the novel components of this research was done through face-to-face interviews, filling questionnaires in hard copy format or online via sharing a signed scanned questionnaire through email. Each submitted questionnaire was coupled with a consent form signed by the expert. The latter primarily aimed at providing the needed evidence that the respondent/expert has no objection to participate in the validation of the research at hand and to inform him/her about the analysis process and its approach in granting anonymity of the responses if desired.

Prior to filling the questionnaires, a brief overview of the research objectives was presented to the expert along with an explanation of the structure of the questionnaire. A copy of the model was provided as an appendix to the questionnaire for ease of reference should the expert decide to look into its details. Accordingly, a number of experts proceeded and filled the questionnaires and handed in the responses in person while others submitted the responses via email. Needless to say, that, an executable version of the questionnaire was developed and shared with the experts who were keen on taking part of the validation exercise, shared it with them and responded accordingly.

8.3.3   Step 3: Determine each Question Response Format

This step focuses on the format of the questions used throughout the validation process. According to the literature, the questions follow two types of format, namely, open-ended and close-ended (Sharp et al., 2002; McDaniel and Gates, 2011; ACAPS, 2016). The open-ended questions are those questions requiring respondents to provide their answers subjectively with supporting explanation as deemed necessary. These questions are mainly used to collect exploratory information for the purpose of either generating new hypothesis (e.g. components) on the subject or for better understanding the problem at hand (McDaniel and Gates, 2011; ACAPS, 2016). The closed-ended questions are used to capture the respondents' opinions about an issue with a predetermined set of options. This type of questions allows the collection of the confirmatory information for the purpose of testing the correctness of previously proposed hypotheses by the research (ACAPS, 2016).

The validation questionnaire is designed using close-ended and open-ended questions. In certain instances, an open-ended question is posed to capture the subjective insight of the expert on a specific subject matter. In other instances, close-ended questions are used and followed-up with open-ended questions aimed at giving the opportunity for the expert to further explain his/her answer and enable the researcher to better interpret his/her response.

8.3.4   Step 4: Establish Questionnaire Flow and Layout

To achieve the best response rate, the logical flow of the questionnaire should be carefully determined. The flow and layout should be designed from the general to the specific (McDaniel and Gates, 2011). The questionnaire used in this research followed this logical flow and reflected it on its layout. It first provides brief information about the research objectives and achievements, collects general information regarding each respondent professional experiences and background knowledge, and then asks each respondent to provide his/her insight on a series of questions, starting from the general ones to more specific. More details regarding the structure of the validation questionnaire are highlighted in Section 8.4.

8.3.5   Steps 5, 6 and 7: Evaluate, Revise, Approve and Finalize Questionnaire

Having completed steps 1 to 4, a draft questionnaire became ready. This underwent a series of changes resulting from discussions with experts on the subject matter. The changes mainly aimed at increasing the efficiency of the questionnaire and decreasing its complexity making it user-friendly for the experts to fill it easily. The main aim was to capture the insights of the experts in as much details as possible during the shortest time possible. Moreover, prior to finalizing and implementing the questionnaire, a dry run for it was considered. The latter assisted in estimating the time needed for the expert to fill the questionnaire and few modifications were introduced accordingly. Taking all the issues raised into consideration, new versions of the questionnaire were developed until the approval of the final one, which was used to undertake the validation exercise. It is important to note that the final copy of the questionnaire used in hard copy format was also made available in a word version using special macros allowing the respondent to select each option online. This version was designed to be used by experts contacted and accepted to contribute to the research validation process via emails. It was also sent to those experts who were not able to fill the questionnaire during their face-to-face interviews as well.

8.3.6   Step 8: Implement the Questionnaire

The final step of the questionnaire design process is putting the validation questionnaire into action, distributing it using one of the methods mentioned in Step 2 of the design process. Once completed, the questionnaires were processed for data analysis and interpretation and a "Thank you" note was sent to each expert who participated in the validation process.

8.4   Validation of the Questionnaire Structure

The validation questionnaire starts with a summary of the research objectives and findings followed by the questionnaire aims and structure. It proceeds by requiring the respondents to provide their personal and professional details using the "Questionnaire Meta-Data" form. The questions are then classified into five main sections. Each section consists of a set of questions focusing on a particular part of the proposed roadmap and framework. The first three sections are devoted to collect data regarding the city vision, readiness, and plan and transformation phases of the proposed models. Remaining two sections captures the needed data in relation to the monitoring, evaluation and sustaining of a transformation process as well as the stakeholders' engagement proposed model.

The first section aims at collecting the general information regarding the SSC transformation process. This includes the experts' point of view in relation to the identification and agreement on the SSC vision, strategies, and objectives; aspects to be considered during a transformation process; examining the current city state and challenges; best technique to be used to present a SSC transformation process added to the challenges that this process may face. The second section is dedicated to the assessment of the current city assets (i.e. checking the city readiness for change). Questions about the main city components that may affect a SSC transformation process and the techniques that can be used to realize the assessment process are asked.

In the third section, questions related to a SSC project planning and phases are considered. Each expert is asked to provide his/her insights regarding the most important dimensions to focus on while planning a SSC solutions and services. This also includes the necessity level of identifying the transformation process assumptions, constrains and risks. One of the questions in this section, specifically the third one, is selected to support the proposed "Generic List of Areas to be improved by a SSC Project".

Questions related to the monitoring, evaluation and sustaining of a SSC transformation process are considered in the fourth section. The need for monitoring and evaluation processes, the time for these to be considered and the techniques to be used to realize this process, and how to sustain a transformation process are captured. Finally yet important, questions to validate the proposed Stakeholder's Engagement Model are considered. This includes rating the significance of engaging different types of stakeholders in a SSC project using effective and efficient engagement process.

8.5   Questionnaire Analysis and Results

8.5.1   Respondents Profile

In order to validate the innovative roadmap and framework, a group of 25 experts from different countries was invited to participate in the validation process. The experts are from Canada, Colombia, Estonia, Germany, India, Italy, Japan, Norway, Russia, United Arab Emirates (UAE), United Kingdom (UK), the United States (USA), and South Korea. The number of experts invited to fill the validation questionnaire and the number of experts who filled it per country is illustrated in Figure 8.3 (a) and (b) respectively.

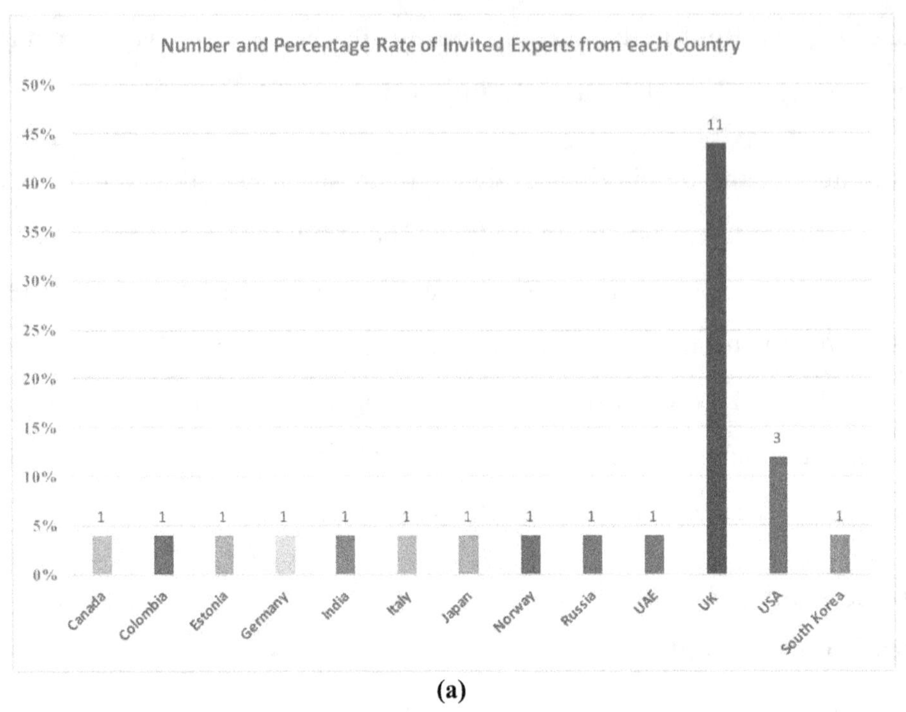

(a)

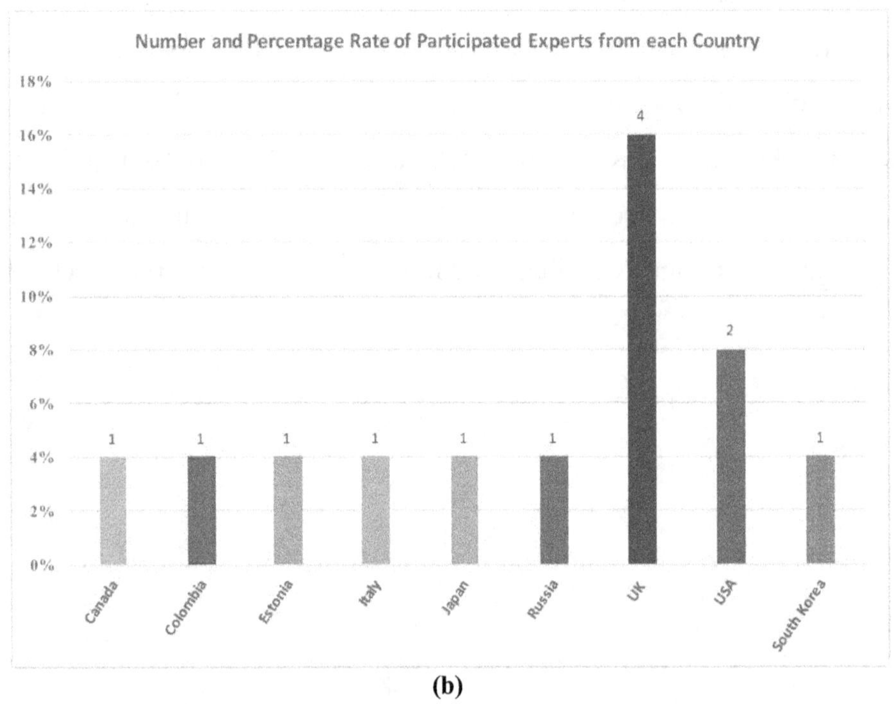

(b)

Figure 8.3: (a) Invited and (b) Participated Experts per Country

The experts were invited to contribute to the validation process face-to-face or via email. Out of the invited 25 experts, only 13 responded, making the response rate equal to 52%. Most of the respondents were male (92%). Of the 13 filled questionnaires, 72% were filled face-to-face while 21% were filled and sent back via email. This illustrates one of the challenges faced throughout this research as meeting with experts in the area and catching their interest to contribute to the validation processes was not easy. Details about the experts who contributed to this research are provided in Table 8.1.

Table 8.1: Overview of Experts Participation in the Research Validation Process

Method Type	Total (#)	Total by Method (#)	Total by Gender (#)		Total Returned Back by Gender (#)	Total Returned Back by Gender (%)	Total Returned Back by Method (#)	Total Returned Back by Method (%)	Overall Returned Back (%)
Face to Face	25	14	Male	12	9	64%	10	71%	52%
			Female	2	1	7%			
Via Email		11	Male	10	3	27%	3	27%	
			Female	1	0	0%			

In addition, the first component of the validation questionnaire collects personal and professional details of each expert. It also asks respondents to rate their professional expertise and knowledge in relation to SSCs, city planning, evaluation and transformation, stakeholders' engagement, and technology and innovation. This is summarized in Table 8.2.

Table 8.2: Overview of Respondents Profiles

Experience	Level of Experience				
	None	Knowledgeable	Advanced	Proficient	Total (Adv. & Prof.)
SSC Concept	0%	31%	54%	15%	69%
Sustainability Concept	0%	8%	23%	69%	92%
City Planning & Evaluation	0%	38%	15%	47%	62%
City Transformation Process	0%	23%	69%	8%	77%
Cities' Stakeholders Engagement	0%	23%	15%	62%	77%
Technology & Innovation	0%	0%	23%	77%	100%

8.5.2 Data Analysis: Quantitative Method

During the data analysis, collected data is revisited, sorted and structured in the most appropriate format in preparation for its analysis (Sharp et al., 2002). To do so, answers were processed and managed using Microsoft® Excel 2015 and followed a simple coding system for close-ended questions noting that the open-ended questions are used for recommendations and future directions.

The answers for closed-ended questions were coded either using a Likert scale (i.e. numerical scale) method or using dummy variables. For the former, each respondent was asked to select an answer from a set of options such as "Very important – Important - Moderately important – Unimportant" or "Strongly agree – Agree – Disagree – Strongly disagree". The options were then coded using the four-point Likert scale values 1, 2, 3, and 4 respectively, represented as $L = \{1,2,3,4\}$. Example of this type of questions is illustrated in Table 8.3.

Table 8.3: Representation of Close-ended Question using four-point Likert Scale

Option	Option	Likert Value
Very Important	Strongly Agree	4
Important	Agree	3
Moderately Important	Disagree	2
Unimportant	Strongly Disagree	1

The close-ended questions that allow a respondent to select one or more options were coded using dummy variables. For example, for the multiple-choice options: "Learning", "Avoid repeating mistakes", "Future improvements", and "Sharing experiences", the dummy variables "L", "A", "F", and "S" were used to code each selection respectively, as illustrated in Table 8.4.

Table 8.4: Representation of Close-ended Question using Dummy Variables

Choice	Dummy Variable
Learning	"L"
Avoid repeating mistakes	"A"
Future improvements	"F"
Sharing experiences	"S"

The data collected through the questionnaires is processed and analyzed following two different statistical techniques namely, the consensus and dissention method, which measures the level of agreement and disagreement on the tested hypothesis, and the frequency method through which the percentage of responses on each Likert scale category regarding each question is calculated and then illustrated using a proper statistical chart or graph. The "consensus and dissention" test is applied on close-ended questions with a single option answer (i.e. the respondent can select only one of the option from the set $L = \{1,2,3,4\}$). The frequency method is applied on all close-ended questions.

It is important to note that a four-point Likert scale was used instead of a five-point scale to eliminate the "Neutral" option to force the expert to provide a meaningful answer following the "forced choice" Likert scale method (Allen and Seaman, 2007).

8.5.3   Data Analysis Results: Consensus and Dissention Method

The Likert scale data has unique data analysis procedures. To understand how to statically analyze data collected based on a Likert scale, there is a need first to understand how data are scaled. Statisticians have grouped the data collected from surveys into four main scales of measurements, known as Steven's Scale of Measurement, that are (Allen and Seaman, 2007; Boone and Boone, 2012):

- **Nominal Scale**: responses are assigned to categories without numerical representation. Examples of nominal data include eye color, gender, and race.
- **Ordinal Scale**: responses can be ordered or ranked and numbers can be assigned to each category to express a "greater than" relationship; noting that the value of how

much a category is greater than others is not implied. Meaning that it is impossible to tell how much "Disagree" is greater than "Strongly Agree". In addition, the exact distance between categories is not measurable. There is no empirical evidence to assume that the distance between *agree* and *strongly agree* is equal to the one between *disagree* and *strongly disagree*. Rankings, such as (unimportant, moderately important, important, and strongly important) are examples of ordinal data.

- **Interval Scale**: data is represented using numbers, which are used to indicate data order as well as reflect distances between points on the scale. An example of this type of data is grades and time intervals. For grades, the difference between 50 and 60 grades is a measurable 10 grades. For time, the increments from a time interval to another is consistent, known, and measurable.

- **Ratio Scale**: with this scale, data are ordered using numeric values where distances, fractions, and decimals between values are measurable. Examples of this type of scales include age, height, weight, and years of experiences.

The Likert scale is a one-dimensional scaling method (Tastle and Wierman, 2007). Meaning that, the scale is represented as a statement (i.e. in our case a question) with choices (i.e. agree, disagree, etc.). In this case, an answer must be made of one and only one choice. With this type of scaling, Likert scale falls into the ordinary scale of measures (Tastle and Wierman, 2006). Therefore, to measure the consensus and dissention of such a scale, there is a need for a measure that can be used to logically analyze ordinal data that are generated from the Likert scale method.

A consensus refers to the similarity of opinions between a group of individuals towards an issue, it is also considered as the general agreement. Dissention, in turn, refers to the difference of opinions towards this issue (Tastle and Wierman, 2007). Consensus is measured as a function of shared insights. Each insight could be captured using the Likert scale. This scale aims at measuring to which extent an individual agrees or disagrees with a given question in a survey questionnaire. For example, categories (i.e. choices) of a four-point Liker scale can be numbered as below, noting that the "Neutral" option is eliminated:

Question 1: *"How important is having and agreeing on a SSC vision"*

1 = Unimportant (UI)

2 = Moderately important (MI)

3 = Important (I)

4 = Very Important (VI)

Question 2: *"Do you agree with the following statement: the quality of city assets affects a SSC planning process"*

1 = Strongly disagree (SD)

2 = Disagree (D)

3 = Agree (A)

4 = Strongly agree (SA)

The degree on consensus/agreement is between zero and one. The value "zero" indicate that there is no consensus/agreement between responses while the value "one" refers to a complete, 100% agreement. A measure of consensus takes into consideration a set of rules as below (Tastle et al., 2005; Tastle and Wierman, 2006):

1. If the number of participant (n) in a survey questionnaire is an even number and an equal number of them separate themselves into two disjoint groups ($n/2$), then respondents are considered to have no consensus/agreement on the posed question; causing the consensus measured value to be zero. For example, half of the respondents selected category "strongly disagree" and the rest selected "strongly agree".

   If the number of participants (n) is an odd number, then there is at least one individual that will break the rule of half-half measure, forcing the consensus measured value to be slightly greater than zero.

2. If all number of participants (n) select the same category, regardless of the category type, then the respondents are considered to have a complete consensus/agreement with 100% degree and consensus measured value equal to one.

3. If ($n/2 + 1$) or more of the participants select the same category of the Likert scale, then the degree of consensus/agreement is greater than zero.

4. As the number of participants that select a specific category increases, the degree of consensus/agreement increases. The maximum value of this degree is one, meaning that all participant place themselves in one category (i.e. select the same choice).

One important issue to note is that the consensus measure method can only be applied on a scale composed of an odd number of categories (i.e. 5-point, 7-point, 9-point Liker scale, etc.) (Tastle et al., 2005). However, as previously mentioned, the designed survey questionnaire is based on a four-point Liker scale, $L = \{1,2,3,4\}$, in which the "Neutral" option was eliminated using the "force choice" technique. Therefore, considering possibilities for conversion of scale from a 4-point scale to a 5-point scale is needed while ensuring the reliability and validity of the collected data. A thorough search of the literature indicates the possibility of doing so by shifting/transforming values while keeping the width between them intact (Tastle et al., 2005).

To start with, the width between the points is equal to 1 (i.e. 2-1 = 1, 3-2 = 1, 4-3 = 1). No matter what shifting strategy is adopted, the width between values should remain unaltered. One possible approach is to shift all values one-step to the right and increase them by 1; adding a new option at the beginning of the scale such as "Neutral" option; and assign to it the rank number equal to 1 and value to 0. By doing so, the four-point Likert scale $L = \{1,2,3,4\}$ is converted to a five-point scale $X = \{1,2,3,4,5\}$, where Neutral = N = 1, UI/SD = 2, MI/D = 3, I/A = 4, and VI/SA = 5. It is worth noting that the Likert scale is an ordinal scale in which these numbers are used for ordering and ranking only; therefore; the addition of "Neutral" has no effect on the nature of the used scale.

This proposed conversion technique is illustrated through an example drawn from the implemented validation questionnaire. Consider the answers for "*Question 2*" provided by the 13 experts using the 4-point scale below:

Expert #	E1	E2	E3	E4	E5	E6	E7	E8	E9	E10	E11	E12	E13
Rating[*]	3	4	3	3	3	3	3	3	3	1	4	2	4

** Key: SD = 1, D = 2, A = 3, and SA = 4*

To convert this 4-point Likert scale into a 5-point scale, each rating value is shifted to the right by increasing its value by 1, keeping in mind that the "Neutral" option, "N", is added to the beginning of the scale. The output of the conversion method is as follows:

Expert #	E1	E2	E3	E4	E5	E6	E7	E8	E9	E10	E11	E12	E13
Shift Rate by 1	3+1	4+1	3+1	3+1	3+1	3+1	3+1	3+1	3+1	1+1	4+1	2+1	4+1
Shifted Rating*	4	5	4	4	4	4	4	4	4	2	5	3	5

Key: N = 1, SD = 2, D = 3, A = 4, and SA = 5

To test the correctness of this conversion process, for each scale the mean and standard deviation are calculated. In fact, although the mean values will not be equal for both scales as the first scale has 4 points while the other consists of 5 points, the standard deviation of both should be equal. The mean (μ) represents the average of all data points in a given set while the standard deviation (σ) represents how distant are the responses of each question from the mean value (Rafalak et al., 2016). The mean and standard deviation of the 4-point scale are 3.00 and 0.784 respectively. The mean and standard deviation of the 5-point scale are 4.00 and 0.784 respectively. By shifting the values by 1 and adding a new option at the beginning of the sacale, the standard deviation remained intact, thus the conversion technique used does not affect the reliability of the collected data and at the same time converts the scale into an-odd numbered categories, a requirement for the use of the "consensus and dissension method".

Having said the above, it becomes possible to use the technique listed in (Tastle et al., 2005; Tastle and Wierman, 2006 & 2007) to calculate the consensus measure. Given a 5-category (i.e. 5-point) Likert scale, $X = \{1,2,3,4,5\}$, where $X_1 = 1$, $X_2 = 2$, $X_3 = 3$, $X_4 = 4$, and $X_5 = 5$, then the width of X, d_X, is calculated using the following formula:

$$d_X = (X_{max} - X_{min}) - 1 \tag{1}$$

where X_{max} and X_{min} refer to the maximum and minimum values of the Likert scale "X" respectively. Subtracting 1 (i.e. a one-point width) from the total width d_x ensures that the addition of the "Neutral" option to the original 4-point scale does not affect the reliability of the collected data. In this case, $X_{max} = 5$ and $X_{min} = 1$; therefore; $d_x = (5 - 1) - 1 = 3$. The mean of X is calculated using the formula:

$$\mu_X = \sum_{i=1}^{n} p_i X_i \tag{2}$$

where p_i is the relative frequency associated with each X_i (i.e. p_i is the relative number of respondents who selected X_i option, where X_i ranges from $1 = $ N, $2 = $ UI/SD to $5 = $ VI/SA) and n is the total number of respondents. The consensus and dissention measures are then calculated as follows:

$$Cns\,(X) = 1 + \sum_{i=1}^{n} p_i \, \log_2 \left(1 - \frac{|X_i - \mu_X|}{d_X} \right) \qquad where\ 0 \le Cns(X) \le 1 \tag{3}$$

$$Dns\,(X) = 1 - Cns(X) \qquad where\ 0 \le Dns(X) \le 1 \tag{4}$$

It is worth noting that the consensus and dissention are related as they are complementary to each other and that, if one of them is known, then the other can be easily calculated. This makes the formula $Cns(X) = 1 - Dns(X)$ true as well. The degree of consensus and dissention measures is a value between 0 and 1. For consensus, the value '0' means that there is no consensus/agreement, leaving the dissention value equal to '1'. The consensus value '1' indicates the existence of a complete consensus/agreement making the dissention value equals to '0'.

Suppose that the consensus and dissention measures are to be calculated for Question 2 above where the 13 responses were as follows: 1 individual chose "Strongly Disagree", 1 individual chose "Disagree", 8 individuals chose "Agree", and 3 individuals chose "Strongly Agree", noting that the "Neutral" option is set to the value 0. Then the mean is calculated using formula (2) as follows:

$$\mu_X = \sum_{i=1}^{13} p_i X_i = \frac{0}{13}\,x\,1 + \frac{1}{13}\,x\,2 + \frac{1}{13}\,x\,3 + \frac{8}{13}\,x\,4 + \frac{3}{13}\,x\,5 = 4$$

Using this calculated mean (μ_X) in addition to the width of X, $d_x = (5 - 1) - 1 = 3$, the consensus measure is calculated using formula (3) as follows:

$$Cns\,(X) = 1 + \sum_{i=1}^{n} p_i \, \log_2 \left(1 - \frac{|X_i - \mu_X|}{d_X} \right)$$

$$= 1 + \frac{0}{13} \, \log_2 \left(1 - \frac{|1 - 4|}{3} \right) + \frac{1}{13} \, \log_2 \left(1 - \frac{|2 - 4|}{3} \right)$$

$$+ \frac{1}{13} \, \log_2 \left(1 - \frac{|3 - 4|}{3} \right) + \frac{8}{13} \, \log_2 \left(1 - \frac{|4 - 4|}{3} \right)$$

$$+ \frac{3}{13} \, \log_2 \left(1 - \frac{|5 - 4|}{3} \right)$$

$$= 0.698$$

In this case, the value of the dissention measure is calculated using formula 4 as:

$$Dns(X) = 1 - Cns(X) = 1 - 0.698 = 0.302$$

The results show that the degree of consensus is equal to 0.698, which falls under rule 3 of the consensus measurement method. This denotes a difference in opinions between respondents. Collected data shows that 8% of respondents strongly disagree with the posed hypothesis, 8% disagree, 62% agree, and finally 22% strongly agree. This makes a good justification for the resulting consensus measure, not too high and slightly greater than the mid value of the interval [0-1]. Results of the consensus and dissention measures of all closed-ended questions are summarized in Table 8.5.

Table 8.5: Consensus and Dissension Measures Results

Section (#)	Questions		Mean 4-point	Mean 5-point	SD (σ)	Consensus (Cns)	Dissention (Dns)
Section 1	Q1		3.538	4.462	0.634	0.684	0.316
	Q2	Q2.1	3.769	4.769	0.421	0.813	0.187
		Q2.2	3.846	4.846	0.361	0.862	0.138
		Q2.3	3.692	4.692	0.462	0.775	0.225
		Q2.4	3.538	4.538	0.499	0.739	0.261
		Q2.5	3.154	3.923	0.769	0.625	0.375
		Q2.6	3.615	4.538	0.625	0.701	0.299
		Q2.7	3.615	4.538	0.625	0.701	0.299
		Q2.8	3.615	4.538	0.625	0.701	0.299
	Q3		3.769	4.769	0.421	0.813	0.187
	Q4		N/A				
	Q5		N/A				
	Q6	Q6.1	3.308	4.154	0.722	0.638	0.362
		Q6.2	3.462	4.385	0.634	0.680	0.320
		Q6.3	3.615	4.538	0.625	0.701	0.299
		Q6.4	3.769	4.769	0.421	0.813	0.187
		Q6.5	3.538	4.462	0.634	0.684	0.316
		Q6.6	3.692	4.692	0.462	0.775	0.225
		Q6.7	3.385	4.308	0.625	0.687	0.313
		Q6.8	3.462	4.462	0.499	0.739	0.261
		Q6.9	3.462	4.385	0.634	0.680	0.320
		Q6.10	3.923	4.923	0.266	0.925	0.075
		Q6.11	3.769	4.769	0.421	0.813	0.187
		Q6.12	3.923	4.923	0.266	0.925	0.075
		Q6.13	3.769	4.769	0.421	0.813	0.187
		Q6.14	3.615	4.538	0.625	0.701	0.299
		Q6.15	3.462	4.385	0.634	0.680	0.320
	Q7		N/A				
Section 2	Q1	Q1.1	3.538	4.385	0.746	0.630	0.370
		Q1.2	3.846	4.846	0.361	0.862	0.138
		Q1.3.1	3.846	4.846	0.361	0.862	0.138
		Q1.3.2	3.385	4.231	0.738	0.623	0.377
	Q2		N/A				
	Q3		3.538	4.462	0.634	0.684	0.316
Section 3	Q1		N/A				
	Q2	Q2.1	3.769	4.769	0.421	0.813	0.187
		Q2.2	3.615	4.538	0.625	0.701	0.299
		Q2.3	3.692	4.615	0.606	0.730	0.270
	Q3	Q3.1	3.692	4.615	0.606	0.730	0.270
		Q3.2	3.692	4.692	0.462	0.775	0.225
		Q3.3	3.692	4.692	0.462	0.775	0.225
		Q3.4	3.615	4.615	0.487	0.751	0.249
		Q3.5	3.615	4.462	0.738	0.651	0.349
		Q3.6	3.462	4.462	0.499	0.739	0.261
Section 4	Q1		3.846	4.846	0.361	0.862	0.138
	Q2		N/A				
	Q3		N/A				
	Q4		N/A				
	Q5		N/A				
Section 5	Q1		3.923	4.923	0.266	0.925	0.075
	Q2	Q2.1.1	3.692	4.692	0.462	0.775	0.225
		Q2.1.2	3.692	4.692	0.462	0.775	0.225
		Q2.1.1	3.769	4.692	0.576	0.771	0.229
		Q2.1.2	3.000	3.846	0.784	0.698	0.302
		Q2.3	3.385	4.385	0.487	0.751	0.249
	Q3	Q3.1	3.692	4.615	0.606	0.730	0.270
		Q3.2	3.538	4.462	0.634	0.684	0.316
		Q3.3	3.462	4.308	0.746	0.621	0.379
		Q3.4	3.538	4.385	0.746	0.630	0.370
		Q3.5	3.538	4.462	0.634	0.684	0.316
		Q3.6	3.308	4.231	0.606	0.707	0.293
		Q3.7	3.462	4.385	0.634	0.680	0.320
		Q3.8	3.692	4.692	0.462	0.775	0.225

** NA = Not Applicable*

8.5.4   Data Analysis Results: Frequency Method

This section focuses on the frequency method through which the percentages of responses on each Likert scale category for each question is calculated and then illustrated using a proper statistical chart or graph. This method was applied on all close-ended questions, including questions with single and multiple selections.

The validation questionnaire consists of five main sections. Each section is divided into a series of questions; each is focusing on a specific part of this research. Data analysis of these questions are provided below.

8.5.4.1   Section 1: General Information & City Vision

The first section aims at collecting data from respondents regarding a SSC concept in general and the main issues that should be considered at an early stage of a transformation process. It starts by asking the respondents to provide their insights in relation to the necessity of having a clear, comprehensive transformation process. About 92% of the respondents emphasized the necessity of having a solid transformation vision, mission, strategies and goals, while the rest rated this as a mandatory important step.

The questionnaire then asks the respondents to rate a list of aspects to be considered while designing a SSC transformation process as a whole, providing the level of significance of each. This includes the economic, environmental, social, governance, and cultural aspects in addition to the quality of life of citizens, urban services, and urban operations. Data analysis shows that all respondents emphasized the necessity of considering the economic, environmental, social, and governance aspects. For cultural aspect, 77% found it as an important aspect to be considered, while 23% viewed it as a moderately important one. As for the quality of life of citizens, urban services, and urban operations, about 92% of respondents agreed on the necessity of considering them during a transforming process. Overview of this question results is illustrated in Figure 8.4, noting that none of the respondents viewed these aspects as unimportant.

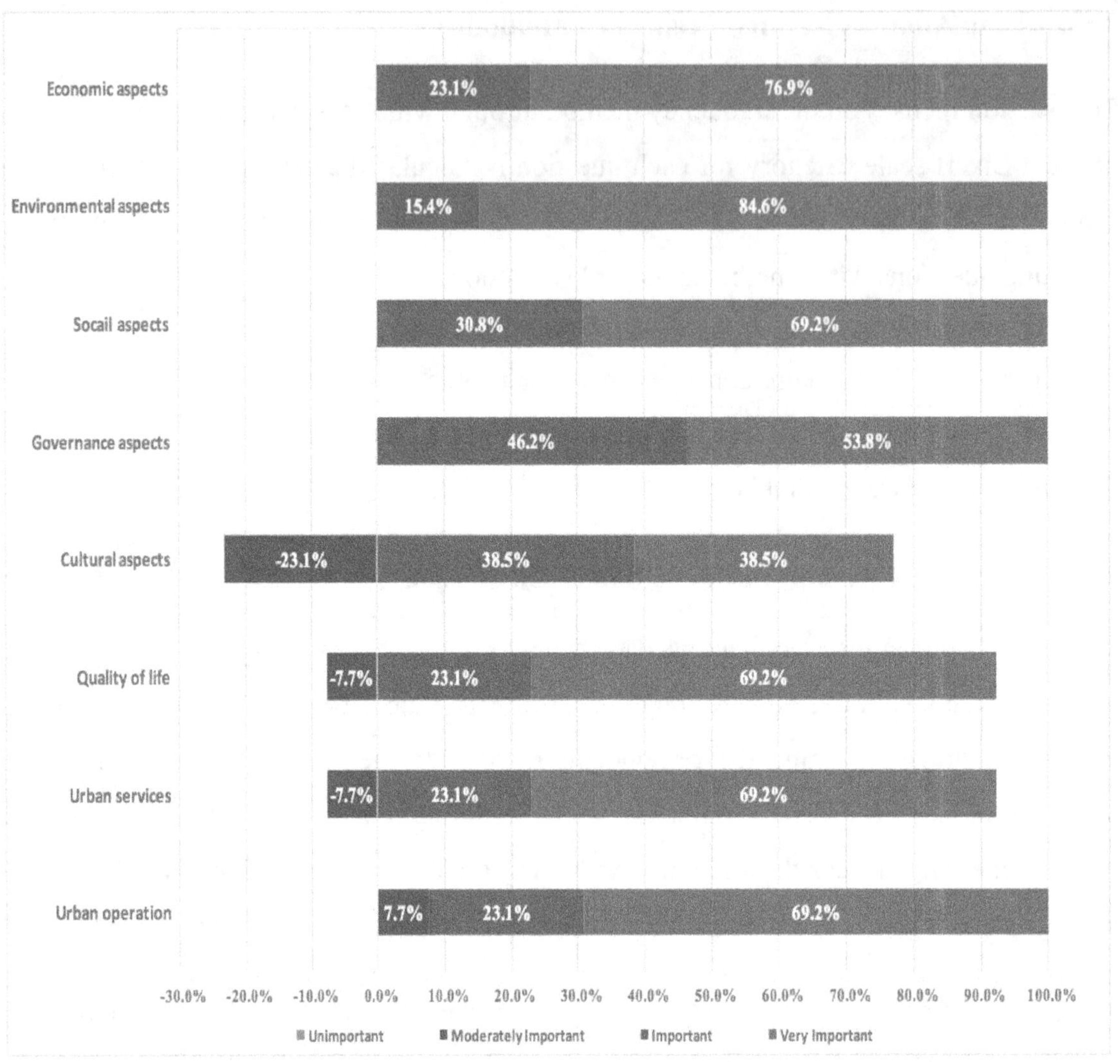

Figure 8.4: Significance of different type of Aspects in a SSC Project

In relation to the necessity of assessing the city current state and challenges, there was an agreement on it with 76.9% and 23.1% rates for "Very Important" and "Important" options respectively, as illustrated in Figure 8.5 (a). To assess the current state and challenges, the experts were asked to provide their insights on whether to use KPIs or KPIs and CSFs. 61.5% considered KPIs as important, while 38.5% emphasized the need for using KPIs and CSFs for this purpose, as illustrated in Figure 8.5 (b).

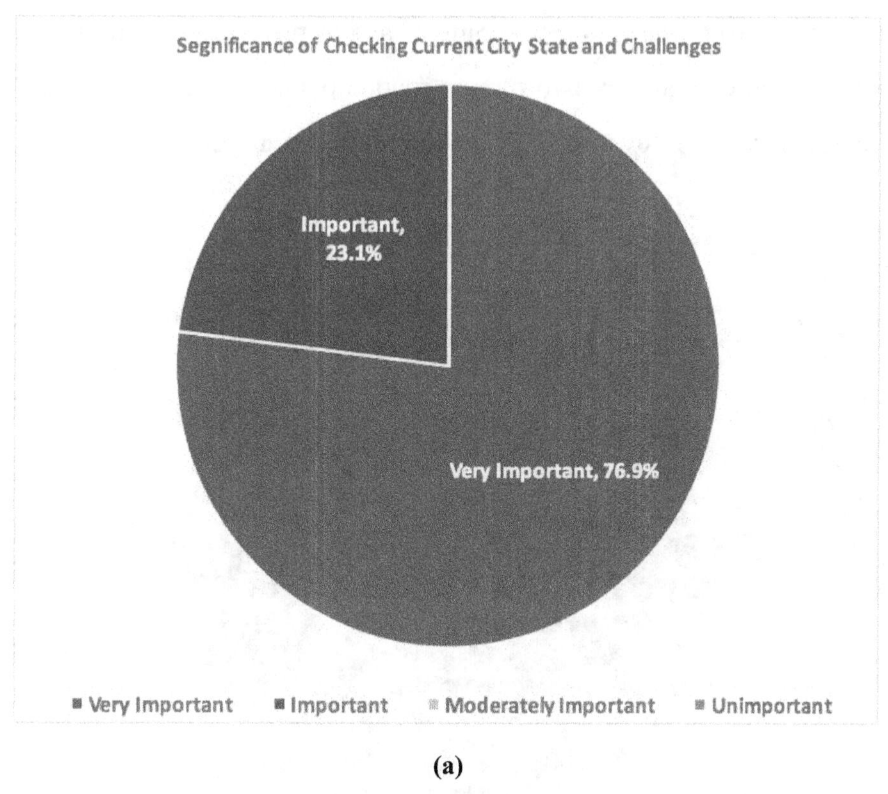

(a)

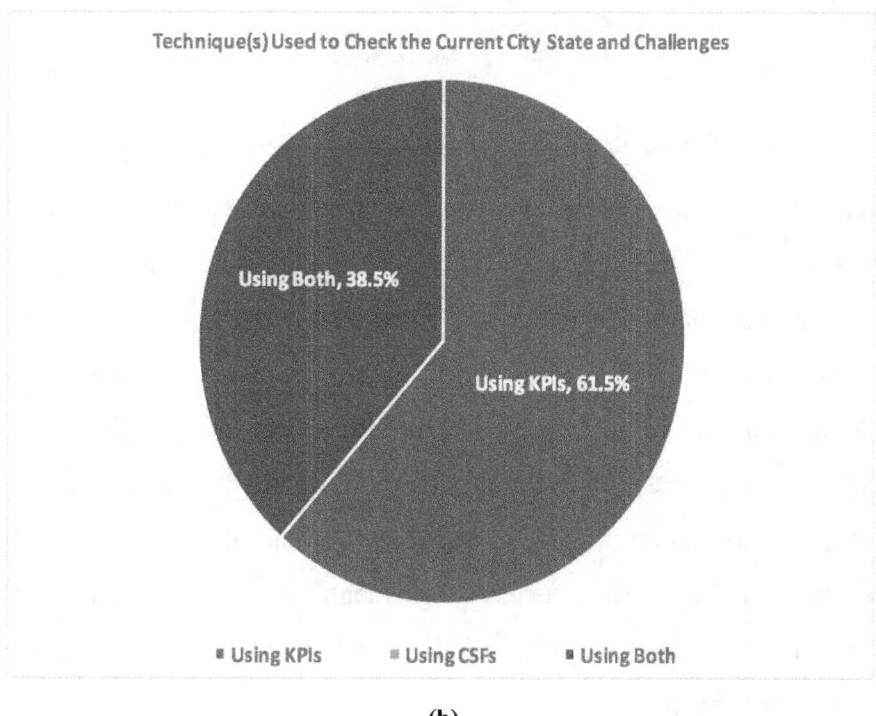

(b)

Figure 8.5: (a) Significance of Assessing Current City State, Using (b) KPIs, CSFs or Both

As for the best ways to represent a SSC transformation process diagrammatically, 92.3% of the respondents noted that a transformation roadmap and a framework could be used to facilitate the transformation towards SSCs as shown in Figure 8.6.

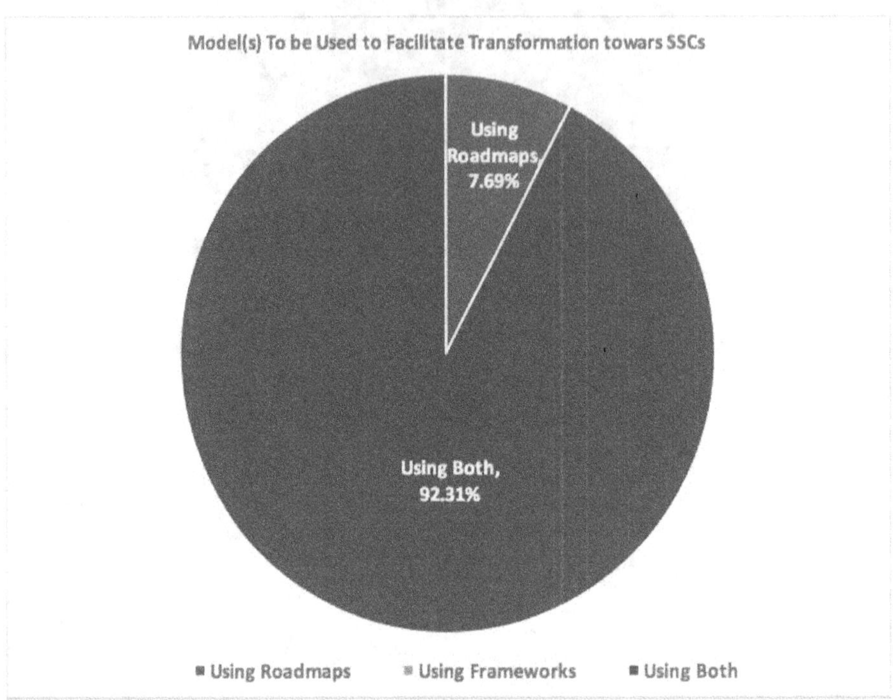

Figure 8.6: Insights on How to Represent a Transformation Process

This section also asks the respondents to provide their insights regarding a set of components proposed to be considered throughout a SSC transformation process and to introduce any missed ones. Although the first question of this section requests the respondents to assess the level of importance of the city vision, mission, strategies, and goals as a single component, this question treats them separately. It first asks about the significance of identifying a SSC vision and mission statements and then the necessity of identifying the transformation process strategies, goals, and objectives. Results show that 85% of responses indicated the necessity of identifying a SSC vision and mission statements while all of them agreed on the need of identifying the transformation strategies, goals, and objects.

Other components to be rated by this question includes the consideration of the city context and needs; engaging of various types of stakeholders; checking current city assets and readiness; identifying relevant CSFs and KPIs; prioritizing transformation activities;

creating a financial feasibility study and action plan; monitoring and evaluation; enhancing a transformation process through continuous improvements; announcing achievements; and producing more changes. The majority of the respondents, with 92%, emphasized the necessity of considering the components related to the city context and needs, stakeholders' engagement, city assets and readiness, CSFs, prioritization of activities, announcing achievements, and producing of more changes. As for the other components, all respondents agreed unanimously on their significance. The analysis of this question is illustrated in Figure 8.7 along with the related spreadsheet.

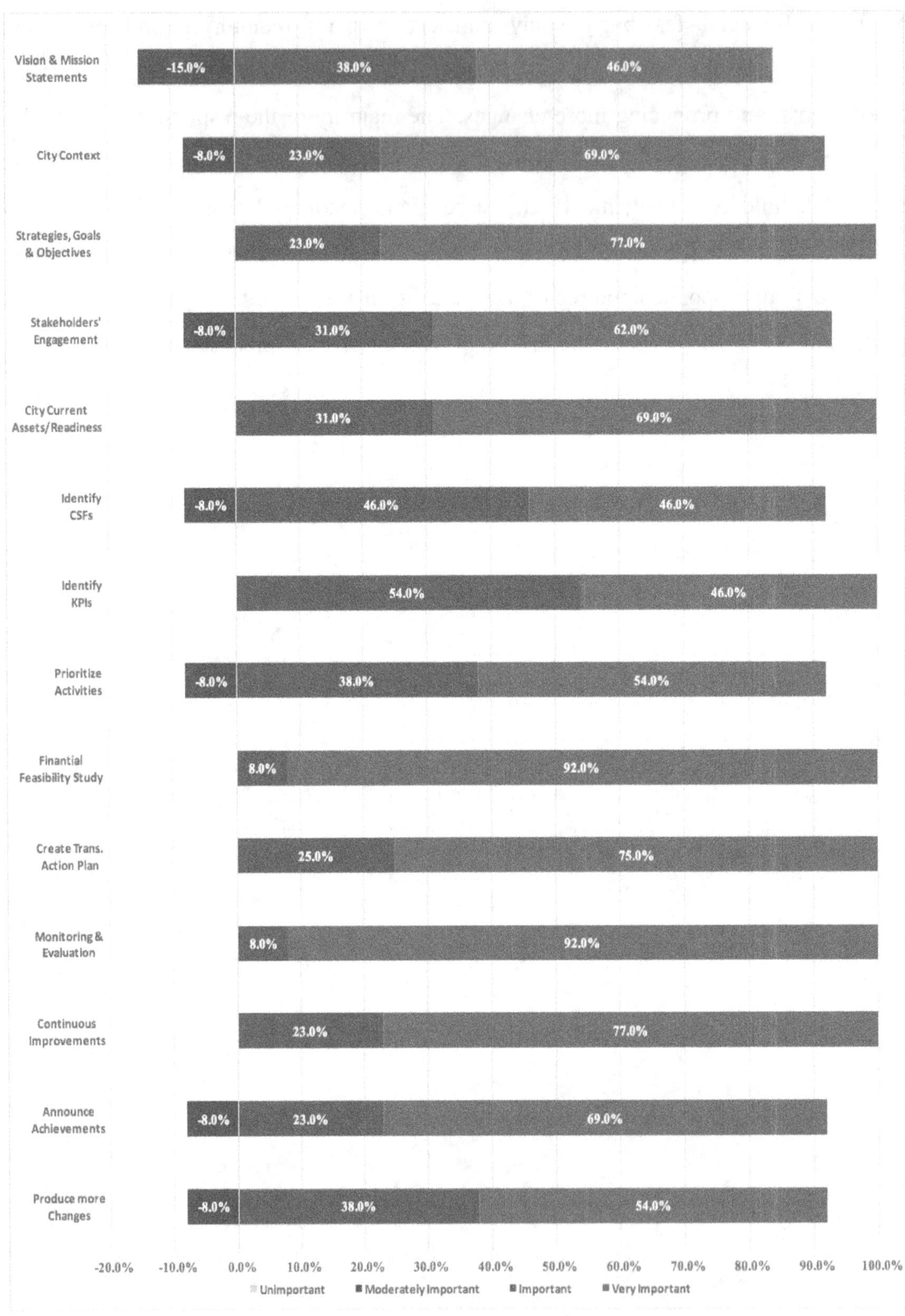

Figure 8.7: Significance of Different Types of Components in a SSC Project

The last question in this section captures opinions regarding the challenges that may face a SSC transformation process. Results show that any shortage in the financial support of a SSC project might harmfully affect a transformation process. The lack of local awareness and shortages in local digital infrastructure only got 54% and 69% respectively, meaning that their effect on the workflow of a transformation process is not crucial. However, increasing the local awareness through citizens' engagement in a SSC project and announcing achievements as well as developing the needed digital infrastructure to close the identified gap are a must. Both, the lack of skilled people and the complexity of integrating SSC systems together got 77%, which is fairly high effect. Some respondents also shed light on other challenges. This includes the lack of decision makers at the government level to provide the support needed to realize a transformation process. In addition to the lack public and private partnerships (PPP), especially to provide the financial support and facilitate the development and delivery of a SSC solutions and services. This is illustrated in Figure 8.8.

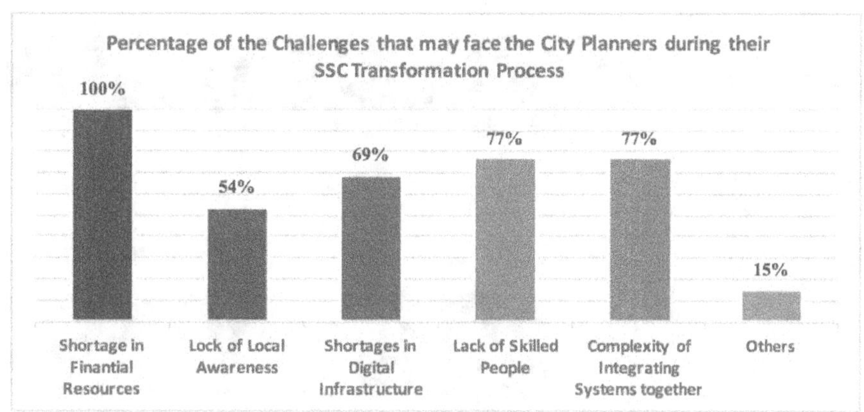

Figure 8.8: Percentages of the Challenges that may face a SSC Project

8.5.4.2   Section 2: City Readiness for Change

For any transformation process to succeed, a minimum set of requirements should be available to boost the realization of this process. In the context of SSCs, availability of these requirements varies from city to another depending on the development level of a city. The latter is measured based on the current city assets regarding its hard, soft, and digital (i.e. hardware and software) infrastructures. The lack of any of these components is denoted as a gap to be closed throughout the SSC transformation process solutions.

This section aims at examining the insights of the experts participating in the validation process in relation to the need for checking the current city assets, when this assessment should take place, and how to measure the readiness of current city assets. As illustrated in Figure 8.9, about 85% of insights tended to assess the hard infrastructure and software component of the digital infrastructure of a city before planning the SSC transformation activities. In turn, there was a collective agreement on the necessity of assessing the soft infrastructure and the digital hardware infrastructure component of a city before planning the activities.

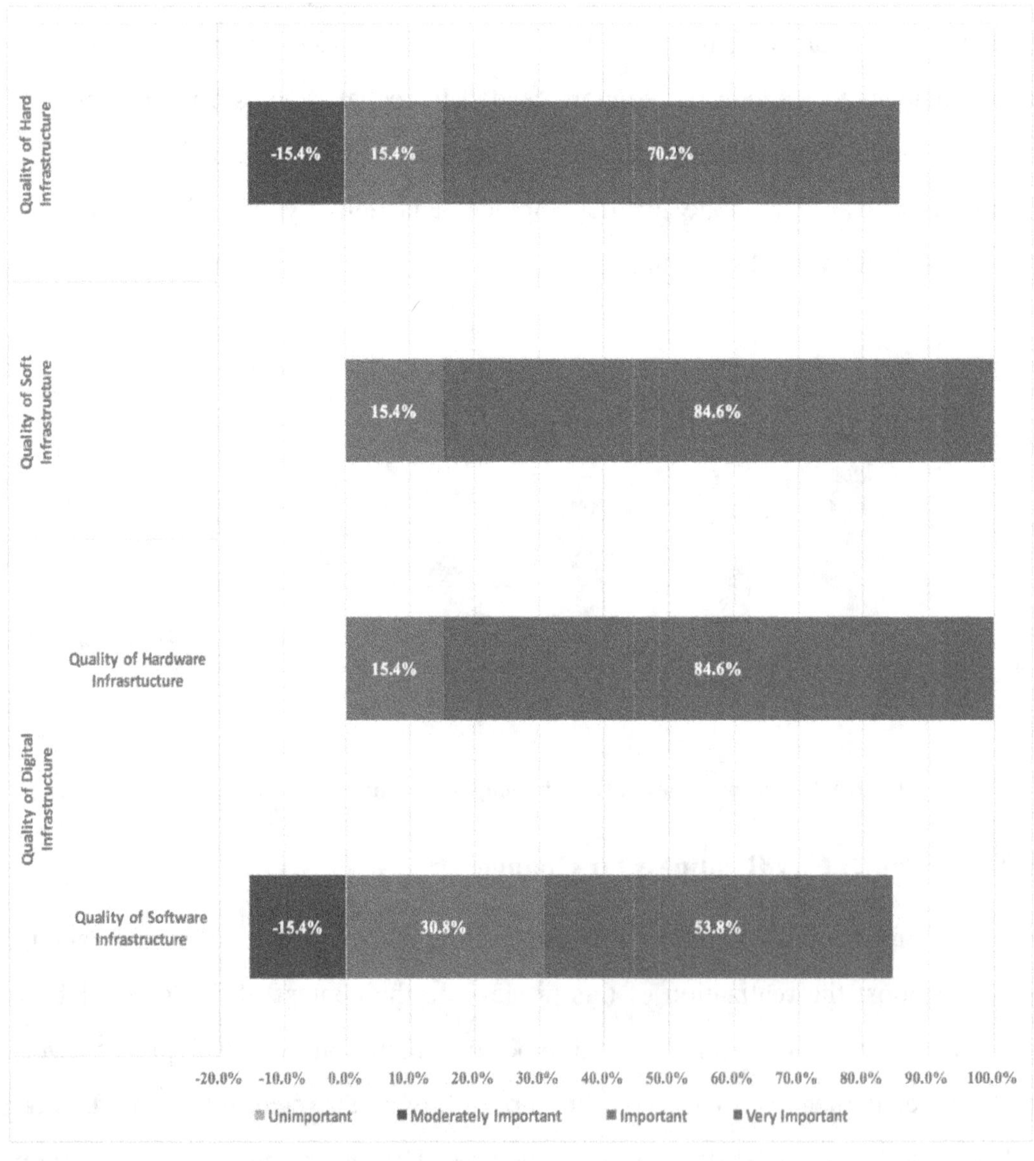

Figure 8.9: Significance of Assessing the Current City Assets

About half of the respondents preferred to check the city assets after the vision phase and before the planning phase of a transformation process. Others stated that this should take place during the vision phase, 38%, or during the planning phase, 8%. Figure 8.10 illustrates the responses regarding the appropriate stage during which to check the city readiness for change.

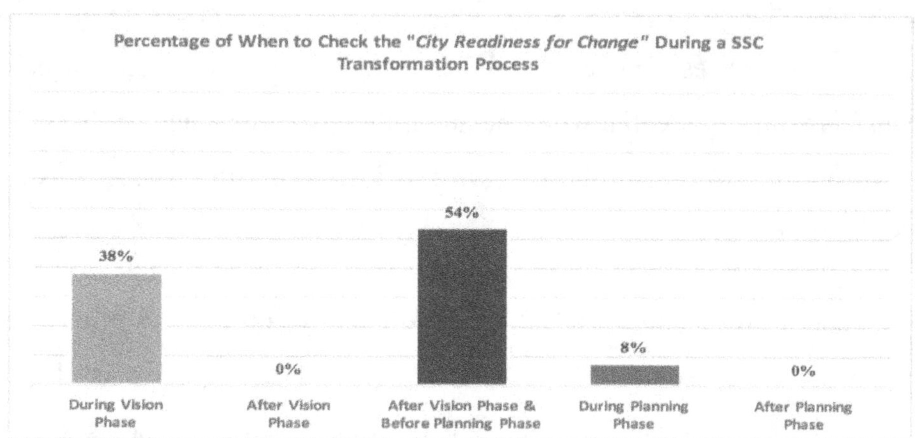

Figure 8.10: Percentage of When to Check the "City Readiness for Change"

Based on most respondents' insights, the quality of the current city assets has a significant impact on the directions of a SSC transformation process, as shown in Figure 8.11. The latter, as suggested by selected respondents, could be measured using a set of appropriate KPIs, surveys, and the Gross Domestic Product (GDP) estimate of a city.

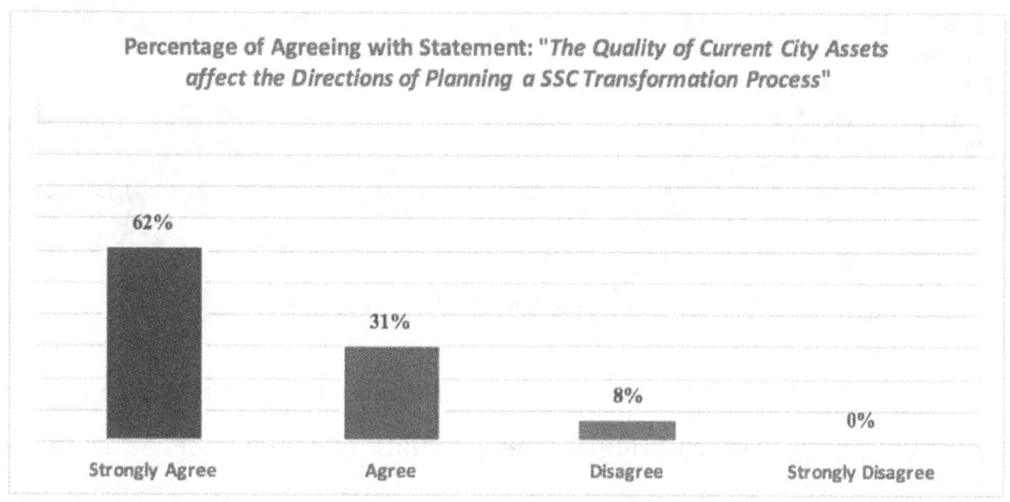

Figure 8.11: Effect of Current City Assets on Transformation Process Planning Directions

8.5.4.3   Section 3: City Plan and Transformation Activities

Transformation towards SSCs leads to different changes at all city levels. The type of changes varies from city to another depending on a city context, attributes, needs, starting point, and SSC objectives to be achieved. These changes are realized through a series of solutions and services to be delivered over the SSC six dimensions. This section aims at capturing the respondents' insights on the impact of the city context on the selection of SSC solutions and services. This also includes their insights on a series of components that are considered to be essential while planning these solutions and services. Finally, it asks the respondents to estimate the necessity of identifying the project's assumptions, constraints and risks.

A notable number of respondents (69%) regarded the city context as a primary engine to identify and plan the SSC solutions and services. Selected experts considered the SSC six dimensions as the core issue while planning the transformation process solutions and services. Figure 8.12 reports on the responses.

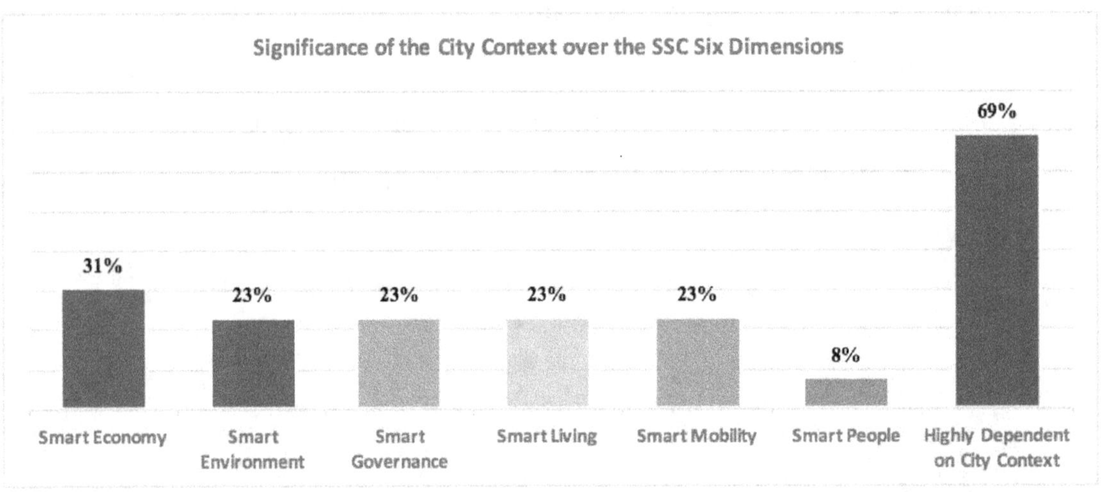

Figure 8.12: Significance of the City Context

There is a set of main issues that should be considered while planning a SSC solutions and services. These include ensuring the sustainability of a city, meeting urban needs, improving quality of life of citizens, considering the SSC six dimension, and city context along with the use of the ICTs to deliver environmentally friendly and viable solutions. The questionnaire asks each respondent to rate each of these components. Results show that the significance rates of considering the sustainability of a city and its context are 92% and 85% respectively. The entire responses, in turn, agreed on the necessity of considering the remaining components as essential issues while planning a SSC solutions and services, as illustrated in Figure 8.13.

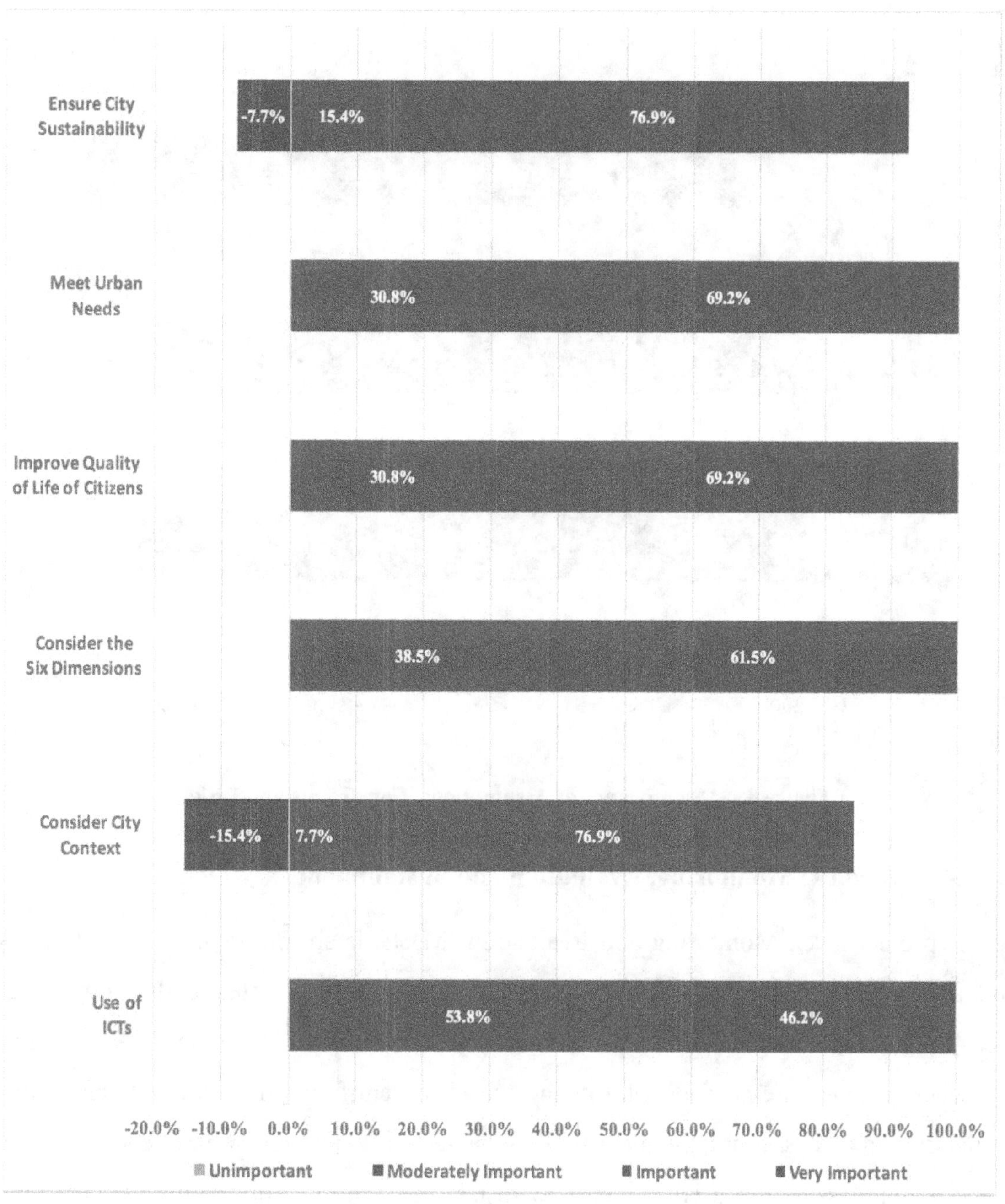

Figure 8.13: Components to consider while planning a SSC Solutions and Services

Finally, the questionnaire asks each respondent to rate the importance level of identifying the transformation process assumptions, constraints, and risks. With a total agreement on the identification of the assumptions, 92% of the respondent emphasized the significance of the identification of the transformation constrains and risks, as illustrated in Figure 8.14.

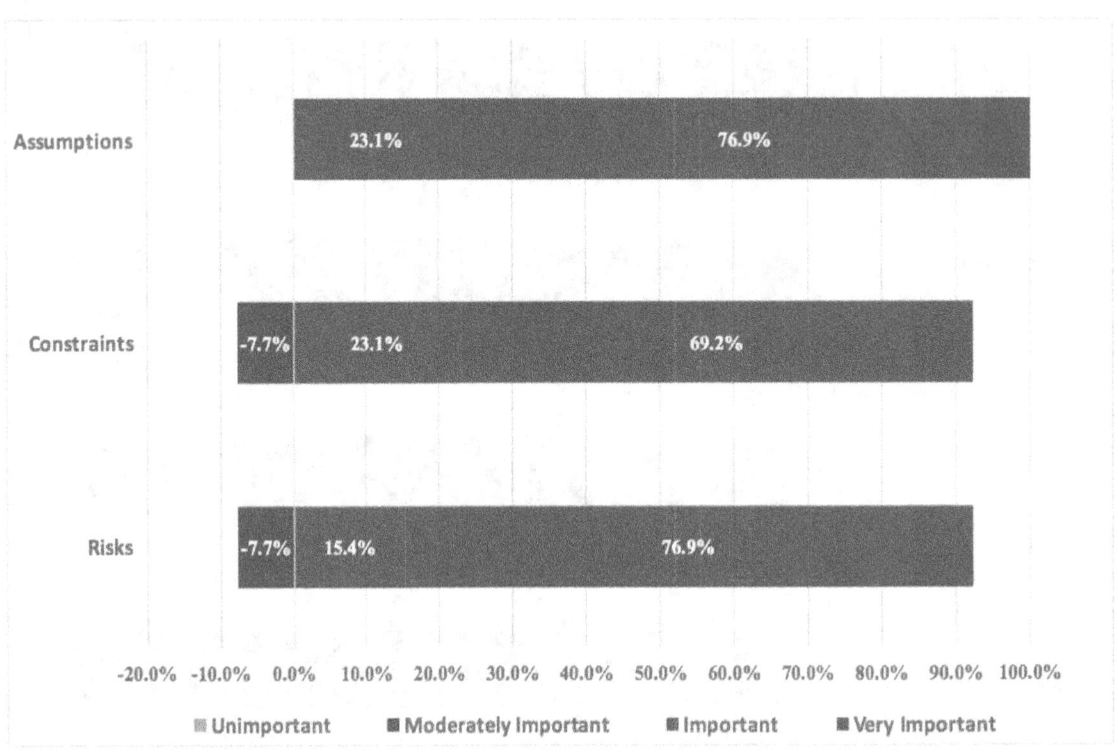

Figure 8.14: Significance of Assumptions, Constraints and Risks

8.5.4.4   Section 4: Monitoring, Evaluation and Sustainment

At the project level, Monitoring and Evaluation (M&E) is an important process to track and assess the implementation and outcomes of the project systemically. It helps in measuring the effectiveness of the project, determining if the project is on track and when and where changes are needed. It forms the basis for identifying the modifications needed on the project and assessing the quality of conducted activities. The report generated from the M&E process is then used as a base to sustain the project through improvements and production of additional changes.

This section focuses on measuring the significance of the M&E in a SSC project and when each should take place and how. It also captures the opinions of the experts in relation to the type of techniques to be used to sustain a SSC transformation process. As for the need for M&E, results show that all respondents unanimously agreed on its importance as shown in Figure 8.15.

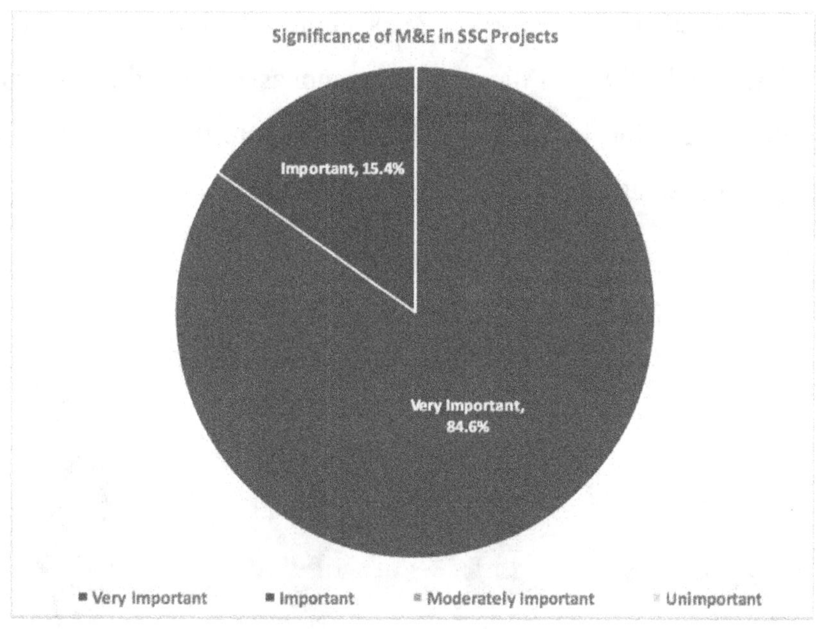

Figure 8.15: Significance of Monitoring and Evaluation in SSC Projects

The next question asks respondents about their insights on when the monitoring and evaluation should take place during a transformation process. For both, each respondent can select all appropriate answers from a set of options that are "During Planning Phase", "After Planning Phase", "During Implementation", and "After Implementation". For monitoring, the percentage of each option was as 65.1%, 53.8%, 76.9%, and 69.2% respectively. In turn, the percentages for evaluation were 30.8%, 38.5%, 46.2%, and 92.3% respectively, as illustrated in Figure 8.16 (a). Although some respondents supposed that the evaluation might start at the planning phase, it is clear from the results that most of them agreed on the necessity of conducting the evaluation after implementing a SSC solutions and services (92.3%). However, answers to the monitoring showed that this practice should take place starting from the planning phase (65.1%) up until finishing the implementation of services (69.2%). As a result, the monitoring could be identified as a continuous process of observations and checking of the progress and quality of a transformation process over a period of time. On the other hand, the evaluation aims at assessing the transformation process outputs and introducing a series of recommendations to decision makers about the current situations and future trends.

Based on the questionnaire analysis, the CSFs and KPIs are used as tools to realize the M&E process, with a rate of 69.2% for the CSFs and 84.6% for the KPIs, as illustrated in Figure 8.16 (b). Although 30.8% of the responses emphasized that the CSFs are used only for evaluation, the discussion in Section 7.2.4 demonstrate that they are often used for both, monitoring and evaluation.

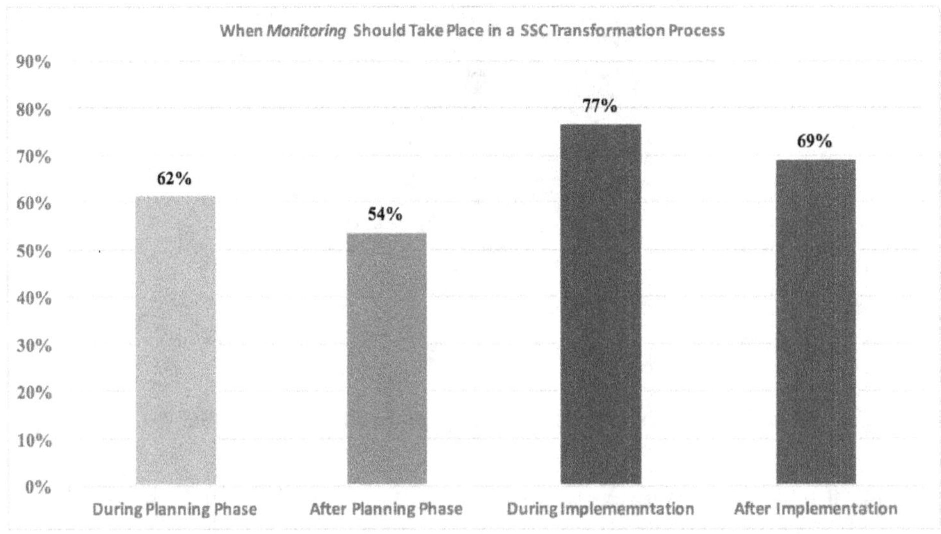

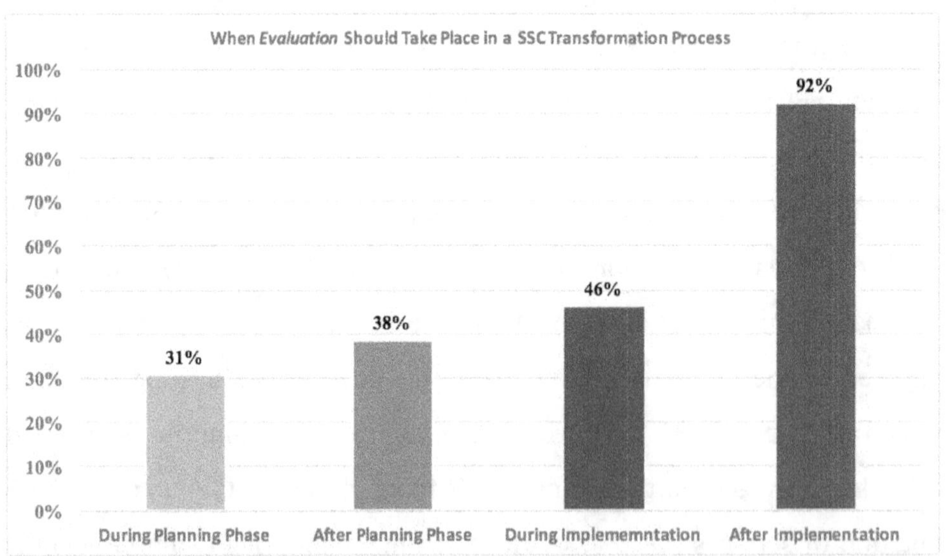

(a)

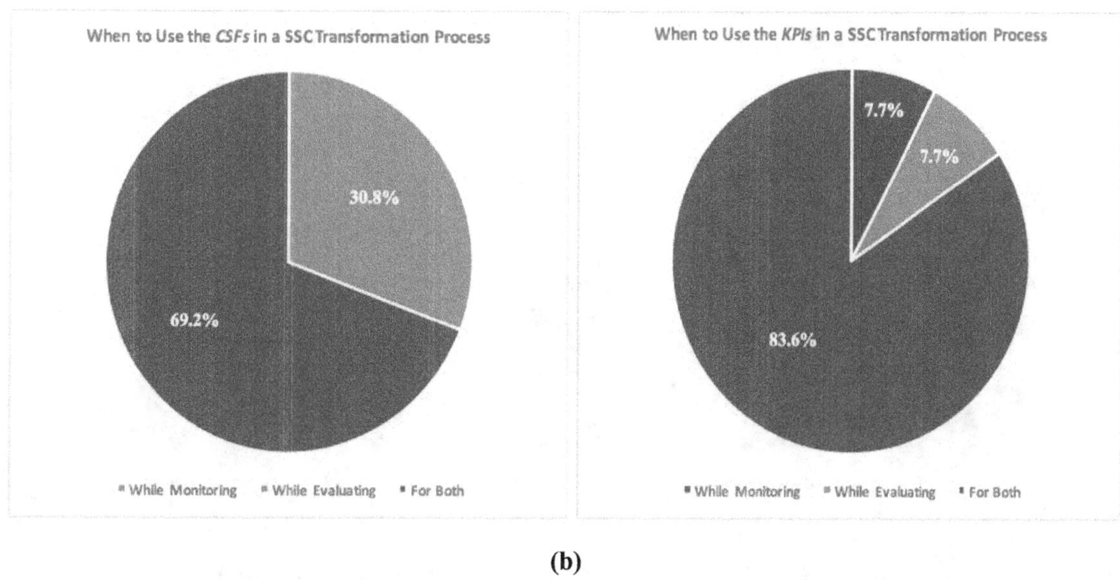

(b)

Figure 8.16: (a) When Monitor & Evaluate should take Place and (b) How to Realize Each

There are many benefits for M&E. This includes learning from previous experiences to avoid repeating the same mistakes and providing a set of recommendations for future improvements. The results of the M&E process might be also shared with others as practices to learn from. The questionnaire asks each respondent to rate this set of benefits and provide any suggestions regarding missing ones, if there are any.

Regarding learning from previous experiences to avoid repeating the same mistakes, the rating of these two components came as 77% and 85% respectively. The benefit of recommendations for future improvements got the highest rate with 92%, while producing of more changes got the lowest rate of 62%. Some respondents suggested other benefits of the M&E, including measuring the impact of a transformation process and ensuring the most efficient and effective use of resources. Figure 8.17 reports on the responses.

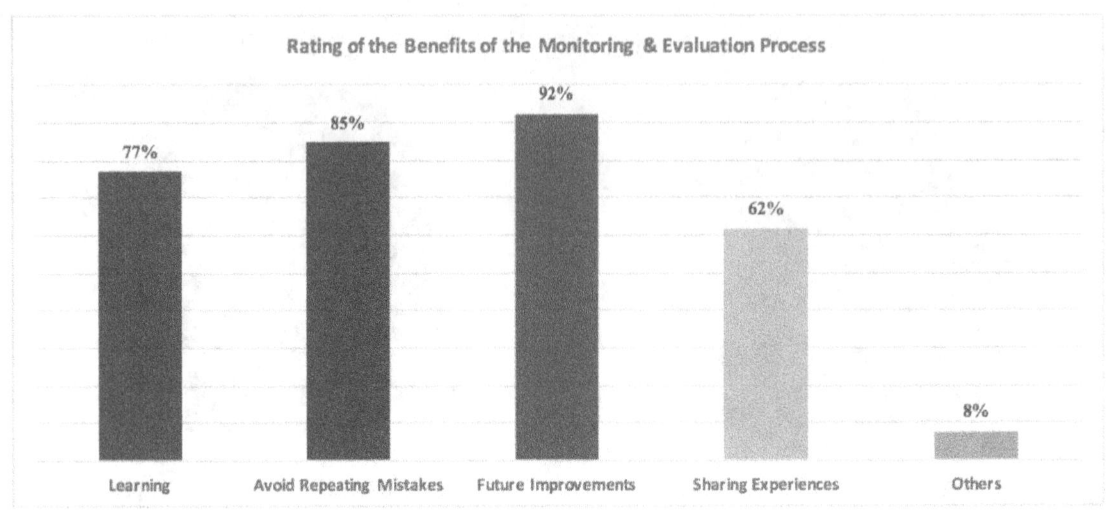

Figure 8.17: Rating of the Benefits of the Monitoring and Evaluation Process

At the final part of this Section, the questionnaire asks the respondents to provide their insights regarding the techniques that could be used to sustain a transformation process. Most of the respondents indicated that this could be achieved through learning from previous experiences (92%), announcing and sharing achievements with others (85%), and through continuous improvements (85%). About half of responses (69%) considered the production of more changes as one of these techniques as well. None of the respondents provided suggestions regarding missed or neglected techniques. Figure 8.18 summarizes the answers of this question.

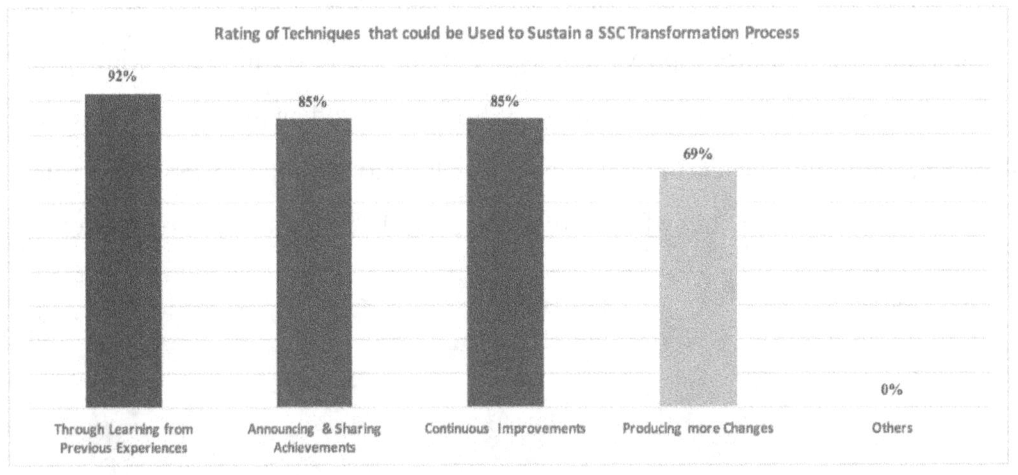

Figure 8.18: Rating of Techniques that could be used to Sustain a SSC Transformation Process

8.5.4.5 Section 5: Stakeholders' Engagement in a SSC Project

The last section of the validation questionnaire is dedicated to highlight the significance of stakeholders' engagement in a SSC transformation process. It includes questions to collect the insights of participants regarding the need for engaging different types of stakeholders in a SSC project and how to realize this engagement process.

The first question captures the opinions of the respondents on the impact of stakeholders in a SSC project. It asks each respondent to provide his/her level of agreement with the statement: *"One of the main issues that affect the success of a Smart Sustainable City project is engaging the key stakeholders in a transformation process"*. Given its importance, there was a collective approval about the crucial impact of stakeholders on a SSC project, as illustrated in Figure 8.19.

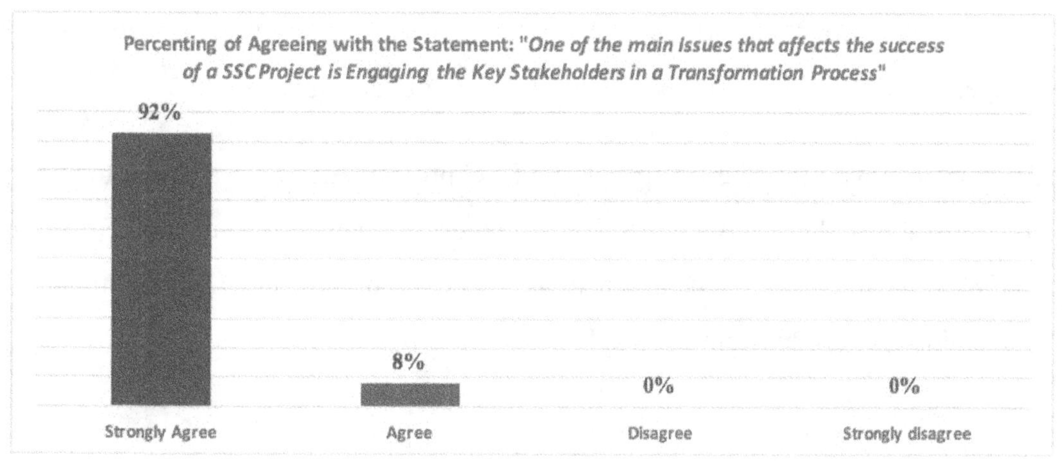

Figure 8.19: Impact of Stakeholders on a SSC Project

Different types of stakeholders should be engaged in a SSC transformation process. The engagement level, in turn, differs from one type to the other based on the effect of this stakeholder on a transformation process and its outcomes. In the context of this research, stakeholders are classified into three main categories, namely, those who have a major effect on a transformation process, those who are affected by a transformation process, and those who may be interested in a SSC project and its outputs.

Stakeholders who have a major effect on a SSC project are divided into two types. The first includes entities or parties involved in the delivery of a SSC project (e.g. the government and ICT companies). Results show that the engagement of this type of stakeholders is a must, with 69% for option "Very Important" and 31% for "Important". The second type of this category includes those who are responsible about determining the context of each activity of a transformation process. This type got the same rating results as that for the first type, as shown in Figure 8.20 (left hand side).

Stakeholders who are affected by a SSC project are either affected directly by a project or may/may not be directly/indirectly affected by it depending on the activity context. 85% of responses indicated the need for engaging all stakeholders that are directly affected by a SSC project by selecting the "Very Important" option, while 8% viewed this engagement as "Important" and 8% as "Moderately Important". For those who may or may not be affected by a SSC project, 23% of respondents viewed their engagement as a must, 62% highlighted the importance of their engagement, 8% treated their engagement as moderately important, and 8% tended to unengaging them in a transformation process at all. Figure 8.20 (middle part) sheds light on these ratings comparisons.

Finally, for those who may be interested in a SSC project, such as academia, media, and social organizations, there was a collective agreement on engaging them in a SSC project. In fact, 38% rated the need to engage them as "Very Important" and 62% as "Important", as depicted in Figure 8.20 (right hand side).

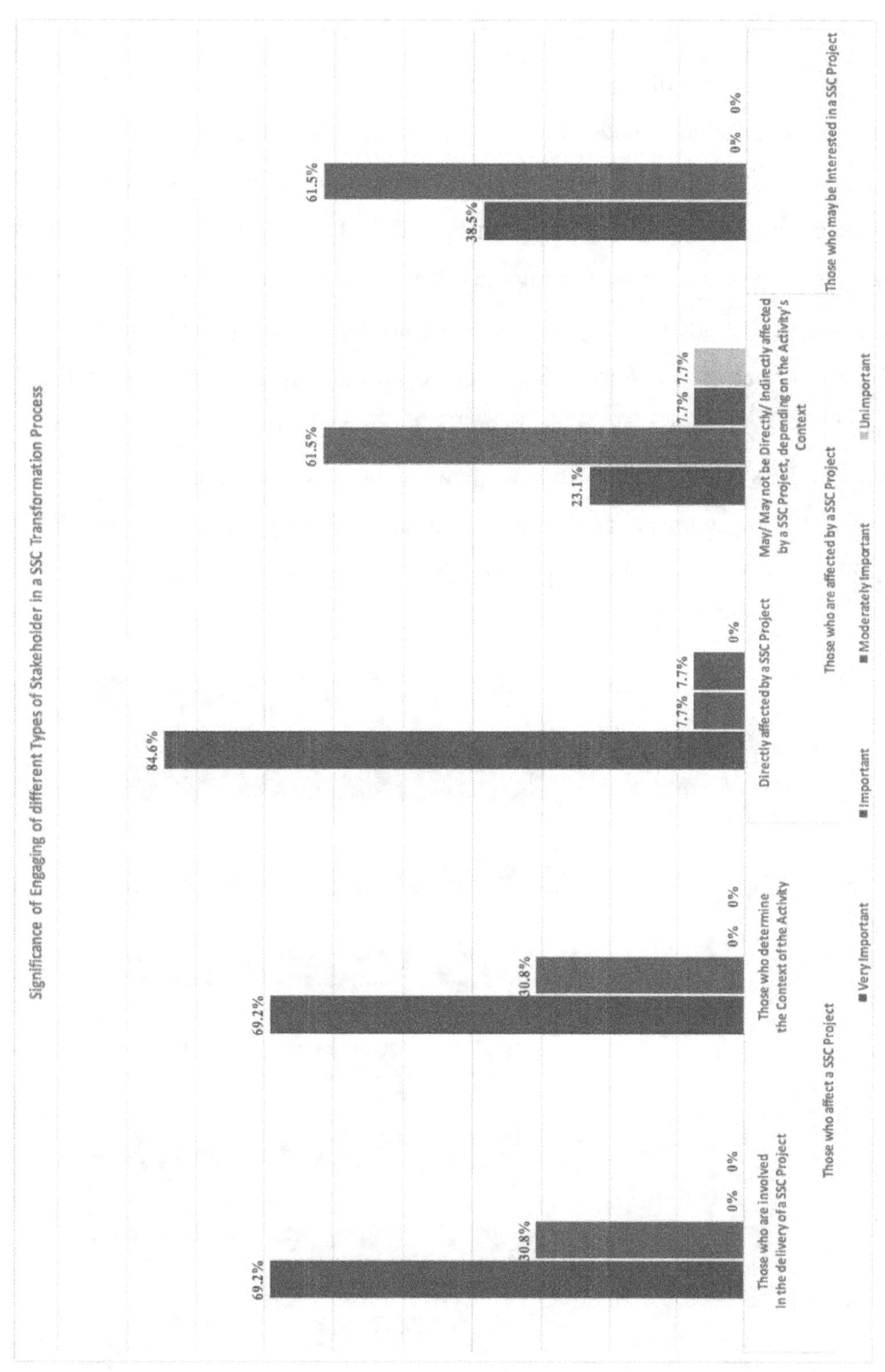

Figure 8.20: Significance of Engaging Different Types of Stakeholders in a SSC Project

259

Last but not least, a solid model is needed to realize an effective and efficient engagement of the different types of stakeholders in a SSC project. This research proposed a new stakeholder engagement model for the benefits of SSC projects as discussed in Section 7.2.1. The last question of the questionnaire is meant to validate the proposed stages and components of this model. As shown in Figure 8.21, 92% of the experts contributing to the validation process considered regarded the proposed stages of the model as necessary with level of importance varying between moderately important, important and very important. About 85% of respondents agreed on the stages of sharing information with stakeholders regarding their roles in a SSC project and mapping them into relevant activities. This is in-line with the newly introduced components related to the stakeholders' engagement model of this research. Finally, all respondents stressed the need for monitoring and evaluating the performance of each stakeholder.

Figure 8.21: Significance of the proposed Stakeholders' Engagement Model Components

8.5.5　Data Analysis: Qualitative Method

Another interesting way to validate the contributions is by undertaking a contextualized analysis. To recall, several experts at the senior level from distinct countries contributed to the validation process. These experts provided their insights on the posed questions from their own perspectives influenced by their own contexts. Studying the conformity or disagreement between experts originating from different contexts would be interesting to capture especially that it is difficult to have access to inside knowledge on top projects. Thus, building on the provided responses as possible constitute a value-added to this research.

When asked about checking the current state and challenges of a city regarding its economic, social, environmental, and political aspects, all experts without exception rated it as important or very important. At the readiness level of the city, this research considered checking the current assets of a city as an essential step before planning the SSC solutions and services. This is in-line with all respondents irrespective of their contexts. The only variance is in the identified level of agreement on the necessity of checking existing city infrastructures. In fact, the expert from Korea (Seoul) strongly agreed on the need of checking the hard, soft, and digital (i.e. hardware and software) infrastructures. The expert from Italy agreed on the hard, soft, and hardware infrastructures and moderately agree on the software ones. The expert from Russia (Moscow) had the same response as that of Korea whereas the expert from Japan strongly agreed on the soft infrastructure and agreed on others. When asked about the importance of engaging different types of stakeholders in a SSC transformation process, all experts rated it as important or very important. In addition, there was an agreement among experts irrespective of their context on the importance of engaging the stakeholders who affect or may be interested in a SSC project. Answers varies in relation to those stakeholders who may be affected by a SSC project. When asked about the significance of assumptions, constraints, and risks, specifically, about identifying the activities, limitations, barriers, and problems that may face a transformation process, all experts agreed. However, the level of agreement varied. All experts strongly agreed on the need of the monitoring and evaluation of a SSC transformation process whereas the experts from Italy and Japan agreed to it. When asked about the techniques that can be followed to sustain a SSC transformation process, experts from Japan and Canada agreed that this could be realized through continuous improvements while all other experts strongly agreed on the importance of this. Answers from the UK were distributed between an agreement and strongly agreement. Moreover, irrespective of the context, all experts, expect the expert from Japan, stated that the best way to represent a SSC transformation process is by creating a transformation roadmap and framework. Expert from Japan stated that this can be represented using only a roadmap.

The above shows that the context has an influence on the answers of the respondents in selected cases. All-in-all, none of the answers of the experts lacked harmony. In fact, the context in selected instances, affected the level of positive agreement between experts as in agreeing or strongly agreeing with the posed question.

This contextual or qualitative analysis added to the presented quantitative analysis show that the responses of the experts are in-line with the contributions of this research.

8.6   Conclusion

The conducted validation survey questionnaire achieved its aims. Its results formed a sense of satisfaction regarding the proposed roadmap and framework. Assessments obtained from the questionnaire represent a success. They confirm the proposed components of the new innovative roadmap and framework.

Although the response rate was low (52%), respondents were selective with wide experiences in the areas related to smart cities, sustainable cities, and urban planning and development. Two methods were used to analyze collected data statistically, namely, consensus and dissention measures method and frequency method. Both methods demonstrated that responses tended to confirm the hypotheses of this research captured through the various posed questions.

The next chapter provides an overall discussion along with its limitations and challenges.

CHAPTER NINE: DISCUSSION AND LIMITATIONS

9.1 Introduction

This book aimed at investigating the emergence of the concept of SSCs as a desired goal for present and future urban development, which is rapidly gaining global attention, especially with the existence of hundreds of SSC initiatives around the world. The research focused on investigating existing transformation models in the literature, identifying a gap in knowledge based on theories, related studies from neighboring disciplines, and observations, and then coming up with a roadmap and framework that capture the essential aspects to be considered while transforming cities into SSCs. Although this study researched its aims, different extensions of this research still deserve further considerations.

This chapter summarizes the research of the book, discusses its findings and contributions, and finally points out its limitations. In Section 9.2, a summary of the book is carried out. Section 9.3 presents discussion on the research findings and contributions. The research limitations are pointed out in Section 9.4. The chapter concludes in Section 9.5.

9.2 Summary of the Book

This book introduced a conceptual roadmap and framework for the transformation towards SSCs. The proposed innovative models were validated using the survey questionnaire instrument, by which a group of experts from different countries in Europe, Americas, and Asia provided their insights regarding the proposed phases, components, and tools of the introduced models. The validation findings showed a high degree of agreement with most of the proposed elements.

Chapter Two reviewed existing definitions and dimensions of a SSC concept, which facilitated the selection of an adequate definition and dimensions to be adopted by this research. The chapter also reviewed existing SSC transformation models. Designers of these models neglected essential aspects that should be considered in a transformation process. Accordingly, the research showed that the existing models are suffering from different types of gaps in knowledge. The role of ICTs as an enabler to realize the SSC initiatives was discussed as well. The final part of this chapter highlighted existing SSC initiatives with a special focus on the Arab region. This also includes the series of challenges that are facing the SSC initiatives globally and in the region. The research methodology was reviewed in details in Chapter Three.

This book investigated existing theories related to the phenomenon of SSCs. Results showed an absence of a specific theory for SSCs. Given the need for a robust theory to focus research, this research proposed a novel link between the ToC and SSCs and used this link to introduce an unprecedented theoretical logic model for the transformation towards SSCs. The latter has been explained in details in Chapter Four.

The fundamental contributions of this research are presented in Chapters Five, Six, and Seven. Chapter Five reviewed existing definitions of the concepts of transformation, roadmap, and framework in the context of SSCs. Results showed inconsistence definitions in the literature. This book, therefore, introduced a new perspective on these concepts. It proposed revised definitions encompasses the essential aspects to consider in a SSC transformation process, including its roadmap and framework. In Chapters Six and Seven, the proposed innovative roadmap and framework were introduced and discussed in details. The roadmap provided the guidance needed to realize a SSC transformation process systematically. The proposed phases and components under each phase presented a comprehensive, systematic transformation process. The roadmap started by examining the current state of the city, identifying its urban challenges that need quick actions, and then drawing the vision and directions to overcome these challenges. It also emphasized the need of assessing the current city capacities regarding the quality of its hard, soft, and digital infrastructures along with the level of its current digital literacy. The need of identifying the transformation process assumptions, constraints, and risks were pointed out as well. The roadmap also affirmed the necessity of sustaining the transformation process through learning from previous mistakes, continuous improvements, sharing of best practices, and production of new changes. The framework, in turn, pointed out and introduced a list of tools for turning the roadmap phases and components (i.e. activities) into actions.

The process of validating the innovative transformation roadmap and framework took place in Chapter Eight. The survey questionnaire instrument was used for this purpose. A group of experts from different countries in Europe, Americas, and Asia was contacted to provide their insights on the proposed transformation roadmap and framework. Findings revealed a high degree of acceptance of the proposals. Some recommendations also provided the potential for the future improvements.

9.3   Discussion

9.3.1   Contribution of the Research

This research records different contributions. Through analytical review of the literature, it provided new definitions for the concepts of transformation, roadmap, and framework in the context of SSCs. It proposed a novel linkage between the ToC and SSCs. Based on this identified theoretical relation, an unprecedented theoretical logic model for the transformation towards SSCs was introduced. This model highlighted the minimum essential elements to be considered during a SSC transformation process. With the aim of closing the identified gap in relation to existing transformation roadmaps and frameworks, this research proposed a coherent, systematic six-phase transformation roadmap along with its related framework. It is important noting that the innovative roadmap and framework were developed to consider all objectives and aspects of a SSC, which were noted and extracted from the definition of a SSC concept.

Through the proposed novel roadmap, the research revealed that assessing the current state of a city regarding its economic, social, environmental, and political challenges is a must before agreeing and stating a city vision. It also revealed that checking the city readiness for change prior to planning a transformation process is essential. The identified gap could then be closed through planning a series of adequate solutions. This results in a more effective, sustainable transformation process. The research showed the necessity of identifying the transformation assumptions, constrains, and risks. This provides a set of predictions regarding the challenges that might be faced by a SSC project and how to overcome or minimize them. In addition, the research demonstrated the need of developing a SSC smart infrastructure and integrated platform. The smart infrastructure in the context of this research refers not only to the digital infrastructure, but also to the hard and soft infrastructures along with the level of the current digital literacy of a city. The integrated platform ensures the connectivity of all city systems, enabling the collection and manipulation of city data and sharing of the extracted knowledge. The innovative smart solutions are to be developed and delivered over a SSC smart infrastructure through the integrated platform. The research argued that at least one smart solution is needed under each of the SSC six dimensions. In addition, it showed that any transformation process should be sustainable; thereby; ensuring a proper quality of life for citizens.

Through the proposed novel framework, the research provided the tools needed to realize a SSC transformation roadmap. The proposed stakeholders' engagement model ensures a systematic, totally managed participation of various types of stakeholder in a SSC project from an early stage. The model starts by identifying, grouping, and mapping stakeholders based on their roles in a transformation process. It also opens the door for looking for partnerships with stakeholders that can support a SSC project. It then ensures the involvement of relevant stakeholders in the monitoring and evaluation process of a SSC project in addition to the necessity of assessing the performance of each stakeholder. The research also proposed a generic list of areas under each of the SSC six dimensions to consider when transforming a city into a SSC. This list, subdivided into sub-lists, could be customized based on the city context, needs, and local interests and used as a reference in a SSC transformation process. The list is a result of intersecting the constituents of the sustainability pillars, city dimensions, quality of life dimensions, and SSC dimensions. It also considers the city context and the role of ICTs in providing innovative solutions that are viable and environmentally friendly.

9.3.2   Importance of the Research Comparing to Others

To our knowledge, this is the first study to examine the necessity of checking the city readiness for change prior to planning the SSC solutions. Only the ITU-T FG-SSC (2015b) recommends to collect relevant data regarding the status of the city's ICT infrastructure and its usage at a city level. However, the ICT infrastructure is not the only resource required in a transformation process (Ruhel, 2014; Vogel, 2012; Kohel, 2016). There are also the city hard and soft infrastructures to be assessed as well. On another note, checking the ICTs usage level in a city is not adequate. The digital literacy of a city is a broader concept. It includes the ICT skills, knowledge skills, information skills, media skills, learning to learn skills, civic skills, among others (UNESCO, 2011).

This research also emphasizes the necessity of examining the current state of the city regarding its economic, social, environmental, and political challenges prior to creating a SSC vision. Only SCC (2015) recommends this as a preliminary stage of a transformation process. Moreover, this research points out the need of identifying the transformation process assumptions, constraints, and risks. The BSI (2014) is the only one that sheds light on the need of the identification of the constraints and risks without mentioning the importance of the assumptions. In addition, this research considers the SSC six dimensions and their related factors. Only EPIC (2013) pointed out its consideration of the six dimensions. However, EPIC provides the SSC services and solutions over the cloud using PaaS and SaaS delivery models. It also controls the solutions delivered over its platform. The services are web-based and controlled by EPIC team. With the different shortages of cloud computing (Apostu et al., 2013), developing a city into a SSC based only on the cloud computing techniques is insufficient.

Finally, this research, to our knowledge, is the first study that provides a systematic model for stakeholders' engagement in a SSC transformation process. Other studied mentioned the necessity of engaging various types of stakeholders without providing any solutions to realize this engagement process. In addition, this study introduces the first generic list of areas under each of the SSC six dimensions to consider when transforming a city into a SSC. Other studies only suggest a series of solutions based on their observations and point of views regarding the needed initiatives to consider throughout a transformation process. However, the proposed list is the first one that is being created based of the objectives of a SSC as a whole. This includes, the sustainability of a city, city attributes, quality of life of citizens, and SSC dimension taking into account the city context and the use of ICTs.

Like other studies, this research emphasizes the necessity of creating a strong city vision and mission statements as well as identifying a set of strategies for turning this vision into reality. It also shows the need of developing a SSC smart infrastructure and integrated platform. Finally, it considers the benefits of learning from previous mistakes to avoid repeating them, continuous improvements of delivered solutions and services, announcing achievements and sharing of best practices with others to learn from, and producing of more changes to ensure the continuing of a transformation process.

9.3.3 Implications and Applications of the Research

The findings of this research can contribute considerably to the transformation of cities from their traditional structures into smart and sustainable ones. It forms a quantum leap in this area of research, opening the door for others to have a holistic overview of the aspects that should be considered during a SSC transformation process. It points out the problems and deficiencies in existing models provides solutions to overcome them.

Practically, the research provides a coherent, systematic roadmap and framework with a step-by-step guidance for city planners, decision makers, and key stakeholders on how to transform their cities into SSCs. The tools needed to support the realization of a SSC transformation process are pointed out and introduced. The proposed roadmap and framework designed to be applied on real cities. Given the time limitation, this was not realized. However, the flexibility of the proposed models as being able to be customized based on the city context makes them suitable for immediate practical application.

9.4 Research Limitations

Although the research has reached its aims, there is a list of limitations to shed light on. To start with, there is no general agreement yet on the definition and dimensions of the SSC concept. The latter have a major effect on the process of transforming cities into smart and sustainable ones. They shape the directions of the transformation models to realize their objectives and elements. Therefore, selecting an adequate definition and dimensions was needed. An extensive literature review on the subject matter was conducted, resulting in selecting the ITU-T definition and Giffinger et al. dimensions, supported by the needed justifications. This opens the door for others to select or propose another definition and dimensions of the concept.

Another limitation is related to the newness of the concept of SSCs. This limit the availability of detailed references related to the transformation roadmaps and frameworks in the literature. Only five roadmaps and four frameworks were found appropriate to be studied and analyzed. Most of existing reports, research papers, articles, books, and publications provide shallow details on the transformation process. Most of them provide only highlights or recommendations to consider without providing detailed, or even illustrations, regarding the transformation process phases, components, and tools. In addition, this research contacted different companies, who are working on Smart and Sustainable Cities projects (e.g. PwC and Deloitte) aiming at getting more details in relation to their used roadmaps and frameworks; however; none of them replied with the needed clarifications.

Another limitation is related to the absence of a theory for the transformation towards SSCs. After studying different theories from neighboring disciplines, such as those used in the sustainable urban development and city planning and management, this research opted the Theory of Change (ToC) as a theoretical foundation to propose a theoretical logic model for the transformation towards SSCs. This opens the door for other researchers to opt another theory or create a new one. In addition, transforming cities into SSCs is a long-term process that cannot be achieved over night. Transformation from traditional cities into SSCs did not fully happen in reality yet. As a result, the innovative roadmap and framework, like many others in the literature, are still in their conceptual forms without being applied or tested over real case studies. This limitation will be considered as one of the future directions of this research.

Finally, given the time limitation of this research it was not applicable to test the proposed models on real cities. To overcome this obstacle, the validation process was carried out using a survey questionnaire instrument. The latter were also faced by a set of limitations. The first limitation related to the minimum number of experts in the area of SSCs, especially in the Arab region. This poses a problem of finding a large number of experts to validate the proposed novel roadmap and framework. Second, many of the contacted experts, including those who are responsible about their cities' SSC projects, refused to contribute to the validation process, explaining that they need a permission from the higher levels in their countries. Last but not least, the minimum number of experts in the Arab region adding to it the challenges of contacting them drove this research to realize the validation process outside the region, specifically, in the United Kingdom. During the visit, the researcher made ace-to-face interviews with experts from different countries around the world, most of them provided their insights on the proposed models by filling out the validation questionnaire. In turn, most of the contacted experts via the electronic emails either refused to contribute or did not even reply to the submitted request.

9.5   Conclusion

This chapter provided an overall discussion on the research. It highlighted the research contributions, its importance comparing to other, its expected implications and possible application, and limitations.

Next chapter is dedicated to the conclusion with a focus on the future directions and recommendations.

CONCLUSION AND FUTURE DIRECTIONS

10.1 Introduction

This book has sought to advance understanding of transformational change within the area of Smart Sustainable Cities (SSCs), particularly, introducing a roadmap and framework for the benefit of transforming cities into SSCs.

Due to the alarming alert of the rapid urbanization along with its associated problems, many cities' leaders and planners are currently seeking to make their cities smarter and more sustainable. This forms a corner stone for the emergence of the concept of SSCs as a desired goal for present and future urban development. SSCs can help in overcoming the urbanization challenges and the limitations of traditional urban development, which is usually tends to manage urban services and infrastructure systems in silos. By leveraging the services that can be offered by the digital technologies, SSCs can help in improving the quality of life of citizens, offering new or enhancing existing city operations and services, and enhancing competitiveness.

Development of SSCs is highly complex. It is challenging and context-specific. The complexity of a SSC is related to its nature as a system-of-systems that integrates all city services together through a digital platform, which collects huge amount of data from different city levels to be analyzed and used based on needs. The challenges, in turn, vary from the sustainable financial investment required to support the development of a SSC to the need for unique governance solutions to make a city functioning as one organism.

Despite its complexity, many attempts are taking place to find an adequate transformation path to SSCs. This includes proposing roadmaps and frameworks to be used as a reference to guide a transformation process. It is worth noting that the transformation from traditional cities to smart and sustainable ones has not really happened yet. Meaning that, all proposed transformation models are currently still in their conceptual form or adopted to be applied on real cities, with no feedback on their efficiency and effectiveness.

This book investigates existing SSC transformation roadmaps and frameworks in the literature. Results show their incompleteness, which denote a gap in knowledge. Some of these models neglect the necessity of assessing the current state of the city regarding its economic, social, and environmental challenges. Others emphasize the need of engaging different types of stakeholders in a SSC transformation process without providing any tools to realize this engagement process. Most of the studies do not consider the six dimensions of a SSC and their related factors. Moreover, some studies list their suggested smart and sustainable solutions according to the analysis of existing literature reports and recommendations while others fully neglected this stage. The suggested solutions are neither context-specific nor selected according to cities' needs. They are also not directly derived for the six dimensions of a SSC, simply they are general solutions with no systematic basis behind their selection. None of the studies consider checking the city readiness for change regarding its current assets prior to planning a transformation process services and solutions. Adoption of a roadmap and framework that neglect essential aspects and objectives of a SSC leads to incomplete transformation process, or worst, it may cause the whole project to fail. As a result, the development of new transformation roadmap and framework that are more coherent and systematic is a must.

Stemming from the above, this book introduced first new definitions for the concepts of transformation, roadmap, and framework in the context of SSCs. It then introduced a new linkage between the ToC and SSCs and used this link to propose a novel theoretical logic model for the transformation towards SSCs. This theoretical model formed the basis for the proposed SSC six-phase transformation roadmap. The related transformation framework that provides the tools needed to realize a SSC transformation process was proposed as well.

10.2 Summary of the Findings

10.2.1 Proposed Definitions

This book proposed new definitions for the concepts of transformation, roadmap, and framework is the context of SSCs, aiming to close the gap in knowledge in existing ones in the literature. Following the literature-based method approach, or desk research technique, the proposed definitions are as below:

1. **Transformation Concept**: *Transformation towards SSCs is a complex multidimensional process through which changes are applied at all city levels; aiming to enhance the sustainability of a city and provide a high quality of life for its citizens through the use of ICTs and other means.*

2. **Roadmap Concept**: *A SSC roadmap provides a high-level view of the objectives and goals of the transformation process and identifies the transformation activities and milestones in order to realize the city's vision for being smart and sustainable.*

3. **Framework Concept**: *A SSC framework is a layered structure that leads city planners and relevant stakeholders throughout a transformation process by providing guidance on city readiness for change and the innovative solutions needed to grant urban sustainability and high quality of life for citizens.*

The proposed definitions aim at guiding city planners, policy and decision makers, and key stakeholders in having an overview understanding of these three concepts in the context of SSCs, helping them in developing and designing their cities transformation processes.

10.2.2 Unprecedented Theoretical Logic Model

This book introduced unprecedented link between the ToC and SSCs. It showed that the ToC elements and stages could be used as a reference to support the identification of a SSC transformation process phases and components. This link takes into consideration the specificity of a SSC as a new emerging field for the urban development through which variety of smart and sustainable solutions to urbanization challenges could be offered.

As discussed in Chapter Three, the introduced Theory of Change for the Transformation towards SSCs (ToSSC) consists of five stages the should be addressed in order, namely, (1) City Context: analyzing the current state (its economic, social, environmental, political conditions and needs), (2) Short, Medium and Long-term Changes, (3) Sequence of Transformation Activities, (4) Assumptions, Constraints, and Risks, (5) Transformational Change Roadmap and Framework.

The proposed theoretical logic model in turn was created based on the introduced link between the ToC and SSCs and existing practices in developing such a model in the literature. It highlights the minimum essential elements and components to be considered during the transformation process, thereby providing a holistic insight to city planners, policy and decision makers, and key stakeholders about how to transform their cities into smart and sustainable ones. The essential elements include considering the city context, examining existing gap in the city infrastructures, planning solutions and allocating resources needed to realize each, engaging stakeholders in a transformation process, monitoring and evaluation, and finally ensuring the continuity and sustainability of a transformation process.

10.2.3 Innovative Six-phase Transformation Roadmap

With the aim of closing a gap in knowledge in existing transformation roadmaps in the literature, this book proposed a six-phase roadmap for the benefits of transforming cities into SSCs. The six phases are named as: (1) City Vision Phase, (2) City Readiness Phase, (3) City Plan Phase, (4) City Transformation Phase, (5) Monitoring and Evaluation Phase, and (6) Sustain Change Phase.

During the "City Vision" phase, analysis of the current state of the city regarding it economic, social, environmental, and political challenges is carried out. After then, the city vision is identified along with the vision and mission statements. A list of strategies to realize the agreed upon vision is also created. At this stage, the roadmap highlights the necessity of communicating the identified vision along with its related strategies with locals, aiming at motivating them to participate into it. The overall objectives and goals of a transformation process are then identified. Finally, this phase shows the require of identifying the mechanisms that ensure an efficient and effective engagement of stakeholders and citizens in a SSC transformation process. It must be stated that this research emphasizes the need of engaging a selected group of relevant stakeholders in the identification of the city vision as well.

The "City Readiness" phase is an unprecedented added phase dedicated to the assessment of the current city assets. It focuses on checking the readiness level of the city current hard, soft, and digital infrastructures along with the level of digital literacy. The hard and soft infrastructures are named as the "Non-ICT based infrastructure" in the proposed innovative roadmap, while the digital infrastructure is denoted as the "ICT-based Infrastructure". This phase also checks the availability of any initiatives being implemented at any city level and could be integrated to a SSC project. The latter aims at ensuring the coherence of a transformation process without the existence of any initiative that is out away. This phase should take place prior to the planning of a SSC services and solutions. The reason behind this is to make sure that the identified gap in relation to existing assets could be closed though well-planned solutions during the "City Plan" phase.

The "City Plan" phase focuses on planning a series of solutions. It starts by identifying the CSFs and KPIs needed to monitor and evaluate a SSC transformation process and its outputs. Assumptions, constraints, and risk are also identified to ensure a consistent transformation process. The transformation from traditional cities to SSCs is context-specific. There is no "one-size-fits-all" solutions. Each city has to identify its essential change solutions along with their implementation priorities. Therefore; the next step sheds light on the necessity of identifying a series of change solutions over the SSC six dimensions with priorities. For each planned solution, resources needed to realize it are allocated and relevant stakeholders are engaged in its implementation process. As urban plans should take into consideration the financial implications of the proposed change activities (i.e. solutions), the required budget, funding mechanisms and other related financial issues that are needed to support each change activity should be defined. This is aggregated in one document named a financial feasibility study. Finally, an overall action plan for the transformation process is created.

During the "City Transformation" phase, the design, implementation, and delivery process have started and the essential solution outputs start coming on stream. This phase focuses on the development of a SSC smart infrastructure and integrated platform aiming to close any identified gap in relation to the current city assets. The short-term (or highly important) solutions are carried out as well. Finally, the integration of existing individual initiatives that are related directly to a SSC project are taking place during this phase.

The "Monitoring & Evaluation" phase handles the evaluation process of a SSC transformation process using the previously identified CSFs and KPIs. The output document(s) of this phase provide the needed analysis and feedbacks. Finally, the aim of the "Sustain Transformation" phase is to ensure the sustainability of a transformation process. The evaluation report(s) are used as a reference to learn from previous mistakes to avoid repeating them. This phase also carries out the continuous improvements of already implemented and delivered solutions, sharing best practices and announcing achievements, and producing of more changes at all city level.

It must be noted that the proposed roadmap is designed to ensure the continuity of a transformation process. The arrows used in Figure 6.1 indicate the necessity of either returning back to update or change the SSCs strategies in case of denoting any errors in stating them or continue the process of designing, implementing, and delivering of additional solutions.

10.2.4 Innovative Transformation Framework

The proposed innovative framework aims at providing the tools needed to realize a SSC transformation process and its related roadmap phases and components. This book proposed a framework that consists at its top-level form five layers, one preparation and four main layers, that are:

(1) *Preparation Activities Layer*: this layer handles all activities related to the "City Vision" phase of the proposed roadmap. One of the activities of this layer is creating a model for stakeholders' engagement in a SSC transformation process. Accordingly, this research proposed the desired model, ensuring the engagement of different types of stakeholders in a transformation process from an early stage.

(2) *Check City Readiness and Gap Analysis*: this layer is dedicated to the tools needed to realize the "City Readiness" phase of the proposed roadmap. It suggested existing international tools to assess the current city assets regarding its ICT-based infrastructure (i.e. hardware and software components in addition to the level of digital literacy of a city), non-ICT based infrastructure (i.e. hard and soft), and

existing related initiatives that are being implemented at the time of establishing a SSC project.

(3) *Develop, Implement, and Deliver Transformation Solutions*: this layer focuses on the identification of solutions to be delivered by a SSC transformation process. It provides the tools needed to realize the "City Plan" and "City Transform" phases. This layer divides the solutions into two main categories, namely (1) the development of a smart infrastructure and integrated platform and (2) the development of the innovative smart solutions. The framework introduces suggested solutions and designs for the former. For the innovative smart solutions, a generic list of areas under each of the SSC six dimensions to consider during a transformation process was proposed. The list takes into consideration the sustainability pillars, city dimensions, quality of life dimensions, and SSC dimensions along with the city context and the ICTs as an enabler.

(4) *Monitoring and Evaluation Layer*: this layer provides recommendation on the tools that can be used to realize the "Monitoring & Evaluation" phase. It sheds light on existing international KPIs to monitor and evaluate a SSC transformation process and its outputs. It also highlights the link between the CSFs and KPIs and how both can be used for the benefits of the monitoring and evaluation process.

(5) *Sustain Transformation and Produce more Changes*: this layer provides solutions to ensure the sustainability of a SSC transformation process. It recommends a series of actions to be taken for this purpose. This includes, learning from previous mistakes, continuous improvements of a transformation process in general and the delivered solution specifically, announcing achievements with locals and sharing of best practices with others, and producing of more changes.

The proposed framework provides insights to understand how to develop a comprehensive, systematic SSC transformation process. It helps city planners, policy and decision makers, and key stakeholders in realizing their cities' visions to be smart and sustainable.

10.2.5 Novel Stakeholders' Engagement Model

Involvement of different types of stakeholders from different levels of a city is essential for the success of a SSC transformation process. To ensure an effective and efficient engagement process, this research proposed a novel stakeholders' engagement model that could be fully or partially adopted by different SSC project teams. The model provides the insights needed for the task of identifying the mechanisms of stakeholders and citizens' engagement of the roadmap 'City Vision' phase. It also provides a series of stages to consider during the engagement process, aiming at ensuring the involvement of different types of relevant stakeholders in all phases of a SSC transformation journey.

The proposed model consists of eight main stages, summarized as below:

(1) *Stakeholders Identification*: during which the stakeholders that can affect or could be affected, directly or indirectly, by a SSC transformation process along with the stakes of each is identified. Based on the identified objectives and goals related to a SSC vision and mission, the identified stakeholders are classified into key or secondary stakeholders.

(2) *Prioritizing Stakeholders*: this stage aims at ranking stakeholders' degree of importance based on their potential impact (i.e. influence) on the success of a SSC transformation process.

(3) *Information Sharing with Stakeholders*: during which a SSC project team share with stakeholders all needed information regarding the SSC transformation process activities and how they can contribute to the activities' success.

(4) *Mapping Stakeholders*: during this stage, a SSC project team maps each stakeholder or group of stakeholders onto the SSC transformation process's strategies and their related activities. This also includes highlighting the effectiveness (i.e. impact) level of each stakeholder in achieving each activity and its related objectives and goals.

(5) *Create Partnerships with appropriate Stakeholders*: this stage aims at seeking partnerships with relevant stakeholders. These partnerships could provide the needed financial of technical support needed to realize a SSC project and help in achieving the desired large-scale transformation process.

(6) *Managing Stakeholders*: the purpose of this stage is to manage stakeholders through managing their relationships with a SSC project. It helps in raising the awareness about a SSC project and make it more prepared to deal with stakeholders needs that are changing throughout the lifecycle of a transformation process. It also makes a SSC project more capable to response effectively and efficiently to issues that must be resolved or difficulties that may arise throughout a transformation process.

(7) *Stakeholders Involvement in Project Monitoring and Evaluation*: this stage ensures that the monitoring and evaluation of a SSC transformation process is taking place with a full coordination and collaboration with key stakeholders. It aims at involving directly affected stakeholders to assess each transformation activity (i.e. solution) impacts for the benefit of enhancing a SSC project transparency and accountability.

(8) *Monitoring and Evaluation of Engagement Process*: this stage helps in evaluating the quality of the impact of each stakeholder in a SSC transformation process. The generated knowledge is then used to decide whether to keep or discard this stakeholder from future activities.

The model captures the main stages needed for the stakeholders' engagement process in a SSC project. It provides a holistic understanding for city planner and decision makers regarding the issue.

10.2.6 Innovative Generic List of Areas of Solutions under a SSC Project

Transformation towards SSCs varies from city to city depending on the development level of each city, availability of resources, willingness to change and reform, and aspirations of city citizens. Therefore, suggesting transformation solutions without any consideration of these issues is insufficient. Existing recommended solutions by different studies in the literature are general, field specific. They are selected based on the lens through which each study is viewing the objectives of a SSC transformation process. None of existing solutions is selected showing how they can be linked to the city context and local aspirations and needs. They are mainly focusing on technologies to enhance existing systems or create new ones, neglecting many required solutions at the hard and soft infrastructures, specifically, laws and regulations, policies, social inclusion, among others.

Thereby, there is a need to a list that can be customized by cities based on their context and needs.

Through logical and coherent analysis, this research proposed a generic list of minimum areas under each of the SSC six dimensions to consider when transforming a city into a SSC. The project team can customize this list based on the city context, needs, and local interest. It is also used as a reference in the SSC transformation process. The proposed list is created taking into consideration the following issues:

1. Ensure sustainability of a city over its economic, social, and environmental pillars.
2. Meet urban needs through improving urban operations and services.
3. Improve quality of life of citizens.
4. Consider the six dimensions of a SSC, namely, smart economy, smart environment, smart governance, smart living, smart mobility, and smart people.
5. City context and the use of ICTs as an enabler to provide solutions that are viable and environmentally friendly.

The list is a result of the intersection of the pillars and dimensions stated in the first four points above. The city context is then used to customize this list, identifying which solutions are missed to be implemented and which are already exist that may need more enhancement or they are sufficient enough. This generic list provides coherent, systematic insights needed for the city planners, policy and decision makers, and relevant stakeholders on the areas to focus on during their cities transformation journey.

10.3 Conclusions on Findings

The analysis of the responses in Chapter 8 demonstrated the necessity of considering different aspects while transforming cities into SSCs. It also provided insights on the degree on the necessity of the proposed components of this research. The questionnaire results reveal and confirm on the following:

1. *The city context should be clearly considered in a transformation process*: this is considered in the proposed roadmap through examining of the current city economic, social, environmental, and political states and challenges at an early stage of a

transformation process, even before the identification of the city vision. The proposed framework, in turn, provides recommendations on how to realize this examination process.

2. *Quality of the current city assets have an essential effect on the transformation process directions*: in an unprecedented manner, the proposed roadmap emphasizes the necessity of checking the city readiness for change before planning a transformation process solutions and services. This includes assessing the current quality of the hard, soft, and digital infrastructures in addition to the level of the digital literacy within a city. It also highlights the significance of closing any existing gap though well-planned solutions. The framework also sheds light on existing international indices that could be used to facilitated the assessment process.

3. *There is a necessity to identify the transformation process assumptions, constraints, and risks*: based of the proposed SSC theoretical logic model (Section 4.5), the proposed roadmap highlights the necessity of identifying the transformation process assumptions, constraints, and risks. It also shows that the assumptions are frequently related to the CSFs and recommends to create a CSF/Assumptions matrix to simplifying the monitoring and evaluation (M&E) process (Section 6.2.3).

4. *Solutions of a transformation process should be planned in a way ensuring the sustainability of a city, meeting the urban needs, improving the quality of life of citizens, and considering the SSC six dimensions and city context along with the use of ICTs, when applicable, to provide solutions that are environmentally friendly and viable*: one of the unprecedented issues that is introduced by the proposed framework is generating a list of minimum areas under each of the SSC six dimensions to be considered while planning a transformation process solutions (Section 7.2.3.2). It is worth noting that the list is created considering all above-mentioned aspects.

5. *The necessity of Monitoring and Evolution of a transformation process and its outputs*: both the proposed roadmap and framework consider the monitoring and evaluation aspects. The proposed roadmap sheds light on the necessity of first identifying the CSFs and KPIs at an early stage of a transformation planning phase,

and then, use these CSFs and KPIs to monitor and evaluate a transformation process as a whole and its delivered solutions. The framework, in turn, suggested existing international KPIs to be used for this purpose. It also explained the relationship between the CSFs and KPIs and how both can be used for the benefits on monitoring and evaluation process.

6. *There is a need to sustain a transformation process*: to ensure the sustainability of a transformation process, the proposed roadmap allocates a separate phase for this purpose, specifically, the last phase. This could be realized through four main techniques, namely, learning from previous experiences to avoid repeating the same mistakes, continuous improvements, announcing achievements, and producing of more changes.

7. *Engagement of different types of stakeholders in a transformation process is a must*: like other studies in the literature, the proposed roadmap emphasized the necessity of engaging stakeholders and citizens in a transformation process from early stages. Unlike others, this research proposed a novel model for stakeholders and citizen's engagement in a SSC transformation process. The proposed model is designed to ensure a systematic, holistic engagement process. It also provides the techniques needed to realize its introduced stages.

8. *Other conclusions*: responses from some experts showed that the current state of a city regarding its challenges could be assessed by examining annual statistical reports or using surveys. Using adequate KPIs dedicated to assess the current city assets can help in realizing checking the city readiness for change phase. Others suggest to check the level of the GDP (Gross Domestic Product) of a city, which is used to measure the health of a country's, thereby a city, economy. The latter is insufficient in this case, as SSCs are not only focusing on improving the economic aspects of a city. This is only one of the aspects to consider (i.e. a SSC is defined across six dimensions, one of them is a smart economy). Finally, other challenges that may be faced by city planners during a SSC transformation process includes the lack of the government/state support and lack of establishing partnerships with private sector

organizations (e.g. IT companies, banks, existing innovation labs, security and safety organizations, among others).

10.4 Recommendations

To ensure an effective and efficient transformation process, this research provides below a list of recommendations to city planners, policy and decision makers, and key stakeholders:

1. **Recommendation 1**: *Perform city state and needs analysis*

   A Current city state report that sheds light on existing economic, social, environmental, and political challenges can be created. This also includes an overall analysis of the city needs and initial suggestions of the smart solutions to be developed.

2. **Recommendation 2**: *Establish robust SSC strategies*

   Robust strategies help in realizing a predefined vision and mission statements. A list of strategies from which measurable, achievable goals and objectives can be created is recommended.

3. **Recommendation 3**: *Check city readiness for change*

   An assessment current city assets report to identify existing gaps is advised. The report must consider checking the readiness level of the current hard, soft, and digital infrastructures in addition to the level of the digital literacy. This may also include a list of initial suggested smart solutions to close identified gaps.

4. **Recommendation 4**: *Engage different types of stakeholders from all city levels*

   Identifying a list of groups of stakeholders that may participate is a SSC transformation process is recommended. This list should consider different types of stakeholders form all city levels. A coherent, systematic engagement process is advised to ensure the involvement of stakeholders in all stages of a transformation process.

5. **Recommendation 5**: *Perform assumptions, constraints, and risks analysis*

   Creating a list of assumptions about expected impacts of a SSC transformation process is preferred. To eliminate or minimize the effect of unplanned circumstances, it is important to identify a list of constrains and risks that may face the transformation process. This also includes suggesting a series of action to be taken in the event of any of these identified obstacles.

6. **Recommendation 6**: *Secure adequate financing for the development of the smart infrastructure, integrated platform, and smart solutions*

   To ensure the continuity of a SSC transformation process, there is a necessity to find adequate financial resources to support the implementation of SSC smart infrastructure, integrated platform, and a series of smart solutions under each of the SSC six dimensions. Without the financial support, a transformation process may be seized, or worse, fail.

7. **Recommendation 7**: *Monitor and evaluate a SSC transformation process*

   To prevent any degradation in the quality and transparency of a transformation process, it is importing to keep an eye on its performance. A recommendation is to identify an adequate list of CSFs and KPIs for this purpose. Monitoring is advised to start from the beginning of a SSC project and continue throughout its lifecycle. Evaluations in turn take place at predefined milestones.

8. **Recommendation 8**: *Announce achievements*

   The investigation revealed that announcing the SSC transformation process achievements is important to ensure its transparency and to increase stakeholders and locals' interest and buy-in into it. Therefore, the advice is to continuously announce achievements once happened as well as share best practices with others to learn from.

10.5 Future Directions

Further studies in the area of this research is necessary; in particular, the tools provided by the transformation framework. One is related to defining a standardized index dedicated to assess the performance of a SSC transformation process. The index must have a list of KPIs that consider all aspects of a SSCs. The KPIs should be divided based on the SSC six dimensions. Indicators for assessing the city hard, soft, and digital infrastructures and the level of the digital literacy should be considered as well. As the transformation towards SSCs differs from one city to another based on the city attributes, needs, and availability of resources (i.e. readiness), one of the recommendations is to create a list of

KPIs that can be customized based on these aspects. In this case, each city can employ the index based on its needs and the sustainability objectives it is seeking to achieve.

More research in the area of the theoretical foundation of the concept of SSCs is needed. This study uses the ToC to focus the proposed research. This opens the door for other researches to investigate existing theories related to the transformational change to be applied on the area of developing cities into SSCs. Others may find a way to introduce a theory dedicated directly to the concept and its transformation process.

Further larger researches regarding the practical application of the proposed transformation roadmap and framework are requisite. This include statistical analysis for the impact of the proposed models on real case studies (i.e. cities). The analysis results help in identifying gaps in the innovative models and to find the ways to overcome them. Although theories provide the underpinning needed for a research, different issues are only detectable through real practices and experiments. A recommendation is to apply the proposed models on different contexts. Cities with different development level can be selected for this purpose. This would provide different insights on the proposed transformation roadmap and framework, allowing to measure the effectiveness and efficiency of these models in different contexts.

APPENDIX A

ITU-T FG-SSC Key Performance Indicators

This Appendix provides the KPIs defined by the ITU-T FG-SSC (2016). Each dimension is labeled as Dx and each sub-dimension is identified using the label Dx.y. The number (x) denotes the dimension and the number (y) denotes the sub-dimension of this dimension. The identified dimension and sub-dimensions are summarized in Table 10.1.

Table 10.1: Dimensions and Sub-dimensions of the ITU-T FG-SSC KPIs

Dimension Label	Dimension	Sub-dimension Label	Sub-dimension
D1	Information and Communication Technology (ICT)	D1.1	Network and access
		D1.2	Services and Information platforms
		D1.3	Information security and privacy
		D1.4	Electromagnetic field.
D2	Environmental Sustainability	D2.1	Air quality
		D2.2	CO_2 emission
		D2.3	Energy
		D2.4	Indoor pollution
		D2.5	Water, soil, and noise
D3	Productivity	D3.1	Capital investment
		D3.2	Employment
		D3.3	Inflation
		D3.4	Trade
		D3.5	Saving
		D3.6	Export/import
		D3.8	Innovation
		D3.9	Knowledge economy
D4	Quality of Life	D4.1	Education
		D4.2	Health
		D4.3	Safety/security public place
		D4.4	Convenience and comfort
D5	Equity and Social Inclusion	D5.1	Inequity of income/consumption (Gini Coefficient)
		D5.2	Social and gender inequity of access to services and infrastructure
		D5.3	Openness and public participation
		D5.4	Governance
D6	Physical Infrastructure	D6.1	Infrastructure/connection to services - piped water
		D6.2	Infrastructure/connection to services – sewage
		D6.3	Infrastructure/connection to services - electricity
		D6.4	Infrastructure/connection to services – waste management
		D6.5	Connection to services – knowledge infrastructure
		D6.6	Infrastructure/connection to services – health infrastructure
		D6.7	Infrastructure/connection to services – electricity
		D6.8	Infrastructure/connection to services – road infrastructure
		D6.9	Housing – building materials
		D6.10	Housing – living space
		D6.11	Building

The core and additional indicators defined for each dimension are summarized below. Each core indicator is identified using the label (Ix.y.z) and each additional indicator is defined using the label (Ax.y.z), where (x) denotes the dimension number, (y) denotes the sub-dimension number, and (z) denotes the indicator number. Noting that the term city inhabitant is used by the ITU-T FG-SSC (2016) to refer to people living in the city.

1. ICT Dimension

The ITU-T FG-SSC defines 11 core indicators and 11 additional indicators for the ICT dimension, including the internet access, wired(less)-broadband subscriptions, computer penetration, social media, privacy protection, information security, among others.

Table 10.2: Core Indicators Defined for the ICT Dimension

Sub-dimension	Core Indicator
D1.1 Networks and access	I1.1.1 Availability of computers or similar devices
	I1.1.2 Availability of Internet access in households
	I1.1.3 Availability of fixed broadband subscriptions
	I1.1.4 Availability of wireless broadband subscriptions
D1.2 Services and information platforms	I1.2.1 Use of social media by the public sector
D1.3 Information security and privacy	I1.3.1 Information security of public services and systems
	I1.3.2 Existence of systems, rules and regulations to ensure Child Online Protection (COP)
	I1.3.3 Existence of systems, rules and regulations to ensure Privacy protection in public service
D1.4 Electromagnetic field	I1.4.1 Compliance with WHO endorsed exposure guidelines
	I1.4.2 Adoption of a consistent planning approval process with respect to EMF
	I1.4.3 Availability of EMF information

Table 10.3: Additional Indicators Defined for the ICT Dimension

Sub-dimension	Additional Indicator
D1.1 Networks and access	A1.1.1 Availability of mobile-cellular telephones
	A1.1.2 International Internet bandwidth
	A1.1.3 Use of Internet by city inhabitants
	A1.1.4 Coverage rate of digital broadcasting network
	A1.1.5 Availability of ultrahigh speed wireline connection
	A1.1.6 Availability of high-speed mobile broadband
	A1.1.7 Availability of WiFi in public areas
	A1.1.8 Availability of smart phones and tablets
	A1.1.10 Quality of mobile broadband
D1.2 Services and information platforms	A1.2.1 Availability of electronic and mobile payment platforms

2. Environmental Sustainability Dimension

The ITU-T FG-SSC defines only 3 core indicators the Environmental Sustainability dimension. These are covering the water resources, air quality, and soil and noise monitoring. Noting that, this dimension has no additional indicators.

Table 10.4: Core Indicators Defined for the Environmental Sustainability Dimension

Sub-dimension	Core Indicator
D2.1 Air quality	I2.1.1 Application of ICT-based monitoring system for particles and toxic substances
D2.5 Water, soil and noise	I2.5.1 Application of city water monitoring through ICT
	I2.5.2 Application of ICT-based noise monitoring

3. Productivity Dimension

The ITU-T FG-SSC defines 8 core indicators and 3 additional indicators for the Productivity dimension. These are covering the expenditure of ICT, ICT companies ration, expenditure of ICT R&D, ICT employees, e-commerce, intangible investment, e-services, and cloud computing.

Table 10.5: Core Indicators Defined for the Productivity Dimension

Sub-dimension	Core Indicator
D3.1 Capital investment	I3.1.1 ICT related Research and Development expenditure
	I3.1.2 Investment intensity in ICT projects enabling SSC
D3.4 Trade	I3.4.1 Application of e-commerce transactions
D3.8 Innovation	I3.8.1 Research and Development intensity in ICT
D3.9 Knowledge economy	I3.9.1 Intangible investments as a proportion of GDP
	I3.9.2 Employees belonging to ICT sector
	I3.9.3 Companies providing e-services
	I3.9.4 Application of computing platforms

Table 10.6: Additional Indicators Defined for the Productivity Dimension

Sub-dimension	Additional Indicator
D3.9 Knowledge economy	A3.9.1 Intangible investments in comparison with total Investments
	A3.9.2 Application of Geographic Information System (GIS)
	A3.9.3 Application of big data

4. Quality of Life Dimension

The ITU-T FG-SSC defines 7 core indicators and 2 additional indicators for the Quality of Life dimension. These are covering the electronic health records, e-learning, sharing medical information, telemedicine, electronic medical records, anti-disaster, and other safety measures.

Table 10.7: Core Indicators Defined for the Quality of Life Dimension

Sub-dimension	Core Indicator
D4.1 Education	I4.1.1 Use of e-learning system
D4.2 Health	I4.2.1 Use of electronic health records
	I4.2.2 Use of electronic medical records
	I4.2.3 Sharing of medical resources and information among hospitals, pharmacies and other health care providers
	I4.2.4 Adoption of telemedicine
D4.3 Safety/security public place	I4.3.1 Adoption of ICT for disaster management
	I4.3.2 Availability of ICT-based safety systems

Table 10.8: Additional Indicators Defined for the Quality of Life Dimension

Sub-dimension	Additional Indicator
D4.1 Education	A4.1.1 Application of e-learning in schools
	A4.1.2 Application of e-learning in academic studies

5. Equity and Social Inclusion Dimension

The ITU-T FG-SSC defines 6 core indicators and 2 additional indicators for the Equity and Social Inclusion dimension. These are covering the support for new city inhabitant, online city information, ICT literacy, civic engagement, support to persons with specific needs, and online administration.

Table 10.9: Core Indicators Defined for the Equity and Social Inclusion Dimension

Sub-dimension	Core Indicator
D5.3 Openness and public participation	I5.3.1 Availability of online city information and feedback mechanisms
	I5.3.2 Online civic engagement
	I5.3.3 Online support for new city inhabitants
	I5.3.4 Existence of strategies, rules and regulations to enable ICT literacy among inhabitants
D5.4 Governance	I5.4.1 Provision of online systems for administering public services and facilities
	I5.4.2 Application of services to support persons with specific needs

Table 10.10: Additional Indicators Defined for the Equity and Social Inclusion Dimension

Sub-dimension	Additional Indicator
D5.3 Openness and public participation	A5.4.1 Existence of strategy, rules and regulations to enable the use of public data
D5.4 Governance	A6.1.1 Availability of visualized real-time information regarding water use

6. Physical Infrastructure Dimension

The ITU-T FG-SSC defines 13 core indicators and 5 additional indicators for the Physical Infrastructure dimension. These are covering the infrastructure including piped water, electricity, buildings, sewage, and road infrastructure.

Table 10.11: Core Indicators Defined for the Physical Infrastructure Dimension

Sub-dimension	Core Indicator
D6.1 Infrastructure/connection to Services - piped water	I6.1.1 Water supply system management using ICT
	I6.1.2 City fresh water sources monitored using ICT
	I6.1.3 Availability of smart water meters
D6.2 Infrastructure/connection to services - sewage	I6.2.1 Sewage system management using ICT
	I6.2.2 Drainage system management using ICT
D6.3 Infrastructure/connection to Services - electricity	I6.3.1 Availability of smart electricity meters
D6.8 Infrastructure/connection to Services - road infrastructure	I6.8.1 Availability of traffic monitoring using ICT
	I6.8.2 Availability of parking guidance systems
	I6.8.3 Availability of real-time traffic information
	I6.8.4 Street lighting management using ICT
	I6.8.5 Gas system management using ICT
D6.11 Building	I6.11.1 Automatic energy management in buildings
	I6.11.2 Integrated management in public buildings

Table 10.12: Additional Indicators Defined for the Physical Infrastructure Dimension

Sub-dimension	Additional Indicator
D6.1 Infrastructure/connection to Services - piped water	A6.1.1 Availability of visualized real-time information regarding water use
D6.3 Infrastructure/connection to Services - electricity	A6.3.1 Electricity supply system management using ICT
	A6.3.2 Availability of visualized real-time information regarding electricity use
D6.8 Infrastructure/connection to Services - road infrastructure	A6.8.1 Availability of visualized real-time information regarding gas use
	A6.8.2 Availability of online bike/car sharing system

REFERENCES

ACAPS (2016). Questionnaire Design: How to Design a Questionnaire for Needs Assessments in Humanitarian Emergencies. The Assessment Capacities Project (ACAPS). Geneva: Austria.

ACCS (2012). *Arlington Country Capital Bikeshare Transit Development Plan – Fiscal Years 2013 – 2018*. Prepares by Foursuare Integrated Transportation Planning for Arlington Country Commuter Services (ACCS). Arlington, VA: USA.

Al-Hader, M. & Rodzi, A. (2009). The Smart City Infrastructure Development & Monitoring. *Theoritical and Empirical Researches in Urban Management*, Vol. (4), No. (2), pp. 87-94.

Albino, V., Berardi, U. & Dangelico, R.M. (2015). Smart Cities: Definitions, Dimensions, Performance, and Initiatives. *Journal of Urban Technology*, Vol. (22), No. (1), pp. 3-21.

Alcatel-Lucent (2012). *Getting Smarter about Smart Cities: Understanding the Market Opportunity in the Cities of Tomorrow*. Alcatel-Lucent. Boulogne-Billancourt: France.

Allen, E. & Seaman, C.A. (2007). Likert Scales and Data Analyses. *Quality* Progress. Web. Accessed, Retrieved from: http://asq.org/quality-progress/2007/07/statistics/likert-scales-and-data-analyses.html.

Allen, W. (2016). Diagramming a Theory of Change. *Learning for Sustainability*, Web. Accessed, Retrieved from: http://learningforsustainability.net/post/diagramming-theory-change/.

Amitrani, C.C., Alfano, A. & Bifulco, F. (2014). New Smart Cities: a focus on some ongoing projects. The 3rd International Virtual Conference, *Conference of Informatics and Management Sciences, (ICTIC)*, Vol. (3), Issue (1), pp. 383-388.

Anastasia, S. (2012). The Concept of 'Smart Cities' – Towards Community Development. *Networks and Communication Studies, NETCOM*, Vol. (26), No. (3-4), pp. 375-388.

Anderson, A. (2004). *Theory of change as a Tool for strategic Planning*. The ASPEN Institute Roundtable on Community Change. New York, NY: USA.

Anderson, A. (2005). *The Community Builder's Approach to Theory of Change: A Practical Guide to Theory Development*. The ASPEN Institute Roundtable on Community Change. New York, NY: USA.

Anderson L. & Anderson, D. (2001). Awake at the Wheel: Moving Beyond Change Management to Conscious Change Leadership. *OD Practitioner*, Vol. (33), No. (3), pp. 40-48.

Anderton, D. (2016). Science in the City Region: Establishing Liverpool's Life Science Ecology. *Regional Studies, Regional Science, Taylor & Francis Online*, Vol. (3), Issue (1), pp. 434-444.

Aoun, C. (2013). *The Smart City Cornerstone: Urban Efficiency*. Schneider Electric, White paper, Web. Accessed, Retrieved from: http://www.digital21.gov.hk/sc/related Doc/download/2013/079%20SchneiderElectric%20(Annex).pdf

Apostu, A., Puican, F., Ularu, G., Suciu, G., Todoran, G., & WSEAS (2013). Study on Advantages and Disadvantages of Cloud Computing – The Advantages of Telemetry Applications in the Cloud. *International Conference, 13th, Applied Computer Science*, pp. 118-123.

Aragón, A.O. & Macedo, J.C. (2010). A 'Systematic Theories of Change' Approach for Purposeful Capacity Development. *IDS Bulletin*, Vol. (41), No. (3), pp. 87-99.

Atzori, L., Iera, A. & Morabito, G. (2010). The Internet of Things: A survey. *Journal of Computer Networks, Elsevier*, Vol. (54), pp. 2787-2805.

Asefeso, A., Lund, S. B. & Parry, H. (2013). The Emperor's New Clothes: A Contemporary Business Life Edition. AA Global Sourcing Ltd, ISBN: 978-1-291-56928-5.

Alawadhi, S., Aldama-Nalda, A., Chourabi, H., Gil-Garcia, J.R., Leung, S., Mellouli, S., Nam, T., Prado, T.A., Scholl, H.J. & Walker, S. (2012). Building Understanding of Smart City Initiatives. *International Conference of Electronic Government, EGOV 2012, Electronic Government*, pp. 40-53.

Backović, N., Milićević, V. & Sofronijevic, A. (2016). Strategic Directions in European Sustainable City Management. *Handbook of Research in Green Economic Development Initiatives and Strategies*, IGI Global, pp. 147-168.

BAH (2012). Components of the Transformation Life Cycle. *Booz | Allen | Hamilton, BAH*. Web. Accessed, Retrieved from: http://www.boozallen.com/consulting /management-consulting/change-management/tlc/tlc-components.

Bal, M., Bryde, D., Fearon, D. & Ochieng, E. (2013). Stakeholder Engagement: Achieving Sustainability in the Construction Sector. *Journal of Sustainability*, Vol. (6), pp. 695-710.

Baller, S., Dutta, S. & Lanvin, B. (2016). *The Global Information Technology Report 2016 – Innovating in the Digital Economy*. World Economic Forum and INSEAD. Geneva: Switzerland.

Banks, J. (1998). *Handbook of Simulation: Principles, Methodology, Advances, Applications, and Practice*. Wiley, John & Sons, Incorporate, 1st Edition.

Baqir, M.N. & Kathawala, Y. (2004). Ba for Knowledge Cities: A Futuristic Technology Model. *Journal of Knowledge Management,* Vol. (8), No. (5), pp. 83–95.

Barrionuevo, J.M., Berrone, P. & Ricart, J.E. (2012). Smart Cities, Sustainable Progress. *IESE Insight*, Issue (14), pp. 50-57.

Basiago, A.D. (1999). Economic, Social, and Environmental Sustainability in Development Theory and Urban Planning Practice. *The Environmentalist, Kluwer Academic Publisher*, Vol. (19), pp. 145-161.

Biech, E. (2008). *ASTD Handbook for Workplace Learning Professionals*. Virginia: VR: American Society for Training & Development, pp. 633.

BIS (2013). *Smart Cities: Background* Paper. Department for Business, Innovation and Skills (BIS), BIS Publications, BIS/13//1209. London: United Kingdom.

Booher, H.R. (2003). *Handbook of Human Systems Integration*. Wiley, 1st Edition, ISBN-13: 978-0471020530.

Boone, H.N. & Boone, D.A. (2012). Analyzing Likert Data. *Journal of Extension*, Vol. (50), No. (2), pp. 1-5.

Borowik, G., Chaczko, Z., Jacak, W. & Luba, T. (Eds.) (2015). *Computational Intelligence and Efficiency in Engineering Systems, Studies in Computational Intelligent.* Cham: Springer International Publishing AG, 1st Edition, pp. 49-59, ISBN-13: 978-3319157191.

BSI (2014). *Smart City Framework – Guide to establishing Strategies for Smart Cities and Communities*. British Standards Institute (BSI), BSI Standards Publication, PAS 181:2014. London: United Kingdom.

Budden, R. (2015). Sustainable Development for Smart Cities: A Geospatial Approach. *Middle East Geospatial Forum, Dubai: UAE.* Web. Accessed, Retrieved from: http://www.megf.org/2015/presentation/16%20Feb/Plenary%201/Richard%20Budde n.pdf

Caragliu, A., Del Bo, C. & Nijkamp, P. (2011). Smart Cities in Europe. *Journal of Urban Technology*, Vol. (18), No. (2), pp. 65-82.

Carpenter, M., Bauer, T. & Erdogan, B. (2009). *Principles of Management*. Flat World Knowledge, Inc., 1st Edition, ISBN-10: 0982043074, ISBN-13: 978-0982043073.

Center for ToC (2013). What is Theory of Change?. *Center for Theory of Change*. Web. Accessed, Retrieved from: http://www.theoryofchange.org/what-is-theory-of-change/.

CEO (2000). *Designing Change Capable Organizations*. Center for Effective Organizations (CEO), Marshall School of Business, University of Southern California. California, CA: USA.

Chris, C., Noakes, L., Westine, C. & Schröter, D. (2011). A Systematic Review of Theory-Driven Evaluation Practice from 1990 to 2009. American *Journal of Evaluation*, Vol. (32), No. (2), pp. 199-226.

Choucri, N., Mistree, D., Haghseta, F., Mezher, T., Baker, W.R. & Ortiz, C.I. (Eds.). (2007). Mapping Sustainability: Knowledge e-Networking and the Value Chain. In Alliance for Global Sustainability Bookseries (pp. 428-429). Springer.

Chourabi, H., Nam, T., Walker, S., Gil-Gracia, R.J., Mellouli, S., Nahon, K., Prado, T.A. & Scholl, H.J. (2012). Understanding Smart Cities: An Integrative Framework. *The 45th Hawaii International Conference on System Science (HICSS)*, pp. 2289-2297.

CISCO (2012). *Smart City Framework - A Systematic Process for Enabling*

Smart+Connected Communities. Cisco Internet Business Solutions Group (IBSG): Falconer, G. & Mitchell, S.

Cohen, B. (2012).6 Key Components for Smart Cities. *UBM's Future Cities*. Web. Accessed, Retrieved from: http://www.ubmfuturecities.com/author.asp?section_id= 219&doc_id=524053.

Conrad, I., Matschinger, H., Riedel-Heller, S., Von Gottberg, C. & Kilian, R. (2014). The Psychometric Properties of the Gernam Version of the WHOQOL–OLD in the German Population aged 60 and Older. Journal of Health and Quality of Life Outcomes, Vol. (12), pp.1-15.

DAFWA (2016). *Improvement Tools: Critical Success Factors and Key Performance Indicators*. Department of Agriculture and Food, Government of Western Australia (DAFWA). South Perth: Australia.

Dameri, R.P. (2013). Searching for Smart City definition: a comprehensive proposal. *International Journal of Computers and Technology*, Vol. (11), No. (5), pp. 2544-2551.

Daszko, M. & Sheinberg, S. (2005). *Survival is Optional: only leaders with new knowledge can lead the transformation (Theory of Transformation)*. Web. Accessed, Retrieved from: http://www.mdaszko.com/theoryoftransformation_final_to_short _article_apr05.pdf

De Santis, R., Fasano, A., Mignolli, N. & Villa, A. (2014). *Smart City: Fact and Fiction*. Munich Personal RePEc Archive, MPRA, Paper No. 54536. Munich: Germany.

Deakin, M.& Al Waer, H. (2011). From Intelligent to Smart Cities. *Intelligent Buildings International,* Vol. (3), No. (3), pp. 140–152.

Debertin, D.L. & Goetz, S.J. (2008). Social Capital Formation in Rural, Urban and Suburban Communities. *Social Capital*, Vol. (1), pp. 60-.90.

Delivered (2015). King Abdullah Economic City. Delivered, *The Global Logistics Magazine*. Web. Accessed, Retrieved from: http://www.delivered.dhl.com/en/ articles/2014/09/king-abdullah-economic-city.html.

Deloitte (2015a). *Smart Cities: How rapid advances in technology are reshaping our economy and society*. Deloitte Touch Tohmatsu Limited (DTTL), Vol. (1). Amsterdam: Netherlands.

Deloitte (2015b). *100 Smart Cities in India – Facilitating Implementation*. Deloitte Touche Tohmatsu India Private Limited (DTTIPL), Indian Chamber of Commerce (ICC). Kolkata: India.

DESA (2013). *Sustainable Development Challenges: World Economic Social Survey 2013*. Department of Economic and Social Affairs, United Nations. New York, NY: USA.

Di Biase, S. A. (Eds.) (2014). Applied Innovation – A Handbook. Chicago: Premier Insights, LLC. pp. 191.

Dias, E., Linde, M., Rafiee, A., Koomen, E. & Scholten, H. (2013). Beauty and Brains: Integration Easy Spatial Design and Advanced Urban Sustainability Models. *Planning Support Systems for Sustainable Urban Development*, Lecture Notes in Geoinformation and Cartography, Springer, pp. 469-484.

DiNapoli, T.P. (2003). *Local Government Management Guide: Strategic Planning*. Office of the New York State Comptroller, Division of Local Government and School Accountability. New York, NY: USA.

Dirks, S. & Keeling, M. (2009). *A Vision of Smarter Cities: How Cities can Lead the Way into a Prosperous and Sustainable Future*. IBM Global Business Services, IBM Institute for Business Value. Somers: NY, USA.

Doherty, P. (2014). *Smart Cities: A new Dynamic for the Middle East*. McGRAW Hill Financial Global Institute, the Digital Group Publications. Tennessee: USA.

Edvinsson, L. (2006). Aspects on the city as a knowledge tool. *Journal of Knowledge Management*, Vol. (10), No. (5), pp. 6-13.

Edwards, R.W., Jumper-Thurman, P., Plesterd, B.A., Oetting, E.R. & Swanson, L. (2000). Community Readiness: Research to Practice. *Journal of Community Psychology*, Vol. (28), No. (3), pp. 281-207.

Earth Institute and Ericsson (2016). *ICT & SDGs: How Information and Communication Technology Can Achieve the Sustainable Development Goals*. The Earth Institute at Columbia University and Ericsson. New York, NY: USA and Stockholm: Sweden.

EC (2015). *In-Depth Report: Indicators for Sustainable Cities*. Science for Environment Policy, European Commission (EC), European Union (EU), Issue (12). Brussels: Belgium.

Eide, E.B. & Rösler, P. (2014). *Rethinking Arab Employment – A Systemic Approach for Resource-Endowed Economies*. World Economic Forum, Ref. (220814).

EIP-SCC (2015). *The European Innovation Partnership on Smart Cities and Communities – Strategic Implementation Plan*. The European Innovation Partnership on Smart Cities and Communities (EIP-SCC). Brussels: Belgium.

El Din, H.S., Shalaby, A., Faroud, H.E. and Elariane, S.A. (2013). Principles of Urban Quality of Life for a Neighborhood. *Journal of Housing and Building National Research Center, HBRC Journal, Elsevier*, Vol. (9), pp. 86-92.

EN & UoB (2013). The Handbook for Economic Lectures. *The Economics Network, University of Bristol (UoB)*, Web. Accessed, Retrieved from: https://www.economics network.ac.uk/handbook/questionnaires/23.

EP (2014). *Mapping Smart Cities in the EU*. European Union (EU), European Parliament's Committee on Industry, Research and Energy, Policy Department A: Economic and Scientific Policy. Brussels: Belgium.

EPIC (2013). *EPIC Roadmap for Smart Cities*. European Union, European Platform for Intelligent Cities (EPIC), Version 1.0, Project no. 270895.

Ericsson (2016). *Lying the Foundations for Smart, Sustainable City*. Ericsson AB. Stockholm: Sweden.

Escher Group (2015). *Five ICT Essential for Smart Cities*. Escher Group. Duplin: Ireland.

ESRC (2007). *Subjective Well-being in Cities: A Cross-Cultural Analysis in Bogotá, Belo Horizonte and Toronto*. Economic & Social Reade arch Council (ESRC), ESRC Research Group on Wellbeing in Developing Countries, Eduardo Wills and Marilyn Hamilton, University of Bath, WeD Working Paper, No. (38). Bath: United Kingdom.

ETS (2007). *Digital Transformation: A Framework for ICT Literacy – A Report for the International ICT Literacy Panel*. Education Testing Service (ETS). Princeton, NJ: USA.

EU-Europa (2014). *The Digital Agenda Toolbox*. European Commission, Joint Research Center, Institute for Prospective Technological Studies. Seville: Spain.

EUREKA (2014). *Smart City: EUREKA's Inter-Cluster in the lead*. A European-wide Network for Market-Oriented Industrial Research and Development (EUREKA). Geneva: Switzerland.

Felderer, M. & Kecheis, J. (2014). Design of a Questionnaire on Testing in ERP Projects. *In: Piazolo F., Felderer M. (eds) Novel Methods and Technologies for Enterprise Information Systems*, Lecture Notes in Information Systems and Organisation, Vol. (8), Springer, Cham.

FoF (2012). *Roadmap Validation Report*. European Forum for ICT in Factories of the Future (FoF) – Research and Innovation. Luxemburg: Luxemburg.

Folke, C., Carpenter, S., R., Walker, B., Scheffer, M., Chapin, T. & Tockstom, J. (2010). Resilience Thinking: Integrating Resilience, Adaptablity and Transformability. *Ecology and Society*, Vol. (15), No. (4): 20.

Freeman, R.E. (1984). *Strategic Management: A Stakeholder Approach*. Pitman Series in Business and Public Policy, Pitman Publishing Inc., Pitman Books Limited, ISBN 0-273-01913-9.

Freeman, R.E., Harrison, J.S., Wicks, A.C., Parmar, B.L. & Colle, S. (2010). *Stakeholder Theory: The State of the Art*. Cambridge University Press, ISBN-13: 978-0521137935.

Friedmann, J. (2000). The Good City: In Defense of Utopian Thinking. *International Journal of Urban and Regional Research*, Vol. (20), No. (2), pp. 460-472.

Fryrear, A. (2015). Survey Results Report: Pie Chart or Bar Graph. *SurveyGizmo*, Web. Accessed, Retrieved from: https://www.surveygizmo.com/survey-blog/pie-chart-or-bar-graph/.

Futaki, K. (2010). *Stakeholder Selection Strategy*. Danube FloodRisk Project, Program co-founded by the European Union.

Geels, F.W. and Kemp, R. (2207). Dynamics in socio-technical systems: Typology of change processes and contrasting case studies. *Technology in Society, ELSEVIER*, Vol. (29), Issue (4), pp. 441- 455.

Gerstenfeld, A. (1979). *Innovation: A Study of Technological Policy*. Washington: University Press of America.

Geyer, H.S. (2009). International Handbook of Urban Policy: Issues in the Developed World. *Edward Elgar Publishing Limited*, Vol. (2), ISBN 978-1-84720-459-2.

Giffinger, R., Fertner, C., Kramar, H., Kalasek, R., Pichler-Milanovic´, N. & Meijers, E. (2007). *Smart Cities: Ranking of European Medium-sized Cities*. Center of Regional Science (SRF), Vienna University of Technology. Graz, AG: Austria.

Giffinger, R. & Gudrun, H. (2010). Smart Cities Ranking: An Effective Instrument for the Positioning of Cities?. *ACE Architecture, City and Environment*, Vol. (4), pp. 7-25.

Girad, L.F., Lombardi, P. & Nijkamp, P. (2009). Creative Urban Design and Development. *International Journal of Services Technology and Management, Special issue*, Vol. (13), No. (2-3), pp. 111-115.

GIZ (2011). *Urban and Municipal Development*. Deutsche Gesellschaftür Internationale Zusammenarbeit (GIZ) GmbH. Eschborn: Germany.

Godin, B. (2015). *Technological Change: What do Technology and Change Stand for?* Project on Intellectual History of Innovations, Working Paper No. (24), INRS: Montreal, Canada.

Gottret, M. (2013). The Urban Development Project theory of Change. *Prezi*, Web. Accessed, Retrieved from: https://prezi.com/iiemlbctsgib/the-urban-development-project-theory-of-change/.

Government Summit (2015). *Smart Cities: Regional Perspective*. The Government Summit - Arab Region. Dubai: UAE.

Grafakos, S. (2015). Developing an Integrated Sustainability and Resilience Framework of Indicators for the Assessment of low-carbon Energy Technologies at the local Level. *International Journal of Sustainable Energy*, Teylor & Francis, pp. 1-27.

Greenfield, A. (2013). *Against the Smart City*. Do Projects. New York, NY: USA.

Hair Jr, J.F., Wolfinbarager, M., Money, A.H, Samouel, P. & Page M.J. (2011). *Essentials of Business Research Methods*. Routledge, 2nd Edition, ISBN-13: 978-0765626318.

Hall, R.E. (2000). The Vision of a Smart City. *Proceedings of the 2nd International Life Extension Technology Workshop*, Paris, France, Sept. 28.

Hancock, T. & Labonté, R. (1999). Indicators That Count! Measuring Population Health at the Community Level. *Canadian Journal of Public Health*, Vol. (90), pp. 22-26.

Harrison, C., Eckman, B., Hamilton, R., Hartswick, P., Kalagnanam, J. & Paraszczak, J. (2010). Foundations for Smarter Cities. *IBM Journal of Research and Development*, Vol. (54), No. (4), pp. 1-16.

Harrington, H.J., Voehl, F. & Voehl, C.F. (2015). Model for Sustainable Change – White Paper. Project Management Institute (PMI), Global Operations Center. Pennsylvania, PA: USA.

Hirani, N. P. and Yavatmal, P. D. (2015). Transformation of Urban Development in to Smart Cities: The Challenges. *Journal of Mathematical and Civil Engineering (IOSR-JMCE)*, Vol. (12), Issue (3), Ver. (2), pp. 24-30.

Hivos (2015). Hivos ToC Guidelines: Theory of Change Thinking in Practice. Hivos publications. The Hague: Netherlands.

Hofstrand, D. (2016). *Vision and Mission Statements – a Roadmap of Where You Want to Go and How to Get There*. Ag Decision Maker, Iowa State University Extension and Outreach, Department of Economics. Ames, IA: USA.

Höjer, H. & Wangel, J. (2014). Smart Sustainable Cities – Definition and Challenges. *ICT Innovations for Sustainably, Advanced in Intelligent Systems and Computing, Springer International Publishing*, Vol. 310, pp. 333-349.

Huang, Y. (2003). Soft vis-à-vis Hard Infrastructure for Economic Growth: Can China Learn from India.? *Carnegie Endowment conference*, Beijing, China.

Huawei (2013). *Huawei Smart City Solution*. Huawei Technologies Co. Ltd. Shenzhen: China.

Huawei (2014). Understanding Top-Level Design for Smart Cities. *ICT Insights, Huawei Enterprise*, Issue (10), pp. 20-23.

IBM (2009). *A Vision of Smarter Cities: How Cities can Lead the way into a Prosperous and Sustainable Future*. IBM Global Business Services, IBM Institute for Business Value. New York, NY: USA.

Ibrahim, M., Al-Nasrawi, S., El-Zaart, A. & Adams, C. (2015a). Challenges facing E-Government and Smart Sustainable City: An Arab Region Perspective. *15th European Conference on e-Government, ECEG*, pp. 396-402.

Ibrahim, M., El-Zaart, A. & Adams, C. (2015b). Paving the Way to Smart Sustainable Cities: Transformation Models and Challenges. *Journal of Information Systems and Technology Management (JISTEM)*, Vol. (12), No. (3), pp. 559-576, doi: 10.4301/S1807-17752015000300004.

Ibrahim, M., El-Zaart, A. & Adams, C. (2015c). Transformation Towards Smart Sustainable Cities. *The 23rd European Conference on Information Systems - Resilience and Information Systems Workshop*. Muenster: Germany, unpublished.

Ibrahim, M., El-Zaart, A. & Adams, C. (2016). Smart Sustainable Cities: A New Perspective on Transformation, Roadmap, and Framework Concepts. *The Fifth International Conference on Smart Cities, Systems, Devices and Technologies (includes URBAN COMPUTING 2016), IARIA 2016*, pp. 8-14, ISBN: 978-1-61208-4763.

Ibrahim, M., El-Zaart, A. & Adams, C. (2017a). Stakeholders Engagement in Smart Sustainable Cities: A Proposed Model. *Sensors, Networks, Smart and Engineering (SENSET), 2017 International Conference on, IEEE Xplore*, pp. 1-4, doi: 10.1109/SENSET.2017.8125067.

Ibrahim, M., El-Zaart, A. & Adams, C. (2017b). Theory of Change for the Transformation towards Smart Sustainable Cities. *Computer and Applications, 2017 International Conference on, IEEE Xplore*, pp. 342-347, doi: 10.1109/COMAPP.2017.8079773.

Ibrahim, M., El-Zaart, A. & Adams, C. (2017c). Smart Sustainable Cities Roadmap: Readiness for Transformation towards Urban Sustainability. *Sustainable Cities and Society*, doi: 10.1016/j.scs.2017.10.008.

Ibrahim, M., El-Zaart, A., & Adams, C. (2018). A Validated Novel Framework for the Transformation towards Smart Sustainable Cities. *International Conference on Information Society and Smart Cities (ISC2018)*, University of Cambridge, Cambridge City, United Kingdom.

Ibrahim, M. (2019). Developing Smart Sustainable Cities: a Validated Transformation Framework. *2019 International Conference on Smart Applications, Communications and Networking (SmartNets), IEEE Xplore*, doi: 10.1109/SmartNets48225.2019.9069773.

.

IDC (2009). *Best Practices: Bringing Stakeholders Together: The Amsterdam Smart City Project*. The International Data Corporation (IDC) Insights, IDC Energy Insights, Framingham, MA: USA.

IEC (2014). *Orchestrating Infrastructure for Sustainable Smart Cities*. International Electrotechnical Commission (IEC), ISBN 978-2-8322-1833-4. Geneva: Switzerland.

IEEE (2015). IEEE Smart Cities. *Institute of Electrical and Electronics Engineers (IEEE)*. Web. Accessed, Retrieved from: http://smartcities.ieee.org/about.html.

IESE (2015). *IESE Cities in Motion Index*. Center for Globalization and Strategy and the IESE Business School, University of Navarra. Navarra: Spain.

IFC (2007). *Stakeholder Engagement: A Good Practice Handbook for Companies Doing Business in Emerging Markets*. International Financial Corporation (IFC). Washington, DC: USA.

Inness, J. E. & Booher, D. E. (2014). A Turning Point for Planning Theory?: Overcoming Dividing Discourses. *Planning Theory & Practice, 14*, pp. 195-213.

Ishida, T. (2002). Digital City Kyoto. *Communications of the ACM*, Vol. (45), No. (7), pp. 78-81.

ISO/IEC (2015). *Smart Cities – Preliminary Report (2014)*. International Organization for Standardization and International Electrotechnical Commission (ISO/IEC). Genève:

Switzerland.

ITU-T FG-SSC (2014a). *An Overview of Smart Sustainable Cities and the role of Information and Communication Technologies.* United Nations, International Telecommunication Union (ITU-T), Focus Group on Smart Sustainable Cities (FG-SSC).

ITU-T FG-SSC (2014b). *Technical Report on Smart Sustainable Cities: An analysis of Definitions.* United Nations, International Telecommunication Union (ITU-T), Focus Group on Smart Sustainable Cities (FG-SSC).

ITU-T FG-SSC (2015a). *Smart Sustainable Cities: a guide for city leaders.* United Nations, International Telecommunication Union (ITU-T), Focus Group on Smart Sustainable Cities (FG-SSC).

ITU-T FG-SSC (2015b). *Standardization Roadmap for Smart Sustainable Cities.* United Nations, International Telecommunication Union (ITU-T), Focus Group on Smart Sustainable Cities (FG-SSC).

ITU-T (2016). *Shaping Smarter and more Sustainable Cities: Striving for Sustainable Development Goals.* International Telecommunication Union Telecommunication Standardization Sector (ITU-T). Geneva: Switzerland.

James, C. (2011). *Theory of Change Review.* A report commissioned by Comic Relief.

Jayashree P. & Hussain, S. (2010). Tracking and evaluating the impact of large scale change initiatives: a proposed approach based on the application of balanced scorecard framework. *Oxford Business and Economics Conference*, OBEC, pp. 1-34.

Kahn, M. (1995). Concepts, Definitions, and Key Issues in Sustainable Development: the Outlook for the Future. *Proceedings of the 1995 International Sustainable Development Research Conference*, pp. 2-13.

Kanter, R.M. & Litow, S.S. (2009). Informed and interconnected: A manifesto for smarter cities. *Harvard Business School General Management Unit, Harvard Business School Working Paper*, No. (09-141).

Kates, R.W., Parris, T.M., Leiserowitz, A.A. (2005). What Is Sustainable Development? Goals, Indicators, Values, and Practice. *Journal of Environment: Science and Policy for Sustainable Development*, Vol. (47), No. (3), pp. 8-21.

Khansari, N., Mostashari, A. & Mansouri, M. (2013). Impacting Sustainable Behaviour and Planning in Smart City. *International Journal of Sustainable Land use and Urban Planning*, Vol. (1), No. (2), pp. 46-61.

Kirkman, G.S., Osorio, C.A. & Sachs, J.D. (2002). The Networked Readiness Index: Measuring the Preparedness of Nations for the Networked World. *In the Global Information Technology Report 2001-2002: Readiness for the Networked World.* Oxford: Oxford University Press.

Kleijnen, J. (1994). *Sensitivity Analysis versus Uncertainty Analysis: When to Use what.?* In Predictability and Nonlinear Modeling in Natural Science and Economics, Springer-Science+Business Media, B.V., ISBN 978-94-011-0962-8 (eBook), pp. 322-333.

Komninos, N., Schaffers, H. & Pallot, M. (2011). Developing a Policy Roadmap for Smart Cities and the Future Internet. *In Proceedings of the eChallenges-2011 Conference*, pp.1-8.

Kohel, K. (2016). *Becoming a Sustainable Organization: A Project and Portfolio Management Approach*. Auerbach Publications, Best Practices and Advances in Program Management (Book 25), ISBN-10: 1498700810, ISBN-13: 978-1498700818.

Kotter, P.J. (1995). Leading Change: Why Transformation Efforts Fail. *Harvard Business Review*, 1st Edition, pp. 92-107.

Kotter, P.J. & Cohen D.S. (2012). *The Heart of Change: Real-Life Stories of How People Change Their Organization*. Harvard Business Review Press, 1st Edition, ISBN-13: 978-1422187333.

KPMG (2015a). *2015 Change Readiness Index: Assessing Countries' ability to Manage Change and Cultivate Opportunity*. KPMG and Oxford Economics. Amstelveen: Netherlands.

KPMG (2015b). *Dubai – a New Paradigm for Smart Cities*. KPMG. Dubai: UAE.

KU (2015). *Access Practical, Step-by-step Guidance in Community-Building Skills*. Community Tool Box, Work Group for Community Health and Development, University of Kansas (KU). Web. Accessed, Retrieved from: http://ctb.ku.edu/en/table-of-contents.

Laing, K. & Todd, L. (Eds.) (2015). *Theory-based Methodology: Using Theories of Change for Development, Research and Evaluation*. Research Centre for Learning and Teaching, Newcastle University. Newcastle: United Kingdom.

Larson, S. & Williams, LJ. (2009). Monitoring the Success of Stakeholder Engagement: Literature Review. In Measham TG Brake L (Eds.). *People Communities and Economies of the Lake Eyre Basin*, DKCRC Research Report 45, Desert Knowledge Cooperative Research Centre, Alice Springs, pp. 251-298.

Lee, J.H. & Hancock, M.G. (2012). *Toward a Framework for Smart Cities: A Comparison of Seoul, San Francisco & Amsterdam*. Stanford Program on Regions of Innovation and Entrepreneurship. Web. Accessed, Retrieved from: http://iisdb.stanford.edu/evnts/7239/Jung_Hoon_Lee_final.pdf.

Leydesdorff, L. & Deakin, M. (2011). The Triple-Helix Model of Smart Cities: A Neo-Evolutionary Perspective. *Journal of urban Technology*, Vol. (18), No. (2), pp. 53-63.

Li, Y., Lin, Y. & Geertman, S. (2015). The Development of Smart Cities in China. *13th International Conference on Computers in Urban Planning and Urban Management*, Cambridge MA, USA.

Lombardi, P. Giordano, S., Farouh, H. & Yousef, W. (2012). Modeling the Smart City Performance. *Innovation – The European Journal of Social Science Research*, Vol. (20), No. (2), pp. 137-149.

Lorenz, H.M., Lohmann, W., Bemard, A. & Göran, A. (2013). Evaluating sustainability of using ICT solutions in smart cities – methodology requirements. *Proceedings of the First International Conference on Information and Communication Technologies for Sustainability*, pp. 175-182.

Lotfi, S & Solaimani, K. (2209). An Assessment of Urban Quality of Life by Using Analytic Hierarchy Process Approach (Case Study: Comparative Study of Quality of Life in the North of Iran). *Journal of Social Science*, Vol. (5), Issue (2), pp. 123-133.

LTS & ITAD (2012). *ESPA Theory of Change*. Economy Services for Poverty Alleviation (ESPA), By LSA International and ITAD. Edinburgh: United Kingdom.

Mackinlay, L., Monbiot, E. & Boxelaar, L. (2013). *World's Vision Theory of Change*. World Vision International. Monrovia, California: USA.

Malamed, C. (2011). Visual Language for Designers: Principles for Creating Graphics that People Understand. *Rockport publishers*, ISBN-13: 978-1-59253-515-6.

Manghnani, N. & Bajaj, K. (2014). Masdar City: A Model of Urban Environmental Sustainability. *Journal of Engineering Research and Applications*, Vol. (4), No. (10), pp. 38-42.

Masdar (2014). Masdar City: Planning a Sustainable, Smart City – An Integrated Approach. *12th International Conference on emerging trends in Sustainable Habitat and Integrated Cities*, Web. Accessed, Retrieved from: http://municipalika.com/wp-content/uploads/2014/Presentations/CS10-Gaurish-Wagle-Presentation.pdf.

Maslow, A.H. (1943). A Theory of Human Motivation. *Psychological Review*, Vol. (5), pp. 370-396.

Maslow, A.H. (1962). Towards a Psychology of Being. *Martino Fine Books*, 1st Edition, ISBN-13: 978-1614270676.

Massam, B.H. (2002). Quality of Life: Public Planning and Private Living. *Journal of Progress in Planning*, Vil. (58), pp. 141-227.

Mathur, V.N., Price, A.D.F., Austin, S. & Moobela, C. (2007). Defining, Identifying and Mapping Stakeholders in the Assessment of Urban Sustainability. In: Horner, M., Hardcastle, C., Price, A., Bebbington, J. (eds.). Proceedings: SUE-MoT Conference 2007: International Conference on Whole Life Urban Sustainability and its Assessment. Glasgow: Scotland.

McDaniel, C. & Gates, R. (2011). Marketing Research. *John Wiley & Sons*, 9th Edition, ISBN 1-118-214-374.

McMichael, A.J., Kjellstrom, T., Slettenhaar, H., Taylor, A., Healy, J., Hansen, E., Taylor, R. &Wilson-Rowan, L. (2000). Goat Island "Sustainability Transition" (GIST) Declaration. *Kluwer Academic Publishers, Global Change and Human Health*, Vol. (1), Issue (1), pp. 59-65.

MEED (2015). *Integrating cities and services with strategies for implementing innovative services and enabling people, connections and networks*. Smart Cities MEED, Web. Accessed, Retrieved from: http://www.meed.com/smart-cities-2015/3192933. article#.

Meikle, S., Ramasut, T. & Walker, J. (2001). *Sustainable Urban Livelihood: Concepts and Implications for Policy*. Development Planning Unit (DPU), University College London, Working Paper, No. (112). London: United Kingdom.

Mesiano, R. (2014). *Green Jobs for Youth Unemployment in the Arab Region*. United Nations Economic and Social Commission for Western Asia (UN ESCWA). Web. Accessed, Retrieved from: http://www.ocemo.org/file/125829/.

Mihalcea, R. & Tarau, P. (2004). TextRank: Bringing Order into Texts. *In Proceedings of the Conference on Empirical Methods in Natural Language Processing (EMNLP 2004),* pp. 404-411.

Mitchell, R.K., Agle, B.R. & Wood, D.J. (1997). Towards a theory of Stakeholder Identification and Salience: Defining the Principle of Who and what Really Counts. *The Academy of Management Review*, Vol. (22), No. (4), pp.853-886.

Monitor Deloitte (2015). *Smart Cities ... Not just the Sum of its Parts*. Monitor Deloitte, Deloitte & Touch (M. E.). Web. Accessed, Retrieved from: http://www2.deloitte. com/content/dam/Deloitte/xe/Documents/strategy/me_deloitte-monitor_smart-cities.pdf

Mosannenzadeh, F. & Vettorato, D. (2014). Defining Smart City – A conceptual Framework Based on Keyword Analysis. *TeMA Journal of Land Use, Mobility and Environment INPUT 2014, Eighth International Conference INPUT – Naples, Special Issue,* pp. 683-694.

Mueller, B. & Urbach, N. (2013). The Why, What, and How of Theories in IS Research. *Thirty Fourth International Conference on Information Systems*, pp. 1-25.

Mureddu, F., Misuraca, G., Osimo, D., Onori, R. & Armenia, S. (2014). Handbook of Research on Advanced ICT Integration for Governance and Policy Modeling: A Living Roadmap for Policymaking. *Government IS&T Books*, pp. 433-460.

Nam, T. & Pardo T.A. (2011). Conceptualizing Smart Sustainable City with Dimensions of Technology, People, and Institutions, *Proceedings of the 12th Annual International Conference on Digital Government Research*, pp. 282-291.

Negre, E., Rosenthal-Sabroux, C. & Gasco, M. (2015). A Knowledge-based Conceptual Vision of the Smart City. *48th Hawaii International Conference on System Science*, pp. 2317-2325.

Neirotti, P., De Marco, A., Cagliano, A.C., Mangano, G. & Scorrano, F. (2014). Current Trends in Smart City Initiatives: Some Stylised Facts. *Journal of Cities*, Vol. (38), pp. 25–36.

Neumann, B. (2016). *Implementing Community Vision Requires Detailed Strategies*. Michigan State University Extension, Web. Accessed, Retrieved from: http://msue.anr.msu.edu/news/implementing_community_vision_requires_detailed_s trategies.

NPC (2012). *Theory of Change: The beginning of Making a Difference*. New Philanthropy Capital (NPC): Kail A. & Lumley, T. London: United Kingdom.

O'Grady, M. & O'Hare, G. (2012). How Smart Is Your City? *Science Magazine*, Vol. (335), No. (6076), pp. 1581-1582.

OECD (2010). *Greener and Smarter: ICTs, the Environment and Climate Change*. Organization for Economic Co-Operation and Development (OECD). Paris: France.

OECD (2016). Better Policies for Sustainable Development 2016: A New Framework for Policy Coherence. *OECD Publishing*, ISBN-13: 978-9264256972.

Okoli, C. & Pawloweski, S. D. (2003). The Delphi Method as a Research Tool: An Example, Design, Considerations and Applications. *Information & Management*, Vol. (42), Issue (1), pp. 14-29.

Olfert, S. (2003). *Quality of Life Leisure Indicators*. Community – University Institute for Social Research (CUISR). Saskatoon, SK: Canada.

Ooredo (2014). *Lusail Smart City Guidance*. Ooredoo Qatar Telecom. Doha: Qatar.

ORS (2007). *A Guide to Measuring Advocacy and Policy*. Organization Research Services (ORS), prepared for the Annie E. Casey Foundation. Seattle, WA: USA.

Osec (2015). *Economic Cities Saudi Arabia*. Osec, Business Network Switzerland, Green Destinations LLC. Dubai: UAE.

Palmer, I., Dunford, R. & Akin, G. (2008). *Managing Organizational Change: A Multiple Perspectives Approach* (2nd ed.). Columbus, OH: McGraw-Hill Higher Education.

PD&R (2013). *Developing Choice Neighborhoods: An Early Look at Implementation in Five Sites*. U.S. Department of Housing and Urban Development, Office of Policy Development and Research (PD&R). Washington, DC: USA.

Pincetl, S. (2015). Cities as Novel Biomes: Recognizing Urban Ecosystem Services as Anthropogenic. *Frontiers in Ecology and Evolution*, Vol. (3), Article (140).

PMI (2013). *Managing Change in Organizations: A Practice Guide*. Project Management Institute (PMI). Pennsylvania, PA: USA.

Polat, E. (2009). A 'New And Soft' Urban Planning Paradigm: The Strategic Spatial Planning. *Debreceni Műszaki Közlemények*, Vol. (6), No. (1), pp. 89-100.

Policy Horizons Canada (2009). *Transitions to a Sustainable Future: Opportunities for Transformational Change in Canada*. Policy Horizons Canada, Web. Accessed, Retrieved from: http://www.horizons.gc.ca/eng/content/transitions-sustainable-future.

Ponterotto, J. G. (2005). Qualitative Research in Counseling Psychology: A Primer on Research Paradigms and Philosophy of Science. *Journal of Counseling Psychology*, Vol. (52), pp. 126-136.

PwC (2010). *Sustainable Urbanization and the Role of ICT in City Development*. PricewaterhouseCoopers (PwC), The Global Strategy Consulting team at PwC (Strategy&). Delhi: India.

PwC (2014a). *Amsterdam: A City of Opportunity*. PricewaterhouseCoopers (PwC) Advisory N.V, KvK 34180287. Delhi: India.

PwC (2014b). *Connect – Rendezvous with the Alumni*. PricewaterhouseCoopers (PwC) Private Limited, AK 237. Delhi: India.

PwC (2015a). *PwC Smart Cities PoV*. PricewaterhouseCoopers (PwC), Web. Accessed, Retrieved from: https://www.rvo.nl/sites/default/files/2015/05/PwC%20Smart%20 Cities%20PoV%20april%202015.pdf

PwC (2015b). *Connecting the Dots: Smart and Sustainable Cities*. PricewaterhouseCoopers (PwC) Private Limited, PD 426. Delhi: India.

PwC & CII (2015). *Making Haryana Smart*. PricewaterhouseCoopers (PwC) Private Limited, SC 311. Delhi: India.

PwC Connect (2015). *Smart Cities: towards a Brighter Future*. PricewaterhouseCoopers (PwC), PwC Connect, Web. Accessed, Retrieved from: http://cloud.pub.pwc.com/ Alumni-Newsletter/focus.html

Queensland Government (2016). *Types of Change*. Queensland Government, Business and Industry Portal, Web. Accessed, Retrieved from: https://www.business.qld.gov. au/business/employing/staff-development/managing-people-through-change/types-change.

Rafalak, M., Bliski, P. & Wierzbicki, A. (2016). Analysis of Questionnaire Results Using Metric Methods. *International Journal of Applied Mathematics & Information Science*, Vol. (10), No. (4), pp. 1255-1270.

Raffay, A. (2007). Stakeholder Involvement in Urban Tourism Development. – a Tale of two Cities. *Doctoral Research Study, University of Derby*. Derby: United Kingdom.

Rakodi, C. & Lloyd-Jones, T. (2002). Urban Livelihoods: A People-centered Approach to Reducing Poverty. *EARTHSCAN Publications Ltd.*, 1st Edition, ISBN-13: 978-1853838606.

Rikerjoe (2009). *Transactional, Transitional, and Transformational Change*. Leading Space, Web. Accessed, Retrieved from: https://leadingspace.wordpress.com/2009/ 12/20/transactional-transitional-and-transformational-change/.

Robinson, S. (1997). Simulation Model Verification and Validation: Increasing the Users' Confidence. *Proceedings of 29th Conference on Winter Simulation*, pp. 53-59.

Rodriguez, S.I., Roman, M.S., Sturhahn, S.C. and Terry, E.H. (2002). Sustainability Assessment and Reporting for the University of Michigan's Ann Arbor Campus. *Center for Sustainability Systems, University of Michigan*. Michigan, MI: USA.

Rogers, P. (2014). *Theory of Change, Methodological Brief: Impact Evaluation No. 2*. UNICEF Office of Research. Florence: Spain.

Roggema, R., Vermeend, T. & Dobbelsteen, A. (2012). Incremental Change, Transition or Transformation? Optimising Change Pathways for Climate Adaptation in Spatial Planning. *Sustainability*, Vol. (4), pp. 2525-2549.

Rubel, H. (2014). *Smart Cities – how to master the world's biggest growth challenge*. The Boston Consulting Group (BCG), Web. Accessed, Retrieved from: http://www.slideshare.net/TheBostonConsultingGroup/smart-cities-35846005.

Safier, M. (2001). *The Inter-Dimensional Analysis of Urban Development: A Guide to the Organization of Cases and Their Linkages*. Development Planning Unit (DPU), University Collage London. London: United Kingdom.

Sairamesh, J., Lee, A., & Anania, L. (2004). Information cities. *Communications of the ACM*, Vol. (47), No. (2), pp. 28-31.

Sargent, R.G. (1981). A Methodology for Cost-risk analysis in the Statistical Validation of Simulation Models. *Communication of the ACM*, Vol. (24), No. (6), pp. 190-197.

Sargent, R.G. (1992). Verification and Validation of Simulation Models. *Proceeding of the 1992 Winter Simulation Conference*, ed. J. J. Swain, D. Goldsman, R. C. Crain, and J. R. Wilson, pp. 104-114.

Satterthwaite, D. & Dodman, D. (2013). Towards resilience and transformation for cities within a finite planet. *Environment and Urbanization*, Vol. (25), No. (2), pp. 291-298.

Saunders, M., Lewis, P., & Thornhill, A. (2009). Research Methods for Business Students. *Prentice Hall*, 5th Edition, ISBN 0-273-71686-7.

SCC (2015). *Smart Cities Readiness Guide: The Planning Manual for Building Tomorrow's cities Today*. Smart Cities Council (SCC). Washington, WA: USA.

Schaffers, H. (2012). Future Internet and Open Innovation for Connected Smart Cities. *FIREBALL, European Commission Project FP7-ICT*, Web. Accessed, Retrieved from: http://fisa.futureinternet.eu/images/2/22/FIREBALL_WP2_Landscape_and_Roadmap_presented_30.09.pdf.

Sharp, J.A., Peters, J. & Howard, K. (2002). The Management of Student Research Project. *Routledge, British Library Cataloguing in Publishing Data*, 3rd Edition, ISBN 0-566-08490-2.

Sirgy, M.J. (1986). A Quality-of-Life Theory Derived from Maslow's Developmental Perspective. *The American Journal of Economics and Sociology*, Vol. (45), Issue (3), pp. 329-342.

Soom, E.V. (2009). *Measuring Levels of Supply and Demand for e-Services and e-Government: a Toolkit for Cities*. The Interreg IVB North Sea Region Programme, Smart Cities Research Brief, No. (3). Brussels: Belgium.

Sproull, L., & Patterson, J. F. (2004). Making information cities livable. *Communications of the ACM*, Vol. (47), No. (2), pp. 33-37.

SSU (2015). *Berlin Strategy: Urban Development Concept – Berlin 2030*. Senate Department for Urban Development and the Environments (Senatsverwaltung für Stadtentwicklung und Umwelt) (SSU). Berlin: Germany.

Staffans, A. & Horelli, L. (2014). Expanded Urban Planning as a Vehicle for Understanding and Shaping Smart, Liveable Cities. *The Journal of Community Informatics*, Vol. (10), No. (3).

Stachowiak, S. (2013). *Pathways for Change: 10 Theories to Inform Advocacy and Policy Change Efforts*. ORS Impact (Organizational Research Services), Center for Evaluation Innovation. Washington: DC, United states.

Steenkamp, A.L. & Kraft, T. (2012). Integrating Conceptual and Empirical Approaches for Software Engineering Research. *In Research Methodologies, Innovations and Philosophies in Software Systems Engineering and Information Systems, British Cataloguing in Publishing Data, British Library*, 1st Edition, pp. 298-319.

Stein, D. & Valters, C. (2012). *Understanding Theory of Change in International Development*. The Justice and Security Research Programme (JSRP). London: United Kingdom.

Sun, Y. (2005). *Development of Neighborhood Quality of Life Indicators*. Community – University Institute for Social Research (CUISR). Saskatoon, SK: Canada.

Tastle, W.J. & Wierman, M.J. (2006). An Information Theoretic Measure for the Evaluation of Ordinal Scale Data. *Behavior Research Methods*, Vol. (38), No. (3), pp.487-494.

Tastle, W.J. & Wierman, M.J. (2007). Consensus and Dissention: A Measure of Ordinal Dispersion. *International Journal of Approximate Reasoning*, Vol. (45), pp. 531-545.

Tastle, W.J., Wierman, M.J. and Dumdum, U.R. (2005). Ranking Ordinal Scales Using the Consensus Measure. *Issues in Information Systems*, Vol. (4), No. (2), pp. 96-102.

Tayntor, B. (2002). Six Sigma Software Development. *Auerbach Publishers Inc.*, 1st Edition, ISBN-13: 978-1420031485.

Theofilou, P. (2013). Quality of Life: Definition and Management. *European's Journal of Psychology*, Vol. (9), No. (1), pp. 150-162.

Thompson, A.A., Peteraf, M.A., Gambie, J.E. & Stickland III, A.J. (Eds.) (2015). *Crafting & Executing Strategy: The Quest for Competitive Advantage: Concepts and Cases*. McGraw-Hill Education, 20th Edition.

Thuzar, M. (2011). Urbanization in South East Asia: Developing Smart Cities for the Future?. *Regional Outlook: Southeast Asia 2011-2012, Institute of Southeast Asian Studies*, pp. 96-100.

Tok, E., Al Mohammad, F. & Al Merekhi, M. (2014). Crafting Smart Cities in the Gulf Region: A Comparison of Masdar and Luail. *European Scientific Journal*, Vol. (2), pp. 130-140.

Toppeta (2010). *The Smart City Vision: How Innovation and ICT can build Smart, "liveable", Sustainable Cities*. THINK! The Innovation Knowledge Foundation, Report 005/2010. Milano: Italy.

Townsend, A.M. (2013). S*mart Cities: Big Data, Civic Hackers, and the Quest for a New Utopia*. Norton & Company. New York, NY: USA.

TunisiaEC (2014). *Tunisian Economic City – About*. Official Tunisian Economic City website. Web. Accessed, Retrieved from: http://www.tunisiaec.com/about-project.

UN (2013). *World Economic and Social Survey 2013: Sustainable Development Challenges*. United Nations, Department of Economic and Social Affairs, Publication Division (E/2013/50/Rev.1, ST/ESA/344).

UN (2014a). *Report of the World Urbanization Prospects: the 2014 Revision, Highlights*. United Nations, Department of Economic and Social Affairs, Publication Division (ST/ESA/SER.A/352).

UN (2014b). *United Nations E-Government Survey 2014: E-Government for the Future We want*. United Nations, Department of Economic and Social Affairs, Publication Division (ST/ESA/PAD/SER.E/188).

UN-DESA (2015). *Sustainable Development Goals*. United Nation Department for Economic and Social Affairs (UN-DESA), Division for Sustainable Development. Web. Accessed, Retrieved from: https://sustainabledevelopment.un.org/sdgs.

UN-HABITAT (1997). *A Reappraisal of the Urban Planning Process*. United Nations Human Settlement Programme (UN-HABITAT): Mosha, A.C.

UN-HABITAT (2010). *Hidden Cities: Unmasking and Overcoming Health Inequities in Urban Setting*. United Nations Human Settlement Programme (UN-HABITAT), World Health Organization, The Who Center for Health Development. Geneva: Switzerland.

UN-HABITAT (2015). *Arab Sustainable Development Report – Making Cities and Human Settlements Inclusive, safe, Resilient and sustainable in the Arab Region*. United Nations Human Settlement Programme (UN-HABITAT), Regional Office for Arab States (ROAS): Schaefer, K.

UNCTAD (2016). *Smart Cities and Infrastructure*. United Nations Commission on Science and Technology for Development (UNCTAD). Budapest: Hungary.

UNESCO (2011). *Digital Literacy in Education*. UNESCO Institute for Information Technologies in Education. Moscow: Russia.

UNICEF (1990). *A UNICEF Guide for Monitoring and Evaluation – Making a Difference?* United Nations Children's Fund (UNICEF). New York, NY: USA.

UNDP (2002). *Handbook on Monitoring and Evaluating for Results*. United Nations Development Programme Evaluation Office (UNDP). New York, NY: USA.

UNDP (2011). *Supporting Transformational Change: Case Studies of Sustained and Successful Development Cooperation*. United Nations Development Programme, Bureau of Development Policy. New York, NY: USA.

UN Rio+20 (2012). *From Transition to Transformation: Sustainable and Inclusive Development in Europe and Central Asia*. United Nations, Rio+20 United Nations Conference on Sustainable Development. New York, NY: USA and Geneva: Switzerland.

UNSDN (2013). *The Urban Opportunity: Transformative and Sustainable Development*. Sustainable Development Solutions Network (UNSDN), a Global Initiative for the

United Nations. New York, NY: USA.

UNTT (2013). *Science, Technology and Innovation for Sustainable Development in the Global Partnership for Development beyond 2015.* The United Nation System Task Team (UNTT), Working group on the global partnership for development beyond 2015, Publication Division. New York, NY: USA.

USMC (2013). *Sustaining the Transformation.* Create Space Independent Publishing Platform, 1st Edition, ISBN-13: 978-1492760498.

Usmani, F. (2013). *Assumptions and Constraints in Project Management.* PM Study Circle, Web. Accessed, Retrieved from: https://pmstudycircle.com/2012/10/assumptions-and-constraints-in-project-management/.

Vedashree, R. & Bose, M. (2015). *Integrated ICT and Geospatial Technologies: Framework for 100 Smart Cities Mission.* NASSCOM Publications, International Youth Center. New Delhi: India.

Ventegodt, S., Merrick, J. and Andersen, N.J. (2003). Quality of Life Theory III. Maslow Revisited. *The Scientific World Journal*, Vol. (3). Pp. 1050-1057.

Vogel, I. (2012a). *ESPA Guide to Working with Theory of Change for Research Projects.* The Ecosystem Services for Poverty Alleviation (ESPA) Programme. Scotland: United Kingdom.

Vogel, I. (2012b). *Review of the Use of 'Theory of Change' in International Development.* The UK Department for International Development (DFID). London: United Kingdom.

WBG (2014). *ICT for Greater Development Impact.* The World Bank Group (WBG), World Bank Group Strategy for Information and Communication Technology 2012-2015. Washington, DC: USA.

Webb, M. (2013). *Smart Cities will ultimately be Driven by Citizens.* The Climate Group. Web. Accessed, Retrieved from: http://www.theclimategroup.org/blogs/smart-2020/smart-cities-will-ultimately-be-driven-by-citizens/

WEF (2015). *The Global Competitiveness Report 2015*-2016. World Economic Forum (WEF). Geneva: Switzerland.

Wei, Y. H. D. (2012). Restructuring for growth in urban China: Transitional institutions, urban development, and spatial transformation. *Journal of Habitat International*, Vol. (36), pp. 396-405.

Weiss, C.H. (1995). Nothing as Practical as Good Theory: Exploring Theory-Based Evaluation for Comprehensive Community-Based Initiatives for Children and Families. *In J. P. Connell, A. C. Kubisch, L. B. Schorr and C. H. Weiss (eds.), New Approaches to Evaluating Community Initiatives: Concepts, Methods and Contexts.* Vol. (1), pp. 65-92. Washington, DC: Aspen Institute.

Wheatley, M. (2012). *Data Driving Transportation System – Changes in IBM Smarter Cities Program.* Data Informed, Web. Accessed, Retrieved from: http://data-informed.com/data-driving-transportation-system-changes-ibm-smarter-cities-program/.

Whetten, D.A. (1989). What Constitutes a Theoretical Contribution?. *Academy of Management Review*, Vol. (14), No. (4), pp. 490-495.

WHO (1999). *Towards a New Planning Process: A Guide to Reorienting Urban Planning towards Local Agenda 21*. World Health Organization (WHO). Copenhagen: Denmark.

Wikström, A. (2013). *The Challenge of Change: Planning for Social Urban Resilience*. Master's Thesis in Urban and Regional Planning, Department of Human Geography, Stockholm University. Stockholm: Sweden.

Withers, M., Williams, M. & Reddington M. (2010). Transforming HR: Creating Value through People. Oxford, Elsevier, 2nd Edition, pp. 132-139.

WKKF (2006). *W.K. Kellogg Foundation Logic Model Development Guide*. W.K. Kellogg Foundation (WKKF). Michigan: USA.

World Bank (1996). *The World Bank Participation Sourcebook*. Environmentally Sustainable Development Publications, ESC Proceedings Series, The World Bank. Washington, DC: USA.

Yigitcanlar, T., O'Connor, K. & Westerman, C. (2008). The Making of Knowledge Cities: Melbourne's Knowledge-based Urban Development Experience. *Journal of Cities,* Vol. (25), No. (2), pp. 63–72.

Yovanof, G.S. & Hazapis, G.N. (2009). An Architectural Framework and Enabling Wireless Technologies for Digital Cities & Intelligent Urban Environments. *Wireless Personal Communications,* Vol. (49), No. (3), pp. 445463.

Yang, Y. (2010). Sustainable Urban Transformation Driving Forces, Indicators and Processes. *Doctoral Research Study, ETH Zurich University*, DISS. ETHO NO. (19161). Zurich: Switzerland.

Yasser (2207). *IT Readiness Assessment for Government Organizations*. The Saudi e-Government Program – Yasser. Riyadh: Saudi Arabia.

ZTE (2014). *ZTE iCity Solution: Sharing Wisdom Enjoying Life*. ZTE. Shenzhen: China.